D0772189

INTO THE
ABYSS

INTO THE
ABYSS

THE STORY
OF THE FIRST
WORLD WAR
VOLUME ONE

G. J. MEYER

AMBERLEY

Dedicated to the memory of my parents,
Cornelia E. and Justin G. Meyer

First published 2006 by Bantam Books
This edition published 2018 by
arrangement with Delacorte Press, an
imprint of Random House, a division of
Penguin Random House LLC.

Amberley Publishing
The Hill, Stroud
Gloucestershire, GL5 4EP

www.amberley-books.com

Copyright © G. J. Meyer 2006, 2018

The right of G. J. Meyer to be identified as
the Author of this work has been asserted
in accordance with the Copyrights,
Designs and Patents Act 1988.

ISBN 978 1 4456 8001 9 (print)
ISBN 978 1 4456 8002 6 (ebook)

All rights reserved. No part of this book
may be reprinted or reproduced or
utilised in any form or by any electronic,
mechanical or other means, now
known or hereafter invented, including
photocopying and recording, or in any
information storage or retrieval system,
without the permission in writing from
the Publishers.

British Library Cataloguing in
Publication Data.
A catalogue record for this book is
available from the British Library.

Maps by Jeffrey L. Ward.
Book design by Virginia Norey.
Origination by Amberley Publishing.
Printed in Great Britain.

Contents

List of Illustrations

Abbreviations for List of Illustrations

CNP   *Collier's New Photographic History of the World's War* (New York, 1918)
CPE   *Collier's Photographic History of the European War* (New York, 1918)
GW   *The Great World War: A History*, edited by Frank A. Mumby (Gresham Publishing Company, five volumes 1915–1917)
HW   *History of the World War* by Francis A. March (Philadelphia, 1918)
IWM   Imperial War Museum
NA   National Archives
NW   *The Nations at War* by Willis John Abbot (New York, 1917)
WW   *Liberty's Victorious Conflict: A Photographic History of the World War* (Woman's Weekly, Chicago, 1918)

List of Maps

Chronology

1914

June 28:	Archduke Franz Ferdinand is assassinated at Sarajevo.
July 5:	Kaiser Wilhelm II gives "blank check" to Austria-Hungary.
July 23:	Austria-Hungary delivers ultimatum to Serbia.
July 25:	Serbia responds to ultimatum and mobilizes. Russia declares Period Preparatory to War.
July 28:	Austria-Hungary declares war on Serbia.
July 30:	Russia and Austria-Hungary order general mobilization.
July 31:	Germany issues "double ultimatum" to France and Russia.
August 1:	France orders general mobilization. Germany mobilizes, declares state of war with Russia.
August 2:	German troops enter Luxembourg.
August 3:	Germany declares war on France. Britain orders general mobilization.
August 4:	Germany declares war on Belgium. Britain declares war on Germany.
August 5:	Austria-Hungary declares war on Russia.
August 6:	Serbia declares war on Germany.
August 7:	French troops invade Alsace.
August 10:	France declares war on Austria-Hungary. Austria-Hungary invades Serbia.
August 12:	Britain declares war on Austria-Hungary.
August 16:	Russian troops invade East Prussia.
August 23:	Germans and British meet in Battle of Mons in Belgium.
August 26:	Battle of Le Cateau.
August 28:	Russian Second Army is destroyed at Tannenberg.
September 3–11:	Russians force Austro-Hungarians out of Lemberg, drive them back to Carpathian Mountains.
September 5:	French-British counterattack opens Battle of the Marne.

September 9:   German withdrawal marks end of Schlieffen Plan offensive.

September 9–14:   Germans defeat Russians in Battle of Masurian Lakes.

October 6:   Belgian troops abandon Antwerp to Germans.

October 19:   Opening of First Battle of Ypres.

October 29:   Turkey enters war on side of Austria-Hungary and Germany.

November 5:   Austria-Hungary invades Serbia.

December 14:   French and British launch general offensive all along Western Front.

1915

January 24:   British-German warships meet at Dogger Bank in North Sea.

February 7–22:   German victory over Russians in Second Battle of Masurian Lakes.

March 10–13:   Battle of Neuve Chapelle in France's Artois region.

March 18:   British-French naval task force fails to force open the Dardanelles.

April 22:   Second Battle of Ypres begins with German offensive.

April 25:   British and French forces land on Gallipoli Peninsula.

May 1:   German offensive at Gorlice and Tarnow in Galicia.

May 9:   British attack Aubers Ridge; French begin Second Battle of Artois.

May 23:   Italy declares war on Austria-Hungary.

June 23:   Italian attack opens First Battle of the Isonzo.

August 5:   German forces occupy Warsaw, climaxing an offensive that began on July 13.

August 6:   British forces land at Suvla Bay in Gallipoli.

September 25:   Massive French offensive begins Second Battle of Champagne and Third Battle of Artois while British attack at Loos.

October 6:   Germans and Austro-Hungarians invade Serbia.

October 14:   Bulgaria and Serbia declare war on each other.

December 17:   Douglas Haig replaces John French as commander of British Expeditionary Force.

Major Characters

Albert I. King of Belgium; commander of Belgian forces during the war

Alexandra. Tsarina of Russia; wife of Nicholas II

Alexeyev, Mikhail. Chief of staff to Nicholas II; commander in chief of Russian armies following the tsar's abdication

Asquith, Herbert Henry. British prime minister, 1908–16

Balfour, Arthur. British Conservative leader; succeeded Churchill as First Lord of the Admiralty in May 1915; succeeded Grey as foreign secretary December 1916

Below, Otto von. German general holding major commands on the Eastern, Western, and Italian Fronts and in the Balkans

Berchtold, Leopold von. Austro-Hungarian foreign minister, 1912–15

Bernstorff, Johann von. German ambassador to the U.S. 1908–17

Bethmann Hollweg, Theobold von. Chancellor of Germany, 1909–17

Bonar Law, Andrew. British Conservative and Unionist leader; chancellor of the exchequer, 1916–18

Briand, Aristide. French politician; succeeded Viviani as premier, October 1915; headed government until March 1917

Bruchmüller, Georg. German artillerist; originator of brilliantly innovative offensive tactics

Brusilov, Alexei. Russian army and army group commander; leader of the 1916 offensive that bears his name

Bülow, Karl von. Commander of German Second Army at the start of the war

Cadorna, Luigi. Chief of general staff of the Italian army, July 1914–November 1917

Caillaux, Joseph. Leader of French political opposition in 1914; arrested by Clemenceau government in 1918

Carden, Sackville. British admiral; commander of Royal Navy forces involved in the start of the Dardanelles offensive

Castelnau, Noël-Edouard de. French army and army group commander

Churchill, Winston. Britain's First Lord of the Admiralty, 1911–15; minister of munitions, 1917–18

Conrad von Hötzendorf, Franz. Austro-Hungarian field marshal; army chief of staff to March 1917

De Robeck, John. British admiral; second commander of Royal Navy forces at the Dardanelles

Driant, Émile. French politician, writer, and lieutenant colonel; killed in opening fighting at Verdun

Enver Pasha. Turkish general; leading member of the Young Turks; minister of war 1914–18, commanding troops in the Caucasus and Middle East

Evert, Alexei. Commander of Russia's Western Army Group from September 1915

Falkenhayn, Erich von. Prussian war minister, 1913–15; army chief of staff, September 1914–August 1916

Fisher, John. British admiral; first sea lord, October 1914–May 1915

Foch, Ferdinand. French general; appointed Allied supreme commander, April 1918

Franchet d'Esperey, Louis. French army and army group commander on the Western Front and, from mid-1918, in Salonika and the Balkans

Franz Ferdinand. Archduke; heir to the throne of Austria-Hungary; assassinated in Sarajevo, June 28, 1915

Franz Joseph. Emperor of Austria and King of Hungary, 1848–1916

French, John. Commander of British Expeditionary Force, August 1914–December 1915

Gallieni, Joseph. French general; key figure in First Battle of the Marne; minister of war, 1915–16

George V. King of Great Britain

Grey, Edward. British foreign secretary, 1905–16

Haig, Douglas. Senior general with British Expeditionary Force from August 1914; commander in chief from December 1915

Hamilton, Ian. British general; commander of Entente forces at Gallipoli, March–October 1915

Hindenburg, Paul von Beneckendorff und von. German field marshal; army chief of staff from August 1916

Hoffmann, Max. Key German military planner and leader on the Eastern Front

Holtzendorff, Henning von. Chief of staff of the German navy, 1915–18

House, "Colonel" Edward. American president Woodrow Wilson's principal adviser on foreign affairs

Hutier, Oskar von. German corps and army commander on Eastern Front, 1915–17; introduced innovative offensive tactics that came to bear his name; commander of Eighteenth Army on the Western Front, 1918

Jagow, Gottlieb von. German foreign minister to March 1917

Jellicoe, John. Commander of Britain's High Seas Fleet, 1914–16; first sea lord, 1916–17

Joffre, Joseph. Chief of French general staff, 1911–16

Kemal, Mustafa. Turkish division commander at Gallipoli; later served in the Caucasus and Middle East

Kitchener, Horatio. British war minister, August 1914–June 1916

Kluck, Alexander von. Commander of the German First Army at the start of the war

Lanrezac, Charles. Commander of the French Fifth Army at the start of the war

Lansing, Robert. U.S. secretary of state, 1915–20

Leman, Gérard. Commander of Belgian defenders at Liège, 1914

Lichnowsky, Karl Max. German ambassador to Britain

Lloyd George, David. British chancellor of the exchequer, 1908–15; minister of munitions, 1915–16; war minister, 1916; prime minister from December 1916

Ludendorff, Erich. German general; chief of staff to Hindenburg, August 1914–August 1916; quartermaster general of the German army, 1916–18; effectively dictator of Germany from mid-1917

Mackensen, August von. German field marshal holding important commands on the Eastern Front, 1914–18

Millerand, Alexandre. French minister of war, August 1914–October 1915

Moltke, Helmuth von. Chief of staff of German army, 1906–September 1914

Nicholas, Grand Duke. Cousin of Nicholas II; Russian general; commander in chief, August 1914–September 1915; then served in the Caucasus

Nicholas II. Tsar of Russia, 1894–1917; executed, 1918

Paléologue, Maurice. French ambassador to Russia, 1914–17

Pasic, Nikola. Prime Minister of Serbia

Pétain, Henri-Philippe. French general; army commander in chief from May 1917

Plumer, Herbert. British corps and army commander, responsible for sector around Ypres

Poincaré, Raymond. President of France, 1913–20

Polivanov, Alexei. Russian general; succeeded Sukhomlinov as war minister, June 1915; dismissed, March 1916

Pourtalès, Friedrich von. German ambassador to Russia

Prittwitz, Max von. Commander of German Eighth Army in August 1914

Putnik, Radomir. Serbian field marshal, war minister, and army chief of staff until 1916

Rasputin, Grigori. Russian monk, mystic, and intimate of the tsar's family

Rawlinson, Henry. British general, serving primarily as commander of the Fourth Army

Rennenkampf, Pavel von. Commander of Russian First Army at Tannenberg, August 1914

Robertson, William. British general; chief of the imperial general staff, December 1915–March 1918

Rupprecht, Crown Prince. Heir to the throne of Bavaria; commander of a German army from August 1914; of an army group from July 1916

Samsonov, Alexander. Commander of Russian Second Army at Tannenberg, August 1914

Sanders, Otto Liman von. German general, commander of Turkish defenses at Gallipoli

Sarrail, Maurice. Commander of French Third Army, 1914–15; Army of the Orient at Salonika, 1916–17

Sazonov, Sergei. Russian foreign minister, 1910–16

Smith-Dorrien, Horace. Corps and army commander with British Expeditionary Force, August 1914–May 1915

Stopford, Frederick. Commander of the landing force at Suvla Bay, Gallipoli, August 1915

Stürmer, Boris. Russian prime minister, February–November 1916; also served as interior minister and foreign minister

Sukhomlinov, Vladimir. Russian war minister, 1909–15

Tirpitz, Alfred von. Prussian naval minister, 1897–1916

Tisza, István. Prime Minister of Hungary, 1913–17

Trotsky, Leon. Leading member of Bolsheviks; principal political adviser to Lenin; head of Russian delegation to Brest-Litovsk negotiations

Viviani, René. Premier of France, June 1914–October 1915

Wilhelm, Crown Prince. Eldest son and heir of Wilhelm II; commander of the German Fifth Army from August 1914 and of an army group from September 1916

Wilhelm II. Emperor of Germany and King of Prussia, 1888–1918

Wilson, Henry. Britain's military liaison with France

Wilson, Woodrow. U.S. president, 1913–21

Zimmermann, Arthur. German deputy foreign minister

THE WAR IN THE WEST

BRITAIN

London
Thames

Southampton

Dov

English Channel

Seine
Fo

Brest

FRANCE

Atlantic Ocean

Loire
Tours

Nantes

0 Miles   50   100
0 Kilometers 50   100

North Sea

Bremen

NETHERLANDS

Amsterdam ✪

GERMANY

Rhine

Zeebrugge
Ostend

Antwerp

Calais
ARTOIS
Boulogne

FLANDERS

Ghent

BELGIUM

Cologne

Yser
Ypres

Brussels ✪

Liège

Koblenz

Frankfurt

Neuve-Chapelle
Loos
Vimy
Arras
Bapaume
Albert
Amiens
PICARDY

Lille

Lens

Cambrai
Le Cateau
Péronne

Somme

Mons

Namur
Meuse

Charleroi

Sambre

ARDENNES

Mosel

Rhine

St. Quentin

Mondidier

Noyon

CHEMIN
DES DAMES

Sedan

ARGONNE

Luxembourg ✪

Compiègne

Aisne

Soissons

Reims

Longwy

Oise

Ourq

Meuse

Verdun

Metz

Chantilly

Marne

CHAMPAGNE

Troyon

Chateau-
Thierry

St. Mihiel

Paris ✪

Nancy

Strasbourg

Seine

LORRAINE

ALSACE

Seine

Yonne

Moselle

Épinal

Rhine

Orléans

Loire

Saône

Belfort

Basel

SWITZERLAND

© 2005 Jeffrey L. Ward

THE WAR IN THE EAST

NORWAY

Stockholm

SWEDEN

DENMARK

Copenhagen

North Sea

Baltic Sea

Königsberg

Danzig

EAST PRUSSIA

Tannenberg

Amsterdam

NETHERLANDS

Elbe

Berlin

Oder

Posen

Vistula

Brussels

BELGIUM

GERMANY

SILESIA

Lodz

POLAND

Luxembourg

Rhine

Danube

Vistula

Krakow

WESTERN

FRANCE

BAVARIA

Munich

Danube

Vienna

AUSTRIA-HUNGARY

Budapest

SWITZERLAND

TRENTINO

Trento

Piave

Caporetto

Isonzo

Milan

Vittorio Veneto

Venice

Trieste

Danube

Po

ITALY

BOSNIA HERZEGOVINA

Sarajevo

Belgrade

Adriatic Sea

Rome

MONTENEGRO

Mediterranean Sea

ALBANIA

FINLAND

⊛ St. Petersburg

Tallinn

Moscow

Riga

LITHUANIA

Kovno

Stalluponen   Vilna   *Lake Naroch*

Gumbinnen   R U S S I A

Masurian Lakes

Baranovitchi

Bug

Warsaw   Brest-Litovsk

Lublin   *Pripet Marshes*

San   Kiev

Tarnow   Przemysl   EASTERN GALICIA

Gorlice

GALICIA   Lemberg (Lvov)

Carpathian Mountains   Czernowitz   *Dniester*

BUKOVINA

Dnieper

TRANSYLVANIA

0   Miles   100   200

0   Kilometers   200

ROMANIA   Bucharest ⊛

Danube   *Black Sea*

SERBIA

Sofia ⊛

BULGARIA

Constantinople ⊛

Salonika   TURKEY

GREECE   © 2005 Jeffrey L. Ward

Introduction

A decade and more ago, when I first set forth on the journey of discovery that has led to the publication of this book, the hundredth anniversary of the start of the First World War was still several years in the future.

Today, as I write these words, that same anniversary lies three years in the past. It is the centenary of the Great War's *end* that now approaches – and will be here in a matter of months.

The interim between then and now has been, for me, a prolonged immersion in what the American diplomat and historian George F. Kennan called the seminal catastrophe of our time, the one from which so many other catastrophes have sprung. Years of study and reflection have changed many things, where my own view of the war is concerned. To say that the conflict has come to look profoundly different than it did when I began is to understate the case by a rather wide margin.

When my immersion began I believed that I already knew a great deal about the war. In fact I probably did know more about it than most people, even most of my fellow amateur students of history, thanks to a fascination with the subject that had begun in my youth and kept me reading about it into advanced middle age. If asked, I might even have said that I thought I "understood" the war, as if anyone could really understand such an infinity of causes and consequences, motives and delusions, twists and turns of fate.

Today I would make no such claim, because I have learned three helpful things. That when I first got down to work in earnest I didn't know nearly as much as I thought I did. That much of what I thought I knew was either so incomplete as to be dangerously misleading or just not true at all. And that some of the most compelling questions about the war have no certain answers and probably never will.

My notions of why Europe's leading powers all plunged into war in August 1914 – notions shaped by my reading and therefore probably pretty consistent with what is generally believed – began to crumble into incoherence as I looked more deeply and widely into original source materials. The standard answers to other questions, too, often made less and less sense as I learned more. Such questions as why the men in power were unwilling or unable even to try to bring the bloodshed to an end as the costs of continuing became almost insupportable and threatened to include the ruin of European civilization. And why the war, to all appearances hopelessly dead-locked in the opening months of 1918, ended in total victory for the Allies before that year had ended.

Et cetera ad infinitum.

As things I had once thought obviously true lost their credibility, my aspirations too began to change. When I began the research that I hoped would provide the foundation for a worthwhile new history of the war, the readership that I had in mind was mainly American. I believed then – as I believe now, this being one opinion that has not collapsed under the weight of better information – that Americans commonly have little understanding of how immense a disaster the Great War was for Europe. The reasons for this are plain enough. United States troops were in combat for little more than the last six months of the conflict, and were engaged on a massive scale for less than half of that half-year. Their casualties, while far from trivial, were extremely modest by the standards of other belligerents. And the American economy flourished not only through the war but because of it, while Europe – the victor nations little less than the vanquished – was financially ruined.

In a word, the American experience of the war was unique. It has always been easy – too easy – for Americans to celebrate the war as a triumph while minimizing if not ignoring its most tragic dimensions. The book I wanted to write might, I thought, contribute to righting the balance.

Eventually it became clear, however, that Americans are not the only people who still have things to learn about the Great War. In Britain too, though the war is certainly remembered as a tragedy, it nevertheless remains in some ways a misunderstood chapter of the national history. Little less than in the U.S., in the United Kingdom some of the most widely accepted explanations of the causes and consequences of the war, of how it evolved and metastasized and finally brought an almost Pyrrhic victory to one side and a bitterly indigestible defeat to the other, stand upon dubious foundations.

This matters. The importance of the lessons of history, of learning from the mistakes of the past so as to have some chance of not repeating them, is so universally acknowledged as to sometimes seem a tiresome cliché. The story of the Great War is rich in lessons for all of us. But we cannot learn those lessons if we have the story wrong.

At times the wrongness can be so flagrant, and so grossly amplified by the media, as to make it seem that perhaps the war's core myths are simply too firmly rooted ever to be displaced. That, at best, more than a single century will be required for popular understanding of the war to align itself with the truth. The memorial observances that began in August 2014 have provided ample grounds for discouragement. An early example was the BBC's documentary series titled "Britain's Great War." As often happens, a book bearing the same title and the byline of the series' on-screen presenter was published simultaneously with the first broadcast. The presenter and presumed author was one of the BBC's most conspicuous personalities, a gentleman whose professional persona is compounded of shrewd, aggressive knowingness, an attitude of intellectual superiority, and an acerbic, sometimes scornful wit.

Commendably, this famous gentleman ended one of the hours of the series by raising a question of high importance:

Did Germany start the war?

"Well," he said, answering his own question with the kind of lofty self-assurance that according to Mark Twain is usually limited to Christians holding four aces, "Germany *did*, after all, invade France and Russia."

What a devastatingly conclusive answer that would have been – if only it were true. Happening to be aware of its untruth, and having witnessed its delivery to millions of viewers not many of whom could have had reason to doubt what they were told, I wrote a brief letter to the famous gentleman. I congratulated him on his mostly unobjectionable treatment of a subject of high importance, and said I had a question of my own;

How was it, if Germany invaded Russia, that the first clashes of German and Russian armies took place on German soil?

I was of course pleased to receive a response. In his first sentence the famous gentleman said he was pleased that I liked the series. In his second and last he said he was passing my question along to the producers. The impression given was that he regarded the question as a mere technicality, and of no possible interest to a personage as eminent as himself.

From this I infer, I hope not too unfairly, that the famous gentleman's knowledge of the First World War appears to be rather narrowly focused. Apparently it does not encompass the outbreak of the conflict, or much in the way of detail about who did what to whom on the Eastern Front. In fact, the story of how Russia's 1914 invasion of Prussia was crushed by outnumbered defenders is neither unknown nor even obscure. It has been told times beyond numbering, most famously by Barbara Tuchman and Alexander Solzhenitsyn. I surmise also that the book bearing the famous gentleman's name, unless ghostwritten by someone whose knowledge is not so specialized, must be a curious work of history indeed.

It is difficult not to wonder, regretfully, if the BBC entrusted an important act of remembrance, not to mention hours of prime broadcast time, to people who could not or would not treat it with the measure of respect it deserves.

Such thoughts are worse than discouraging. No book on the Great War will ever reach – or influence, one must presume, nearly as many people as the famous intellect's televised pronouncements.

Not all important questions about the Great War have indisputable answers, of course. Not everything we want to know is knowable. There will never be agreement on just when in July 1914 it became inevitable that Britain, France and Russia on one side, Germany and Austria-Hungary on the other, were all going to enter a conflict that none of them wanted and all of them feared. Or on whether it all might have ended differently – sooner, with less terrible results – if the Ottoman Empire had not been drawn in on the side of the Germans, or Italy on the side of the Allies.

Again, et cetera ad infinitum.

Still, the absence of answers does not excuse an ignoring of the many facts that *are* settled. Or the mindless repeating of things the propagandists declared to be true a century ago but have since been shown to fabrications.

The aim of the pages that follow is to separate fact from fabrication, shed new light on the former when new light is called for, and consign as much as possible of the latter to that most venerable of receptacles, the dustbin of history. And to do so in a way that the reader will find not only illuminating, not only interesting, but an enjoyable experience. I am grateful for the opportunity to do my bit in this regard.

G. J. Meyer
Mere, Wiltshire

PART ONE

July 1914

Into the Abyss

Franz Ferdinand and Sophie.

Chapter 1

June 28:

The Black Hand Descends

"It's nothing. It's nothing."
—Archduke Franz Ferdinand

Thirty-four long, sweet summer days separated the morning of June 28, when the heir to the Austro-Hungarian Empire was shot to death, from the evening of August 1, when Russia's foreign minister and Germany's ambassador to Russia fell weeping into each other's arms and what is rightly called the Great War began.

On the morning when the drama opened, Archduke Franz Ferdinand was making an official visit to the city of Sarajevo in the province of Bosnia, at the southernmost tip of the Austro-Hungarian domains. He was a big, beefy man, a career soldier whose intelligence and strong will usually lay concealed behind blunt, impassive features and eyes that, at least in his photographs, often seemed cold and strangely empty. He was also the eldest nephew of the Hapsburg emperor Franz Joseph and therefore—the emperor's only son having committed suicide—heir to the imperial crown. He had come to Bosnia in his capacity as inspector general of the Austro-Hungarian armies, to observe the summer military exercises, and he had brought his wife, Sophie, with him. The two would be observing their fourteenth wedding anniversary later in the week, and Franz Ferdinand was using this visit to put Sophie at the center of things, to give her a little of the recognition she was usually denied.

Back in the Hapsburg capital of Vienna, Sophie was, for the wife of a prospective emperor, improbably close to being a nonperson. At the turn of the century the emperor had forbidden Franz Ferdinand to marry her. She was not of royal lineage, was in fact a mere countess, the daughter of a noble but impoverished Czech family. As a young woman, she had been reduced by financial need to accepting employment as lady-in-waiting to an Austrian archduchess who entertained hopes of marrying her own daughter to Franz Ferdinand. All these things made Sophie, according to the rigid protocols of the Hapsburg court, unworthy to be an emperor's consort or a progenitor of future rulers. The accidental discovery that she and Franz Ferdinand were conducting a secret if chaste romance—that he had been regularly visiting the archduchess's palace not to court her daughter but to see a lowly and thirtyish member of the household staff—sparked outrage, and Sophie had to leave her post. But Franz Ferdinand continued to pursue her. In his youth he had had a long struggle with tuberculosis, and perhaps his survival had left him determined to live his private life on his own terms. Uninterested in any of the young women who possessed the credentials to become his bride, he had remained single into his late thirties. The last two years of his bachelorhood turned into a battle of wills with his uncle the emperor over the subject of Sophie Chotek.

Franz Joseph finally tired of the deadlock and gave his consent. What he consented to, however, was a morganatic marriage, one that would exclude Sophie's descendants from the succession. And so on June 28, 1900, fourteen years to the day before his visit to Sarajevo, Franz Ferdinand appeared as ordered in the Hapsburg monarchy's Secret Council Chamber. In the presence of the emperor, the Cardinal Archbishop of Vienna, the Primate of Hungary, all the government's principal ministers, and all the other Hapsburg archdukes, he solemnly renounced the Austro-Hungarian throne on behalf of any children that he and Sophie might have and any descendants of those children. (Sophie was thirty-two, which in those days made her an all but hopeless spinster.) When the wedding took place three days later, only Franz Ferdinand's mother and sister, out of the whole huge Hapsburg family, attended. Even Franz Ferdinand's brothers, the eldest of whom was a notorious libertine, self-righteously stayed away. The marriage turned out to be a happy one all the same, in short order producing a daughter and two sons whom the usually stiff Franz Ferdinand loved so unreservedly that he would play with them on the floor in the presence of astonished visitors. But at court Sophie was relentlessly snubbed. She was not permitted to ride with her husband in royal processions or to sit near him at state dinners. She could not even join him in his box at the opera. When he, as heir, led the procession at court balls, she was kept far back, behind the lowest ranking of the truly royal ladies.

But here in Bosnia, a turbulent border province, the rules of Vienna could be set aside. Here in Sarajevo, Franz Ferdinand and Sophie could appear together in public as royal husband and wife. It was a rare experience, and they were enjoying it as much as any pair of small-town shopkeepers on their first vacation in years. They were staying in the nearby seaside resort town of Bad Ilidz, and on Saturday they had browsed the local antique markets. They had started Sunday with mass in an improvised chapel at their hotel, after which the archduke sent a telegram to the children, Sophie, Max, and Ernst. Momma and Poppa were well, the wire said. Momma and Poppa were looking forward to getting home on Tuesday.

Franz Ferdinand, his wife Sophie, and two of their children *"Sophie dear, don't die! Stay alive for our children!"*

And now on this brilliant morning, the air crisp and clear after a week of rain and chill, the streets lined with people some of whom cheered and some of whom merely looked on in silence, Sophie was seated beside the archduke in an open car as they rode toward the town hall. They looked less imperial than like characters out of a comic opera: an overweight middle-aged pair, Franz Ferdinand faintly ridiculous in an ornate military headpiece and a field marshal's tunic that stretched too tight across his ample torso, Sophie's plump face smiling cheerily under a broad bonnet and the dainty parasol that, even in the moving car, she held above her head.

Suddenly there was a loud crack: the sound, as police investigators would later determine, of the percussion cap on a Serbian-made pocket bomb being struck against a lamppost. A small dark object was seen flying through the air: the bomb, thrown by someone in the crowd. It was on target, but the driver of the royal car saw it coming and accelerated, so that it fell inches behind the archduke and his wife. Franz Ferdinand too saw it, swung at it with his arm, and deflected it farther to the rear. It exploded with a shattering noise as the car sped off, damaging the next vehicle in the procession and injuring several people. A tiny fragment of shrapnel grazed Sophie's neck.

In the crowds along the route of the motorcade that day were six young men who had traveled to Sarajevo for the purpose of killing the archduke. Five of them, including the one who had thrown the bomb, were Bosnian Serb teenagers—youths born and raised in Bosnia but of Serbian descent. All five were sick with tuberculosis, curiously enough, and all were members of Young Bosnia, a radical patriotic organization linked to and supported by a deeply secret Serb nationalist group formally called Union or Death but known to its members as the Black Hand. Though the Black Hand had been active for years, Austria-Hungary's intelligence services still knew nothing of its existence. Its purpose was the expansion of the Kingdom of Serbia, a smallish and ambitious young country adjacent to Bosnia, so that all the Serbs of the Balkans could be united. Its ultimate goal was the creation of a Greater Serbia that would include Bosnia, and its members were prepared to use terrorism to achieve that goal. The assassins of June 28 had been assembled just across the border in the Serbian capital of Belgrade, armed with bombs and Belgian revolvers, and slipped into Sarajevo well in advance of the archduke's arrival.

June 28, as it happened, was an awkward day for a Hapsburg to be visiting Bosnia. It was St. Vitus Day, which for more than five hundred years had been an occasion of mourning for the Serbs. On St. Vitus Day in 1389 a Serbian kingdom that had flourished through the Middle Ages was defeated by the Ottoman Turks at the Battle of Kosovo, on the so-called Field of Blackbirds. The Serb army was not merely vanquished but slaughtered. Soon afterward the kingdom ceased to exist. The Serbs became subjects—slaves, really—of their savagely harsh Turkish conquerors. Kosovo was avenged in 1912, when the Turks were driven out of the Balkans at last, but it would never be forgotten—certainly not while so many Serbs were still under alien rule. There could be no better day than this one to strike a blow against the oppressors—which now meant a blow against the Hapsburgs, the Turks being gone from the scene.

Between the throwing of the bomb and the motorcade's arrival at the town hall, the car carrying Franz Ferdinand and Sophie drove past three more members of the gang. They were armed but did nothing. Later two of them, after being arrested, made excuses for their failure to act. The third, probably the most truthful, said he had lost his nerve.

After a standard ceremonial welcome—the mayor, absurdly, didn't deviate from a script declaring that everyone in Sarajevo honored the archduke and was delighted by this visit—Franz Ferdinand announced a change in his itinerary. He insisted on going to the hospital where the people injured by the bomb had been taken. It was the right Hapsburg gesture, a demonstration of concern for servants of the crown. Franz Ferdinand asked Sophie to stay behind, out of any possible danger. She refused, saying that her place was with him. This did not seem reckless. The military governor of Bosnia, who was riding in the same car with the couple that morning, had already declared his confidence that there would be no further trouble. If he knew anything about the Serb fanatics, he said, it was that they were capable of only one assassination attempt per day.

The motorcade set out once again. The route originally

planned by the authorities was still cleared of traffic, and the lead driver mistakenly took it rather than the road to the hospital. The others followed. They passed still another would-be assassin, but he too did nothing. When the governor, seated in front of Franz Ferdinand and Sophie, discovered that they were going the wrong way, he ordered their driver to stop. The driver brought the car to a halt, shifted gears, and prepared to turn around. By a coincidence that has reverberated down the decades, he had stopped less than five feet from Gavrilo Princip, nineteen years old, the one remaining member of the assassination gang and its leader. Princip pulled out his revolver, pointed it at the stopped car, and fired twice.

Husband and wife remained upright and calm in their seats. The governor, seeing no signs of injury and thinking that they must have escaped harm, shouted again at the driver, telling him to turn around.

Suddenly a thin stream of blood came spurting out of Franz Ferdinand's mouth.

"For heaven's sake!" cried Sophie. "What's happened to you?" Then she slumped over, her head falling between her husband's knees. The military governor thought she had fainted, but somehow the archduke knew better.

"Sophie dear, Sophie dear, don't die!" he called. "Stay alive for our children!" Other members of the party surrounded him, struggling to open his tunic to see where he had been shot. "It's nothing," he told them weakly. "It's nothing."

Gavrilo Princip meanwhile tried to shoot himself in the head but was stopped by a member of the crowd. In the struggle that followed, he managed to swallow his vial of the cyanide that all the members of the gang had been given. The cyanide was old: it would make him vomit but not kill him. He was quickly captured.

Within minutes Franz Ferdinand and Sophie were both dead. (Princip, in prison, would express regret at Sophie's death, which he had not intended; the bullet that killed her had passed through the door of the car before striking her in the groin and severing an artery.) The news caused a sensation, of course, but there was little sense of crisis. In Vienna the eighty-three-year-old emperor, Franz Joseph, seemed almost grateful when he heard. He had long regarded Franz Ferdinand as a nuisance, not only because of the marriage problem but also because of the archduke's unpleasantly advanced ideas. (He had even wanted, ironically, to give the Hapsburgs' Slavic subjects, the Bosnian Serbs included, a voice in the governance of the empire.) Apparently Franz Joseph believed at first that the Sarajevo murders had simplified things, had even put them right. "A higher power," his private secretary would remember him saying, "has re-established the order which I, alas, could not preserve."

Germany's Kaiser Wilhelm II, when he learned of the assassination, ended his sailing vacation off the coast of Norway and headed for home. He did so more because he and the archduke had been friends than because he foresaw an emergency; he and his wife had been guests at Franz Ferdinand and Sophie's country estate just weeks before.

From his royal yacht the *Standart,* Tsar Nicholas II of Russia declared three weeks of mourning in honor of the slain archduke. Beyond that he showed little interest; he had other things on his mind. His ten-year-old only son had a few days earlier twisted his ankle in jumping aboard the *Standart* for a family cruise in the Gulf of Finland. The injury activated the hemophilia that the boy had inherited from his mother, who in turn had inherited it from her grandmother, Queen Victoria of England. By June 28 he was in intense pain from internal bleeding. His parents, not for the first time and not for the last, feared for his survival.

The murders aroused little interest in Britain and France. Both countries were focused on other stories, London on a crisis over Ireland, Paris on a sensational murder trial that combined sex with political scandal. And assassinations were not unusual in those days. In the two decades before 1914, presidents of the United States, France, Mexico, Guatemala, Uruguay, and the Dominican Republic had been murdered. So had prime ministers of Russia, Spain, Greece, Bulgaria, Persia, and Egypt, and kings, queens, and empresses of Austria, Italy, Serbia, Portugal, and Greece. People had grown accustomed to such things and to expecting that their consequences would not be terribly serious.

Across the Atlantic in the United States, yet another killing of people no one had ever heard of in a place no one had ever heard of could hardly have seemed less important. President Woodrow Wilson had only somewhat more interest in European affairs than most of his fellow citizens, though he was inclined to believe that he might be the man to enlighten the Old World and save it from its foolish ways. During the summer his personal emissary, a Texan who styled himself "Colonel" Edward House despite never having served in any military capacity, spent two months visiting the capitals of the great powers and conferring with some of their most important men. "My purpose," House confided to his diary, perhaps somewhat smugly, "was to plant the seeds of peace." What he found, he reported to Wilson, was "militarism run stark mad. Unless someone acting for you [it is not difficult to guess who he thought that someone might be] can bring about a different understanding, there is some day to be an awful cataclysm."

House would depart for home having accomplished essentially nothing. He returned to an America that appeared to be on the verge of war with Mexico (U.S. troops had forcibly occupied the coastal town of Veracruz in April), was embroiled in violent labor disputes (also in April, Wilson had sent troops to Colorado to crush a strike by coal miners), but was as confident as the president of its uniquely virtuous, uniquely pacific role in the world. William Jennings Bryan, Wilson's secretary of state, saw it as "the imperative duty of the United States . . . to set a shining example of disarmament." In January the influential *Review of Reviews* had

Col. Edward House,
confidant to Woodrow Wilson
*"There is some day to be
an awful cataclysm."*

confidently told its readers that "the world is moving away from military ideals; and a period of peace, industry and world-wide friendship is dawning," while statesman and Nobel Peace Prize winner Elihu Root wrote unhappily that, even for educated Americans, "international law was regarded as a rather antiquated branch of useless learning, diplomacy as a foolish mystery and the foreign service as a superfluous expense."

None of these people had even the faintest idea, as June ended, of what lay just ahead. But they are hardly to be blamed. What was coming was unlike anything anyone had ever seen.

THE SERBS

NO ONE COULD HAVE BEEN SURPRISED THAT trouble had broken out in the southeastern corner of Europe, or that the Serbs were at the center of that trouble. In 1914, as before and since, the Balkan Peninsula was the most unstable region in Europe, a jumble of ill-defined small nations, violently shifting borders, and intermingled ethnic groups filled with hatred for one another and convinced of their right to expand. By 1914 the Balkans were exploding annually. The little Kingdom of Serbia, seething with resentment and ambition, was never not involved.

The roots of the trouble went deep. Almost two millennia ago the dividing line between the Eastern and Western Roman Empires ran through the Balkans, and so the dividing line between the Catholic and Orthodox worlds has run through the region ever since. Later, after the Turks forced their way into Europe, the Balkans became another of the things it continues to be today: the home of Europe's only indigenous Muslim population, the point where European Christendom ends and Islam begins. Through many generations the Balkans were a prize fought over by Muslim Turkey, Catholic Austria, and Orthodox Russia. By 1914, Turkey having been pushed almost entirely out of the region, the contest was between Russia and Austria-Hungary only, with Turkey waiting on the sidelines in hope of recovering some part of what it had lost.

The Russians wanted Constantinople above all. In pre-Christian times it had been the Greek city of Byzantium, and it then became the Eastern Roman capital until falling to the Turks. It dominated the long chain of waterways—the Dardanelles, the Sea of Marmara, the Bosporus—that linked Russia's Black Sea ports to the Mediterranean. Possession of Constantinople would make the *tsar*—the word means "caesar" in Russian, as does *kaiser* in German—what Russia's rulers had long claimed to be: rightful leader of the whole Orthodox world, rightful heir to the old eastern empire. It was largely with Constantinople in mind that the Russians anointed themselves patrons and protectors of the Slavic and Orthodox populations in the Balkans, the Serbs included. As the nineteenth century unfolded and the Turkish empire entered a terminal state of decay, it was mainly Britain that kept the Russians from seizing Constantinople. The British were motivated not by any affection for the Turks but by simple self-interest. They feared that Russian expansion to the south would threaten their own position in the Middle East and ultimately their control of India.

The Serbs had been part of a wave of so-called South Slavs (Yugoslavs, in their language) that moved into the Balkan region during the seventh century, when the Eastern Roman Empire was beginning to totter (Rome itself had collapsed much earlier) and many tribal groups were on the move. In the centuries that followed, the Serbs built a miniature empire under their own tsar. For a time it was uncertain whether all the Serbs would be Orthodox or some would be Roman Catholic, but eventually they settled into the Orthodox faith. Thereby they helped to ensure that a thousand years hence their descendants would identify themselves with the greatest of Slavic and Orthodox nations, Russia, and would look to the Russians for protection. They assured also that religious differences would contribute to separating them from Catholic Austria and from the Magyars (many of them Calvinist Protestants) who dominated Hungary.

From the late Middle Ages, in the aftermath of their defeat at Kosovo, the Serbs were trapped inside the empire of the Ottoman Turks. By the eighteenth century the Turks, the Austrians, and the Russians were entangled in what would turn into two hundred years of bloody conflict in and over the Balkans. In 1829 a Russian victory over the increasingly incompetent and helpless Turks made possible the emergence of a new principality that was, if almost invisibly tiny, the first Serbian state in almost half a millennium and a rallying point for Serbian nationalism. In the 1870s another Russo-Turkish war broke out, with Serbia fighting actively on the side of Russia this time and gaining more territory as a result. Now there was once again a Kingdom of Serbia, a rugged, mountainous, and landlocked little country surrounded by the whole boiling ethnic stew of the Balkans. Its neighbors were Europe's only Muslims, Catholics, and Orthodox Christians some of whom thought of themselves as Serbs and some of whom did not. Among those neighbors were Magyars, Bulgars, Croats, Albanians, Macedonians, Romanians, Montenegrans, Greeks, and—just across the border in Bosnia—brother Serbs suffering the indignity of not living in Serbia. Despite the inconvenient fact that Serbs were only a minority of the Bosnian population (fully a third were Muslims, and one in five was Croatian and therefore Roman Catholic), the incorporation of Bosnia into an Orthodox and Slavic Greater Serbia became an integral part of the Serbs' national dream. The fact that under international law Bosnia was the possession of two of the great powers—officially of the Ottomans but actually of the Austrians in recent years—mattered to Serbia not at all.

As the years passed, trouble erupted with increasing frequency, and sometimes with shocking brutality. At the start of the twentieth century Serbia had a king and queen who were friendly to Hapsburg Vienna. In 1903 a group of disgruntled army officers staged a coup, shot the royal pair to death, threw their naked bodies out the windows of their Belgrade palace, and replaced them with a dynasty loyal to Russia.

In 1908 Austria-Hungary enraged Serbia by annexing Bosnia and the adjacent little district of Herzegovina, taking them from the Ottoman Turks and making them full and presumably permanent provinces of the Hapsburg empire. Serbia turned to Russia for help. The Russians, however, were still recovering from a 1905 war with Japan in which total and humiliating defeat had exposed the incompetence of both their army and their navy, forced the abandonment of their ambitions in the Far East, and ignited a revolution at home. As a result—and to its further humiliation—the Russian government felt incapable of doing anything to support the Serbs.

In 1911 the same conspirators who had murdered Serbia's royal family founded Union or Death, the Black Hand. Then in 1912 came the First Balkan War. Serbia joined with several of its neighbors to drive the Turks all the way back to Istanbul. The victory doubled the kingdom's size and raised its population to four and a half million. A year later, in the Second Balkan War, Serbia defeated its neighbor and onetime ally Bulgaria. Again it grew larger, briefly seizing part of the Dalmatian coast but being forced to withdraw when the Austrians threatened to invade. Serbia was still getting not nearly as much support as it wanted from Russia, but France, seeing a strategic opportunity in the Balkans, was now providing money, arms, and training to the Serbian army. France's motives were transparent: to make Serbia strong enough to tie up a substantial part of the Austro-Hungarian army in case of war, so that France and its ally Russia (and Britain too, if everything went perfectly) would be free to deal with Germany alone.

To what extent did the government of Serbia know in advance of the plot to kill Franz Ferdinand? To what extent could Belgrade therefore be held responsible? As with many parts of this story, the answer is neither clear nor simple. Prime Minister Nikola Pasic, a shrewd old man with a majestic white beard, did hear about the plot weeks before the shooting, but he emphatically disapproved. He put out the word on the Belgrade grapevine that the plot should be called off. On the other hand, Serbian officialdom was not entirely innocent. The leader of the Black Hand was the country's chief of military intelligence, one Colonel Dragutin Dimitrijevic, a monomaniacally dedicated Pan-Serb nationalist whose physical strength had caused him to be nicknamed "Apis" after a divine bull in ancient Egyptian mythology. Apis had been the mastermind behind the strategy that led to Serbia's successes in the Balkan wars. Now, in 1914, he was the mastermind behind the plot to kill Franz Ferdinand. But there has never been any evidence that Pasic's cabinet was involved.

On the contrary, Apis and his allies in the Black Hand and the military saw Pasic as an obstacle, even as an enemy. The prime minister's lack of enthusiasm for extreme measures, for another round of war, was contemptible in their eyes. Pasic was so unacceptable to the Serbian army's high command that in June 1914 the generals forced him out of office. He was almost immediately restored, but only at the insistence of the Russians and the French, who regarded him as sane and sensible and therefore as a badly needed man in the Balkans. Pasic's return to office was a defeat for Apis, an indication that his influence was waning. Apis may have seen the assassination of Franz Ferdinand as a way of precipitating a crisis that would cause Pasic's government to fall, and if the crisis led to war, he would not have been likely to regard that as too high a price to pay. Pasic, on the other hand, understood that Serbia was physically and financially exhausted after two wars in as many years—its casualties had totaled ninety thousand, an immense number for such a small country— and that the army was in no condition to challenge the Austrians. In case of war, Serbia would be able to muster only eleven badly equipped divisions against Vienna's forty-eight. And of course Pasic

Serbian Prime Minister Nikola Pasic
"Our cause is just. God will help us."

was mindful of Russia's failure to come to Serbia's aid in 1908, in 1912, and again in 1913.

Why didn't Pasic intervene more actively to stop the assassination? Actually, he went so far in that direction as to put himself at risk. He sent out an order that the three conspirators whose names had become known to him should be stopped from crossing the border into Bosnia. But the answer came back that he was too late—the three were already across. He then directed his ambassador in Vienna to deliver an oral warning. But this ambassador, himself an ardent Serb nationalist, had no great enthusiasm for such a mission. He met with Austria's finance minister rather than with someone better positioned to take action on such a matter. He expressed himself so vaguely—he said he was concerned that "some young Serb might put a live rather than a blank cartridge in his gun, and fire it," never indicating that

Belgrade had knowledge of an actual plot and even knew the names of conspirators already in Sarajevo—that the finance minister could see no reason for alarm and was given no basis on which to do anything. It must have seemed to Pasic, who could have known nothing of how his warning had been diluted, that there was nothing more he could do. That summer Serbia was in the midst of an election. The result would decide whether Pasic remained as prime minister. It would have been suicide, certainly politically and perhaps literally, for him to become known as the enemy—the betrayer, even—of the most violently passionate patriots in the kingdom.

By then no one but the assassins themselves could have stopped the assassination. Not even the Black Hand, not even Apis himself, was now in control. On June 14 Apis told a meeting of the Black Hand executive committee of his plans for Sarajevo in two more weeks. The committee's members did not react as he expected. They voted that the plot must be called off. Like Pasic, they realized that the assassination could lead to war with the empire next door, and undoubtedly they understood that the prime minister had reason to be opposed. Apis, through a chain of intermediaries, managed to get word to the assassination gang to abandon its plot. Now it was his turn to be ignored. Gavrilo Princip, in an interview with a psychiatrist as he lay dying of tuberculosis in an Austrian prison midway through the war (an interview in which, strangely, he often spoke of himself in the third person), would say that in going to Sarajevo "he only wanted to die for his ideals." He had been happy to accept the Black Hand's weapons but unwilling to obey when instructed not to use them.

Chapter 2

Never Again

*"In 1908–1909 we would have been playing cards
up, in 1912–1913 we still had a clear chance,
now we have to go for all or nothing."*
—Austrian Field Marshal Franz Conrad

Leopold von Berchtold and Franz Conrad were polar opposites as men, and over the years they had often been at odds over how Austria-Hungary should deal with its Serbian problem. But in the days following the assassination, their differences disappeared and they became partners. To understand how this happened is to understand much about the origins of the war.

Conrad (Conrad von Hötzendorf was his full family name, but the *von* part was an addition, an honorific that had come with his grandfather's elevation to the nobility) was a soldier to the marrow of his bones, sometimes even a rather fanatical one. His father had been an officer; he himself began his military training at age eleven, and he became chief of the Austro-Hungarian general staff in 1906 at the age of fifty-four. He looked the part: a compact, tidy figure with a fierce mustache that turned up at the corners and pale hair cut in a brush. He was an almost neurotically hard worker, intent upon trying to turn the hodgepodge Austro-Hungarian armies into a modern and effective fighting force, constantly drawing up and issuing new orders and war plans, painfully conscious that the empire was militarily weak and its status among Europe's great powers no longer assured. He was certain that the empire could save itself only by asserting itself in the Balkans—above all by eliminating Serbia's endless subversion and, if possible, by eliminating Serbia. Time after time, until Emperor Franz Joseph grew sick of hearing it, he had urged attacks on the Serb kingdom. At times he even wanted to attack the recently created Kingdom of Italy, which officially was Austria's ally but had taken over a great expanse of what had previously been Hapsburg territory and was obviously hungry for more. In 1911 Conrad had been dismissed from his position as chief of staff because of his obsessive aggressiveness. But a year later war in the Balkans made his talents and his energy seem indispensable. And so he was recalled to duty and showed himself to be no less bellicose than before. In the course of 1913 he made no fewer than twenty-five proposals for war on Serbia.

Count Berchtold, by contrast, was an enormously wealthy, deeply cultivated, pleasure-loving aristocrat of ancient family. And he too looked the part: polished, serenely self-assured, a vision of elegance in spotless collars and cuffs and diamond stickpins. He spoke German, French, Hungarian, Czech, and Slovak, and he had married a Hungarian heiress. (Unusually, he held both Austrian and Hungarian citizenships, and when asked his nationality, he said he was "Viennese.") He owned a racing stable and was famous for his charm and his success with women. He was also widely regarded as weak, lazy, frivolous, and unreliable. He

Conrad von Hötzendorf
Chief of Staff of
Austro-Hungarian Army
Frustrated by Austria's
passivity during the
two Balkan Wars.

had spent much of his early career as a diplomat in Paris and London, splendid places for a wealthy young nobleman eager to indulge his many appetites. He became the Austro-Hungarian ambassador to Russia in 1907 and was appointed foreign minister in 1912, when he was fifty years old. His conduct in the Balkan crises of that year and 1913, when Serbia enlarged itself at the expense of the Turks and the Bulgarians while Vienna stood by watching, had cemented his reputation for passivity and vacillation. Conrad among others came to be convinced that Berchtold lacked the backbone to protect Hapsburg interests in the slippery world of great power diplomacy. Berchtold himself was well aware by then that important people regarded him as unworthy to be foreign minister and that he needed to repair his reputation. He was ready to believe what Conrad had always believed: that the monarchy had squandered too many opportunities in its area of greatest vulnerability, the Balkans. He expected good opportunities to be far less plentiful in the years ahead, now that Serbia had grown bigger and Russia was recovering its strength, and he was as determined as Conrad not to let the next one slip away. He had become, in short, dangerous: a weak man determined to appear strong. Within forty-eight hours of the assassination he was calling for "a final and fundamental reckoning with Serbia."

Austria-Hungary in 1914 was a second-rate and declining empire trying desperately to hang on to its traditional place among the nations that recognized one another as Europe's leading powers. In the half-century leading up to the Sarajevo assassinations, it had been displaced as leader of the German states—had been, in effect, evicted from Germany—by Otto von Bismarck, Prussia's great chancellor and the creator of the new German Empire. Then it had lost great hunks of territory—Tuscany, Lombardy—to a new Kingdom of Italy that, although also militarily weak, was supported in its expansion by France. Austria-Hungary had become a paradox, simultaneously obsolete and ahead of its time. In an era of nationalism run rampant, it was not a nation at all but a cobbled-together assortment of thirteen nationalities that spoke sixteen languages, belonged to five major religions, and were organized into seventeen "lands" served by twenty parliaments. But it had the potential to provide a model for a Europe in which diverse peoples could live together in peace and might even, one day, think of uniting. Archduke Franz Ferdinand, as much as Franz Joseph disliked him, had appeared to understand that potential. His murder left the empire without the one man who might possibly have been strong and canny enough to lead it through the crisis of 1914. The archduke had always disliked Conrad's lust for military adventures and almost certainly would have restrained him. He was "a man," as Berchtold would observe sadly amid the ruins of postwar Europe, whom "the monarchy needed."

Just across Hungary's southernmost border was the nightmare Kingdom of Serbia, stirring unrest whenever it could. For many Austrians, and not only for such hawks as Field Marshal Conrad, the empire faced a simple choice: it could maintain a strong position in the Balkans, or it could allow itself to be gradually undone by implacably hostile, Russian-sponsored Balkan troublemakers. The threat was not only external—every new Serbian success seemed an incitement for the many ethnic minorities inside Austria-Hungary to seek either independence or union with whatever Balkan nation they felt themselves to be linked to by culture, religion, blood, and geography. The situation was a recipe for trouble, and throughout the decade leading up to 1914, one development after another added new poisons to the mix.

The first of these developments, when it came in 1906, was a Gilbert and Sullivan–style affair that came to be known, in suitably comic fashion, as the Pig War. Serbia was still a tiny country at that time, but its position on Bosnia's border gave it opportunities for mischief that the expansionists were delighted to exploit. Exasperated officials in Vienna, almost desperate to find some way to strike back, decided that they could punish and perhaps even subdue Serbia economically by refusing to import its livestock, pigs included. They enacted an embargo that went on for five years and accomplished nothing except to make Vienna look ridiculous. The Serbs were able to find so many new markets for their animals that their exports increased. They learned—or thought they learned, which came down to the same thing—that they could defy the mighty Hapsburgs and pay no price for doing so.

Things turned in a more serious direction in 1908. Austria, having had no success in stopping Serbia from making trouble in

Bosnia and Herzegovina, became increasingly concerned about the fact that, in strict legal terms, these two southernmost pieces of its empire didn't belong to it at all. According to international law, they were still provinces of the Ottoman Empire, though Austria had occupied and administered them since 1878, when the Turks had been forced to withdraw after suffering another in their seemingly endless series of defeats. Vienna saw that it had good reason to fear the consequences if somehow this territory ever became part of Serbia. And the aggressiveness of the Serbs, coupled with the increasingly decrepit state of the Ottoman Empire, made such a development far from unimaginable. So Vienna announced that it was annexing Bosnia and Herzegovina into the Austro-Hungarian Empire. Serbia, predictably, howled in protest and appealed to Russia. But Russia was still recovering from its disastrous war with Japan and the revolution that followed and therefore was powerless to intervene.

Conrad, who was by then entering his third year as the Austrian army's chief of staff, wanted to send his troops into Serbia and regarded victory as assured. He had at his disposal a standing army of more than three hundred and sixty thousand men, while Serbia at this point had fewer than twenty thousand. Even more important, he had the full support of the Germans, who understood the extent of Russia's impotence and were increasingly worried about Austria's slow decline. The time seemed right for eviscerating Serbia, perhaps for partitioning her out of existence. Characteristically, Conrad started saying that scores might be settled with other neighbors too: with tiny Montenegro, for example, another Balkan nuisance and an ally of Serbia's. And perhaps even with Italy, which had its own territorial ambitions in the Balkans but would have been hopelessly outmatched in a war with Austria.

Not everyone in Austria and Berlin wanted war. Emperor Franz Joseph, in his sixtieth year on the throne by then, had experienced far more military humiliations than triumphs in the course of his long life and had little appetite for a new adventure. The Hungarians were always opposed to any move that might disturb the status quo. They feared that a military victory that brought still more Serbs into the empire would dilute their influence by turning the dual monarchy into a three-cornered system with the Slavs as equal partners. This was not an idle idea: it had powerful advocates in Vienna. People who knew Franz Ferdinand well were convinced that he planned to bring the Slavs into a triple monarchy upon succeeding to the throne.

Germany ended the crisis by issuing an ultimatum: unless the Russians approved the annexation, Germany would regard Vienna as justified in moving against Serbia. Resentfully, Russia yielded. It had no choice.

Supposedly this was a great diplomatic victory. Conrad, however, regarded it as a disaster. Others agreed, among them some of Germany's leading generals. And they had persuasive arguments on their side. Austria had come out of the crisis without acquiring one inch of territory and without having done anything to weaken Serbia. The annexation had, on the other hand, infuriated both the Kingdom of Serbia and those Serb nationalists living in Bosnia. It had subjected Russia to a fresh humiliation—this was the first time in its history that Russia had had to yield to the demands of another European nation. It showed Russia the importance of building up its army as quickly as possible, clinging to its alliance with France, and becoming capable of demonstrating that it was not a useless ally.

Three years after the annexation crisis, the Balkans began to convulse. It is a measure of just how far the decay of the Ottoman Empire had advanced that in 1912 the minuscule nation of Montenegro launched an attack on the once-invincible Turks. Serbia, Bulgaria, and Greece all joined in, and in a single stunning month the Turks were driven from a region they had dominated for more than five hundred years. The map of the Balkans was redrawn. Immediately the victors doubled in size. Serbia was now big enough to be, not a major power certainly, but a real military problem for Austria.

This First Balkan War began and ended before Austria was able to mobilize its army and become involved. Thereafter the balance of power shifted significantly not only in the Balkans but in Europe as a whole, and in ways that were not at all to Vienna's advantage. No longer was there an Ottoman presence in the Balkans to balance Russia's, and Russia's Balkan allies had grown more powerful than ever. Again there had been demands in Vienna for military action, and of course Conrad had been in favor.

Berchtold, now the foreign minister, had opposed him. So had Franz Ferdinand, who was shrewd enough to understand that making war on Slav neighbors was no way to win the loyalty of Vienna's tens of million of restive Slavic subjects. Once again nothing was done. One reason for Vienna's failure to act was the mobilization, by a Russia that was nonetheless extremely fearful of war, of many thousands of troops. Another was a conspicuous absence of support from Berlin. The kaiser's government told the Austrians that there was no popular support in Germany for a war in the Balkans, so that hostilities were politically impossible.

One of the winners of the 1912 war, Bulgaria, was a rival of Serbia's and therefore a potential ally for Austria: this was a world in which the enemy of your enemy was sometimes your only friend. Bulgaria was not satisfied with its gains in the war, and in 1913, less than a month after the finalization of the peace agreement, it launched a surprise attack on Serbia. Greece and Montenegro both came to Serbia's aid. So did Romania, which had not been involved in 1912. Even Turkey, hoping to recoup some of its losses, came in against Bulgaria, which quickly went down to defeat. It was all over before Austria could even ready its army for action. Serbia's gains this time included part of the Adriatic coast—like Bosnia and Herzegovina, one of the prime objectives of the Serb expansionists. When peace was restored, Vienna insisted that Serbia withdraw from the coast. Serbia refused. Austria, almost petulantly determined to stop Serbia from getting *everything* it wanted, issued an ultimatum: If Serbia didn't get out of Albania, it would be attacked. Again Serbia turned to Russia for help, and again the Russians showed themselves to be reluctant. Finding that even Britain and France opposed their occupation of the coast, and infuriated despite their other gains, the Serbs pulled back. The area they gave up became the new nation of Albania.

By the summer of 1914 the Balkans were a region in which nobody was satisfied and everyone found reason to be angry and afraid. The Turks had lost almost everything they had ever possessed in the region; Bulgaria had lost much of its spoils from 1913; and although Greece had kept its gains, it did not think it had been given enough. The region was as unstable as it had ever been.

Russia and Austria both were aggrieved as well: Russia because it was seen as having failed the states whose patron it wanted to be; Austria because, only five years after it let slip its best opportunity to crush Serbia, it had been able to do nothing while the part of the world where it felt most threatened was reshaped to Serbia's advantage. Certain that their credibility would be destroyed if they permitted any such thing to recur, both empires resolved never to be so weak and passive again.

The Austrians concluded also that the international conferences that ended both Balkan wars had done them no good. Only their ultimatum to Serbia, their direct threat of war, had made a difference. They had learned to regard peace conferences as traps.

Finally, the Austrians were disgusted by Germany's failure to support them. Germany knew this; it was something that Berlin now had to take into account. Feeble though it might be, Austria-Hungary was the only even marginally dependable ally that Germany had in all of Europe. If the Germans again failed to support Austria-Hungary in a crisis, if they lost their junior partner as a result, they would be alone and surrounded by enemies. The conclusion, for Berlin, was obvious. Never again must Vienna have reason to doubt the value of its alliance with Germany.

Never again. For three weeks and more following the assassination of Franz Ferdinand, that was the German position.

THE HAPSBURGS

IN 1914 EMPEROR FRANZ JOSEPH WAS IN HIS SIXTY-sixth year at the head of the most successful family in the history of Europe. He ruled an empire that extended from what is now the Czech Republic and deep inside what is now Poland to the Italian port city of Trieste. He did so from grand palaces in and near Vienna, a city as cosmopolitan, as culturally rich, and as beautiful as any in the world. He had been doing so since he was eighteen years old, which made him one of the longest-reigning monarchs in the history of the world.

He was not only very old, however, but also sad, tired, lonely, and profoundly bored with life. He had always been the most conscientious of autocrats; even at eighty-four he rose daily before dawn, was at his desk by five A.M. after saying his morning prayers on his knees, and worked around the clock. And what he had to look back on, after so many decades of dull toil, was enough disappointment and failure to blight any three lives. Little wonder that he spoke, in unguarded moments, of yearning for death. It was almost as if he knew that his dynasty was now near the end of its thousand-year run.

But what a run it had been. The Hapsburgs had been kings of Austria and other places (Bohemia, Germany, Hungary, and Spain, to name just some) for six and a half centuries. With minor interruptions, they had been emperors for more than four and a half centuries. At their apex in the 1500s they had dominated Europe and the New World as no family has done before or since.

The name of the first member of the line to appear in recorded history, one Guntram the Rich, makes clear that even in his time, a century before the Norman conquest of England, the family was prospering to a far-from-common degree. In 1273 a descendant of Guntram's became the first Hapsburg monarch, King Rudolf I of Germany. One of Rudolf's sons succeeded him on the German throne, and another became King of Austria. Thereafter the Hapsburgs were never less than royal; the only question, from then on, was how many kingdoms the family would rule at any given time.

From the year 800, when the barbarian chief of a Germanic tribe called the Franks went to Rome and had himself crowned Emperor Charles (we remember him as Charlemagne, the Germans as Karl der Grosse), the rulers of Germany had fancied themselves successors to the ancient emperors of Rome. As a result of their ancestors' success in overrunning the Roman Empire in the fourth and fifth centuries, they controlled much of Italy. They did so through the Dark and Middle Ages and on through the Renaissance into modern times. The highest possible honor for a German was to become Holy Roman emperor, a title that continued to represent supremacy over the fragmented German states even when the men who held it no longer controlled Rome. The last German emperor to be crowned in Rome was a member of the Hapsburg family's Austrian branch. He became Emperor Frederick III in 1440, and though the throne was "elective" (the only voters were the hereditary rulers of major German states, including Austria), from that point on the Hapsburgs had so much

Emperor Franz Joseph
*"All are dying,
only I can't die."*

wealth and power that until 1711 not a single non-Hapsburg was elected to it.

Apparently thanks to his mother, Frederick III was the first member of the line to display the famous "Hapsburg lip," a sometimes grotesque protuberance of the lower lip and jaw that became a mark of the family as its members had increasing difficulty finding spouses worthy of their exalted status and so, increasingly, married one another. He was also distinguished by his success in raising the Hapsburg practice of making advantageous marriages to a level never equaled. The Hapsburgs were not warriors or adventurers; rather, they were congenitally risk-averse. They expanded their holdings less by the sword than by matrimony. In the days when every educated European knew Latin, a saying about the Hapsburgs became famous: *Bella gerant alii, tu felix Austria nube.* "Let others wage wars; you, happy Austria, marry."

First Frederick III married his son Maximilian to the heiress to the Netherlands, Luxembourg, and the Artois and Burgundy regions that are now parts of France. Then, a generation later, he married Maximilian's son Philip to the eldest daughter and heir of Ferdinand and Isabella of Spain. By this marriage the family acquired not only Spain, not only the kingdoms of Naples and Sicily and Sardinia, but all of Spain's vast possessions in the New World. That Philip's Spanish bride happened to be insane scarcely seemed to matter.

All this was inherited by Philip's son, Emperor Charles V, who thereby ruled more of the world than any man ever had and along the way added the kingdoms of Portugal and Milan to his domain. Charles ultimately found his possessions to be more than one man could manage, so he divided them. His son Philip II was based near Madrid as King of Spain (and was married for a time to Mary Tudor, the queen of England called Bloody Mary, failing however to produce a child with her and thereby to secure that promising little realm for the Hapsburgs). Charles's brother Ferdinand became Holy Roman emperor and took charge of the eastern, German branch of the family business.

It was downhill from there. The Spanish line of the Hapsburgs died out after a few generations, evidently the victim of inbreeding (a practice that also weakened the German line, though not to the point of extinction) and of the insanity brought into the family through the marriage that had given it Spain in the first place. The last Hapsburg king of Spain, Charles II, married three times but failed to reproduce. The Austrian line was more vigorous but beset with problems. France under Louis XIV seized all of the Hapsburgs' possessions west of the Rhine, including the provinces of Alsace and Lorraine. The Ottoman Turks invaded Europe, conquered most of the Balkans, and twice reached the gates of Vienna before being turned back. The Reformation cast Catholic Austria into the role of enemy in newly Protestant northern Germany. This was particularly convenient for Prussia, the leading Protestant state on the continent, which grabbed important pieces of the Hapsburg inheritance. Finally there came the rise of Napoleon Bonaparte. He occupied Vienna twice, stripped away many of the Hapsburgs' southern possessions, and, determined to produce an heir, took a juicy little Hapsburg princess (the grandniece of Marie Antoinette, also a member of the family) as his bride.

Napoleon ended the fiction of the Holy Roman Empire, and from that point forward the Hapsburg monarchs bore the humbler title of hereditary emperors of Austria. The Congress of Vienna that followed the fall of Napoleon, as part of its program of restoring the old order across Europe, returned to the Hapsburgs some of their most important southern holdings, including northern Italy. After that things remained relatively tranquil for more than thirty years.

Then came the Revolution of 1848, an upheaval in which, from France to Russia, people demanding reform rose up against their rulers. Most of the major cities of the Hapsburg empire revolted, and for a time the survival of the dynasty was in question. The childless emperor at the time abdicated, and a younger brother was passed over in favor of his son Franz Joseph. The royalists hoped that this attractive boy, tall, vigorous, and only eighteen years old, could win the loyalty of his subjects. Their hopes were fulfilled. Franz Joseph, born during the presidency of Andrew Jackson and crowned twelve years before the election of Abraham Lincoln, was still on the throne when Woodrow Wilson moved into the White House.

Both personally and politically, however, Franz Joseph's reign was almost as sorrowful as it was long. Everything went wrong for him in the end. As a young man, he married the most beautiful princess in Europe, Elizabeth of Bavaria, but after six happy years and four children he passed on to her the gonorrhea that he had contracted on one of his disastrous Italian campaigns. Formalities aside, that was the end of the marriage.

In 1859 Austria was driven out of Lombardy in northern Italy by the rising forces of Italian nationalism. Shortly thereafter it lost Tuscany and Modena as well.

In 1866 Prussia defeated Austria and forced it to abandon its ancient claim to leadership over Germany. At this point, fearful of further losses, Franz Joseph entered into a compact under which Hungary became not merely one of the empire's possessions but an equal partner in a new and peculiar kind of dual monarchy. The ruler would be not only emperor of Austria but also "apostolic king" of Hungary. Austria and Hungary each would have its own prime minister and parliament, though the war, finance, and foreign affairs ministries would be centralized in Vienna. This arrangement was successful insofar as it gave the Magyars, who dominated Hungary, a more powerful and secure position in European politics than they could possibly have had otherwise. It gave them a reason to want the empire to survive. But it also created problems. It greatly complicated the process of making policy: all the most important decisions had to be approved not only in Vienna but in the Hungarian capital of Budapest as well. It also gave Hungary reason to oppose anything that might weaken its position within the empire. Thus Hungary would resist the transformation of the dual monarchy into a three-cornered arrangement that included the Slavs. It would do so despite the fact that by 1914 fully three-fifths of the empire's subjects were Slavic: Poles, Czechs, Slovaks, Ukrainians, Serbs, and others.

In 1867 Franz Joseph's younger brother Maximilian, who three years earlier had quixotically accepted an invitation to go to Mexico and become its emperor, was shot to death there by a firing squad.

In 1870, with Austria on the sidelines looking on, Prussia led a confederation of German states in a swift and stunning victory over France. The Franco-Prussian War led to the creation of a new German Empire in which the King of Prussia was elevated to kaiser and from which Austria was excluded. From this point Vienna could not hope to be more than the distinctly junior partner of a Berlin that had risen to first place among the continental powers.

In 1889 Archduke Rudolf, Franz Joseph's only son, intelligent and talented but also frustrated, rebellious, neurotic, a drug addict, and syphilitic (he not only followed his father in infecting his wife with venereal disease but sterilized the lady in the process), committed suicide with his teenage mistress, leaving no male heir.

Nine years later Empress Elizabeth was stabbed to death by an Italian anarchist who had hoped to kill King Umberto I of Italy but, unable to raise the train fare to Rome, settled for her.

Two years after that came the refusal of Archduke Franz Ferdinand, the soldierly nephew who had become heir after Rudolf's death, not to marry Countess Sophie Chotek, mere lady-in-waiting to a Hapsburg cousin.

In his seemingly endless old age Franz Joseph was a kindly but inflexible man, devoted to preserving the traditions of his ancestors, ardently hoping to live out his remaining days in peace. He remained doggedly faithful to his responsibilities if only because they were his heritage and he had no one to share them with. Once, reminiscing with Field Marshal Conrad about a general both of them had known, he said plaintively that "all are dying, only I *can't* die." When Conrad offered a courtly response, expressing gratitude for the emperor's long life, Franz Joseph replied, "Yes, yes, but one is *so* alone then."

Chapter 3

Setting Fire to Europe

"I don't believe we are heading for a great war.
France and Russia are not ready for war."
—Kaiser Wilhelm II

O n the day after the assassination, crowds of non-Serb
Bosnians, mainly the Muslims and Catholic Croats who
together made up a majority of Bosnia's population, marched
through the streets of Sarajevo holding up black-draped Austro-
Hungarian flags and pictures of the slain archduke and his wife.
Gangs of hooligans attacked buildings housing the institutions
of the Bosnian Serb community—vandalizing schools, newspaper offices, and a hotel, breaking windows at the residence of the
city's leading Orthodox priest. Some fifty people were injured,
and one was killed. There were demonstrations in other cities of
the dual monarchy, and in Munich and Berlin as well, but they
were smaller and nonviolent and quickly subsided.

In the Serbian capital of Belgrade, the uproar was more intense. An Austrian diplomat reported that the Serbs were falling
"into one another's arms in delight." Disorderly crowds roamed
the city, and as news arrived of the disturbances in Sarajevo, their
jubilation was laced with anger. Belgrade's newspapers fueled
the fires, "behaving shamefully" according to a British diplomat
on the scene, telling their readers that ten thousand of the Serbs
living in Austria-Hungary had been injured or killed and that Serbian women were being subjected to outrages. (This was all untrue.)

It is easy to make too much of all this. Even in Sarajevo the demonstrations came to an end after a few hours, and in Vienna the government promptly announced that victims would be compensated for their losses. The Serbian government conducted itself responsibly, attempting to discourage the demonstrations. In Vienna life quickly returned to normal. The slain archduke had been too cold and stiff a public figure ever to become popular, and there were few signs that his death was mourned. "The event almost failed to make any impression whatever," said one observer. "On Sunday and Monday, the crowds in Vienna listened to music and drank wine as if nothing had happened." Franz Ferdinand and Sophie were interred at their country estate with so little fanfare that the late archduke's friends were offended and the emperor found it necessary to explain his failure to do more.

The Austro-Hungarian leadership, though determined to take action against Serbia, was not yet ready to do so. The forty-eight hours after the assassination brought meeting after meeting—Foreign Minister Berchtold, Field Marshal Conrad, Hungarian prime minister István Tisza, Emperor Franz Joseph, and others conferred and dispersed in a continuous round robin, but no consensus emerged. Berchtold and Conrad wanted an attack on Serbia, and they wanted it to happen speedily. The emperor was uncertain; Tisza was opposed. The one point on which they agreed was that nothing could be decided until certain preliminaries had been attended to.

First, the support of Germany had to be made certain. Nothing would be possible without it. Any Austrian action against Serbia was sure to be of concern to Russia, and Vienna alone was not nearly powerful enough to deter the Russians from intervening or to deal with their enormous army if they did intervene.

It was just as essential to get Hungary on board, and that was likely to be at least as difficult. Under the clumsy arrangements of the Hapsburg system, Vienna could not make war without the consent of Budapest, and the Hungarians were sure to have little interest. Failure in such a war would be a disaster, obviously, but from the Hungarian perspective even success could be regrettable.

Finally, no action would be possible until the Austrian army had been mobilized. Mobilization in 1914 was a cumbersome, difficult, expensive undertaking. It required calling up and organizing hundreds of thousands of reserve troops, commandeering entire national railroad systems for the movement of soldiers and supplies, and getting the most enormous and mechanized military machines the world had ever seen into motion according to timetables so intricate that years had been required for their development. Either of the Austro-Hungarian mobilization plans (Vienna was unusual in having two such plans, one for war against Serbia only and the other for war in conjunction with Germany against Serbia and Russia) would take weeks to implement. Part of the problem was that many thousands of soldiers had been sent home, as was customary each summer before the mechanization of agriculture, to help bring in the harvest. Conrad feared that calling them back to their units earlier than planned would alert Serbia and Russia to what was in process.

Further complicating the situation—and a particularly exasperating complication because it was sheer bad luck—was the fact that the President of France, Raymond Poincaré, was going to be paying a state visit to the Russian capital, St. Petersburg, from Monday, July 20, to Thursday, July 23. If Austria-Hungary took any steps against Serbia before the end of that visit, if it mobilized before then or even signaled that it intended to mobilize, the leaders of France and Russia would be given a unique opportunity to coordinate their response and cement their alliance at the moment of decision. Thus, mobilization being the unavoidably slow process that it was in Austria-Hungary, the army could not be ready for action until mid-August, a month and a half after the assassination. By that time whatever sympathy the assassination had generated for Austria would be largely dissipated.

There was no need for delay, however, in securing Germany's support, and soon there seemed no need for concern about the extent of that support. Kaiser Wilhelm had liked and admired Archduke Franz Ferdinand, who understood the dangers of the Balkans and had been more restrained, more thoughtful, than Conrad. The kaiser and the men around him needed no reminding that, with Russia and France allied against them and Britain leaning the same way, Germany needed Austria and needed to help Austria defend itself against the centrifugal force that was

Balkan nationalism. The Germans were far more ready to support Austria-Hungary than they had been during the Balkan wars of the preceding two years, more conscious of being surrounded by enemies who were growing in strength.

Wilhelm had been racing his new sailboat, the *Meteor V,* off the coast of Norway when word reached him of the assassination. Returning almost immediately to his palace at Potsdam outside Berlin, he began to monitor events. There was not much to monitor, actually—not a great deal was happening in Vienna or elsewhere once the initial disturbances had played themselves out. As it became clear that the assassins were Bosnian Serbs who had been prepared for their mission in Belgrade, Wilhelm went into one of his belligerent moods. It was his practice to write in the margins of diplomatic dispatches as he read them, and his comments were often wildly dramatic; it was a way of blustering, of playing his beloved role of All-High Warlord, and also of letting the foreign office know where he stood. "Then he's a false rascal!" he would soon be saying of Britain's foreign secretary in one such note. "He lies!" "Rot!" When at the beginning of July he received a wire in which the German ambassador in Vienna reported having urged the Austrians not to be too quick in moving against Serbia, Wilhelm exploded. "Who authorized him to act that way?" he wrote. "Serbia must be disposed of, and that right soon!"

Word of this reaction soon spread and reached official Vienna. The Austrians, of course, were delighted, especially as Berlin was sending similarly strong signals of support through other channels. The German ambassador, Heinrich von Tschirschky, had been shown the error of his ways: he knew now that the kaiser wanted him to be tough and to urge the Austrians to be tough as well. Tschirschky welcomed the lesson, actually. He was one of the many members of the old Prussian aristocracy who believed that Germany's position in Europe was rapidly becoming unsafe. He feared that Austria-Hungary was weakening almost to the point of collapse. "How often have I asked myself," he had lamented in one of his dispatches, "whether it really is worthwhile to commit ourselves to this state, creaking in all its joints, and to continue the dreary work of dragging it along."

On July 5 and 6 Wilhelm and Germany's deputy foreign

minister, Arthur Zimmermann, met separately with emissaries from Vienna. Wilhelm made no effort to tell the Austrians what to do. What he did tell them, emphatically, was what they wanted to hear: that this time something had to be done about Serbia, that action should be taken *soon,* and that the Austrians could count on Germany's support whatever they decided. "It was his opinion that this action must not be delayed," the Austrian ambassador said of Wilhelm II immediately after their meeting. "Russia's attitude will no doubt be hostile, but for this he [Wilhelm] had been for years prepared, and should a war between Austria-Hungary and Russia be unavoidable, we might be convinced that Germany, our old faithful ally, would stand at our side. Russia at the present time was in no way prepared for war, and would think twice before it appealed to arms." This report became famous as the "blank check"—the promise that Berlin would be with Vienna no matter what.

Apparently the Austrians had made no effort to explain what exactly they intended to do, or when. It is unlikely that they could have done so if asked; not yet having come to an agreement with Hungary, they had no settled policy or plan. Neither the kaiser nor Zimmermann took the trouble to ask—one indication among many that at this point the Germans did not regard the situation as being serious enough to require much thought or care. War Minister Erich von Falkenhayn, after being briefed on the meetings and the contents of a letter from Franz Joseph and an accompanying memorandum from Berchtold (these dealt less with the Sarajevo crisis than with Vienna's long-term plans for changing the balance of power in the Balkans through alliance with Bulgaria), said that what he had learned "did not succeed in convincing me that the Vienna Government had taken any firm resolution." Like a number of his colleagues, Falkenhayn thought it likely that the Austrians were going to have to be prodded into action.

The Austrians, armed with the kaiser's unqualified promise of support, would from this point feel free to proceed autonomously. They would be slow at best in telling Berlin of their plans. The Germans, for their part, would continue to be slow to ask. The Austrian envoys to Berlin hadn't even explained that they regarded any action as impossible until after the French visit to St. Petersburg. The Germans continued to assume that Austria intended to proceed without delay to strike at Serbia, after which it would be free to move almost all of its forces to its border with Russia.

Everything known about Kaiser Wilhelm and his closest associates indicates that in early July they saw little possibility of a general European war. Falkenhayn's skepticism about whether Vienna would in the end actually do anything reflected widespread German doubt, based on much experience, about the Hapsburg empire's ability to take action to save itself. Recent experience also encouraged the Germans to be equally skeptical—scornful, perhaps—about Russia. Evidently it was all but inconceivable to them that this time, unlike 1908 or 1912 or 1913, the Russians would feel not only capable of taking military action but compelled to do so. Almost immediately after his talks with the Austrians, when Falkenhayn asked the kaiser if military preparations were necessary, Wilhelm said no. He soon returned to his boat-racing vacation off Norway, telling one of his admirals before departing that "I don't believe we are headed for a great war. In this case the tsar's views would not be on the side of the prince's [Franz Ferdinand's] murderer. Besides this, France and Russia are not ready for war."

German chancellor Theobold von Bethmann Hollweg, an intelligent and conscientious servant of the crown but a statesman of limited vision, also went on vacation. Army Chief of Staff Helmuth von Moltke had not even been called back from the spa where he was recovering from a bronchial infection, and the head of the German navy went off to a spa of his own. Thus scattered, the principal figures in the German government and military were incapable of making or coordinating plans, of responding to anything done by other countries, or even of staying abreast of developments. At the July 5–6 meetings they had shown less interest in the Serbian problem than in Berchtold's arcane scheme for using Bulgaria as a lever to pry Romania out of its alliance with Russia.

In Vienna, where Germany's promise of support was received as the best possible news, attention swung next to the Hungarians. At center stage now was Hungary's prime minister, Count Tisza, a gruff but politically adroit man who cared little about the Hapsburg empire except insofar as its existence benefited the Hungarians. Tisza was so absolutely opposed to any Austro-Hungarian expansion into Serbia that he had once warned Emperor Franz Joseph that any effort in that direction would ignite civil war in Hungary. (Conrad, always ready for a fight, reacted by saying that after thrashing Serbia, Austria would probably have to thrash the Hungarians as well.)

On July 7 Austria-Hungary's council of ministers was assembled by Berchtold to discuss measures to "put an end to Serbia's intrigues once and for all" and, he hoped, to approve a course of action. Tisza surprised no one when he showed himself willing to do little. He tried to divert attention to Berchtold's plans for Bulgaria and Romania. (Such diplomatic intrigues, typical of eastern Europe in the years before the war, are almost impossible to explain briefly.) When he saw that everyone had lost interest in such long-term speculative ventures, that nothing short of a showdown with Serbia would satisfy the Austrians, Tisza groped for ways to slow things down. He insisted that nothing be done until he had an opportunity to prepare a memo explaining his objections to Franz Joseph, who was away at his summer retreat. Berchtold and the council had no choice but to agree. Tisza was, after all, the head of the Hungarian government and not to be ignored.

Much of the discussion focused on the idea, with which none of the council members disagreed, that Serbia should be presented with a set of demands. At issue was whether these demands

Hungarian Prime Minister
István Tisza
"Our exactions may be hard, but not such that they cannot be complied with."

should be framed in such a way that Serbia could reasonably be expected to accept and act on them. Again Tisza was alone: "Our exactions may be hard," he said, "but not such that they cannot be complied with. If Serbia accepted them, we should have a splendid diplomatic success." Such a success, he added, "would decidedly improve our situation and give a chance of initiating an advantageous policy in the Balkans." A failure to limit the conflict to diplomatic measures, he warned, could lead to "the terrible calamity of a European war."

No one had any interest in going along with what Tisza proposed. The Austro-Hungarian war minister responded that "a diplomatic success would be of no use at all" and would be "interpreted as weakness." According to a summary of the proceedings, everyone except Tisza agreed that "a purely diplomatic success, even if it ended with a glaring humiliation of Serbia, would be worthless." It was finally decided, therefore, that "such stringent demands must be addressed to Serbia" that refusal would be "almost certain."

Implicit in all this was the assumption that an Austro-Hungarian invasion would lead without complications to the defeat of Serbia. This led to the question of Serbia's fate after it was defeated. Tisza's position was that "by a war we could reduce the size of Serbia, but we could not completely annihilate it." Here he carried the council with him, probably because of the reason he offered: "Russia would fight to the death before allowing this." But all agreed that Serbia was to be made smaller. Parts of it were to be given to Bulgaria, Greece, and Albania. What remained, though formally an autonomous state, was to be an Austro-Hungarian satellite. In this way Berchtold—always too clever by half—thought that he could proceed with the destruction of Serbia while promising Russia and the world that Vienna did not want an inch of Serbian territory.

The summary of the council's proceedings makes plain the near-desperation of the men participating. They were genuinely afraid of Serbia—convinced that, if Serbia were not crushed, it would be impossible to keep their South Slav subjects from fighting to break free of Hapsburg control. Another striking aspect of the discussion is the attention *not* given to how the other great powers—even Germany—might react to what was being planned. At the opening of the meeting, Berchtold had acknowledged that a "decisive stroke" of the kind he and Conrad wanted "cannot be dealt without previous diplomatic preparation." But by this he meant only that Vienna could not proceed without an assurance of German support, and he had already been given that assurance. The council did not recognize the advisability of keeping Germany informed. Nor, beyond assuming that Russia would not intervene unless Vienna tried to absorb Serbia, did the ministers pay the slightest attention to the need to try to prepare Russia for what lay ahead. The emphasis, instead, was on secrecy. On secrecy, and on surprise, and on deceit: in the weeks to follow not even the Germans would be told of the council's decision to dismember Serbia after taking it by force. To the contrary, all the great powers would be assured—falsely but repeatedly—that Austria had no territorial aspirations where Serbia was concerned. Even Tisza appears to have decided in the end to go along with this approach. Late in the meeting he told the council that he "was anxious to meet the others halfway and was prepared to concede that the demands addressed to Serbia should be hard indeed, but not such as to make our intention of raising unacceptable terms clear to everybody else." The shift in his tone is striking. Tisza was no longer insisting that the demands be acceptable, only that Vienna's real intent be concealed from *everybody else*. In the case of Germany, the results of this secrecy would be unfortunate. They would keep the Berlin government from understanding what Vienna was doing until it was very nearly too late. In the case of Russia, the results would be disastrous. The Austrians' duplicity assured that, when their intentions became clear at last, the Russians would be shocked, panicked, and—not without reason—convinced that they had been betrayed.

This meeting was followed by a period of quiet waiting. For the sake of secrecy, and to Conrad's consternation, little could be done to ready the Austro-Hungarian army for action. Tisza remained nettlesome. On the day after the council meeting he wrote to Franz Joseph, warning that an attack on Serbia "would, as far as can humanly be foreseen, lead to an intervention by Russia and hence to a world war." He reverted to his original position that the demands to be made of Serbia should be "stiff but not impossible to meet, and that further action should be taken only if Serbia refuses." Berchtold, occupied with drafting the demands, paid him no attention.

By July 13 Vienna's ambassador in Berlin was reporting that the Germans were growing nervous about Vienna's failure to act. Berchtold ignored this report too. A day later, when Tisza pointedly objected to the use of the term *ultimatum* in connection with the demands, Berchtold cheerfully offered a compromise. The document he was drafting would be a "note with time limit," not an ultimatum. It was a distinction without a difference, and it cost Berchtold nothing. Serbia would be given forty-eight hours to respond and would be told nothing about what Vienna intended to do if the response proved unsatisfactory. Austria's ambassadors were under instructions to assure Russia and even Germany that Vienna was planning nothing that would cause concern. Again Berchtold was being too clever, deceiving friends and prospective enemies alike.

On July 19 the council of ministers met again in Vienna. Members reviewed Berchtold's draft note and gave their approval. It included ten demands. At least half were entirely reasonable. A few, however, were susceptible to being interpreted as requiring Serbia to compromise its sovereignty. The most objectionable called for direct Austrian involvement in Serbia's handling of the assassination investigation and related internal matters. Its rejection was, in practical terms, nearly inevitable. The council agreed that Berchtold should have the note delivered to the Prime Minister of Serbia in Belgrade on July 23, immediately after the departure of France's President Poincaré from St. Petersburg. Tisza was no longer objecting. Germany's promise of support had neutralized his warnings, and on top of that (the complexities of the Balkans being almost infinite) he was beginning to see Serbia—specifically, Serbia's friendly relations with Romania—as a threat to Hungary's control of Transylvania, which had a large Romanian population increasingly restless for union with what it saw as its true homeland.

The delivery of the note to Serbia, when the evening of Thursday, July 23, finally arrived, was a sad little comedy of errors. Prime Minister Pasic had—not necessarily by coincidence, as he had been alerted that a communication from Vienna was coming—left Belgrade on an electioneering trip into Serbia's newest provinces. His foreign minister, when told to expect an important visit by the Austrian ambassador at six p.m., tried to contact Pasic by telegram but got no answer.

Vienna's ambassador to Belgrade, another of the many Austrian officials who had long regarded war with Serbia as not only inevitable but desirable, was a baron with the interesting name Giesl von Gieslingen. Upon arriving, he was taken to see the foreign minister. An interpreter was on hand because the minister spoke neither German nor French. Giesl began to read his government's note, a lengthy document that opened with a preamble complaining that the behavior of Serbia had been intolerable and would in fact no longer be tolerated. He read slowly, with frequent pauses for the benefit of the interpreter. The foreign minister, more and more alarmed by what he was hearing, began to interrupt. Again and again he complained through the interpreter that he could not accept a communication this important, that only Pasic could do so. Giesl, out of patience, said that in that case he could only leave the note and go. In departing he said that no response other than unconditional acceptance would satisfy Austria, and that Serbia's response was required by six p.m. on Saturday.

News of the Austrian demands had little impact except in Russia. The government of faraway Britain, ensnared in a violent crisis having to do with Irish Home Rule, had scant attention to spare for the Balkans. The London newspapers, never friendly toward Serbia, dealt generously with Austria's demands, in most cases describing them as appropriate and responsible. The British foreign secretary, Sir Edward Grey, suggested only that Austria's deadline ought to be extended.

There was even less interest in France. President Poincaré, having completed his visit with Tsar Nicholas and his ministers, was at sea, somewhere between St. Petersburg and home. In Paris the public and even the government were fixated on a scandal that had erupted when the wife of a former prime minister shot and killed a newspaper editor.

Berlin too was quiet. Kaiser Wilhelm, back to his customary weeks of summertime sailing, didn't learn about the Austrian note until news of it reached him through the Norwegian newspapers.

He was, understandably, angry at not having been informed by his own foreign office. For the first time he showed signs of serious concern. He proposed canceling a planned visit of the German High Seas Fleet to Scandinavia but was dissuaded. Chancellor Bethmann Hollweg urged him not to interrupt his vacation a second time. Wilhelm refused and started for home.

At this point Wilhelm still knew nearly nothing about what the Austrian note said. Requests for a copy had gone out from Berlin, but when a copy reached Foreign Minister Gottlieb von Jagow on the evening of July 22—less than twenty-four hours before the delivery to Serbia—it proved to be incomplete and unaccompanied by any indication that the Austrians were determined to reject the Serbian response. Bethmann didn't bother to read it. Vienna had not consulted Berlin, now virtually no time remained for questions or objections, and the man whose questions would have mattered most—Kaiser Wilhelm—knew less than anyone. Berchtold, almost certainly, had planned things this way. Having succeeded in getting his government to commit to action despite Tisza's initial resistance and the deadly inertia of the dual monarchy's dual bureaucracy, he was determined to make further complications impossible. Thus he compounded his earlier mistakes. Not only had he left the Russian government completely unprepared for the harshness of his note, he had actively encouraged the Russians to expect something very different. He had done nothing to help newspapers across Europe, and thereby the European public, understand why Austria was taking action at last. Little had been disclosed, and less had been publicized, about Vienna's success in tracing the assassination plot back to Belgrade and establishing the likelihood that officials of the Kingdom of Serbia had been involved. Vienna had made no public complaints about Belgrade's failure to investigate the assassination. Thus the news of Vienna's note, when it flashed across the continent, came as more of a surprise than an invasion of Serbia might have done in the immediate aftermath of the Sarajevo shootings. By July 23 the assassination was three and a half weeks in the past. Tempers had cooled, and people in cities far from Sarajevo had moved on to other things. They were no longer disposed to regard the murder of the archduke and his wife as such an outrage as to require a military response.

In St. Petersburg, Russia's foreign minister, the mercurial Sergei Sazonov, went into a rage when he learned of the Austrian note. He complained that he had been deceived, that Russia couldn't possibly stand by while Serbia was humiliated or worse, that Austria couldn't possibly have sent such a note without the knowledge and approval of Germany, and that both countries must be plotting to drive Russia out of the Balkans. "You are setting fire to Europe!" Sazonov told the Austrian ambassador. The Prince Regent of Serbia, meanwhile, was sending wires to Tsar Nicholas asking for help.

How could Russia *not* help Serbia? Nicholas was being told that his people would not tolerate another abandonment of their brothers, the South Slavs. Russia would be disgraced, would have no more friends in the Balkans, no respect in Europe. A failure of such magnitude might trigger a revolution worse than the one in 1905.

One solution suggested itself. If Russia showed enough firmness, perhaps Austria would hold back. By Friday, July 24, the day after the delivery of Austria's note, the day before Serbia was supposed to reply, Sazonov was telling the Russian army's chief of staff to get ready for mobilization.

It was at this point that the Balkan crisis became a European one.

Russian Foreign Minister
Sergei Sazonov
*"The curses of the nations
will be upon you."*

THE HOHENZOLLERNS

THE FLAMBOYANT AND ERRATIC KAISER WILHELM II owned and loved to show off more than three hundred military dress uniforms. He would cheerfully change his costume a dozen or more times daily. One of the jokes that made the rounds in Berlin was that the kaiser wouldn't visit an aquarium without first putting on admiral's regalia, or eat a plum pudding without dressing as a British field marshal. He really could be almost that childish, even in 1914, when he was in his early fifties and had ruled Germany for a quarter of a century. Not surprisingly, many of the men who were sworn to serve him regarded him not just as immature but as mentally unstable.

Wilhelm was only the third member of the Hohenzollern family to occupy the throne of Imperial Germany; the second had been kaiser for only months. The Hohenzollerns, unlike the Hapsburgs, were in 1914 a still-rising family at the top of a rising nation. Despite interruptions that at times had brought them to the brink of ruin, they had been rising for five hundred years, slowly emerging from obscurity in the late Middle Ages and eventually surpassing all the older and grander dynasties of Europe. They had always been more vigorous than the Hapsburgs, more warlike, rising through conquest and ingenuity rather than through matrimony. They had a remarkable history not just of ruling countries but of *inventing* the countries they wanted to rule. It is scarcely going too far to say that the Hohenzollerns—assisted, of course, by their brilliant servant Otto von Bismarck—invented modern Germany. Centuries earlier they had invented Prussia, a country so completely artificial that at the end of World War II it would simply and forever cease to exist.

The first Hohenzollern of note was one Count Friedrich, a member of the minor nobility who in the early fifteenth century somehow got the Holy Roman emperor to appoint him Margrave of Brandenburg, an area centered on Berlin in northeastern Germany. In his new position Friedrich was an elector, one of the hereditary magnates entitled to choose new emperors. His descendants increased their holdings during the next century and a half, expanding to the east by getting possession of a wild and backward territory called Prussia.

Inhabited originally by Slavs rather than by Germans, Prussia had been conquered and Christianized in the 1200s by a military religious order (there were such things in those hard days) called the Teutonic Knights. It happened that, when the Protestant Reformation swept across northern Germany, the head of the Teutonic Knights was a member of the Hohenzollern family, one Albert by name. In 1525 this Albert did what most of the nobles in that part of Europe

Kaiser Wilhelm II
Still immature after a quarter-century on the throne.

were doing at the time: he declared himself a Protestant. Simultaneously he declared that Prussia was now a duchy, and that he—surprise—was its duke. This Albert of Hohenzollern's little dynasty died out in the male line after only two generations, at which point a marriage was arranged between the female heir and her cousin, the Hohenzollern elector of Brandenburg. (The Hapsburgs must have nodded in approval.)

The first half of the seventeenth century was a low point for the family: Brandenburg found itself on the losing side in a North European war and for a while was occupied by Sweden. Better times returned with Friedrich Wilhelm, called the Great Elector, who was margrave from 1640 to 1688 and originated the superbly trained army that forever after would be the Hohenzollern trademark and would cause Napoleon to say that Prussia had been hatched out of a cannonball. Friedrich Wilhelm made Brandenburg the most powerful of Germany's Protestant states, second only to Catholic Austria to the south.

In 1701 the Hapsburg Holy Roman emperor found himself in a struggle over who would inherit the throne of Spain. He needed help—he needed the tough little army of Brandenburg. The Hohenzollern elector of the time, another Friedrich (the Hohenzollerns rarely went far afield in naming their sons), wanted something in return: he wanted to be a king. This presented difficulties, but the emperor's need was real and so things were worked out. He decided that Friedrich could have a kingdom, in a way, but that the intricate rules of imperial governance required calling it Prussia rather than Brandenburg. The rules required also that, although Friedrich could not be king *of* Prussia, it would be acceptable for him to style himself king *in* Prussia. This was nearly the feeblest way imaginable of being a king, one that made Friedrich's new status seem faintly ridiculous. But it was a step toward real kingship, and Friedrich settled for it. He became King Friedrich I, the first Hohenzollern to be a monarch, if only in a way.

It was not until two generations later that the Hohenzollerns became kings *of* Prussia. This happened during one of the most remarkable reigns in European history, that of Friedrich II, who by the age of thirty-three was known to all of Europe as Frederick the Great.

Frederick the Great is too big a subject to be dealt with in a few paragraphs. Suffice it to say that he was a writer, a composer of mu-

sic that is still performed today, and a "philosopher king" according
to no less a judge than Voltaire (who became his house guest and
stayed so long that the two ended up despising each other). He was
the first monarch in all of Europe to abolish religious discrimina-
tion, press censorship, and judicial torture. He was also a ruthless
adventurer all too eager for glory, and he and his kingdom would
have been destroyed except for the lucky fact that, in addition to
all his other gifts, Frederick happened to be a military genius. In the
course of his long life he teetered more than once on the brink of
total failure—at one point he was at war with Austria, France, Russia,
and Sweden simultaneously—but after any number of hair-raising
escapes he raised Prussia to the ranks of Europe's leading powers.
He made the Hohenzollerns one of the leading dynasties of Europe
despite never having—and giving no evidence of ever wanting—
children of his own. When he died in 1786, just before the French
Revolution, the crown passed to an untalented nephew.

The wars of Napoleon undid all of Frederick's achievements. They
reduced Prussia first to a state of collapse, then to submissive vassal-
age to France. By piling humiliations upon all the German states,
however, Napoleon ignited German nationalism. This led to an uprising after Napoleon's disastrous invasion of Russia. The Prussian
army, lethal as always, contributed significantly to the defeat of the
French first at Leipzig and finally at Waterloo. Hohenzollern princes
were conspicuous on the field of battle; one of them was killed leading a cavalry charge. In 1815 the Congress of Vienna restored Prussia to major power status but in a new way: some of the kingdom's
easternmost holdings were given to Russia and Austria and replaced
with others in the west. Prussia thus became the only major power
almost all of whose subjects were German. This was important at a
time when nationalism was starting to be a powerful political force,
and when Germans everywhere were beginning to talk of unifica-
tion. The big question was whether there would be a Greater Germany led by Austria or a Lesser Germany from which Austria, with its
millions of non-German subjects, would be excluded.

The century following the defeat of Napoleon brought triumph
after triumph to the Hohenzollerns. In 1864, guided by Bismarck,
Prussia took the disputed but largely German provinces of Schleswig
and Holstein from Denmark. Two years after that it fought Austria
and won so conclusively as to put its claim to leadership among

the German states beyond challenge. The Hohenzollern realm now stretched across northern Germany all the way to the border with France and included two-thirds of the population of non-Austrian Germany. In 1870 the French emperor Napoleon III, in trouble politically and desperate to find some way of reversing his fortunes, was seduced by Bismarck into committing the folly of declaring war. Prussia and the German states allied with it—Austria emphatically not included—were more than ready. They astonished the world by demolishing the French army at the Battle of Sedan. In the Hall of Mirrors at the Palace of Versailles, the assembled German princes declared the creation of a new German empire, a federation within which such states as Baden, Bavaria, Saxony, and Württemberg would continue to have their own kings but over which there would now be a Hohenzollern emperor.

As part of the spoils of war, the German princes wanted to take from France—to take *back* from France, they would have said—the province of Alsace and part of the province of Lorraine. This territory was not of tremendous importance economically or in any other real way, but many Germans believed it had been stolen by Louis XIV two centuries before and was German rather than French. Bismarck, architect of everything Prussia had achieved over the preceding decade, foresaw that France would never forgive the loss. He predicted that to keep what it had won, Germany would have to fight another war after a half-century had passed. He was right, as usual, but made no serious effort to block the annexation.

The first ruler of the newly united Germany, King Wilhelm I of Prussia, proved to be surprisingly unhappy about his elevation, even sullen. In his opinion being King of Prussia was as great an honor as any man could ever want. But an empire required an emperor, and he had no choice but to agree. He remained King of Prussia while assuming his new title, however, and Prussia continued to be a distinct state with its own government and military administration. It continued to be dominated by a centuries-old Prussian elite, the Junkers, whose sons went into the army and the civil administration and swore loyalty not to their country but to its king.

At that point, 1871, the Hohenzollerns stood at the pinnacle of Europe. Kaiser Wilhelm I, a man so stolid and methodical that the people of Berlin learned to set their watches by his appearances at his window, ruled what was unquestionably the most powerful and vigorous country in Europe. And he had a worthy heir: his son, Crown Prince Frederick, an able, conscientious, and loyal young man who in the centuries-old tradition of his family had led armies through all the great campaigns leading up to the creation of the empire and had been rewarded with the Iron Cross and a field marshal's baton. The crown prince was happily married to the eldest and best-loved daughter of England's Queen Victoria. She was a serious-minded young woman who had won her husband over to the idea of one day, after they had inherited the throne, transforming Germany into a democratic monarchy on the British model. Together, meanwhile, they were producing yet another generation of Hohenzollerns. Their eldest child was a boy who bore his grandfather's name. He had a withered, useless left arm—a troubling defect in the heir to a line of warrior-kings—but he was healthy otherwise and not unintelligent. When his grandfather became emperor, the boy Wilhelm was twelve years old, his father barely forty. But only seventeen years later, filled with insecurities but determined to prove himself a mighty leader, a worthy All-High Warlord, this same boy would ascend to the throne as Wilhelm II.

Chapter 4

July 25 to 28:

Secrets and Lies

"This was more than one could have expected.
A great moral victory for Vienna!"
—Kaiser Wilhelm II

As the details of Austria's demands became known, three and a half weeks of drift came abruptly to an end. Actions and reactions began to follow one another at an accelerating pace. The possibility of war became increasingly real. Not only in Vienna, Berlin, and St. Petersburg but also in London, Rome, and Paris, awareness dawned that this was a genuinely dangerous crisis.

Men with the power to decide the fate of Europe did the things that brought the war on and failed to do the things that might have kept the war from happening. They told lies, made mistakes, and missed opportunities. With few if any exceptions they were decent, well-intended men, and almost always they acted for what they thought were the best of reasons. But little of what they did produced the results they intended.

Saturday, July 25

Measured by the headlines that it generated, this was an extraordinary day. The Kingdom of Serbia, forty-eight hours almost to the minute after receiving Austria-Hungary's demands, presented its response. It agreed outright to only half of the ten demands. The Austro-Hungarian ambassador to Serbia, Baron Giesl, followed his instructions to find this unacceptable and broke off diplomatic relations immediately. His bags had been packed in advance, and in less than half an hour he was on a train. Less than ten minutes later the train crossed the border into Hungary.

Both countries announced that they were mobilizing. (Serbia had started mobilizing hours before delivering its response.) Russia then declared what its military planners called a Period Preparatory to War—not yet mobilizing but moving ominously in that direction. Army units on summer maneuvers were returned to their barracks, officers on leave were recalled, and the military districts of Kazan, Kiev, Moscow, and Odessa were ordered to make ready. More secretly, preparations also began in the Warsaw, Vilna, and St. Petersburg districts. The last development was particularly dangerous, as those three districts threatened Germany directly.

But there was even more to July 25 than that.

The Serbian response to Austria's demands, far from being defiant, was actually conciliatory, respectful, and at times almost submissive in tone. But it was also long, and its language was artfully oblique. ("The most brilliant example of diplomatic skill I have ever known," an annoyed Berchtold called it.) It explained that while Serbia could agree unconditionally to a number of the demands, it had questions about several others—not objections, just questions—and was unable to accept only one: predictably, the one that would have involved Austria directly in Belgrade's search for and prosecution of the assassination plotters. But even here the wording was far from bellicose. "The Royal Government cannot accept such an arrangement, as it would be a violation of the Constitution and the law of criminal procedure," it stated. "Nevertheless, in concrete cases communications as to the results of the investigation in question might be given to the Austro-Hungarian agents."

As positive as it was in many ways, and as clever as it may have been as an attempt to hold off the Austrians while impressing the rest of the world with Serbia's willingness to cooperate, the response can fairly be regarded as one of the mistakes that led to war. By declining to yield, the Serbs gave Berchtold, Conrad, and their cohorts the one thing they wanted: an excuse for military action. Worse, they did this unnecessarily. They might have responded differently—not more shrewdly, their document being nothing if not shrewd, but more effectively—had they not been receiving reports about how Russia wanted them to stand firm. These reports were wishful thinking on the part of Serbia's combative ambassador to Russia, who was being manipulated by France's ambassador in St. Petersburg, Maurice Paléologue. They certainly were not in accord with the thinking of Russian officialdom. Tsar Nicholas was leery of a major war because he was fearful of its likely consequences—social and economic strains so severe that they could spark revolution. So was Foreign Minister Sazonov. Both men believed that Russia was years from being ready to fight the Germans. Though Russia was greatly expanding its already huge army and was also, with the help of France, building a new network of railroads designed to improve its ability to wage war, such projects would not be completed until 1917 at the earliest. But Sazonov especially believed that Austria-Hungary was acting not independently but as the tool of Berlin, that the Germans were determined to precipitate a preventive war, and that Russia could protect itself only by reacting forcefully and quickly.

The Serbian response also might have been different if someone other than Nikola Pasic had been responsible for preparing it. Because of his prior knowledge of the Black Hand's plot, and also because of the efforts he had made to stop the assassination, Serbia's prime minister had abundant reasons for not wanting Austria-Hungary to become involved in any investigation. It would be bad for him, and probably bad for Serbia, if Austria discovered how much he had known and started asking why he had not done more. It might be even worse for him if the Black Hand learned that, in attempting to stop the assassination, he had actually tried to alert the Austrians. To all this was added Pasic's need to show himself willing to stand up to the Austrians in the run-up to the Serbian election.

The Austrian mobilization that followed put into motion a plan for assembling twenty divisions—some three hundred thousand troops—just a few miles from Belgrade. In deploying his forces in this way, Conrad left himself with only twenty-eight divisions for Galicia to the north, where Austria-Hungary would have to face much larger numbers if Russia went to war. This alarmed the German general staff when it became known in Berlin. It meant—contrary to what Conrad had indicated in earlier consultations with the German high command—that the German army in the east would have painfully limited Austrian support in case of a Russian attack. It showed Conrad's blind determination to believe that Russia was going to stay out, and that he was therefore free to give the Serbs the thrashing that he had been wanting to give them for years.

Russia, in declaring its Period Preparatory to War, took the steps that would enable it to get its troops into action more quickly if it too mobilized. And if its actions were "preparatory," they were far from trivial. They involved the mustering of 1.1 million troops in the four districts nearest to Austria-Hungary. Serbia's mobilization, necessarily much smaller, was based on the mistaken but eminently rational assumption that Austria was preparing to attack within a few days. The same assumption prompted the Serbs to begin moving their government out of Belgrade and away from the border.

Mobilization, a momentous word in those days, meant something short of—but not always a great deal short of—declaring and going to war. The degree of difference varied from nation to nation, and in this fact lay a world of trouble. For Russia, geographically vast and systemically inefficient, mobilization was an almost glacial affair. It was a matter of calling up reserves (no simple matter where railways were few and men reporting for duty might have to travel hundreds of miles), assembling divisions and armies in their assigned positions, and getting them ready to advance against the enemy or face an enemy advance. Crucially, an invasion of enemy territory was not integral to Russia's mobilization arrangements; that was to be decided according to circumstances. Even after mobilization, the Russian leadership would continue to have options. Its mobilized armies could be kept in place on Russian soil without disruption of their ability to act.

The sprawling Austro-Hungarian Empire faced transport problems similar to, though not quite so serious as, those of Russia. And again like St. Petersburg's, Vienna's mobilization plans gave it a measure of flexibility. Conrad had divided his forces into three groups: one for use against Serbia, one for Galicia and engagement of the Russians, and a third to be deployed to either front depending on need. It was by deciding to send his third group to the south that Conrad was able to assemble twenty divisions for an attack on Serbia.

Germany, in 1914 the most modern and efficient of Europe's industrial giants, could mobilize with a speed that was dazzling by comparison with either Russia or Austria-Hungary. Its planners were convinced that in case of war the country's survival would depend on that speed. Ever since 1894, when France and Russia had first become allies, the Germans had been faced with the likelihood that war with either would entail war with both. They also assumed—this was arguable but not unreasonable—that they could not expect to win a protracted war against both. For this reason their mobilization plan was focused on a single overriding objective: to knock France out of action in the west in no more than six weeks, before Russia could launch a major attack from the east. Germany's plans, therefore, included the start of a drive on Paris. Once started, such a drive would be nearly impossible to stop or even significantly modify without reducing all the arrangements to chaos. For Germany alone, mobilization equaled war.

But mobilization was bound to be dangerous, regardless of which power undertook it. It was inherently threatening. Even if undertaken by Austria-Hungary, the least of the great powers, and even if directed at a mere Balkan kingdom, it was certain to draw some kind of response.

The start of Austria-Hungary's mobilization caught the chief of the Serbian army, the aged Field Marshal Radomir Putnik, on his way home from a summer vacation in the Austrian province of Bohemia. The authorities in Budapest detained him. But Emperor Franz Joseph demanded not only that Putnik be allowed to proceed but that a special train be made available to return him to Belgrade. It was a charming gesture of Old World courtliness, one that the new world of industrialized warfare would soon render obsolete. As Putnik took charge of the Serbian defenses, Conrad and his troops would have reason to regret their emperor's chivalry.

Sunday, July 26

This was a day when no headlines were made, a day when little, supposedly, was happening. Again, however, things were less simple than they appeared, particularly in Austria and Russia, whose leaders were now putting their military machines in motion and hoping that the other powers would understand their actions as they wanted them to be understood.

Austria mobilized in part to start the clock ticking on a process that would require sixteen days to bring the army to readiness. But it also wanted to demonstrate that the situation was serious, that if France and Britain wanted to avoid something worse than a localized Balkan problem, they had better restrain Russia. France mattered even at this early stage because it was Russia's one powerful ally, and because everyone understood that without French support the Russians would be reluctant, probably even unwilling, to risk war with an Austria-Hungary acting with German support. Britain mattered because it was powerful despite having only a small army, because it had allied itself with France and Russia in a loose and informal way, and because it was certain to want to avoid a general war.

The second of Vienna's purposes could not possibly be achieved. France's President Poincaré was still at sea. With wireless communications still primitive (and with Germany attempting to jam radio transmissions), he was nearly incommunicado. Britain's foreign secretary, Sir Edward Grey, was both cautious by nature and paralyzed by divisions within the government of which he was a member. In the near term, no one in Paris or London was going to be pressuring St. Petersburg—or Berlin or Vienna for that matter—to do anything. Grey's own position, which he expressed within the cabinet only, was that the greatest threat to British security was German dominance in Europe. He believed that if war were to break out between Austria and Russia and lead to war between Germany and France, Britain would have to side with France. This did not mean, however, that he wanted war.

On July 26 Grey felt that the most he could do was communicate his concerns to the German ambassador in London, Prince Karl Lichnowsky, and suggest a conference of Britain, France, Germany, and Italy as a means of resolving the crisis. Lichnowsky, whose position in London permitted him to see almost from the start that Grey and other British leaders were likely to oppose Germany in a showdown, seized on this suggestion. "I would like to call your attention to the significance of Grey's proposal of a mediation *à quatre* between Austria and Russia," he said in a telegram to Berlin. "I see in it the only possibility of avoiding a world war, in which for us there would be everything to lose and nothing to gain."

Russia's declaration of a Period Preparatory to War had a less subtle purpose than the Austrian mobilization. Its goal was, simply, to make the Austrians reconsider. St. Petersburg was also eager to make Berlin believe that it was not being threatened, but German intelligence soon learned that the Russian military was doing much more than it would admit to. Its secret preparations in the military districts closest to Germany reflected the Russian government's fear that, as Foreign Minister Sazonov told Tsar Nicholas, it faced not just a dispute over Serbia but "a question of the balance of power in Europe, which is seriously threatened." But they also bore an uncomfortably close resemblance to an undeclared mobilization. When the German military attaché in St. Petersburg made inquiries, however, he was given lies in response. As more was learned about how much the Russians were doing, and as the Russians continued to pretend that they were doing very little, Berlin grew increasingly nervous. It became progressively less willing to accept the assurances of goodwill coming from St. Petersburg.

Maurice Paléologue, France's ambassador in St. Petersburg, was able to keep himself informed of the extent of Russia's preparations. The Russians had a responsibility under their Entente with France to tell Paris in advance of any mobilization plans, but Paléologue did not remind them of this fact. He appears to have been unwilling to do anything that might discourage them from proceeding. He did not even tell his own government what he knew; he didn't want anyone in Paris to restrain the Russians either. A similar game was being played in Vienna by Germany's Ambassador Tschirschky, a onetime foreign minister who had decided that it was his duty to encourage Austrian aggressiveness without doing so openly.

It happened that Kaiser Wilhelm's younger brother, Prince Heinrich of Prussia, was in England on this Sunday, attending the annual yacht races at Cowes and lunching as the guest of his first cousin, King George V. Afterward—heedless of the fact that the king had little voice in foreign policy—Heinrich sent a message to Berlin reporting that "Georgie" had given him the impression that London wanted to stay neutral. The prince, a naval officer by profession, had already earned a reputation as a not entirely reliable reporter, and his message contradicted warnings being sent by Ambassador Lichnowsky. The German foreign ministry, however, had never taken Lichnowsky seriously. Its leading figures saw him as a gullible Anglophile, a wealthy dilettante who owed his position to his long friendship with the kaiser. They were predisposed to find the views of Prince Heinrich more credible because they were so very much more pleasing.

And so the final week of peace had begun with Austria mobilizing while sending signals that no one was available to receive; with Russia in the first stages of mobilizing while pretending not to be; with Germany beginning to feel directly threatened; and with France's ambassador urging the Russians as well as the Serbians on. Britain was sending ambiguous signals that the continental powers were free to interpret as they wished. Berlin and Paris were both, for the time being, effectively leaderless. Nothing irreversible had happened, but neither was anyone quite in control.

Monday, July 27

This was yet another day when, so far as the public knew, nothing much of importance was happening.

But in fact it was the day when the Austro-Hungarian Council of Ministers met in secret and voted to declare war on Serbia. This was a strange because utterly unnecessary decision. Even Conrad, eager as he was for action, questioned it. He couldn't see the point of declaring war more than two weeks in advance of the completion of Austria's mobilization. But Berchtold, determined to commit the dual monarchy to military action before Germany's position softened or the mediation proposals coming out of Britain could have an effect, brought Conrad around.

The declaration of war was to be announced on Tuesday and

required the approval of Franz Joseph. When Berchtold and Conrad went to see him, he proved to be reluctant. They told him lies about Serbian attacks. Actually there had been nothing more than a brief and meaningless exchange of gunfire at an insignificant border town. Persuaded by this tale that war had begun and that Serbia was responsible, the emperor signed. In preparing to do so, he trembled so badly that he had difficulty putting on his glasses.

In London, Grey read the text of Serbia's response to the ultimatum and found it promising. He met with Lichnowsky and repeated his suggestion of a conference of the powers. Lichnowsky again relayed the suggestion to Berlin, urging that it be pursued. Chancellor Bethmann Hollweg, who disliked the proposal but didn't want to offend the British, indicated by return wire that he was forwarding it to Vienna. But he explained to Austria's ambassador in Berlin "in the most decided way" that the German government wanted nothing to do with Grey's ideas, "that on the contrary it advises to disregard them, but that it must pass them on to satisfy the English." The Germans and Austrians had reason to be skeptical about the proposed conference. At least two of the four countries that would participate, France and Italy, would have little reason to look sympathetically on Austria's grievances. A third, Britain, seemed unlikely to do anything to damage its relations with France and Russia. At best, the Germans and Austrians believed, a conference would substitute talk for action, degenerating into a sterile debate over the wording of the Austrian note and Serbia's response. In the end, they feared, Serbia would dance away scot-free, with Austria-Hungary looking on as helplessly as in 1912 and 1913. Serb activists both within and outside the Hapsburg empire would be encouraged to continue making trouble, and Austria-Hungary's other minorities would be encouraged to do the same.

The Austrians had financial reasons too for resisting mediation. Theirs was a financially starved administration—Conrad had never been given enough money to keep the armies of Vienna competitive with the other great powers in size, equipment, or technology—and the mobilizations during the two Balkan wars had been as costly as they had been fruitless. By 1914 all the great powers, but Austria-Hungary especially, were creaking under the weight of an arms race that was becoming constantly more onerous as the machinery of war grew more massive and complex. Vienna could not afford to be mobilizing year after year. It wanted to be sure that this time it got something for its money.

In the afternoon Kaiser Wilhelm arrived home from his vacation cruise. Chancellor Bethmann and Gottlieb von Jagow, the head of the German foreign ministry, were not delighted by his return. They had urged him to stay away, telling him that a premature end to his vacation might alarm the other powers. What they really feared, probably, was that the unpredictable kaiser would interfere in their handling of the crisis.

With or without the kaiser's presence, Bethmann and Jagow were not an ideal pair to be steering the most powerful state in Europe through such difficult straits. Bethmann was a tall, dour career civil servant who five years earlier had been raised to the chancellorship despite having no experience in foreign affairs and despite being disliked by the kaiser. ("He was always lecturing me," Wilhelm complained, "and pretends to know everything.")

German Foreign Minister
Gottlieb von Jagow
*"Nothing has helped.
I am appointed."*

Like many Germans in high places, he was terrified by the presence of unfriendly powers to the east and west and convinced that Germany could only grow more vulnerable with the passage of time. Jagow was a frail hypochondriac who had used an elder brother's connections to get into the foreign service and had then successfully leveraged those same connections to get a series of plush and undemanding assignments in Rome and elsewhere. When summoned home to head the foreign ministry, he had pulled every string he could reach in a futile effort to escape. "Nothing has helped," he had said despairingly at last. "I am appointed."

Late in the night Vienna sent word to Berlin of its decision to declare war. When the message reached Bethmann and Jagow, they were not astonished. The Austrians were doing at last what Berlin had been urging from the start: they were taking action. No effort was made to inform the kaiser. This was, after all, exactly what he too had demanded at the start.

Tuesday, July 28

Wilhelm II was back in his office, seated in his saddle chair. (Wanting no doubt to be the perfect Hohenzollern warrior-king, and proud no doubt of the agonies he had endured in boyhood to become a skillful horseman in spite of his crippled arm, he claimed to be more comfortable in a saddle than in a conventional chair.) He had much work to catch up on. First he read the most recent wire from Lichnowsky in London: it quoted Sir Edward Grey as saying that an Austrian attack on Serbia would have disastrous consequences, but that the Serbian response to Austria appeared to provide a basis for negotiations. Then he read the Serbian response itself. Perhaps in part because he had just seen Grey's thoughts on the subject—Wilhelm was one of those men who tend to agree with whoever talked with them last—his reaction was much the same as Grey's. "This was more than one could have expected," he declared. "A great moral victory for Vienna; but with it every reason for war drops away, and Giesl might have remained quietly in Belgrade. On the strength of this *I*"—he underlined the pronoun, implicitly rebuking the Austrians—"should never have ordered mobilization!"

Seeing an opportunity and eager to seize it, Wilhelm sent a

handwritten note to Jagow declaring the Serbian response "a ca-
pitulation of the most humiliating kind," so that *every cause for
war* falls to the ground!" He instructed the foreign ministry to
prepare a message to go out over his name informing Vienna that
a basis now existed for resolving the crisis through mediation, and
that he was prepared to help. He added an idea that a member
of his military staff had suggested to him at the start of the day.
Because the Serbs could not be trusted ("Orientals," Wilhelm
called them, "therefore liars, tricksters and masters of evasion"),
Austria should send its army across the border and occupy Belgrade but then go no farther. In possession of Serbia's capital,
the Austrians would be in a position of strength as mediation
proceeded. This would come to be called the Stop-in-Belgrade
proposal, and soon Grey too would be suggesting it. It offered
a solution much like the one that ended the Franco-Prussian
War in 1871. The German armies had remained in France until
Berlin's terms were met—the payment of immense reparations
plus the surrender of Alsace and Lorraine—then paraded through
the streets of Paris and gone home.

Bethmann and Jagow, incredibly, had still not told Wilhelm
that an Austrian declaration of war was only hours away. The
kaiser assumed that such a declaration would not come for another two weeks if at all. Just as incredibly, Bethmann and Jagow
prepared the kaiser's message to Vienna as instructed but surreptitiously delayed its transmission for twelve hours, making
certain that it wouldn't be received until after the Austrians issued
their declaration.

Though Bethmann and Jagow had deceived the kaiser, depriv-
ing him of any chance of intervening before Austria declared war,
their motives may well have been good. As clumsy as their behavior had been at a crucial juncture where nothing less than brilliance was required, they knew Wilhelm all too well—his childish
arrogance, his unpredictability, his history of reversing himself and
even breaking down in the midst of a crisis. (He had done so in
1908, 1911, and again early in 1914, sinking so low that he had to be
talked out of abdicating.) No doubt they thought they had a better
grasp of the situation than he. Having been in Berlin while he was
still away, they definitely were better informed, if only because
they had gone to such lengths to keep him uninformed. And they

had reason to think that, in their support of the Austrians, they had been carrying out the kaiser's wishes. They must have felt that involving him more directly at this late hour could only complicate an already confusing situation.

The Austrian declaration, issued in the middle of the afternoon, changed everything. It was one of the two or three most important blunders committed by any of the great powers during the days leading up to war. And, as with the delivery of the Austrian note to Serbia five days earlier, there was a farcical aspect to how it happened. Berchtold, knowing that the Serbian government had withdrawn from Belgrade to the interior and not knowing how to make contact with that government wherever it now was, sent a telegram, uncoded and in French, informing Prime Minister Pasic that a state of war now existed between their two countries. He addressed this message to Pasic via Serbian army headquarters. Shortly thereafter, in an abundance of caution, he sent a second, identical telegram via the Serbian foreign ministry. The two messages reached Pasic separately after being routed through Romania. The first was handed to him as he was having lunch at a provincial hotel. After reading it he got to his feet and addressed the room. "Austria has declared war on us," he said gravely. "Our cause is just. God will help us." When the second telegram arrived a short time later, Pasic became suspicious. Never having heard of one nation declaring war on another in such a manner, he began to think that the whole thing might be a hoax. The German ambassador, when asked, replied that he knew nothing about a declaration of war. (He was being truthful; not even the kaiser, as we have seen, was informed in advance of Austria's declaration.) The authenticity of the telegrams was confirmed soon enough. News of the declaration sparked anti-Serbian demonstrations in Vienna and even in Berlin, but there was no movement of Austrian troops. Conrad merely began shelling Belgrade from the Bosnian side of the border.

The kaiser met with Bethmann after learning the truth. The chancellor, a visibly unhappy man afterward, immediately began steering a new course. He composed a long telegram to Tschirschky in Vienna, complaining that the Austro-Hungarian government "has left us in the dark concerning its intentions, despite repeated interrogations" and that its declaration of war had put

Germany in "an extraordinarily difficult position" that could cause it to "incur the odium of having been responsible for a world war." He instructed Tschirschky to urge the Austrians to respond positively to what was now Grey's, not just the kaiser's, Stop-in-Belgrade proposal. No doubt Tschirschky, who shortly after the assassination had been rebuked for urging caution on the Austrians, was taken aback. Berchtold was more than taken aback. For three weeks the Germans had been prodding him to act. Now at last he was taking action—and suddenly the Germans wanted him to stop.

The day brought one additional misfortune, and a serious one. Russia's ambassador to Austria, having been kept waiting since Monday, finally was allowed to meet with Berchtold. He wanted to discuss a number of ideas that were being passed around among the various capitals: a suggestion by Sazonov that he and Vienna's ambassador to St. Petersburg should review the original Austrian note to see if it might be modified enough for Serbia to accept it, for example, and Sir Edward Grey's proposal that the Serbian reply be used as a starting point for negotiations rather than a reason for war. Everyone was distracted by the rush of events, however, and Berchtold and his visitor apparently lost track of exactly which idea they were discussing at various points in the conversation. The result was misunderstanding. Berchtold, when the meeting was over, believed that he had made it clear that while he would not negotiate with Serbia, he was prepared to do so with Russia. But the ambassador came away with a distinctly different impression. He reported to Sazonov that Berchtold was not willing to negotiate even with Russia. Probably for no other reason than that both parties had too much on their minds and were approaching exhaustion, an important door had been inadvertently closed.

So Tuesday ended badly. Vienna, with its declaration of war, had convinced Sazonov in St. Petersburg that it was mobilizing not merely to underscore its grievances but to destroy Serbia (which was, in fact, not far from the truth where Berchtold and Conrad were concerned). The Russians had accelerated their preparations for war, Sazonov had been told that it was not even possible to talk with Vienna, and he took this as further evidence that war had become inevitable. Meanwhile he was also being told by France's Ambassador Paléologue that Paris wanted him to stand firm, by Germany's Ambassador Friedrich von Pourtalès that if Russia proceeded with its military preparations Germany would have to mobilize as well, by Serbia's ambassador that the Austrians were bombarding Belgrade, and by Russia's generals that Germany was preparing for war and they must do the same. In important ways, Sazonov was being deceived. French prime minister René Viviani, from the ship on which he and President Poincaré were returning from St. Petersburg, had sent a telegram urging Paléologue to do everything possible to resolve the crisis without war. Paléologue, so determined to encourage Russian belligerence that he was in effect creating his own foreign policy, instead told Sazonov of the "complete readiness of France to fulfill her obligations as an ally in case of necessity."

Paléologue's motivation in all this is clear enough. Notoriously excitable, so inclined to take the darkest possible view of every situation that he was widely distrusted (he owed his appointment to a lifelong friendship with Poincaré), he had been warning even before the July crisis that a European war was inevitable by year-end. Among the terrors that tormented him was the thought that, if France failed to demonstrate a willingness to support Russia almost unreservedly, St. Petersburg would abandon the Entente and seek to ally itself with Berlin. Thus he saw himself as preventing the collapse of France's entire foreign policy, and therefore of France's security.

THE ROMANOVS

IN 1914 THE ROMANOV FAMILY HAD JUST COMPLETED the celebration of its three hundredth year on the Russian throne. It had been a turbulent, often bizarre three centuries. Geniuses and degenerates had worn the crown by turns, amazingly strong women succeeded by alarmingly weak men. There had been royal murders and assassinations, questions about whether a tsar who was presumably dead and buried had actually died at all, and enough sexual irregularity to make it uncertain whether the Romanovs of the twentieth century were even related to the founders of the dynasty. By fits and starts Russia had changed from a remote and exotic eastern kingdom into one of Europe's dominating powers—still only half modern, still not entirely European, but an empire of immense wealth reaching from Poland to the Pacific Ocean. By 1914 the Romanovs had been, by the standards of Russian history, stable and respectable for five generations. The reigning tsar, Nicholas II, was a far more virtuous man than many of his predecessors. He was also, unfortunately, far weaker and less capable than the best of them.

The first Romanov tsar was Michael, crowned in 1613 when he was sixteen years old. He was given the crown because Russia's previous royal family had died out; because after fifteen years of leaderless disorder the country's most powerful factions were desperate for stability; and because no better choice was available. If Michael's blood was not quite royal, it was nearly so: his aunt Anastasia, his father's sister, had been the beloved first wife of Ivan the Terrible and the mother of the last tsar in Ivan's line. Grief over her death is supposed to have been a factor in Ivan's transformation into a homicidal maniac of almost inconceivable savagery.

The Romanovs did not burst upon the European scene until almost a century later, when Peter I, Peter the Great, became tsar. He was a gigantic figure in every sense: more than six and a half feet tall, immensely strong, infinitely energetic, violent, a reformer of everything and at the same time a ruthless tyrant. He was so determined to force Russia into the modern Western world that he moved its capital from Moscow to a swampy piece of wilderness on the coast of the Baltic Sea. Here he built a magnificent new city that was laced with canals and became known as the Venice of the North. He named it St. Petersburg because that was more Western than the Russian equivalent, Petrograd. There was nothing that he wasn't determined to change, and when his ministers weren't quick enough in doing what he wanted, he would lash even the most exalted of them with his stick. He forced the men of Russia to shave their beards and adopt Western dress; the traditionalists were scandalized. He modernized the government and the military. He conquered and developed seaports not only on the Baltic but on the Black Sea, beginning the long process of pushing the Ottoman Turks southward back toward their capital of Constantinople. By the time of his death in 1725, he had transformed Russia into a major player among the nations of the world.

As a young man Peter had married a woman from the Russian nobility, but he soon found her tedious and eventually sent her to a convent. He replaced her with a mistress, a Lutheran girl named Marta who had begun her life as a humbly born orphan in Latvia. She had become a prisoner when an invading Russian army captured her hometown, was given to a man who happened to be close to Peter, and so was taken back to St. Petersburg, where she was discovered by the tsar. Marta and Peter had twelve children together (only two, both of them daughters, survived to adulthood), and she came to be the one person in whom he had complete confidence. She was rechristened in the Orthodox faith and given the baptismal name Catherine, and was married to Peter in 1712, when she was twenty-eight and he fifty. He had her crowned his empress consort in 1724 (Peter was the first tsar to call himself emperor), and upon Peter's death she was proclaimed Empress Catherine I in her own right. Her career has to be considered among the more remarkable in history.

The story becomes fuzzy in the years following Catherine's death. The Romanovs became extinct in the male line (Peter had his heir, a son by his first wife, tortured until he died), and in time the crown went to an obscure German princeling whose mother had been Peter's and Catherine's daughter. This new tsar, Peter III, was a drunkard, a fool, probably sexually impotent, and an ardent admirer of

The Russian royal family: Nicholas, Alexandra, their four daughters and son

Russia's enemy Frederick the Great of Prussia. Not surprisingly, the Russian nobility despised him. He matters in history for one reason only: before becoming tsar, he had married a fifteen-year-old German princess—another Catherine, as it happened—who quickly succeeded him on the throne. (Plotters from the army, in collusion with this second Catherine, murdered him less than a year after his coronation.) She became Catherine the Great, the second monumental figure of the Romanov era.

She was a physically tiny woman whose appetites and ambitions equaled those of Peter the Great. She became more Russian than the Russians, and during her thirty-four-year reign the empire expanded tremendously and again was prodded along the road to modernization. Like Peter the Great, she reached out to the West. She corresponded with such Enlightenment giants as Voltaire and Diderot. She brought John Paul Jones from the New World to take command of her Black Sea Fleet and use it against the Turks. It was with Catherine that the Russians began to aspire seriously to the role of patron of the Christian peoples of the Balkans. And under Catherine they first dreamed of driving the Turks out of Constantinople, the ancient and holy imperial city of the East.

Like Peter the Great before her and like many of her own descendants, Catherine was a perplexing mixture of reformer and tyrant. She was also a woman of great intellect and cultivation, as well as a libertine. She had multiple lovers before her husband's death, and it is at best questionable whether her son and heir, Paul, was actually the son of Peter III. Her long string of handsome young lovers, most of them playthings whom she was far too shrewd to take seriously except in the boudoir, continued until her death of a stroke at sixty-seven. Unprovable stories about her sexual encounters with a horse have come down to the twenty-first century.

Catherine had no confidence in her son Paul; in fact, she despised him. She took charge of the upbringing of Paul's sons, especially the eldest, Alexander. She carefully supervised his preparation for the throne. When she died, Paul succeeded. But he was soon murdered, just as his father had been—assuming that Peter III was in fact his father. He was then succeeded, as Catherine had intended, by the tall, handsome, and intelligent young Alexander I.

In what would become something of a Romanov pattern, Tsar Alexander began his reign as a reformer of whom great things were expected, then took alarm at the forces of change all around him, and finally turned into the most iron-handed kind of reactionary. His first fifteen years on the throne were turbulent in the extreme, with Napoleon marching his armies up and down Europe and finally occupying and burning Moscow. It fell to Alexander to save Russia and his dynasty, and he succeeded brilliantly. In the end he outwaited and outwitted the French emperor. At one point he even pretended to consider offering his sister to Napoleon, though in fact giving a Romanov princess to such an upstart was unthinkable. After Napoleon took an Austrian bride instead (even the mighty Hapsburgs turned out to be more submissive than Alexander) and finally was driven into exile, Alexander was more influential than any other monarch in restoring the old order.

Intriguing questions hang over the end of Alexander's life. In 1825, childless but at the peak of his power, he was suddenly reported to have died in a town where he had been staying far from the capital. When his coffin arrived in St. Petersburg, his brothers refused to have it opened. There were rumors that he had not died at all but had done something that he had long talked yearningly of doing—withdrawn into a monastery in Siberia to spend the rest of his life in contemplation. Nothing of the sort was ever proved. But toward the end of the twentieth century, when his coffin was finally opened in St. Petersburg's Peter and Paul Fortress, it was found to be empty.

Alexander's heir was his brother Constantine, but because this archduke refused the crown, it was passed to a third and much younger brother who thereby became Nicholas I. This Nicholas, lacking even ephemeral reforming instincts, was a reactionary in all ways from the start. When he died in 1855, he was called the man who had frozen Russia for thirty years.

His son Alexander II was also conservative but more intelligent and therefore able to understand the need for change. He began his career as a reformer and even something of an idealist, abolishing the serfdom that had long been the shame of Russia. Gradually he too turned in the direction of reaction and repression, taking such severe measures against a movement of young reformers that some became bomb-throwing radicals. In the last years of his reign there were repeated attempts on his life, but Alexander never completely abandoned his efforts to move Russia closer to if not quite into the modern world. In 1881, shortly after he had approved the creation of a parliament-like body that was to be allowed to advise on legislation without actually passing laws, a bomb thrown by a young Pole blew him apart.

Still alive but oozing blood from every part of his body, one leg gone and the other shredded, his torso torn open and his face disfigured, the tsar was carried to his palace. There he died, horribly, in the presence of his family, including his eldest son, who then became Alexander III, and the latter's eldest son, thirteen-year-old Nicholas. He was the third tsar to be murdered in six generations.

Alexander III was a huge and bearlike man, powerful enough to bend a poker and roll pieces of silverware into balls with his bare hands. On succeeding to the throne he declared his "faith in the power and right of autocracy," and he was as good as his word. He dedicated himself unreservedly to reversing as many of his father's reforms as possible (a restoration of serfdom was not among the possibilities), refusing any innovations that might reduce the power of the Romanovs, and clamping down in almost totalitarian fashion on every form of dissent. Newspapers were not even allowed to print the word *constitution*.

Alexander III's son Nicholas was improbably unlike his father in almost every respect: physically slight, something of a playboy in his youth though in fairly innocent ways, and utterly lacking in self-confidence. He was, however, given the same tutor who had taught his father, an archconservative named Constantine Pobedonostsev, known as the High Priest of Social Stagnation. "Among the falsest of political principles is the principle of the sovereignty of the people," Pobedonostsev taught. "It is terrible to think of our condition if destiny had sent us the fatal gift—an all-Russia Parliament. But that will never be." Young Nicholas listened, and like his father he believed. He learned that it was not only the tsar's right but his sacred duty to be a strong father to all the Russians, to yield power to no one. But he had a clear sense of his own limits, knew that he could never be like his father, and had absolutely no wish to succeed him.

There appeared to be no cause for worry on that score. In 1894, with Nicholas in his mid-twenties and preparing to marry Princess Alix of Hesse-Darmstadt (his parents were not at all happy about the match, though the bride was a granddaughter of Queen Victoria of Britain and therefore Wilhelm II's first cousin), Alexander III was not yet fifty and a fountain of vitality. It seemed likely that he would rule for another twenty years or more, and his own expectation that this would be so was reflected in his failure to do anything to prepare his heir for the responsibilities of government. (Nicholas himself demonstrated no wish to learn.) But then, abruptly, he went into a swift decline—the problem was diagnosed as nephritis—and soon died. His heir was shattered, and not only because he had lost the father he idolized.

"What am I going to do?" he asked. "I am not prepared to be a tsar. I never wanted to become one. I know nothing of the business of ruling. I have no idea of even how to talk to the ministers."

Chapter 5

July 29 to 31:

Fear Is a Bad Counselor

"Think of the responsibility which you are asking
me to take! Think of the thousands and thousands of
men who will be sent to their death!"
—Tsar Nicholas II

Wednesday, July 29

At one o'clock in the morning Tsar Nicholas sent a telegram to Kaiser Wilhelm. It was signed "Nicky," and it expressed indignation that an "ignoble war has been declared on a weak country." It asked the kaiser "in the name of our old friendship to do what you can to stop your allies from going too far." While this wire was making its way to Potsdam, Wilhelm sent one of his own to the tsar. It was signed "your very sincere and devoted friend and cousin, Willy." In it the kaiser declared his hopes for peace and said, "I am exerting my utmost influence to induce the Austrians to deal straightly to arrive to [sic] a satisfactory understanding with you."

This exchange was promising, though in his marginal scribblings the kaiser dismissed Tsar Nicholas's message as "a confession of his own weakness, and an attempt to put the responsibility on my own shoulders." The two monarchs wrote to each other in English, a language in which they could not have been more fluent if born and raised in London. In any case, like every glimmer of hope during this exhausting and interminable week, the exchange would soon be submerged in the rush of events. The tsar's foreign minister, Sazonov, continued to be under intense pressure from all sides. He needed little persuading when, later in the morning, War Minister Vladimir Sukhomlinov and the army's chief of staff came to him with their solution to the crisis: mobilization. Mobilizing the army, they said, would put Austria-Hungary on notice in the strongest possible way. Not mobilizing, on the other hand, would leave the army unable to respond if Austria's troops entered Serbia. In case of a wider war, the army would be totally unprepared. Sazonov was quick to agree.

The chief of staff then took the train to Tsar Nicholas's summer palace (the tsar, capable of a strange degree of detachment when terrible things were happening around him, had not visited the capital once since Franz Ferdinand's assassination) and got his signature on two decrees. One ordered the mobilization of twelve army corps, fifty-five divisions, in the four military districts where secret preparations were already most advanced. This was a massive force, bigger than the entire Austro-Hungarian army, but it would include less than half of Russia's troops and so was not intended as a threat to Germany. The other decree would put in motion a general mobilization involving all districts including those nearest Germany and thereby drastically escalate the crisis. Nicholas believed he was merely putting in place the paperwork necessary for possible action later. He told his visitor that neither order was to be executed without specific authorization from him. That night army headquarters was preparing for execution of the general mobilization—and Sazonov was telling lies to the British ambassador, assuring him that Russia was considering no action that could possibly distress the Germans—when the tsar sent word that he had made a decision. Only a partial mobilization, he said, would be allowed; there must be no move against Germany. Nicholas was continuing to exchange telegrams with "Willy," who was continuing to assure him—truthfully—that he was trying to slow the Austrians down.

On this same day President Poincaré of France and Prime Minister Viviani landed at Dunkirk and hurried to Paris by train. They were surprised to learn that Austria had declared war, surprised too by the crowds that had gathered to greet them and were shouting "To Berlin!" Here as in other capitals, the man in the street was giving every appearance of being eager for the fighting

Raymond Poincaré
President of France
*Determined to bring
Britain into the war.*

to begin. Crowds were gathering in Vienna too and in Berlin and Hamburg and London, where a young bank clerk returning from vacation observed that the city was in "a state of hysteria." The enthusiasm was not universal, however. Bertrand Russell, also in London, said he "discovered to my horror that average men and women were delighted at the prospect of war." Across Europe Socialist leaders were mustering their followers in opposition to the impending conflict. Even among the political and military elites, the mood was generally grim. Sir Edward Grey, from his office at the foreign ministry, made his famous comment that "the lamps are going out all over Europe. We shall not see them lit again in our lifetime." (Ironically, long before the war's end Grey would have to retire from public life because he was going blind.) Poincaré, though touched by the fervor of the Paris crowds and determined to give the Russians no reason to doubt his government's support, was equally determined to avert hostilities if possible. He and Viviani sent a telegram to St. Petersburg urging that the Russians do nothing that might provoke a German mobilization; this arrived, however, after the tsar's approval of partial mobilization.

Among the holders of high office, one man at least did not share the sense of glum foreboding: the ebullient—sometimes excessively ebullient—young Winston Churchill. "I think a curse should rest on me," he wrote to Prime Minister Asquith's wife, obviously believing nothing of the kind, "because I *love* this war. I know it's smashing & shattering the lives of thousands every moment—& yet—I *can't* help it—I enjoy every second of it."

Churchill was still a little premature in writing of "this war." As Wednesday ended, the outlook appeared to be slightly less dark, the likelihood of war diminishing if only slightly. The kaiser and the tsar were not only communicating but cooperating in an attempt to impose restraint. Only two things now seemed necessary for a resolution of the crisis to remain possible. Russia must refrain from general mobilization; the kaiser seemed willing to accept, temporarily, limited Russian measures that did not threaten Germany directly. And Austria must agree to something akin to the Stop-in-Belgrade plan. This second condition was likely to be met eventually, simply because Germany wanted it to happen; Austria would find it difficult to proceed without Berlin's support. It all came down, therefore, to the question of whether the Russians would mobilize and stampede the Germans into doing likewise. The German military authorities remained divided. War Minister Erich von Falkenhayn, frightened by the dangers of allowing a Russian mobilization to go unanswered, was urging preliminary steps toward mobilization. But for Chief of Staff Moltke (sometimes accused, unjustifiably, of having plotted from the start to provoke a preventive war), the greatest fear at this point was of doing anything that might cause the Russians to mobilize. In a memorandum dated July 29 he told Chancellor Bethmann Hollweg that if war came, "the leading nations of Europe would tear one another limb from limb . . . in a struggle that would destroy the culture of almost all of Europe for decades to come." Bethmann, who needed no persuading, sent an evening telegram instructing Ambassador Pourtalès to "kindly impress upon M. Sazonov very seriously that further progress of Russian mobilization measures would compel us to mobilize and that then European war could scarcely be prevented."

Thursday, July 30

The European public was now fully awake to the possibility of war. Runs on banks were becoming widespread. Austria, Germany, and Russia were all withdrawing their reserves from foreign banks. The financial markets in Berlin and Brussels had to be shut down because of panic selling.

Even the Nicky-Willy telegrams were beginning to go wrong. In one of his middle-of-the-night messages, in a maladroit attempt to assure the kaiser that Russia had no hostile intentions where Germany was concerned, Tsar Nicholas told him that "the military measures which have now come into force were decided on five days ago for reasons of defense on account of Austria's preparations." Wilhelm concluded from this that Russia "is almost a week ahead of us," and that "that means I have got to mobilize as well."

In the morning the leaders of the Russian general staff came back to Sazonov with bad news. They said there was no acceptable way of executing the kind of partial mobilization that the tsar had approved, one supposedly directed at Austria-Hungary alone. Any such mobilization would have to be done off the cuff and would throw Russia's armed forces into a state of confusion that might leave them helpless in case of a German attack. In practical terms only general mobilization was possible, and it must be postponed no longer. When Sazonov accepted this argument—its validity has been a bone of contention ever since—the chief of the general staff telephoned the tsar and again asked him to approve a general mobilization. Nicholas refused, saying that the question was closed. He was persuaded, grudgingly, to meet with Sazonov at three p.m. Sazonov was soon on his way.

The meeting was a long one, with the foreign minister arguing the generals' case. Austria, Sazonov said, was preparing to destroy Serbia and refusing to talk. Germany was playing a double game, appearing to restrain the Austrians but really just trying to buy time for its own preparations: Germany was far along with an undeclared mobilization of its own. Russia could not afford not to respond. Russia also could not mobilize in any way short of fully—the result of trying such a thing could be disastrous. Sazonov was wrong about almost everything except Austria's determination to attack Serbia. He was not lying, but he was dangerously misinformed.

Nicholas continued to refuse, and Sazonov continued to plead. The tsar, conscious of the magnitude of what he was being asked, agonized aloud. "Think of the responsibility which you are asking me to take!" he declared. "Think of the thousands and thousands of men who will be sent to their death!"

Finally, probably inevitably, Nicholas was worn down. He was a stubborn but not a strong man, and even the strongest of men would have found it difficult to resist when being told that war could no longer be avoided regardless of what they did and that nothing less than national survival was at stake. Perhaps Sazonov's most powerful argument—another falsehood that he believed to be true—was that a general mobilization would not necessarily drive Germany to war. What neither Sazonov nor Nicholas understood was that Russia's mobilization would arouse in Germany's generals a panic indistinguishable from the fears driving the Russians, and that those generals would demand a German response. Far worse, neither of them had any way of knowing how fast the Germans would be able to mobilize, or how inflexible and therefore dangerous the German mobilization plan was. Not even Kaiser Wilhelm or Chancellor Bethmann Hollweg understood clearly at this point that Germany was literally incapable of mobilizing without invading its neighbors to the west and thereby igniting the continental war that all of them dreaded. The final tragedy is that the tsar's decision was based largely on the things that Sazonov told him about Germany's preparations for war, when in fact Germany remained the only one of the continental powers to have taken no military action at all.

Russia's general mobilization, decided just a little more than forty-eight hours after Austria's declaration of war on Serbia, added nine hundred thousand active-duty troops to the number that would have been affected by partial mobilization. It also called up the Russian reserves—a staggering total of four million men, enough to frighten any nation on earth. By making German mobilization—and therefore war—a near-certainty, it drastically reduced the possibility that the Willy-Nicky telegrams or any of the other increasingly desperate efforts to defuse the situation (cables were flying among the capital cities around the clock) could produce results before it was too late. It all but ended the hope of negotiations, or of a compromise based on Stop-in-Belgrade.

Tragically, Russia's mobilization, while dictated by military considerations, was not only militarily unnecessary but counterproductive. Tactically it was a gift to the Austrians (or would have been, if Conrad had taken advantage of it), relieving them of the anguish of not knowing whether they needed to prepare to fight the Russians or were free to focus on Serbia alone. Strategically it was an act of high folly. In no real sense had the security of Russia ever been threatened by the July crisis. Even the destruction of Serbia—something that certainly could have been averted without resorting to war—would have had little impact on Russia's strategic position. Russia would still have had the biggest army in the world by a huge margin, and it would still have been in the beginning stages of a program aimed at expanding that army by 40 percent within three years.

Tsar Nicholas was shown a telegram that the monk Rasputin had sent to Tsarina Alexandra. Rasputin, who had maneuvered himself into being almost a member of the imperial family, was at his home village deep in the interior of Russia, just beginning to recover from a stab wound that had nearly taken his life. Because of his distance from the capital and the state of his health, he could not possibly have known what was happening in St. Petersburg or Vienna or elsewhere. Thus his telegram, like so many other things about this strange and sinister man, continues to mystify even today. "Let Papa [Rasputin's name for Nicholas] not plan war," the telegram said. "With war will come the end of Russia and yourselves, and you will lose to the last man." The tsar read it and tore it into pieces.

British foreign secretary Sir Edward Grey, alarmed by the deepening seriousness of the crisis, finally stopped being so diplomatic as to be nearly incapable of saying anything. Speaking without the knowledge of the British cabinet, he told Germany's Ambassador Lichnowsky that in his opinion, quite unofficially, "unless Austria is willing to enter upon a discussion of the Serbian question, a world war is inevitable," and that he would expect such a war to bring Britain in on the side of France and Russia. When the kaiser and Bethmann Hollweg learned of this, they abandoned any lingering hopes that war if it came could be a "local" one involving only Austria-Hungary and Serbia, and they intensified their attempts to restrain the Austrians. If Grey had been this forthright just a few days earlier, Berlin almost certainly would have changed its position more quickly and firmly. Austria might then have deferred its declaration of war, and Russia would have had little reason to mobilize. Now, however, it was all but too late. Also too late, Bethmann awakened to the fact that the Russians were laboring under a misunderstanding about Vienna's willingness to talk. He cleared this up by having Tschirschky alert Berchtold to the problem, but with things now happening so fast and diplomacy being submerged under the concerns of the generals, there was little chance that talks could be got under way in time to avoid disaster.

Bethmann was peppering Tschirschky with telegrams, each one more urgent and exasperated than the last. In one he instructed the ambassador to make clear to Berchtold that any Austro-Hungarian refusal to negotiate with Russia would be not only a "serious error" but "a direct provocation of Russia's armed intervention." "We are, of course, ready to fulfill the obligations of our alliance," he said in another, "but must decline to be drawn wantonly into a world conflagration by Vienna, without having any regard paid to our counsel." But here again the remedies were coming too late—all the more so because Berchtold had withdrawn into an almost total silence. He was bent on war and wanted no discussion.

The tension continued to increase. President Poincaré, concerned about jeopardizing France's alliance with Russia, sent assurances to St. Petersburg through Ambassador Paléologue that Russia could depend on France. Paléologue hurried to tell Sazonov. Not yet knowing that Russia had already mobilized (if Paléologue knew, he did not deign to inform Paris), Poincaré also told his ambassador to urge the Russians to proceed cautiously. This Paléologue had no interest in doing.

Paris and St. Petersburg continued to receive reports of extensive military preparations within Germany, reports that continued to be untrue. France was beginning to prepare, but it was doing so extremely tentatively, to avoid alarming the Germans or, what Poincaré cared about even more at this point, giving the British any cause to see France as an aggressor. No reserves were called up, and no movement of troops by train was permitted. Determined to bring Britain to France's assistance if war started, and mindful that this would require casting Germany in the role of aggressor, Poincaré ordered that all troops be kept six miles back from the border. When the French commander in chief, General Joseph Joffre, requested permission to mobilize, he was refused. Even limited movements of troops toward the six-mile limit were not permitted—until Joffre, later in the day, threatened to resign.

Poincaré summoned the British ambassador to his office. He asked for a firmer line in London. He said that if Britain would declare its intention to support France, Germany might be deterred and war averted. The ambassador, aware of how divided the government in London remained, was able to say nothing more than "how difficult it would be for His Majesty's government to make such a statement."

General Helmuth von Moltke, chief of the German general staff, checked on the status of Austria's mobilization. When he learned that Conrad was still deploying unnecessarily large numbers of his mobilized troops to the south—the field marshal continued to be unable to put aside his dream of invading Serbia—Moltke panicked. As things stood, the Austrian troops on the Russian border would, if fighting began, be outnumbered by two to one. Moltke sent a wire to Conrad, urging him to shift his main force to the north—to mobilize against Russia, in effect. Unless Conrad did so, Germany, in beginning a war against France, would be unprotected in its rear. Getting into matters that were not supposed to be the business of generals, Moltke also warned Conrad that Vienna must refuse to be drawn into the Stop-in-Belgrade proposal. That proposal, of course, was exactly what Bethmann Hollweg had been pushing Berchtold to accept. "What a joke!" Berchtold exclaimed when he learned of Moltke's warning. "Who's in charge in Berlin?"

At nine p.m. Moltke took Erich von Falkenhayn, the war minister, with him to the chancellor's office. The two generals told Bethmann that German mobilization had become imperative, that a postponement would put the country at risk, and that at a minimum a State of Imminent War (Germany's equivalent of Russia's Period Preparatory to War) must be declared. Bethmann, reluctant to commit to military action but equally unwilling to assume responsibility for leaving Germany undefended, promised a decision by noon on Friday. He too was coming to regard war as inevitable, and his focus was shifting from preserving the peace to preparing for hostilities. Knowing that Conrad had declared Stop-in-Belgrade to be infeasible and was supported in this by Berchtold, he, like Moltke, was yielding to a fatalistic acceptance of the notion that if Germany's enemies were determined to make war, now was better than later.

Friday, July 31

When they learned of Russia's mobilization—unofficial reports reached Berlin almost immediately—the German generals intensified their demands. Germany continued to be the only European power not to have undertaken any military preparations at all, and the situation was becoming intolerable. Even Britain was on the move, First Lord of the Admiralty Churchill having ordered the Grand Fleet to take up a position in the North Sea from which it could respond quickly to any forays by the German High Seas Fleet and protect France's Channel ports.

Holes were appearing in Germany's war plans. No one had foreseen a situation in which Russia mobilized without declaring war, or in which war erupted between Germany and Russia with France waiting on the sidelines. No one was sure what to do. The generals, of course—Chief of Staff Moltke included—were all but howling for action. Germany, they argued, was in a better position to win a two-front war now than it would be after a few more years of French and Russian military buildup, and with every day of delay it was being drawn deeper into a death trap. Kaiser Wilhelm refused mobilization but agreed to declare a State of Impending War, which put in motion a variety of measures (securing borders, railways, and Germany's postal, telephone, and telegraph systems, and recalling soldiers on leave) in the expectation that mobilization would follow within forty-eight hours. He did so with the same deep reluctance shown by Franz Joseph when asked to declare war on Serbia, and by Tsar Nicholas when begged for mobilization. Like his fellow emperors, he yielded only because the military men, now taking charge in Berlin, St. Petersburg, and Vienna, were insisting that there was no alternative. Bethmann too, desperately worried about keeping Britain out of any war and bringing Italy in on the side of Germany and Austria-Hungary, agreed only when, minutes before noon, the earlier reports of Russia's mobilization were confirmed.

Berlin continued to ask Vienna to demonstrate some willingness to negotiate on the basis of various proposals being offered by London and St. Petersburg (such proposals had become numerous and complex), but Berchtold maintained his silence. Short-circuiting diplomatic channels, Wilhelm sent a telegram directly to Franz Joseph, requesting his intervention. After conferring with Berchtold and Conrad, the Hapsburg emperor replied that Vienna could not do more than it had already done. He did not explain that Austria-Hungary too was now caught in the snares of its own military planning. Just as Russia had been unable to limit its mobilization to Austria because (as the generals claimed) it had no plan that would permit it to do so, and just as Germany had no way of mobilizing without attacking its neighbors, Austria had no plan that would send its army into Belgrade but no farther. Conrad feared, as the Russian generals had feared before their mobilization and as Germany's generals would soon be fearing with equally fateful consequences, that attempting to change his arrangements could lead only to disorder. Vienna could not regard this as a tolerable option with Serbia mobilizing and the Russians assembling immense forces along their common border. In important regards, however, Conrad was not in touch with reality. Even as war with Russia became likely, he remained obsessed with punishing Serbia. Just as foolishly, he clung to the delusion that Italy would be entering the war on the side of the Central Powers, providing hundreds of thousands of additional troops.

All options except the military ones were shutting down. Power was moving into the hands of the soldiers and away from the diplomats and politicians. The soldiers were motivated mainly by fear. And as the Austrian ambassador to France had observed on Thursday in a message to Berchtold, "Fear is a bad counselor."

In a display of German diplomacy at its ham-handed worst, Berlin informed London that if Britain remained neutral, Germany would promise to restore the borders of both France and Belgium (though not any overseas colonies that Germany might seize) at the end of whatever war might ensue. This was ominous—no one had even mentioned Belgium until now.

Grey, an English gentleman of the old school whose passions were fly-fishing (he had written a book on the subject) and bird-watching, saw the offer as nothing better than a crude attempt at bribery, an insult to be rejected out of hand. His anger is transparent in his instructions to the British ambassador in Berlin:

"You must inform German Chancellor that his proposal that we should bind ourselves to neutrality on such terms cannot for a moment be entertained. He asks us in effect to engage to stand by while French colonies are taken and France is beaten so long as Germany does not take French territory as distinct from the colonies. From the material point of view such a proposal is unacceptable, for France could be so crushed as to lose her position as a Great Power, and become subordinate to German policy without further territory in Europe being taken from her. But apart from that, for us to make this bargain with Germany at the expense of France would be a disgrace from which the good name of this country would never recover."

To this warning he added assurances that German assistance in averting war would be rewarded. "If the peace of Europe can be preserved and this crisis be safely passed," he said, "my own effort would be to promote some arrangement to which Germany could be a party, by which she could be assured that no hostile or aggressive policy would be pursued against her or her allies by France, Russia and ourselves, jointly or separately." He appeared to be pointing toward fundamental changes in the overall system of European alliances, changes calculated to make this the last crisis of its kind. The implication was that until now Grey had not understood the intensity of Germany's fear of encirclement, but that his eyes had been opened.

Grey next took a step that would give Bethmann much reason to regret having broached the question of Belgium. With the approval of the cabinet, he asked France and Germany to declare their intention to respect Belgian neutrality in case of war. France was able to agree without difficulty. Its plans for an offensive against Germany were focused far to the south of Belgium in the area of Alsace-Lorraine, and Poincaré understood that British support in case of war would be infinitely more valuable than any possible use of Belgian territory. Germany, trapped by the inflexibility of its mobilization plan, was unable to respond at all. Thus was the first major step taken toward Britain's entry into the war.

Germany now sent what would become known as its double ultimatum to France and Russia. This was a message warning that German mobilization "must follow in case Russia does not suspend every war measure against Austria-Hungary and ourselves within twelve hours." France was asked for a declaration of neutrality. The deadline for responses was Saturday afternoon.

The double ultimatum was in part Berlin's desperate final effort to escape mobilization and in part an effort to precipitate a breakdown in diplomatic relations to help justify the westward invasion that must follow mobilization. As directed to Russia, it was a straightforward request for cooperation. As directed to France, it was a kind of wild theatrical gesture aimed at making clear to the world that if war with Russia came, Germany and France would be at war also. It was intended to explain, in the court of public opinion, a German attack on France. What it actually looked like was overbearing German bluster. The likelihood that Berlin never expected Paris to accept it is supported by the outrageous additional demand that the German ambassador to France was instructed to make in case of acceptance: France's temporary surrender of its great fortresses at Verdun and Toul, in return for a promise that they would be returned at the end of Germany's fight with Russia. Bethmann would intimate as much in his memoirs. "If France had actually declared her neutrality," he wrote, "we should have had to sit by while the French army, under the protection of a specious neutrality, made all its preparations to attack us while we were busy in the East."

There came a final flurry of Nicky-Willy telegrams. The kaiser told the tsar that he was continuing to try to mediate in Vienna, and that "the peace of Europe may still be maintained by you, if Russia will agree to stop the military measures which must threaten Germany and Austria-Hungary."

Once again, messages between the two emperors crossed in midair. Nicholas told Wilhelm that it was "technically impossible" to stop Russia's mobilization but that Russia did not want war and still did not see war as unavoidable. "So long as the negotiations with Austria on Serbia's account are taking place, my troops shall not take any provocative action. I give you my solemn word for this. I put all my trust in God's mercy and hope in your successful mediation in Vienna for the welfare of our countries and for the peace of Europe."

As soon as the kaiser's message reached the tsar, Nicholas sent back an answer. He said he understood that Russian mobilization might require Germany to mobilize as well. He said he accepted this, but it need not mean war. He asked Wilhelm for "the same guarantee from you as I gave you, that these measures do not mean war and that we shall continue negotiating for the benefit of our countries and universal peace dear to all our hearts. Our long proved friendship must succeed, with God's help, in avoiding bloodshed. Anxiously, full of confidence await your answer."

It was obviously heartfelt and must have seemed the richest of opportunities. But nothing would come of it. Because of all that had already happened, nothing could.

THE OTTOMAN TURKS

IT IS ONE OF HISTORY'S LITTLE JOKES, SURELY, THAT Turkey and the Ottoman Empire that it ruled had no part to play in the July crisis that brought on the Great War. For the crisis could never have unfolded as it did if not for the profound impact that the empire of the Turks had had on the development of eastern Europe. And no one would be affected by the war itself more profoundly than the Turks and the many peoples who, century after century, had been their unhappy subjects.

Without the decline of the Ottoman Empire, the Hapsburgs would not have been in Bosnia at all, and there could have been no Kingdom of Serbia. There would have been no power vacuum in the Balkans. Russia and Austria-Hungary could never have been pulled into that vacuum or into such dangerous conflict with each other.

To go back further, without the *rise* of the Ottomans the whole bitter saga of the Balkans would have been unimaginably different. The Turks had ruled the peninsula for five hundred years, reaching at their height westward into Italy, northward into Austria, Hungary, and Russia, and all the way around the Black Sea. For a time they seemed destined to conquer the whole eastern half of Europe, if not the entire continent. When the Great War began, their empire, while maintaining only a toehold in Europe proper, still extended across the Middle East to the Arabian Peninsula.

The empire reached its pinnacle, and its decline began, with the life of a single man, Sultan Suleiman the Magnificent. (That was what Christian Europe called him—to his own people he was Suleiman the Lawmaker.) He ruled from 1520 to 1566 and led the Ottomans to their zenith both culturally and geographically. He was ten generations removed from the Turkish-Mongol chieftain named Osman who had founded the dynasty three hundred years before and given it his name. In every one of those ten generations, in an unbroken sequence of achievement that no other family has ever approached, the Ottoman Turks were led by yet another dynamic, heroic, conquering figure. Generation after generation, starting where Osman had first emerged from obscurity in what is now eastern Turkey and from there moving outward in all directions, the dynasty took control of more and more of the world around it. The sultans forced their way into Europe for the first time in 1354, and ninety-nine years later they captured Constantinople, the heart of the Byzantine Empire. From then on Constantinople was their home. Its mighty basilica of Hagia Sophia, perhaps the greatest architectural achievement of the Roman era, became an Islamic mosque.

The Ottomans continued their expansion for another century after taking Constantinople, conquering among other places all of eastern Europe south of the Danube. Suleiman's father, Selim I, doubled the size of the empire by winning a single battle that made him the master of Syria, Palestine, Egypt, and Algeria. The domain that he passed on to Suleiman included among its major cities Alexandria, Algiers, Athens, Baghdad, Cairo, Damascus, Jerusalem, and Smyrna. The Ottomans had become not only the political and military masters of the Islamic world but also—what put their supremacy beyond challenge—the custodians of Mecca and Medina and the other holy places associated with the Prophet Muhammad.

As its power increased, the dynasty evolved into something that was not a family in any ordinary sense of the term but a chain of fathers and sons who never married. Instead of taking wives, the sultans kept scores and even hundreds of women who were property rather than spouses. These women lived as prisoners in a harem. They were allowed contact with no men except the rulers who owned them and an army of custodians, many of them black Africans, whose sexual organs had been surgically removed.

Suleiman, a contemporary of Henry VIII of England, took this strange heritage to a peak of vitality. Like his forebears, he was a warrior, personally leading his army in thirteen campaigns. He pushed deeper into Europe, capturing Belgrade and Budapest and completing the conquest of the Balkans. He besieged Vienna, the keystone of central Europe, and would have captured it too if torrents of rain had not made it impossible for him to bring his heavy guns north. He was a poet, a student of the works of Aristotle, and a builder who made Constantinople grander and more beautiful than it had ever been. The opulence of life in his Topkapi Palace beggars the imagination.

Suleiman had some three hundred concubines, as well as a promising young son and heir named Mustafa, when he was given a red-haired Russian girl named Ghowrem, who came to be known as Roxelana. She came into his harem as part of his share of the booty from a slave-gathering raid into what is now Poland, and she must have been a remarkable creature. (Not surprisingly, in light of the power she acquired in Constantinople, she eventually won a second new name: "the witch.") Almost from the day of her arrival, Suleiman never slept with another woman. Eventually and amazingly, he did something that no sultan had done in centuries: he married. Their love story would have been one of the great ones if it hadn't ended up taking the dynasty and the empire in such a sordid direction.

Mustafa gave every indication of developing into yet another mighty branch on the family tree. At an early age he showed himself a bold military leader adored by his troops, a capable provincial governor, and a popular hero. But he stood in the way of the son whom Roxelana had borne to (presumably) Suleiman, and so he was doomed. Working her wiles, Roxelana persuaded Suleiman that Mustafa was plotting against him. (He was doing nothing of the kind.) With his father looking on, Mustafa was overpowered and strangled by five professional executioners whose tongues had been slit and eardrums broken so that they would hear no secrets and could never speak of what they saw. And so when Suleiman died some years later, master of an empire of almost incredible size and power, he was succeeded by Roxelana's son, Selim II. Nothing was ever the same again.

Selim the Sot was short and fat and a drunk. He never saw a battlefield and died after eight years on the throne by falling down and fracturing his skull in his marble bath. His son, Murad III, was also a drunk and an opium addict as well; during a reign of twenty years he sired 103 children and apparently did little else. His heir, Mahomet III, began his reign by ordering all of his many brothers, the youngest of them mere children, put to death, thereby introducing that custom into Ottoman royal culture. Having done so he followed his father in devoting the rest of his life to copulation. And so it went. Every sultan from Roxelana's son forward was a monster of degeneracy or a repulsive weakling or both. The abruptness and permanence of the change, the sharpness of the contrast between the murdered Mustafa and his half-brother Selim II, has given rise to speculation that perhaps Roxelana's son was not Suleiman's son at all.

In the post-Suleiman empire, a new breed of craven sultans came to live in terror of being overthrown by rivals from within the dynasty. Appalling new traditions emerged, to be observed whenever one of them died. All the women of the deceased sultan would be moved to a distant place and kept in even deeper solitude for the rest of their miserable lives. Any who happened to be pregnant would be murdered (generally by being bundled in sacks and drowned), and the younger brothers and half-brothers of the new monarch (often a large number of men, boys, and infants) were murdered as well (generally by strangulation).

The rulers erected a windowless building called the Cage in which their heirs were confined from early childhood until they died or were put to death or, having been taught nothing about anything, were released to take their turns on the throne. The result was as inevitable as it was monstrous: an empire ruled year after year and finally century after century by utterly ignorant, utterly incompetent, sometimes half-imbecilic, half-mad men, some of whom spent decades in the Cage before their release and all of whom, after their release, were free to do absolutely anything they wanted, no matter how vicious, for as long as they remained alive. They commonly indulged their freedom to kill or maim anyone they wished to kill or maim for any reason—for playing the wrong music or for smoking, for example—or for no reason at all.

Throughout the three and a half centuries from the death of Suleiman until the Great War, only one sultan displayed some of the fire and strength of the men who had built the empire. This was Murad IV, who reigned from 1623 to 1640. He became sultan when he was only ten years old—too young to have been incapacitated by the Cage—and he grew into a man of immense courage and physical power. He was the first sultan since Suleiman to be a soldier, leading his army into Persia, where he savagely put down an uprising. He was also even more insanely cruel than most sultans. In just one year of his reign, 1637, some twenty-five thousand of the empire's subjects were executed, many of them by Murad's own hand. He claimed the right to kill ten innocent people per day, and occasionally he would sit on the wall of his palace shooting randomly at passersby. At night he would make incognito visits to the taverns of Constantinople, where anyone found smoking would be executed on the spot. "Wherever the sultan went," says Noel Barber in his book *The Sultans,* "he was followed by his chief executioner, Kara Ali, whose belt bulged with nails and gimlets, clubs for breaking hands and feet, and cannisters containing different kinds of powder for blinding."

Almost uniquely among the Ottomans, Murad produced no children, and on his deathbed he ordered the death of his brother and heir, Ibrahim, who had been living in the Cage from the age of two. This order was not obeyed, Ibrahim being the last living member of the dynasty, but from that point there were few further signs of vitality in the Ottoman line. Ibrahim devoted himself to building up a harem of 280 beautiful young women. Then, acting on a dubious report that one of these women (no one could say which one) had become romantically involved with a eunuch, he had all of them drowned. And so it continued.

Not surprisingly, the empire rotted from within under this kind of leadership and became an increasingly inviting target. Young General Napoleon Bonaparte first showed Europe just how impotent the Ottomans had become when, in 1798, he invaded and almost effortlessly conquered Egypt. Also suggestive of what lay ahead was the fact that Napoleon was driven out of Egypt not by the Turks or their Egyptian subjects but by the British navy. From then on, and increasingly, the survival of the sultans and their decaying empire depended less on themselves than on the jealousies and rivalries of the European powers. The Ottomans hung on through the nineteenth century less through any acts of their own than because Britain and France blocked Russia from finishing them off.

Even so, the hundred years leading up to 1914 brought uninterrupted losing wars: with the empire's own Turkish satraps as they tried for autonomy in Egypt, Syria, and elsewhere; with Arab chieftains seeking independence; with Persia; with the Christian peoples of the Balkans; and—four times between 1806 and 1878—with a Russia hungering for Constantinople.

In 1830 the French seized control of Algeria in North Africa. At about that same time the British began building a power base in Arabia and the Persian Gulf. In 1853 Russia, tempted by what appeared to be easy pickings, invaded the Ottoman provinces south of the Danube. The Ottoman presence in Europe might have come to an end then if not for the Crimean War, in which Britain and France intervened to stop the Russians.

Britain, fearful that its position in the eastern Mediterranean and control of India might be lost if Russia broke through to the south, saved the Ottomans from destruction yet again in 1878. But by that time several European countries, Britain included, were feasting on the Turkish empire's extremities. Austria-Hungary took possession of Bosnia and Herzegovina, literally preparing the ground for the Sarajevo assassination. France, with British support and in the face of such strong German opposition that for a time the issue threatened to spark a war, took Tunisia and Morocco in North Africa. Britain took Egypt and Cyprus, and finally even Italy reached across the Mediterranean to grab Tripoli (today's Libya), along with islands in the Aegean and Mediterranean. Germany meanwhile, having arrived too late to share in this plunder, focused on building ties with the Turks. It began work on a Berlin-to-Baghdad railway, and Kaiser Wilhelm II paid a state visit to Constantinople and Jerusalem.

In 1908, the year when Austria-Hungary formally annexed Bosnia and Herzegovina, a group of would-be reformers called the Young Turks (their leader, an army officer named Enver Pasha, was only twenty-seven years old) seized control of the government in Constantinople and introduced a constitution. In 1912 the First Balkan War drove the Turks almost entirely out of the Balkans. This, and the failure of the Constantinople regime to deliver the reforms expected of it or to stop the disintegration of the empire, gravely damaged the prestige of the ruling faction, which was replaced by nationalist extremists once again led by Enver. Some of it was regained the following year, however, when the Second Balkan War led to Turkey's recovery of the city of Adrianople on the European mainland. The sultan was at least as ridiculous a figure as the sorriest of his predecessors. (He had been deemed a safe choice for the throne after boasting that he had not read a newspaper in more than thirty years.) No one even pretended that he mattered. In January 1914, Enver Pasha left the army to become minister of war, and in July he took his empire into a secret defensive alliance with Germany.

Enver Pasha
War Minister
and Young Turk
*Eager to recoup the
Ottoman Empire's
humiliating losses
in the Balkans
and elsewhere.*

Astonishingly in light of all the humiliations it had experienced, the Ottoman Empire of July 1914 was still bigger geographically than France, Germany, and Austria-Hungary combined. It still ruled Arabia, which soon would emerge as the world's greatest source of oil. If war did erupt, no one knew if the empire would enter it or, if so, on which side. It would be a coveted ally—or a rich, probably easy conquest.

Chapter 6

Saturday, August 1:

Leaping into the Dark

"If his Majesty insisted on leading the whole army eastwards, he would have a confused mass of disorderly armed men."

—Helmuth von Moltke

Why didn't the Germans seize upon Tsar Nicholas's eleventh-hour offer? Why didn't they agree to do as the Russians were doing, mobilize their forces but at the same time pledge not to attack? Why didn't they wait, pressuring Austria-Hungary to be sensible while Russia put pressure on Serbia and some sort of settlement was worked out? It was a splendid opportunity. Seizing it could have put Germany in a solid bargaining position.

It all came to nothing in part because of the unmanageable difficulties that mobilizing and then waiting would have created for Germany and Germany alone. An open-ended postponement of hostilities after the great powers had mobilized would have destroyed Germany's chances of defeating France before having to fight Russia. It would have given Russia especially, but France as well, an advantage that could only grow as time passed. The high command of the German army would, understandably, have called any such postponement an act of madness. When the kaiser suggested something like it, Army Chief of Staff Helmuth von Moltke came close to calling the idea insane.

Ever since becoming chief of staff, Moltke had been developing a highly secret plan for fighting a two-front war. This came to be called the Schlieffen Plan, after the general who first conceived and proposed it, but it was Moltke who made it Germany's only military option. By 1914 he had spent a decade immersed in it, tinkering with it, torturing himself about how to make it work. No matter how often or in how many ways he introduced new refinements, the plan continued to have one unchanging thesis at its center: speed was everything. Anything that slowed the Germans down, anything that might allow Russia to get into a war before France had been taken out, was regarded as likely to be fatal.

For this reason the tsar's promise to "take no provocative action" while mobilizing was, from the German perspective, nonsense. General mobilization meant, by definition, that Russia was marshaling its forces for an attack on Germany. Every day of mobilization brought Russia closer to being ready to strike at Germany from the east as soon as Germany was ready to engage France in the west. Viewed from Berlin, Russian mobilization *was* a provocative action of the most serious kind. It was inherently threatening to an extent that the tsar and his advisers could not possibly have understood. And while the Russians hoped that mobilization, by demonstrating the gravity of the situation, would increase the willingness of the Central Powers to negotiate, actually it worked in the opposite direction. The Germans— fearful like all the great powers of appearing weak—were unwilling to give the appearance of having been forced to negotiate by the threat of Russian action.

But Germany's mobilization problems went even deeper. Moltke, over the years, had transformed Schlieffen's idea for a lightning-fast attack on France from an option into an inevitability in case of war. Any delay after mobilization had gone from being a danger into being an impossibility. Moltke and his staff gradually lost the ability to imagine situations in which delay might become advisable. Their planning became so rigid that it left Germany—today this can seem almost impossible to believe—with no way of mobilizing without invading Luxembourg and Belgium en route to invading France.

This was the self-created trap that the Germans found themselves in on August 1—a trap that gave the army's high command no choice except to tell the kaiser that Tsar Nicholas was asking Germany to do the one thing that Germany absolutely could not do. Only Russia could now prevent war, the generals told Wilhelm, and Russia could do so only by agreeing to the terms of the double ultimatum.

At midday on the fifth Saturday since the murder of Franz Ferdinand, the deadline for the double ultimatum arrived without an answer from Russia or France. Kaiser Wilhelm, at the urging of Moltke and Falkenhayn and with the reluctant agreement of Chancellor Bethmann Hollweg, approved a declaration stating that because of St. Petersburg's continued mobilization a state of war now existed between the two empires. This declaration was wired to Friedrich von Pourtalès, Berlin's ambassador to Russia, with instructions to deliver it at six p.m. (It would not reach Pourtalès until five-forty-five, and he had to decode it before taking it to Sazonov.)

Later in the afternoon, when the German ambassador in Paris called on Viviani and asked for his government's response to the ultimatum, he was told icily that "France will have to regard her own interests." An hour later the French government declared a general mobilization—General Joffre, chief of the French general staff, was warning that every twenty-four hours of delay would cost ten or twelve miles of territory when the fighting began—and fifteen minutes after that Kaiser Wilhelm agreed to mobilization as well.

The German mobilization order was made public at five p.m. The kaiser had made its signing a solemn and, in an improvised way, a formal occasion, inviting Bethmann Hollweg and a number of Germany's most senior military officials to serve as witnesses. After handshakes and words of firm resolution by men with tears in their eyes, they remained together to wait for word from Pourtalès. Their conversation turned into a discussion of what should be done next, which soon became a heated and somewhat confused argument. Long-bearded old Admiral Alfred von Tirpitz, father of the High Seas Fleet that had poisoned relations with Britain, said that neither mobilization nor a war declaration was needed at this point—that all reasonable possibilities of a negotiated settlement should be allowed to play out. Almost everyone except the kaiser, who appeared to be uncertain, disagreed with Tirpitz, but not always in the same way or for the same reasons. Moltke and Falkenhayn remained firm on the need for mobilization without delay. Bethmann, who never would have assented to mobilization if Russia's earlier mobilization had not been confirmed without possibility of doubt, said that a formal declaration of war was what was needed now.

The dispute was interrupted by the arrival of Gottlieb von Jagow, the head of the foreign office. Bursting into the room, he announced that a message had just arrived from Ambassador Lichnowsky in London. It was still being decoded but would be ready in minutes. It appeared to be important.

It was a good reason to delay the mobilization, said Tirpitz, at least until they knew what it was all about.

Rubbish, said Moltke and Falkenhayn, and they departed. They were off to oversee the mobilization.

The message from London proved to be not just important but astonishing. Lichnowsky reported that the British foreign secretary, Sir Edward Grey, had just telephoned him with a momentous question. Grey wanted to know, the ambassador said, "if I thought I could assure him that in case France should remain neutral in a Russo-German war, we would not attack the French." The question had come just in advance of a meeting of the British cabinet, and Lichnowsky had assured Grey "that I could take responsibility for such a guaranty, and he is to use this assurance at today's cabinet session."

The kaiser, when he had absorbed this, was almost beside himself with joy. So was Bethmann: it seemed almost too good to be true. It placed at Germany's feet an historic diplomatic victory. The Germans were now free to bring Russia to heel virtually without risk and to restore Austria-Hungary's position among the powers.

Moltke and Falkenhayn were intercepted and summoned back to the palace. The message from London was read to them. Then the kaiser gave new orders to Moltke:

"We shall simply march the whole army east!"

These words came as a blow to Moltke. He was the nephew and namesake of Field Marshal Helmuth von Moltke, one of the greatest figures in German military history. The elder Moltke had led the Prussian army to victory over Austria in 1866, thereby establishing Prussia as the leader of the German states. He had then, in 1870, led the armies of Prussia and the German states allied with it in the defeat of France. His nephew had always enjoyed a special place in the army simply because of his name. It was almost certainly his name, in fact, that had propelled him to the top of the general staff. He was a stolid, insecure man, gloomy and filled with fear of the future, convinced that Germany's enemies were growing stronger so rapidly that within not many more years the empire's position would be hopeless. This fear had caused him to toy with the idea of preventive war (an idea that Bismarck had ridiculed as "committing suicide out of fear of death"), though he had never actually advocated or prepared for such a war. He was sixty-seven years old in 1914, with heavy jowls and too much flesh on what had once been his impressively martial frame, a weary man recovering from a bronchial infection, devoid of the slightest trace of charisma. No one had ever mistaken him for a military genius.

All the same he was a competent, conscientious, experienced soldier. And now he could scarcely believe what the kaiser was telling him. Stop this enormous army? Smash all the clockwork plans for transporting it and feeding it and making certain that at every point it would have what it needed to fight? Turn it around? March it *east*? Call off the great wheeling movement to the west that was the whole and only point of German mobilization and almost certainly Germany's sole hope of victory?

Moltke collected his wits and began to speak. "I assured his Majesty," he would write later, "that this wasn't possible. The deployment of an army of a million men was not a matter of improvisation. It was the product of a whole year's work—of timetables that once worked out could not be changed. If his Majesty insisted on leading the whole army eastwards, he would not have an army ready to strike, he would have a confused mass of disorderly armed men without commissariat." Not only would his army be a confused and disorderly mass of troops, he added, but once facing eastward it would have at its back sixty-two French army divisions ready for action and equipped with their own carefully developed plans for the conquest of Germany. How could Britain, how could anyone, guarantee that France would not seize such an opportunity?

The kaiser, his withered left arm tight against his side as usual, the waxed points of his great hornlike mustache reaching upward almost to his eyes, answered Moltke in the most wounding way possible.

"Your uncle," he said, "would have given me a different answer."

"This pained me a good deal," Moltke would recall, "for I have never pretended to be the equal of the great Field Marshal." He tried to explain that once the mobilization plan had been executed, it would become possible to start moving troops to the east, adding that he could not accept responsibility for the military consequences of halting its execution. Bethmann interrupted in a way that Moltke could not have welcomed, saying that he could not accept political responsibility for a failure to respond positively to Britain's remarkable offer. Finally and with difficulty, a compromise was worked out. Falkenhayn took Moltke into a side room and quietly argued that some slowing of the mobilization process had to be possible. The invasion force could be stopped at least briefly at the Luxembourg border, surely. Moltke gave in. This could work for a while—for hours, though not for days.

Before the slowdown could create serious problems, causing troops and trains that were supposed to be advancing to back up on one another and wreck all the timetables, Berlin learned that what is usually true of things that seem too good to be true applied in this case: the message from London was the result of a tangle of misunderstandings. The origins of these misunderstandings remain hard to unravel even today. It seems certain that Grey, in raising the question of possible French and British neutrality, had not regarded himself as offering anything like a formal proposal. But he like everyone else had been willing to clutch at straws by this point, and apparently he had tossed out an idle thought to see what kind of response it might draw. Perhaps, enmeshed as he was in the struggle going on within the British government and exhausted by long days and nights of searching for a resolution to the continental crisis, he had been less than clear in what he said. Certainly it could never have occurred to him that his idea would be seized by the Germans as an opportunity to delay fighting with France in order to crush Russia first; what he probably had in mind, rather, was an arrangement in which Germany would stand on the defensive on both fronts while the Austro-Russian dispute was worked out.

Perhaps Lichnowsky, who throughout the crisis had displayed exceptional understanding of its dangers and exceptional courage in telling his government truths that it did not want to hear, had been too eager to believe that Grey was telling him what he most wanted to hear. As early as 1912, even before taking up his post in London, he had told the kaiser that "it is understandable that each increase in Serbian power and her expansion towards the sea is regarded with alarm by the Austrian statesmen; but it would be incomprehensible if we should run even the faintest risk of becoming involved in a war for such a cause." His feelings on the matter were even stronger in 1914, and he never hesitated to say so.

For a few blissful hours an exultant Kaiser Wilhelm was able to occupy himself with grandiose new schemes. The German foreign ministry cabled Lichnowsky that Britain would be required to *guarantee* French neutrality, that it had until seven p.m. on Monday to make the necessary arrangements, and that until then Germany would refrain from attacking. Finally, all such fantasies were brought crashing down by another message from London. Lichnowsky reported that Grey, after meeting with the cabinet, had told him that a German violation of Belgian neutrality "would make it difficult for the Government here to adopt an attitude of friendly neutrality." Germany's failure to promise that it would not enter Belgium, Grey had added, "has caused an unfavorable impression." He had again raised the question of whether it might be possible for France and Germany "to remain facing each other under arms, without attacking each other, in the event of a Russian war," but there was no further suggestion that Britain was promising neutrality in return.

Grey was offering, in a word, nothing. Obliquely but clearly enough, he was indicating that Britain would likely join with France in case of war—especially a war that took German troops into Belgium. The kaiser, after venting his rage about the deceitful English (his feelings about Britain had always been a mess of admiration, envy, and resentment), put everything back on track. Moltke was told that the mobilization could go forward as

German Ambassador Lichnowsky making his last
call on the British Foreign Office

originally intended. Later, in making his marginal comments on
Lichnowsky's last message, the kaiser gave particular attention
to Grey's mention of an "unfavorable impression" having been
created in London. "My impression," he wrote, "is that Mr. Grey
is a false dog who is afraid of his own meanness and false policy,
but who will not come out in the open against us, preferring to let
himself be forced by us to do it." His childish language aside, the
kaiser did have a point.

Shortly after seven p.m. in St. Petersburg, Germany's Ambassador Pourtalès was admitted to the office of Foreign Minister Sazonov. The two men were friends, though throughout July
their meetings had sometimes been volcanic. Pourtalès had been

in St. Petersburg for seven years and had developed an affection for Russia. Like diplomats and politicians in all the capital cities, he had had almost no sleep in days. He was an old man, already preparing for retirement when the crisis began, and by Saturday he was approaching collapse. Quietly, he asked Sazonov if Russia was prepared to answer the double ultimatum.

Sazonov, exhausted himself, overwrought, and a volatile personality under the best of circumstances, had just come from a meeting at which he had been trying to assure the British ambassador that Russia's mobilization did not necessarily mean war. He answered Pourtalès by echoing what the tsar had earlier told the kaiser: although it was not possible to stop mobilization, Russia wanted to continue negotiations. Russia remained hopeful of avoiding war.

Pourtalès took from his pocket a copy of Germany's ultimatum, read it aloud, and added that the consequences of a negative reply would be grave.

Sazonov repeated his first answer.

Pourtalès too repeated himself: the consequences would be grave.

"I have no other reply to give you," said Sazonov.

Pourtalès took out more papers. "In that case, sir, I am instructed by my government to hand you this note." In his hands he held two messages, both of them declarations of war. One was for use if Russia gave no answer to the ultimatum, the other a reply to a negative answer. In his distress and confusion he pressed both on Sazonov and burst into tears.

Or so Sazonov wrote years later in his memoirs. Pourtalès's recollection was that Sazonov wept first. Whatever the sequence, apparently both men cried. They embraced, then pulled apart and began to exchange accusations.

"This was a criminal act of yours," Sazonov said. "The curses of the nations will be upon you."

"We were defending our honor."

"Your honor was not involved."

Finally they parted forever, Sazonov helping the distraught Pourtalès to the door.

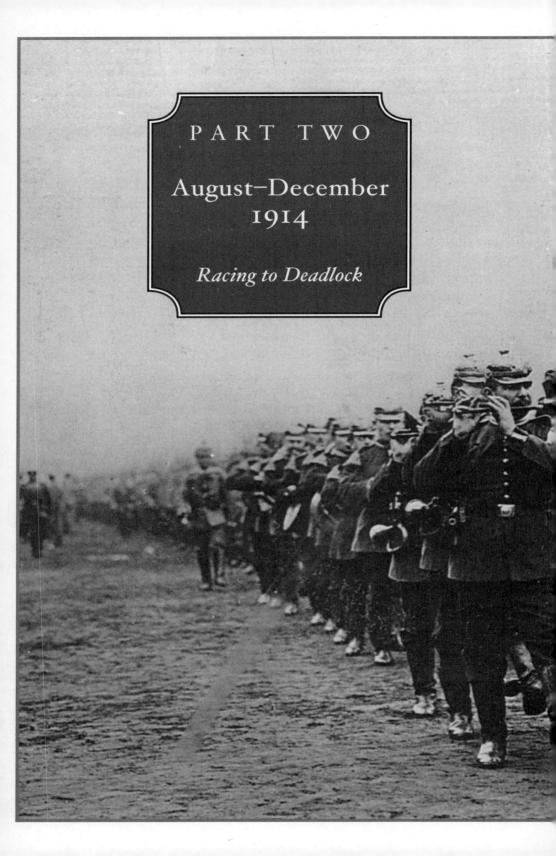

PART TWO

August–December 1914

Racing to Deadlock

Bound for glory: the troops of imperial Germany, adorned with the pickelhaube *headgear that will soon be replaced with more practical steel helmets, marching off to start the war.*

Chapter 7

The Iron Dice Roll

"If the iron dice roll, may God help us."
—Chancellor Theobold von Bethmann Hollweg

Before every commander of the armies that went to war in August 1914 there lay the possibility of becoming a hero, a giant, a deliverer of his people. Likewise there lay before every one of them the very real possibility of everlasting disgrace.

This was nowhere more true than in the case of Helmuth von Moltke, who as the war began was sixty-six years old, in questionable health, and approaching the ninth anniversary of his appointment as head of the German high command. His long service as chief meant that he was responsible not only for winning the war but for the plans—the inconceivably intricate plans, including among much else the timetables of the eleven thousand trains that would have to be moved to complete German mobilization—according to which the war was to be prosecuted. All of it was on his shoulders. And Moltke went to war without a trace of Napoleonic zest. Throughout most of the July crisis he had been a voice for restraint. Though Russia's mobilization turned him into a strident advocate of military action, even then he was motivated not by any hunger for conquest or expectation of victory but by fear of a kind that was far from uncommon in the upper reaches of the German civil and military administration. This fear rose out of the belief, the conviction, that Germany was encircled by enemies who were growing stronger at an alarming rate, and that if the showdown were delayed just a few years more there might be no possibility of victory, even of survival. Far from looking forward to a quick and easy victory, Moltke said that if war came it would be "a long weary struggle with a country that will not acknowledge defeat until the whole strength of its people is broken, a war that even if we should be the victors will push our own people, too, to the limits of exhaustion."

This prognosis was consistent with Moltke's innate pessimism; he was so notorious for his gloomy outlook that the kaiser had long made a joke of it. His pessimism even extended, and always had, to his own abilities; in 1905, when it was beginning to appear that he would be promoted to head of the general staff over capable and more experienced rivals, Moltke had confided to the German chancellor of the time that he regarded himself as "too reflective, too scrupulous, and, if you like, too conscientious for such a post." He said he did not possess "the capacity for risking all on a single throw" that marked great commanders. About that he appears to have been right; he was less a man of action

Helmuth von Moltke
"Too reflective, too scrupulous, and too conscientious."

than an intellectual and aesthete, more cultivated than Prussian generals were expected to be. "Art is the only thing I live for," he once commented, revealing just how remote his values were from those of the Junkers whose sons made up Germany's military elite. But he was also right about what lay ahead. The accuracy of his dark prophecy reflected not only his disposition but his acumen, his grasp of the realities of twentieth-century warfare.

It is not only ironic but mystifying, in light of what he foresaw, that Moltke had committed himself and his nation to a strategy focused exclusively on the achievement of a lightning-fast victory over France. This strategy was embedded in the deeply secret Schlieffen Plan, originally the work of Field Marshal Count Alfred von Schlieffen, Moltke's predecessor as chief of the general staff. He had developed it before his retirement in 1905 in response to the formation of the Franco-Russian Entente and the resulting likelihood that, if war came, Germany was going to find itself fighting on two fronts. He based it on simple assumptions: that even with Austria-Hungary on its side Germany could not expect to win a protracted war against both France and Russia; that Russia would be unable to mobilize rapidly; and that the immense size of the Russian empire meant that any invader looking for a quick and decisive victory was likely to be as disappointed as Napoleon had been after capturing Moscow in 1812. Out of these assumptions rose the conclusion that Germany had to crush France before Russia became capable of mounting an offensive. It could then shift its forces to the east and crush Russia in its turn.

Moltke had adopted the plan upon succeeding Schlieffen, and in the years that followed he changed it substantially. As a result of his changes, and ultimately as a result of the failure of the altered plan to deliver Paris into German hands within the forty days that Schlieffen had set as his deadline, Moltke's assigned place in history has generally been among the fools and weaklings. Schlieffen, by contrast, has been enshrined as a strategist of much brilliance, the creator of a key to glory that Moltke proved incapable of using. If such judgments are not flagrantly unfair, they are at a minimum arguable. It would be absurd to think that Moltke should have regarded the plan he received from Schlieffen as too sacred to be altered as circumstances changed. Schlieffen had handed his ideas over to Moltke at a point when Russia was weaker than it had been in generations. It had just lost its war with Japan and was faced with a popular uprising that had shaken the Romanov regime. Schlieffen had good reason to assume that Russia might be unable to put an effective army into the field at all, never mind speedily.

By 1914 the situation had changed. For five years the Russian government had been spending a third of its revenues on its army and navy. The so-called Grand Program, initiated in 1913, provided for the addition of 585,000 men to the tsar's armies annually, with each recruit to remain on active duty for at least three years. By 1914, 1.4 million Russian troops were in uniform, with several million more reservists available in case of mobilization—enough to form as many as 150 divisions. Russia had also made great strides in industrializing, French capital was financing a radical improvement of the Russian rail system in ways directly threatening to Germany, and France itself was growing both in strength and in confidence. Moltke would have had to be a fool not to fear that the Russians might be capable of fighting their way to Berlin before the Germans reached Paris.

Moltke's uncle and namesake, the architect of Germany's victories over Austria and France almost half a century earlier, had seen things very differently from Schlieffen. In his last years he came to believe that in a two-front war Germany should stand on the defensive in the west, attack in the east just enough to drive the Russians out of Poland, and then allow its enemies to wreck their armies by hurling them against walls of fire and steel. He believed that such a war would end not in victory but in a negotiated peace with exhausted but undefeated foes—and that that was all Germany should hope for. "We should exploit in the West the great advantages which the Rhine and our powerful fortifications offer to the defensive," he had said as early as 1879, "and should apply all the fighting forces which are not absolutely indispensable for an imposing offensive against the east." This remained German doctrine until Schlieffen, an austere and solitary man with few interests outside military history and strategy, became head of the army and gradually set Moltke's thinking aside.

The validity of the new strategy was, however, something less than self-evident, as Schlieffen himself acknowledged. His commentaries, which he continued to produce and share with the general staff throughout the years after his retirement, make clear that he was far from certain that it could succeed. It bet everything on an overwhelming right wing made up of seven out of every eight soldiers available for the fight with France. This massed force was to punch like a fist through three neutral countries—Holland, Belgium, and tiny Luxembourg—on its way into France. It would swing counterclockwise in a great wheeling motion, first to the west and then southward into France, overrunning whatever enemy forces confronted it, encircling and cutting off Paris, and finally swinging back to the east to take whatever remained of the French army in the rear and destroy it.

The plan was majestic in conception and breathtakingly bold but also fraught with problems not all of which were military. From a narrowly military standpoint the invasion of the three neutral countries was sensible: it would enable the Germans to move across northern Europe's flat and open coastal plain, avoiding the powerful fortresses that the French had constructed in the rough hill country just west of their long border with Germany. In terms of grand strategy and international politics, however, it was dangerous in the extreme. It gave no weight to the possibility that a violation of the treaties guaranteeing the neutrality of Belgium and Holland might provoke Britain to intervene. If Schlieffen considered the possibility of British intervention, he obviously regarded it as an acceptable risk. Britain's army was small (Bismarck had joked that if it ever invaded Germany, he would have it arrested). If Germany could wrap up the war in the west on Schlieffen's timetable, the British would have little opportunity to become a factor.

The French general staff was equally alert to the attractions of Belgium as a route into its enemy's heartland. But it did not have the autonomy that allowed Schlieffen and then the younger Moltke to consult with no one; hard experience with two Bonapartist empires had made republican France wary of placing too much authority over strategy in the hands of the military. As late as 1913 the French Supreme War Council was exploring a possible invasion of Germany through Belgium, but it was obliged to keep the Paris government informed as it did so. By this time the French and British were well along in planning joint operations, and the French government was determined to bring the

British in on its side in case of war. Therefore Paris checked with London about the War Council's idea and was sternly warned off. Any such move, France's friends on the British general staff said, would destroy even the possibility of support from Britain. And so the council stopped all work in that direction.

In Germany no such course correction was, in practical terms, even possible. No German chancellor since the young Wilhelm II's dismissal of Bismarck in 1890 had ever attempted to question, never mind challenge, the war planning of the general staff. As Bethmann Hollweg wrote in self-defense after the war, "for the civilian side to have tried to foil a thoroughly thought-out military plan described as absolutely essential would have entailed an intolerable responsibility. In the event of a subsequent failure, such a policy would have been considered its sole cause." Bethmann's administration was afraid to interfere with the army's plans even when those plans entailed terrible political risks. There is no better example of how the governmental machinery created by Bismarck proved inadequate to deal with the dangers and complexities of the twentieth century, when Bismarck's strong hand and towering intellect no longer controlled the levers of power.

In his splendid isolation Schlieffen assumed that Germany's enemies were intent not just on her defeat but on her destruction, and that as a result she was justified in doing things that under less harrowing circumstances would not have been thinkable. The seizure of the Dutch and Belgian roads and railways became not only desirable but imperative. Nothing less could save Germany, and anything else would increase Germany's peril. "If we were to attack along the entire Belfort-Montmédy front [along the line of French fortresses] with blind faith in the sanctity of neutrality," Schlieffen wrote, "we would soon be effectively enveloped on our right flank by a realistic and unscrupulous enemy advancing through southern Belgium and Luxembourg." The "unscrupulous enemy" was, of course, France. Schlieffen's guiding principle was that if Germany declined the benefits of violating the neutrality of its neighbors, France would happily seize them.

If Schlieffen had few concerns about the price of invading Belgium and Holland, he had many about whether his plan was militarily feasible. The outer edge of his right wing, in sweeping toward Paris, would have to advance more than two hundred miles through enemy territory in no more than forty days, defeating whatever enemies it encountered along the way. The infantry would have to do this mainly on foot, each soldier carrying seventy or more pounds of equipment every step of the way. If the horse-drawn artillery failed to keep up, if the huge amounts of food and fodder and ammunition and replacements needed by all these hundreds of thousands of men and their scores of thousands of horses were not always near at hand, if good order was not maintained, the entire venture would collapse of its own weight under the guns of the enemy.

Schlieffen calculated that the German army would need ninety divisions to execute his plan. (It had only about sixty in 1905.) He concluded that if the right wing did manage to reach Paris, the effort would likely drain it of the strength and mobility needed for a final swing to the east and the climactic battle that was the plan's whole point. "Before the Germans reach the Somme or the Oise," he wrote when his plan was still in gestation, "they will have realized, like other conquerors before them, that they are too weak for the whole enterprise." Even after his retirement, Schlieffen never stopped tormenting himself with such questions. Part of his legend is that in January 1913, as he lay dying, he became conscious just long enough to say, "It must come to a fight. Only keep the right wing strong!"

The younger Moltke, like Schlieffen a bookish and introspective man, unlike Schlieffen a man with many nonmilitary interests (he was an accomplished cellist, followed his wife into occult religious practices, and raised Prussian eyebrows by taking books by Goethe on maneuvers), inherited not only the plan but his predecessor's obsession with it. By 1911 he decided that it would be unnecessary and unwise to invade Holland; the Germans could neither take the time to defeat the Dutch army before advancing on France nor allow that army to stand undefeated and hostile on the northern edge of the route to Paris. Moltke said, too, that Germany would need neutral Holland as a "windpipe" through which to get access to supplies. In doing so he again exposed his doubts about the plausibility of the entire plan: a campaign that ended in victory after six weeks would have no need for a windpipe.

The most challenging aspect of Moltke's change was that it

would crowd the armies of the Schlieffen right wing—more than half a million men with all their artillery and support—into a twelve-mile-wide passage south of Holland and north of the Ardennes Forest. This would give them far fewer roads and rail lines to use—no small complication when hundreds of thousands of troops and their supply trains had to be moved great distances as rapidly as possible. It also meant that the Germans would be unable to go around, but would have to attack and destroy, the powerful network of fortresses that the Belgians had constructed at Liège just inside their border with Germany. For this reason German mobilization required an immediate invasion of Belgium: Moltke's entire strategy would collapse if the Belgians were given time to ready their Liège defenses. The Schlieffen Plan itself, Moltke had said, "will hardly be possible unless Liège is in our hands. The fortress must therefore be taken at once . . . the possession of Liège is the *sine qua non* of our advance."

Moltke came to believe that Germany could not afford to concentrate such an overwhelmingly large part of its forces in the attacking right wing. As the years passed, he altered the distribution of his troops so that the right wing would be only three times the size of the left, not seven as Schlieffen had prescribed. In its 1914 iteration the plan entailed positioning fifty-five divisions north of the fortified city of Metz, which lay directly to the east of Paris, with twenty-three divisions in a defensive posture farther south. Schlieffen, with fewer divisions to deploy, had assigned fifty-nine to the north and only nine to the left. This change, though controversial ever since, was certainly rational; after 1910 the French army, like the Russian, had become much more formidable than it had been in Schlieffen's day. It was bigger, better trained, better equipped, better led, and more professional overall. It was sure to be ready with an offensive of its own, and Moltke and his staff guessed rightly that its attack force would be concentrated somewhere south of Belgium and therefore opposite the relatively weak German left wing. If the French broke through into Germany, they might then be able to swing to the north, cut the German right wing off from its home base, and achieve their own quick victory.

But in broad terms, and without any apparent enthusiasm or even anything approaching real confidence, Moltke embraced

Schlieffen's approach. There is no evidence that he ever seriously considered *not* keeping it—that he ever thought through, for
example, the potentially immense advantages of reverting to his
uncle's idea and standing on the defensive in the west at least for
a while, forcing the French to attack him if they wanted a war.
In 1913 he abandoned an alternative plan that his staff had until
then been updating regularly and keeping ready for use—one for
directing Germany's offensive capabilities toward Russia. When
the crisis came, therefore, he *had* no alternative.

Perhaps he was unable to think through the ramifications of
the strategic situation in Europe (one such ramification being the
certain fact that Britain would never have gone to war if France
had attacked Germany rather than vice versa). More likely he was
in the grip of a fever that infected all the military planners of Europe in the years leading up to 1914, the French especially but the
Germans and others to a more limited extent. This was "the cult
of the offensive"—the belief that the only way to succeed in war
was to attack your enemy as quickly as possible and then stay on
the attack regardless of the consequences. This belief was rooted
in what everyone took to be the lessons of the Franco-Prussian
War, in which many of the most senior generals of 1914 had taken
part at the beginning of their careers. In that war the forces of
Napoleon III had allowed the Prussians to seize and keep the
initiative, and the results had been disastrous. Probably this idea
played some part in Molke's strategic decisions. It is also possibly
true, for all that even Moltke's severest critics really know, that
no alternative to his final version of the Schlieffen Plan could have
produced better results.

In the thirty days following the start of the war, mobilization
increased the German army from its peacetime strength of seven
hundred and sixty-one thousand men to slightly more than two
million. This ocean of humanity was organized into eighty-seven
infantry divisions averaging some eighteen thousand men each,
plus another eleven cavalry divisions. These divisions formed
eight field armies, each commanded by a full general. Seven took
up positions along Germany's western border, and the last stood
alone in faraway East Prussia with responsibility for holding off
whatever Russia threw at it. To the south of East Prussia, separated from it by Russian Poland, was Austria-Hungary, with an

initial mobilized force of 1.3 million men—forty-nine infantry and eleven cavalry divisions under Conrad von Hötzendorf. Farther south still was Serbia, with a tough, experienced, and almost fanatically dedicated army of some two hundred and fifty thousand troops making up twelve and a half divisions. Also opposing Germany and Austria was a Russian army whose three and a half million troops were organized into 114 infantry and thirty-six cavalry divisions and had the potential, given Russia's immense population, to grow much larger. This was "the Russian steamroller," the sheer size of which made it a chilling threat for the German and Austrian planners. To the west, thirty days after mobilization, France had 1.8 million men under arms (all the numbers given here would soon be dwarfed by floods of new volunteers and conscripts) and organized into ninety divisions—eighty infantry and ten cavalry.

Even without possible British and Belgian involvement, therefore, the Germans and Austrians began at an overwhelming manpower disadvantage in the east. In the west the German armies were at best equal in size to those of the French. In their advance on Paris they would be facing the only military organization in the world that was comparable to theirs not only in manpower but in fighting capability as well—a huge modern army whose generals had a secret plan of their own for swift and conclusive victory.

PARIS IN 1914

THE START OF THE WAR CAME AS A FAR GREATER shock to Paris than to Berlin, Budapest, St. Petersburg, or Vienna. Until almost the end of the July crisis, the French paid it little attention. They, and the newspapers they read, were focused instead on a lady named Henriette Caillaux.

Not that the lady and the war are entirely unrelated. Among the what-ifs of 1914 is the intriguing possibility—remote to be sure, but real nonetheless—that the war might have been averted if not for six pistol shots fired by Madame Caillaux 101 days before the assassination of Franz Ferdinand.

Madame Caillaux was the wife—the second wife, importantly, just as he was her second husband—of Joseph Caillaux, a former French premier who in early 1914 was making a serious bid to become once again the head of the government. In arm's-length partnership with a brilliant and charismatic Socialist leader named Jean Jaurès, Caillaux was campaigning to displace the men who, a year earlier, had enacted a controversial measure aimed at improving France's readiness for war. This measure was a requirement, demanded by President Poincaré and the leadership of the army, that every military conscript (and France was drafting 80 percent of its eligible men by that time, as opposed to 56 percent in Germany) must spend three years on active service, rather than two as in the recent past. The change had been one expression of a surge of patriotic fervor that arose in the wake of a French-German showdown over control of Morocco in 1911 and swept Poincaré into the presidency two years later. (When the Germans ended that showdown by backing down, in large part because Britain was siding with France, it seemed proof that France's long period of weakness on the international stage had ended at last.) Supporters of the extension were convinced that unless France maintained its credibility as a military power, it would lose the confidence of its Russian ally and be left to face Germany alone. Jaurès was insistent that the European arms race was madness, that a general war would be ruinous for everyone involved no matter who won, that it was ridiculous for the only republic in Europe to tie itself to a regime as antediluvian as tsarist Russia, and that it was not impossible for France and Germany to come to an understanding. Though Caillaux had not pledged himself to repeal the extension, the conservatives convinced themselves that he would do so if given the opportunity. They did everything in their power to turn him into what the writer-politician Maurice Barrès said he already was: "the most hated man in France."

A national election was scheduled for early summer. It would decide the membership of the Chamber of Deputies, which in turn would choose the next premier. (The premiership, a position analogous to that of British prime minister, changed hands more or less annually as shifting coalitions of France's many factions caused governments to rise and fall. It is not to be confused with the presidency, an elective office with a fixed six-year term and roughly comparable to Britain's monarch.) The election became a referendum on the three-year-service question and, by implication, on France's place in the European balance of power.

Joseph Caillaux, the leading opponent of the Poincaré camp, was an interesting figure if not an altogether appealing human being. Trained in accounting and as an auditor, meticulous as only a dedicated accountant can be, he had followed his father into politics and had risen to cabinet rank on the basis of hard work and his knowledge (unusual in the Chamber of Deputies) of the intricacies of budgeting, taxation, and finance. At an early age he became minister of finance, an office to which his unrivaled competency would cause him to be returned repeatedly over the years. Haughty to the point of insufferable arrogance, rich, impeccably honest and therefore able to survive the numberless accusations hurled at him over the years, he remained throughout his career the very picture of stuffy, almost comic *haut bourgeois* respectability.

Paradoxically, by 1914 Caillaux had moved about as far to the left as it was possible for a French politician to move in those days and still be a contender for the highest offices of government. This had happened gradually, as a result of his mastery of finance. He had conducted a study of the tax system and, offended by its inadequacy to the needs of a modern state, had proposed an income tax. The idea horrified the conservatives, who predictably had no interest in surrendering their exemption from being taxed. But it won Caillaux so many new friends in the so-called Radical faction (which in fact was not radical at all but barely left of center) that he became for a time premier.

Caillaux's tenure as premier included the 1911 Moroccan crisis, and he had been firm and effective in negotiating a settlement with the Germans. Though his enemies accused him, inevitably, of bending under German pressure, he had won for France the colony of Morocco at the lowest price Berlin was prepared to accept short of war. It was also during Caillaux's premiership that General Joseph Joffre was made head of the French general staff, which meant that, in the years just before the war, the army had a commander who insisted on better training, better equipment, and promotion on the basis of ability and performance. Even in his skepticism about the military service extension, Caillaux never challenged the idea that France should be militarily strong. His questions were about how strength could best be achieved. Keeping many thousands of men on active duty for an additional year required heavy spending for barracks and other facilities, but it did little to increase the size of the army upon mobilization. Caillaux wanted to invest in artillery (in which France was seriously deficient) and innovations such as aircraft.

One other thing was paradoxical about Joseph Caillaux. Behind his invincible facade of fashionable propriety, behind his cold and eccentric public persona, he was an adventurous womanizer. He did not marry until he was into middle age. When he did, his choice was a divorcée older than himself who had been his mistress for some years. Not long afterward he entered into an affair with a married woman, Madame Henriette Claretie. Their liaison was not frivolous. With some difficulty the two divorced their spouses and were married.

All these currents—hatred for Caillaux's taxation proposals, conservative belief that the future of the nation hinged on the service extension, questions about the alliance with Russia, and the support given to Caillaux by Jaurès and the Socialists—came together in the 1914 election. In the words of Barrès, Caillaux was a menace because he was the one man who could "bring Jaurès's pacifist dream down from the clouds, to make the theories of working-class internationalism and the fraternity of all people both practical and realizable."

The campaign was more than spirited. As a Caillaux victory loomed, his enemies cast aside what little restraint was customary in the politics of France. The conservative press attacked him relentlessly. Characteristically, Caillaux disdained to reply; he would coolly assert his innocence of whatever the latest charge happened to be but go no further. He was coasting toward a victory that would lead to a reappraisal of national policy and possibly to the resignation of Poincaré (who threatened just such a step). But then his private life was brought into the political arena, and everything changed.

Caillaux's first wife, a woman spurned and vengeful, made available to Gaston Calmette, the editor of the conservative publication *Le Figaro,* letters that Caillaux had sent to her in 1901 when she was still his mistress and married to another man. Calmette, who had been attacking Caillaux viciously, now promised his readers a "comic interlude" that he opened by printing one of the letters. Its content was not scandalous in any sexual sense; Caillaux had boasted of appearing to fight for his income tax proposal while actually assuring that it could not pass. This raised questions about possible duplicity on his part (unless of course he was simply trying to impress his paramour), but it was hardly a smoking gun. Much was made of the fact that Caillaux signed himself *Ton Jo,* "Your Joe." The *ton* was inappropriately intimate when used by a gentleman in addressing a married lady, but even by the standards of its day it was something less than outrageous.

The second Madame Caillaux, however, was not amused. Despite her affair and divorce and remarriage, Henriette cared greatly about her reputation and place in society. She hated the world of politics and the abuse to which it exposed her husband. Lately, when in public, she had found herself hissed and laughed at when people learned that she was the spouse of that traitor to his class, the man who wanted to tax incomes. She complained of being unable to eat or sleep, and when she tried to talk with her husband about what was happening, he (as he ruefully acknowledged later) did not take her seriously.

What terrified Henriette about the publication of the letter, apparently, was the possibility that it would be followed by love letters that she and Caillaux had exchanged while still married to other people. There was gossip to the effect that these letters too had been given to *Le Figaro.*

On the afternoon of March 16 she dressed elegantly, went by chauffeured auto to the shop of a Paris gun dealer, and there purchased a small Browning automatic pistol. The dealer took her to his basement for instruction in the pistol's use. From there she went to the offices of *Le Figaro,* where, her hands and her weapon concealed in a fur muff, she created consternation by identifying herself and asking to see Calmette. The editor was out, as it happened, and she had to wait hours for his return. When at last he arrived through a rear entrance, he was told of his visitor and urged not to see her. He gallantly replied that he would not deny a lady. Upon being admitted to his office, Henriette asked Calmette if he knew why she wanted to see him. When he replied that he did not and offered her a chair, she took out her pistol and squeezed the trigger until its six bullets had been discharged. Calmette was hit four times and killed. Later Henriette testified that, intending only to frighten him, she had closed her eyes before firing and pointed the pistol at the floor. Calmette, unfortunately for both of them, had fallen to the floor as soon as he saw the gun and so put himself in the line of fire. When members of the *Figaro* staff came running into the office, Henriette surrendered her weapon but imperiously maintained her dignity. "Do not touch me," she declared. "I am a lady." When the police were preparing to take her to jail, she refused to enter their wagon. She had a vehicle suitable to her station, she said, and would travel in it. The police agreed.

It was the most sensational story in years, one that combined murder and sex with wild speculation about what had motivated Henriette and what further scandals might be revealed. It monopolized the attention of the Paris newspapers all that spring and summer. Its first effect was to sideline Caillaux politically: he immediately resigned from the cabinet and announced (he would later change his mind) that his political career was over.

In spite of the scandal, the election turned out to be a disaster for Poincaré and the conservatives and a triumph for Caillaux's Radicals and their Socialist allies. Under ordinary circumstances, Caillaux would have become premier. But now someone else had to be found for the job, and with Caillaux out of the running, no one was holding Poincaré to his threat to resign. For two weeks, as the formidable Poincaré used his constitutional authority to block a succession of candidates who were opposed to the service extension,

France remained without a government. Finally, grudgingly, Poincaré agreed to the appointment of René Viviani, a onetime socialist and a rising but inexperienced political star who in 1913 had voted against the extension but now promised to withdraw his opposition. In the weeks ahead Viviani would show himself to be emotionally fragile (his career would end in insanity) and willing to follow Poincaré's guidance in dealing with the July crisis.

Henriette's trial, from its start early in July, was an early specimen of full-bore media circus, obsessing press and public alike, making the news about yet another crisis in the distant Balkans seem dreary and pointless by comparison, and constantly giving rise to new sensations. (One of the trial judges challenged another to a duel.) Then came the state visit that Poincaré paid to St. Petersburg, taking Viviani with him and using the long days at sea to instruct the new premier in the importance of military readiness and the alliance with Russia.

Even if there had been no trial and no voyage to Russia, French passivity throughout the crisis undoubtedly would have been to Poincaré's liking. The president was the closest thing to a true master of French politics to have emerged in decades. He had begun his career as the youngest lawyer in the country, became the youngest member of the Chamber of Deputies at twenty-six, was elected premier in his forties, and in 1913, at age fifty-two, became both the youngest president in the nation's history and the first to be elected while serving as premier. In 1914 he was mindful of what General Joffre had told him: that France was now strong enough to win a war with Germany if Serbia tied up a substantial part of the Austro-Hungarian army, Russia took the field against the Germans, and Britain too came in on France's side. The British factor made it essential that France stand aside during the diplomatic crisis. Paris could have changed the outcome of the crisis only by discouraging the Russians from being so quick to mobilize. Caillaux, as premier, almost certainly would have done this. The tsar's reluctance to mobilize makes it at least possible that Caillaux could have succeeded.

The magnitude of the international crisis finally came crashing in on Paris on Wednesday, July 29. A chivalrous jury found Madame Caillaux not guilty, and France's newspapers awoke from their trance to discover that Europe was on the brink of war. Poincaré and Viviani returned to Paris, finding the capital burning with war fever. July

29 was also the day on which Tsar Nicholas first ordered and then temporarily canceled general mobilization. Thanks to the scheming Ambassador Paléologue, Paris had only limited knowledge of what was happening in St. Petersburg, and the Russians had no reason to think that the French government was not enthusiastic about their mobilization. By Friday full mobilization was under way in Russia, but no word of it appeared in the Paris newspapers. The papers were, however, carrying excited and unfounded reports that Germany was mobilizing secretly. Joffre was demanding French mobilization.

With Caillaux out of the picture and the final slide into war under way, there was in all of France only one man of importance who not only thought that war might be prevented but was committed to preventing it if he could. This was Jean Jaurès, whose gifts were so prodigious that it seemed briefly possible that even now, far into the eleventh hour, he might make a difference.

As a leader, a thinker, and simply as a human being, Jaurès stood out like a giant in the summer of 1914. Like Caillaux he was widely hated, but only for the most honorable of reasons: he had dedicated his life to the achievement of democracy and genuine peace not only in France but across the continent. But he was respected too—respected and loved to an extent remarkable for a man whose socialist convictions had put him permanently outside the boundaries of political respectability. Everyone who knew him and has left a record of the experience tells of a sunny, selfless, brilliant personality, bearded and bearlike and utterly careless of his appearance, indifferent to personal success or failure but passionately dedicated to his vision of a better, saner world.

Born in provincial obscurity, he had been sent to Paris on scholarship and excelled at the most elite schools to be found there. He had gone first into an academic career and then into politics, earning a doctorate along the way. Drawn by his sense of the injustices of industrial society into the Socialist Party, he soon became its dominant figure and a practical, nondogmatic adapter of Marxist thought. He was opposed to imperialism, colonialism, and militarism, all of which he saw as a waste of resources that could be used for better purposes. But he was not opposed to nationalism, envisioning a Europe of autonomous democracies working together for a prosperity in which the poor and the powerless could share. He believed that political liberty was meaningless without economic liberty, that the power

of the industrialists, banks, big landowners, and church must be cur-
tailed, and that small family businesses and farms must be preserved.
An anticlerical, he nevertheless opposed the efforts of his associates to
bar Catholics from teaching in the universities. Above all he was opposed to the secret alliances of the great powers, France included. He
foresaw how disastrous a general war would be with a clarity that can
still astonish anyone who reads the things he wrote and said. He was
widely regarded as the greatest orator of his time, and by consistently
demonstrating his integrity and indifference to personal advantage,
he had unified France's leftist factions and made the Socialist Party a
force in national politics. By late July France appeared to be divided
into two camps: one that regarded Jaurès as a public danger, another
that was ready to follow him. In the midst of mounting hysteria he
was the one prominent figure calling for restraint, deliberation, and a
search for a way out of war—for *sangfroid*. "The danger is great but
not insuperable if we keep our clearness of mind and strength of will,"
he wrote in his last newspaper column, which appeared on Friday,
July 31, "if we show the heroism of patience as well as the heroism
of action."

France's conservative voices, meanwhile, were anything but calm.
"We have no wish to incite anyone to political assassination," the
newspaper *Action Française* had declared on July 23 in what was
becoming the characteristic tone of Jaurès's enemies, "but M. Jean
Jaurès may well shake in his shoes! His words may perhaps give some
fanatic the desire to settle by the experimental method the question
of whether anything would be changed in the invincible order
of things if M. Jean Jaurès were to suffer the fate of M. Calmette." Another paper told its readers that "if on the eve of war a General were
to detail half a dozen men and a Corporal to put Citizen Jaurès against
a wall and to pump the lead he needs into his brain at point-blank
range—do you think that General would be doing anything but his
elementary duty?"

On the evening of July 31, just back from a hurried trip to Brussels
where he had addressed an emergency meeting of Socialists from
several countries, including Germany, Jaurès and a small group of
his associates went to the foreign ministry, where they met with vice
minister Abel Ferry and demanded every possible effort to keep Russia from mobilizing. By this time the government not only knew of
the Russian mobilization but had received, via the German ambas-

sador, Berlin's warning that it too would mobilize if the Russians did not reverse course. Viviani, after consultation with Poincaré, had given the Germans his promise of an answer by one P.M. tomorrow, Saturday. Now Ferry simply told Jaurès that it was too late, that "everything is finished, there is nothing left to do."

"To the very end," Jaurès answered angrily, "we will continue to struggle against war."

"No," Ferry replied. "You won't be able to continue. You will be assassinated on the nearest street corner."

Two hours later a twenty-nine-year-old man named Raoul Villain, well educated but aimless, confused, and unemployed, was walking along the Rue Montmartre when he saw several men enter the Café du Croissant. Among them was Jaurès, and Villain recognized him. As he watched, Jaurès took a seat with his back to an open window. For half an hour, while Jaurès ate his dinner and conferred with the editors of his newspaper, L'Humanité, about what should be said in the Saturday edition, Villain paced outside. He was armed; inflamed by the hysteria all around him, he had been planning to travel to Germany and shoot the kaiser. Here, suddenly, was an opportunity to demonstrate his patriotism and strike a blow for France right at home.

Inside the restaurant a man rose from his place at another table and approached the Jaurès group. He was a friend of one of Jaurès's companions, and he wanted to show off a photo of his baby daughter.

"May I see?" Jaurès asked. He examined the picture, smiled, asked the child's age, and offered congratulations. At that instant Villain, standing just outside the window, fired two shots into the back of his head. Jaurès was dead before the police arrived, and the next day France and Germany mobilized. The Socialists in both countries, now without anyone capable of bringing them together, supported the move to war.

Chapter 8

First Blood

"All the courage in the world cannot prevail against gunfire."
—Captain Charles De Gaulle

The war began in earnest on August 2, when an advance force of German cavalry moved into Luxembourg to seize its network of railways. That same day Germany delivered an ultimatum to Belgium, demanding unobstructed passage for its armies. Young King Albert refused. His little army, which could put only seven divisions totaling one hundred and seventeen thousand troops into the field, began blowing up bridges and rail lines leading into Belgium from Germany. Suddenly the little city of Liège, always locally important as a center of road, rail, and water transportation, became the most important place on the continent. Its defenses, on high bluffs looming over the River Meuse, dominated the narrow passage through which the Schlieffen right wing had to pass on its way westward. Unless these defenses were overcome, and quickly, the German advance would be blocked almost at its starting point and the entire offensive reduced to a shambles.

Liège was no ordinary city but a ring of twelve massive forts that together made it one of the most formidable military strongpoints in the world. Each of these forts contained eight or nine big guns under armored turrets, and each was built of reinforced concrete and designed to withstand direct hits from the heaviest artillery then in existence. General Gérard Leman, the elderly Belgian commander at Liège, had some eight thousand troops inside the forts plus, as a mobile force, a division of twenty-four thousand infantry, five hundred cavalry, and seventy-two field guns. The Germans, as part of their mobilization plan, had formed, trained, and stationed near the border a special strike force of thirty thousand men plus mobile field artillery whose sole mission was to attack and neutralize the forts. When the lead elements of this force moved on Liège from the south on August 4, they were greatly outnumbered by the defenders but immediately launched a night assault. They met ferocious fire and were thrown back. They quickly attacked again and were again repulsed. This put the Germans in a desperate situation.

Leman, ordered by King Albert to hold his position at all costs (a term meaning death before surrender or retreat), learned of the appearance of German cavalry to his north and concluded that he would soon be surrounded. To keep his mobile force from capture, he sent it off to join the main Belgian army. This removed almost a quarter of Belgium's total fighting forces from danger of encirclement and capture, but at a price: it ended any possibility that Leman would have enough troops to keep the Germans at a distance from which their guns would be unable to do their worst.

There now arrived on the scene, and on the world stage, an obscure German officer who quickly established himself as the hero of the siege and with startling speed would become one of the most important men in the German army. This was Erich Ludendorff. (Note the absence of a *von* in the name—he was not a member of Prussia's Junker aristocracy.) Recently promoted to major general, a tall, portly, double-chinned forty-nine-year-old, Ludendorff was on temporary assignment as liaison between the Liège assault force and the German Second Army, which was still assembling on the German side of the border. There had been good reason for giving Ludendorff this assignment: a few years earlier, as a key member of Moltke's staff, he had developed the plans for the reduction of the Liège fortifications. (With typical thoroughness, he had once spent a vacation in Belgium in order to examine the defenses at first hand.) In the German army, unlike the French, it was customary to send staff officers into the field, into combat, where they could observe their plans in action, assist in making adjustments when reality began to intrude, and learn from the experience. But Ludendorff was constitutionally incapable of remaining a mere observer or adviser. It was he who had sent the cavalry that, by showing itself north of Liège, had caused Leman to send most of his troops away. Then, coming upon a brigade whose commander had been killed in one of the early attacks, he put himself in charge. Bringing howitzers forward and directing their fire on the Belgian defenses, he led an assault that gave him possession of an expanse of high ground from which the city and its central citadel were clearly visible.

When he could see no sign of activity around the citadel (Leman had moved to one of the outlying forts), Ludendorff drove to it. He shouted a demand for surrender while pounding on the gate with the pommel of his sword. Astoundingly, he was obeyed in spite of being greatly outnumbered. Thus the centerpiece of the Liège defenses fell into German hands almost without effort. Though the circle of forts was still intact, all were now isolated and without any support except what they could give one another. Ludendorff then hurried back into Germany to see to it that more and bigger guns were brought forward without delay.

Moltke's seven western armies, meanwhile, were forming up on a north-south line just inside the German border south of Holland. Picture a clock with Paris at its center. The line of armies was in the upper-right portion of the clock's face, extending, roughly, from one to three o'clock. The biggest and northernmost of these armies, positioned to the north and east of Liège, was commanded by General Alexander von Kluck, tough, aggressive, irascible, and sixty-eight years old, a hardened infantryman who had begun life as a commoner and had been elevated to the nobility in reward for decades of distinguished service. Remarkably for a high-ranking German officer, Kluck had never had a tour of duty on the high command's headquarters staff. His First Army, almost a third of a million men strong, was assigned to be the outer edge of the right wing. It would have the longest distance to travel as it moved westward across Belgium and then looped toward the southwest. If things went perfectly it would, on its way to Paris, move around and past the westernmost end of the French defensive line. It would then continue southward, circle all the way around Paris, and move back to the east. Finally it would hit the French line from the rear, pushing it into other German armies positioned at two and three o'clock and crushing it in a great vise.

The Germans did students of the war a lasting favor by arranging their armies in numerical order. Next to Kluck, immediately to his south during the mobilization (later to his east, as the Schlieffen wheel made its great turn), was the Second Army under General Karl von Bülow, a member of the high Prussian aristocracy who also was in his late sixties. Then came the Third Army, the Fourth, and so on down to the Seventh, which was almost as far south as Paris and had the Swiss border on its left. The first three of these armies made up the right wing, and though that wing no longer included as big a part of the German army as Schlieffen had intended, it was still an awesome force of seven hundred and fifty thousand troops. This was war on a truly new scale; the army with which Wellington defeated Napoleon at Waterloo had totaled sixty thousand men.

The First, Second, and Third Armies would be side by side as they drove forward. Their left would be protected by the rest of the German line. Though their right would be exposed, this would be no problem if Kluck could get around the equally exposed French left. His primary assignment, until he had circled Paris, was not to engage the enemy but to *keep moving*. If circumstances developed in such a way as to permit him to strike at the flank of the French left as he advanced, perhaps crippling it, so much the better. That would be secondary, however. The goal was Paris.

The two armies on the German left, the Sixth and the Seventh, were not intended to be an attack force. Their role was to absorb an expected advance by the French into Alsace and Lorraine, stopping the invaders from breaking through while keeping them too fully engaged to spare troops for the defense of Paris. Between the three armies of the right wing and the two on the left were the Fourth and Fifth Armies, the latter commanded by Imperial Crown Prince Wilhelm, the kaiser's eldest son. They were to provide a connecting link between the defensive force in the south and the right wing, keeping the line continuous and free of gaps. They would be the hub of the wheel on which the right wing was

King Albert of Belgium

moving, and they would not have to move either far or fast. They would be an anchor, a pivot point, for the entire campaign. Ultimately they were to become the killing machine into which Kluck was to drive the French after his swing around Paris.

French General Joffre, for his part, had his million-plus frontline troops organized into five armies. They too were forming up in a line and were in numerical order, with the First on the right just above Switzerland. The French Second Army was immediately to its north, the Third above it, and so on northward and westward in a great arc that ended approximately midway between Paris and the starting point of Kluck's army. Joffre's First, Second, and Third Armies, as they took up their positions, faced eastward toward Alsace and Lorraine with their backs to the chain of superfortresses (Verdun, Toul, Épinal, and Belfort) that France had constructed between Switzerland and Belgium. The Fourth and Fifth, being to the north and west of these forts, had no such strongpoints to fall back on. The position of the Fifth, commanded by Joffre's friend and protégé Charles Lanrezac, was problematic. It was the end of the French line in exactly the same way that Kluck's army was the end of the German, with no significant French forces to its north or west. Its left flank ended, as tacticians say, "up in the air"—out on a limb. This position carried within it the danger that the Germans might get around Lanrezac's left, exposing him to attack in the flank or from the rear. In the opening days of the war, however, this danger seemed so hypothetical to Joffre as to be unworthy of concern.

Neither Lanrezac nor Joffre had any real way of knowing what the Germans were going to do. Aerial reconnaissance, like military aviation generally, was barely in its infancy in the summer of 1914. Until mobilization was completed, it would not be possible to make much use of the cavalry that was supposed to function as the eyes of the army. The commanders on both sides could do little more than make educated guesses, using whatever information came in from spies or could be gleaned from the questioning of captured soldiers. The sheer size of their armies and of the theater of operations, and the unavoidable remoteness from the front lines of headquarters responsible for the movements of hundreds of thousands of men, compounded the intelligence problem.

GERMAN ADVANCE *of* 1914

ENGLAND

North Sea

Amsterdam ✪

NETHERLANDS

GERMANY

Calais •   FLANDERS   Ypres •

BELGIUM

• Antwerp

Brussels ✪

Cologne •

GERMAN 1st

• Aachen

Lille •

Mons •

Charleroi •

Meuse

Liège •

GERMAN 2nd

Rhine

Koblenz •

Namur •

Sambre

Maubeuge •

Le Cateau •

GERMAN 3rd

GERMAN 4th

Somme

Guise •

Ardennes
Forest

LUXEMBOURG

Mosel

Amiens •

PICARDY

Noyon   Oise

Aisne

Meuse

• Luxembourg

FRANCE

Soissons •

Ourcq

Reims •

Argonne Forest

GERMAN 5th

Seine

FRENCH 6th

Château Thierry •

Marne

Épernay •

Verdun •

• Metz

Paris ✪

Petit Morin

Grand Morin

Marsh of
St. Gond

St. Mihiel •

FRENCH 3rd

Nancy •

GERMAN 6th

GERMAN 7th

Strasbourg •

BRITISH

FRENCH 4th

FRENCH 9th

Toul •

FRENCH 2nd

FRENCH 5th

Aube

Moselle

Épinal •

Rhine

FRENCH 1st

Belfort •

Mülhausen •

—— Front Line September 5, 1914

– – – Front Line September 14, 1914

0   Miles   25   50   75

0   Kilometers   50   75

© 2005 Jeffrey L. Ward

SWITZERLAND

The Armies and Their Commanders:

British Expeditionary Force—John French

France at start of war:

First Army—Auguste Dubail
Second Army—Noël de Castelnau
Third Army—Pierre-Xavier Ruffey
Fourth Army—Fernand de Langle de Cary
Fifth Army—Charles Lanrezac

Organized during the Battle of the Marne:

Sixth Army—Michel Maunoury
Ninth Army—Ferdinand Foch

Germany:

First Army—Alexander von Kluck
Second Army—Karl von Bülow
Third Army—Max Klemens von Hausen
Fourth Army—Albrecht, Duke of Württemberg
Fifth Army—Crown Prince Wilhelm of Germany
Sixth Army—Crown Prince Rupprecht of Bavaria
Seventh Army—Josias von Heeringen

The individual armies, too, would be half-blind as they went into action. And they would be far more vulnerable than their size would suggest. A mass of infantry on the move is like nothing else in the world, but it may usefully be thought of as an immensely long and cumbersome caterpillar with the head of a nearsighted tiger. (The monstrousness of the image is not inappropriate.) It is structured to make its head as lethal as possible, ready at all times to come to grips with whatever enemy comes into its path. A big part of an army commander's job is to make certain that it is in fact the head that meets the enemy, so that the tiger's teeth—men armed with guns and blades and whatever other implements of destruction are available to them—can either attack the enemy or fend off the enemy's attack as circumstances require.

An advancing army's worst vulnerability lies in the long caterpillar body behind the head. (*Long* is an inadequate word in the context of 1914: a single corps of two divisions included thirty thousand or more men at full strength and stretched over fifteen miles of road when on the march.) Great battles can be won when a tiger's head eludes or even accidentally misses the head of its enemy and makes contact with its body instead. When this happens the enemy is "taken in the flank," and if an attacking head has sufficient weight it can quickly tear the enemy's body apart, finally reducing even the head to an isolated, enfeebled remnant. Much the same can happen when an army on the move is taken in the rear, or surrounded and cut off from its lines of supply. Hence the importance that Moltke and Joffre attached to arranging their armies in an unbroken line, so that each could protect the flanks of its neighbors. Hence too the dangers inherent in the fact that both generals would begin the war with one end of their lines unprotected.

Joffre, like Moltke, was intent upon taking the offensive. His master plan, approved in 1913, reflected the French government's refusal to permit any move into neutral territory. It assumed that the Germans too would stay out of Belgium and Luxembourg, and so it assumed further that the first great clash of the war would take place on the French-German border, somewhere between Verdun to the north and the fortress of Belfort to the south. Joffre's five armies were more than sufficient to maintain a solid line while attacking from one end of that border to the other, and so he saw no reason to be concerned about Lanrezac's left, which would be anchored on Luxembourg.

Joffre's advantage was that he was not irrevocably committed to attacking at any specific place or time or even to attacking at all. Unlike Moltke he had options—he could change his plans and the disposition of his armies according to how the situation developed. This ability quickly proved important: when the Germans moved into Luxembourg and then on to Liège, Joffre was able to order the Fourth and Fifth Armies to shift around and face northward. He now expected the Germans to come from the northeast, through Belgium's Ardennes Forest toward the French city of Sedan. His left wing would move north to meet them.

Lanrezac was not so sure. As word reached him of the intensifying assault on Liège, he could think of no reason for it unless the Germans needed to clear a path to the west. As early as July 31—before war was declared—he had sent a message to Joffre expressing concern about what would happen if the Germans advanced westward while his army stayed south of the Belgian border or moved east to join in the French offensive. "In such a case," he warned, "the Fifth Army . . . could do nothing to prevent a possible encircling movement against our left wing." Joffre did not respond; he was certain that no such thing would happen. A week later, with the Germans continuing to concentrate troops opposite Liège, Lanrezac sent another appeal. "This time there can be no doubt," he said. "They are planning a wide encircling movement through Belgium. I ask permission to change the direction of the Fifth Army toward the north." He had it exactly right, but Joffre remained unpersuaded, confident that whatever was happening around Liège must be a German feint intended to lure his forces out of position. His attention was focused on launching an attack by his right wing into Alsace and Lorraine—the capture of France's lost provinces would be a tremendous symbolic triumph. As a precaution, though, he did send cavalry on a scouting expedition into Belgium. When this foray found no evidence of German activity—inevitably, the Germans not yet having moved beyond Liège—Joffre felt free to proceed with his own plans. His First Army began crossing into Alsace as early as August 7, the day Ludendorff captured the Liège citadel, and it made good progress. Another week passed, and the direction of the German right wing became undeniable, before Joffre at last responded to Lanrezac's warnings, telling him almost laconically that "I see no objection (to the contrary) to your considering the movement that you propose." Even then he added, with thinly veiled annoyance, that "the threat is as yet only a long-term possibility and we are not absolutely certain that it actually exists." Lanrezac started northward, not knowing that it was already too late for him to escape being outflanked in exactly the way he had feared from the start.

The Germans, by this time, had hauled into Belgium the weapons that would decide the fate of Liège, two new kinds of monster artillery: 305mm Skoda siege mortars borrowed from Austria, plus an almost unimaginably huge 420mm howitzer secretly developed and produced by Germany's Krupp steelworks. Neither gun had ever been used in combat. The bigger of the two weighed seventy-five tons and had to be transported by rail in five sections and set in concrete before going into action. It could fire up to ten 2,200-pound projectiles per hour, each shell carrying a hardened head and a delayed-action fuse so that it penetrated its target before exploding. It had a range of nine miles, its projectiles following such a high trajectory that they came down almost vertically. It had to be fired electrically so that the two-hundred-man crew operating it, their heads covered with protective padding, could move three hundred yards away and lie down on the ground before detonation. Once "registered"—its elevation and direction set so that every round landed on target—it was a hellishly destructive weapon, capable of breaking apart even the strongest of the Liège forts and vaporizing the men inside. It was a fitting opening act for a hellishly destructive war.

The big guns arrived at Liège on August 10, but two days more were needed to get them in place. By this time, off to the south, Joffre's Alsace offensive had captured several towns, but on August 11 the Germans counterattacked and brought the advance to a stop. The day after that Austria's Field Marshal Conrad, launching the punitive campaign that he had so long craved, sent three armies totaling four hundred and sixty thousand men into Serbia, where they soon were moving rapidly across easy terrain toward the mountains to the east.

On August 13, after taking several shattering hits, Fort Chaud-fontaine at the southeastern corner of the Liège circle surren-dered, with only seventy-six of the 408 members of its garrison still alive. Later on the same day two more of the forts, similarly devastated, also surrendered. On August 15 Fort Lonçin ceased to exist when the twenty-third 420mm shell fired at it penetrated its ammunition stores and set them off. Taking possession, the Germans found Belgian General Leman lying in the wreckage.

The Austrian 305mm Skoda siege mortar
One of the weapons that broke the defenses of Liège.

As he was being carried away, he opened his eyes. "I ask you to bear witness," he said to the German commander, "that you found me unconscious." Though a few of the forts had not yet surrendered or been destroyed, their ability to interfere with the German advance was at an end. Moltke's armies were ready, the road to the west was open, and the right wing went into motion almost exactly on Schlieffen's schedule. German engineers hurried to repair rail lines destroyed by the Belgians, and trains rolled

forward one after another, carrying the mountains of supplies needed to support the offensive. More than five hundred trains were crossing the Rhine every twenty-four hours; in the first sixteen days after troop movements began, 2,150 trains crossed a single bridge at Cologne—one every ten minutes. And with good reason. Kluck's First Army alone required five hundred and fifty tons of food every day. Its eighty-four thousand horses consumed eight hundred and forty tons of fodder daily.

Things now started happening at an accelerating pace and on an expanding scale, and it became uncommon for anything to happen as anyone had expected or intended. By August 16, in a heroically speedy if tragically premature response to the French government's calls for the opening of a second front, Russia inserted its First Army into East Prussia. This move was far in advance of what the Germans had thought possible; obviously other Russian armies would be arriving soon, and so Moltke was faced with a possible disaster in the east long before the fight in the west could be decided. That same day a Serbian counterattack stopped the Austrians and threw them back in disorder. Suddenly major developments were occurring daily.

August 17: A collision of German and Russian troops at Stallupönen in East Prussia ends inconclusively; the Germans are forced into a retreat that disrupts their plans, but they take three thousand prisoners with them.

August 18: Joffre broadens his eastward offensive by sending the French Second Army into Lorraine. The invasion makes good progress, but only because Moltke has ordered the German Sixth Army to fall back. He too has a plan for Lorraine: to allow the French to advance until they are between his Fifth Army to the north and Seventh Army to the south. Then they can be hit on both flanks and destroyed. This trap, if successful, could produce a victory on the German left so decisive that the success of the Schlieffen right wing might become unnecessary. The Austrians are hit again in Serbia and suffer another severe defeat. Four Russian armies enter Galicia, the Austrian part of Poland (there being no country of Poland in those days—it was long ago divided among Russia, Germany, and Austria). The Austrians are not nearly as prepared as they should be for this offensive because of Conrad's decision to invade Serbia.

August 19: The French continue to advance in Lorraine.

August 20: Crown Prince Rupprecht of Bavaria, commander of the German Sixth Army in Lorraine and temporarily in command of the Seventh Army as well, watches as the French offensive overextends itself and runs out of momentum. Unable to resist so tempting a target ("We cannot ask our Bavarian soldiers to retreat again," he complains, "just when they feel absolute superiority over the enemy facing them"), he orders a counterattack that proves to be brilliantly successful, inflicting tremendous casualties on the French and driving them back across the border to the city of Nancy. Even Nancy is nearly abandoned. It is saved by a defense and counterattack organized by a corps commander named Ferdinand Foch, another sudden hero who will loom ever larger in the years of war to come (and will receive word this very week that his son-in-law and only son have been killed in combat). Rupprecht's counterattack, for all its success, is a serious mistake. It neither destroys the French Sixth Army nor captures anything of strategic importance. Instead it pushes the French backward out of Moltke's trap, returning them to their line of fortresses. The latest developments in technology have, as time will prove, made these fortresses capable of standing up even under the kinds of guns that broke Liège, and in the weeks ahead their strength will permit Joffre to shift troops from his right wing to his imperiled left. The Germans' chances of achieving a breakthrough are vanishingly small, but Rupprecht thinks otherwise. Wanting to press his advantage, he asks—all but demands—that Moltke send him more troops. Moltke, in one of his departures from a Schlieffen Plan in which all possible manpower was supposed to be concentrated in the right wing, agrees.

On this same day the Austrian invasion of Serbia is transformed from a failure into a humiliating rout: the Austrian forces take fifty thousand casualties, including six thousand men killed, and flee back across the border. The Russians and Germans collide again in East Prussia, this time at a place called Gumbinnen, and again the fighting is bloody but inconclusive. The Germans pull back, but the Russians do not pursue. The commander of the Eighth Army, Max von Prittwitz, telephones Moltke and reports that he is in trouble and needs to withdraw from East Prussia. This is disastrous news tactically, strategically, and in terms of morale. East Prussia is the homeland of the Junkers, Prussia's hereditary elite, and as such it is the cradle of Germany's general staff. The thought of the Junker farms being left to the mercies of rampaging Cossack horsemen is horrifying. But once again, as with Rupprecht, Moltke decides that he is too far from the action and too lacking in reliable information to disagree. He does not challenge Prittwitz's decision, does not tell him to stand and fight.

In Belgium, meanwhile, things continued to go well for the Germans. Having done their work at Liège, the big guns were quickly moved westward to Namur, a cluster of nine forts nearly as strong as Liège and a junction of six rail lines. Namur surrendered after five days of shelling. The Germans, however, had something to regret: their failure to cut off and destroy the Belgian army before it slipped off to Antwerp, near the coast. Now Kluck had to reduce his army by two corps in order to keep the Belgians from coming back south and threatening his lines of communication. But the French and Belgians had made an equally serious mistake in failing to send troops to Namur while it still might have provided them with a fortified base from which to block the German advance. Such a move, with enough troops involved, would have had a good chance of succeeding. Now, with that opportunity gone, Lanrezac was going to have to find a way to stop the Germans in open country.

As the Germans took possession of Brussels, they paused to give themselves a parade—the first such celebration since the Franco-Prussian War. From there, while continuing westward, they began to bend their route toward the south, toward Paris. In their wake they were leaving a trail of killings that, even after the truth was separated from the exaggerations of propaganda, would disgrace them in the eyes of the world, give their enemies reason to argue that this was a war for civilization, and begin the long process that would end with the United States entering the war against them. They destroyed towns. They took civilian hostages, including women and children. They killed many of these hostages—in some cases machine-gunning them by the score. They killed priests simply because they were priests (while claiming that they were leaders of a guerrilla resistance). They destroyed the storybook city of Louvain, with its exquisite medieval university and irreplaceable library.

To the extent that such acts can be explained—not excused, but explained—they had tangled origins. In the Franco-Prussian War the Germans had suffered significant casualties at the hands of *franc-tireurs,* civilian snipers and guerrillas, some of whom were urged on by French priests. They were determined not to have a repeat. When they encountered guerrillas in Belgium, they lashed out viciously. The German newspapers carried sensational accounts of German soldiers being mutilated and killed by Belgian townsfolk. These stories were read by the troops, angering and frightening them and causing them to respond with further violence. And senior officers were fixated on the same idea that had made the violation of Belgian neutrality possible in the first place—the idea that Germany was in a life-or-death struggle and so had no choice but to take extreme measures. "Our advance in Belgium is certainly brutal," Moltke observed. "But we are fighting for our lives and all who get in the way must take the consequences."

Wherever enemy armies were believed to be approaching, in Belgium and in France, in southwestern Germany and in East Prussia, in Serbia and in Poland, the civilian populations fled by the hundreds of thousands in whatever way they could. Roads became clogged with refugees and their livestock and whatever possessions they could load onto wagons and carts. Whenever armies wanted to use those same roads, the civilians had to make for the fields and woods.

But Europe was focused on the fortunes of the armies, not the savagery and suffering that the war was already visiting on the innocent, as the middle of August passed. By August 21 things seemed to be moving rapidly to a climax. On that day a second Russian army entered East Prussia and began taking town after town. The Russians' plan was obvious: their two armies would converge on Germany's one eastern army, which they vastly outnumbered, and obliterate it. The road to Berlin would then be open, and the Germans would have no way of saving themselves except by pulling apart their long wall of armies in the west. Kaiser Wilhelm was almost unhinged by the news from East Prussia. After nervously pacing the garden out-

Belgian civilians, displaced by war, crowd the docks of Antwerp
waiting for passage to Britain

side his headquarters, he seated himself on a bench and told his companions—the heads of his military and naval cabinets—to sit down as well. The two men, no doubt trying to be properly deferential to their emperor, pulled up a second bench and sat on it. "Do you already hold me in such contempt that none will sit beside me?" the kaiser cried. It was an early sign, the first of many, that he was not going to stand up well under the strain of war.

It was on August 21, too, that Joffre launched a new offensive, sending the Third and Fourth Armies that formed the center of his line northward into the Ardennes. By now it had become obvious that the Germans' main attack would not be coming from that direction, and Joffre guessed that their center couldn't possibly be very strong. His intelligence bureau had estimated that the Germans would begin the war with sixty-eight combat-ready divisions in the west—not seventy-eight infantry and ten cavalry divisions plus fourteen brigades of territorial militia, as was actually the case. It assumed incorrectly that the Germans would, like the French, regard their newly mobilized reserve troops as too green for action on the front lines. Joffre therefore reasoned that if the Germans had enough strength on their left to push back his offensive in Alsace-Lorraine and enough on their right for a drive across Belgium, the center had to be vulnerable. By thrusting upward into southeastern Belgium, he thought, he could penetrate far enough to strike the German right wing in its flank and separate it from its sources of supply and reinforcement.

The fourteen French divisions sent into the Ardennes ran head-on into exactly fourteen German divisions that found strong defensive positions in the region's rough wooded hills and were well equipped with machine guns and artillery. The French attacked and attacked again under increasingly hopeless conditions until finally, weakened by appalling casualties, they had no choice but to stop. The fight at the town of Rossignol was sadly typical: of the fourteen thousand crack colonial troops thrown at the Germans there, nearly a third were shot dead. Lanrezac's Fifth Army might have been mangled in this offensive as well, if not for his warnings and appeals and Joffre's grudging decision to allow him to stay farther west.

Now the Fifth was the only French army not fully engaged. And by now it was clear that Lanrezac had been right all along: the main German invasion force was to his north, moving through Belgium virtually unopposed. A seventy-five-mile shift had taken Lanrezac's left to a point across the River Sambre from the town of Charleroi. Lanrezac didn't know where the Germans were and had little in the way of instructions from Joffre, and so he did something that was extremely unfashionable in the French army of 1914: he had his troops take up defensive positions. It was fortunate that he did. The next day his army was hit by advance units of Bülow's Second Army coming out of the east. The striking fact here is that Lanrezac, at the far left end of the French line, had met not the end of the German right wing under Kluck but the army on Kluck's left. Important as Lanrezac's move to the north was, it had not reached far enough to intercept the outer edge of the German right. All five French armies were now locked in combat, but this was true of only six of Germany's. Kluck's army was out somewhere to the north and west, beyond Lanrezac's reach and meeting no serious resistance as it plowed its way forward.

By this point all of Joffre's offensives had been beaten back, several of them ending in severe disorder. French casualties for the war's first month are believed to have totaled two hundred sixty thousand, of whom seventy-five thousand were killed (twenty-seven thousand on August 22 alone).* Among the dead were more than 10 percent of France's regular and reserve officers. The cult of the offensive was not delivering its promised results. As a young French captain named Charles De Gaulle would say of the fight in which he was wounded and had his eyes opened, "In a moment it is clear that all the courage in the world cannot prevail against gunfire."

The Germans, except on their right where continued movement was essential, tended to rely on their artillery and let the French attack first. In this way they held their own at worst and took significantly fewer casualties overall: eighteen thousand of their troops were killed on the Western Front in August, a fraction of the French and British total.

And Kluck, with Bülow keeping pace on his left and the German line unbroken all the way to Switzerland, was pounding to the southwest on schedule. The Schlieffen Plan was being achieved. It was actually happening. The stage was set for Kluck to swing around Lanrezac and continue on to Paris.

Or so it seemed until Sunday, August 23. Then, suddenly, Kluck crashed into a mass of dug-in riflemen freshly arrived from England. It must have been a shock. Kluck hadn't known that British troops were in the neighborhood. He hadn't even known, until the day before, that they were in France in sufficient numbers to take the field.

---

*Historians of a statistical bent have been moving the Great War's casualty figures upward and downward for generations. In many cases definitive information is not available. France never specified its losses for August 1914; the records of Austria-Hungary, Russia, and Turkey are often disorderly or worse; some archives are lost, and those that survive sometimes conflict. Anything approaching exactness, especially for whole nations and whole years, is in many cases forever unattainable.

LONDON IN 1914

FOR ALEXANDER VON KLUCK, THE UNEXPECTED collision with British troops on August 23 was not a great deal more than a serious inconvenience. The men of the British Expeditionary Force were some of the world's best soldiers, hardened in their empire's colonial wars, but there were simply not enough of them to stop the avalanche-like advance of Kluck's First Army.

For the French, politicians and generals alike, the very fact that Britain was in the war was a dream come true, something toward which they had been bending national policy for years. It meant that, if the war turned out to be a long one, they would have on their side the richest nation in Europe and the world's greatest navy.

For the British themselves, both those in favor of war and those opposed, the whole thing must have seemed strangely improbable. Nothing had been less inevitable, as Berlin and Paris and St. Petersburg and Vienna stumbled toward catastrophe in July 1914, than that London would be drawn in as well.

Though Sir Edward Grey's foreign office had involved itself in the crisis from the start, its efforts had been directed at preserving the peace. To that end it had maintained a posture of almost excessive impartiality, doing nothing to inflame public opinion. The attention of the public, and of most of the government in London, had been focused meanwhile on a crisis closer to home—one that involved Ireland, the nearest and most troublesome part of the British Empire.

Legally, officially, Ireland was no longer a British possession at all, no longer a colony but rather as integral a part of the United Kingdom as Scotland and Wales. Its elected representatives sat in Parliament. They were numerous enough not only to influence policy but, when the House of Commons was narrowly divided, to cause governments to rise and fall. For the mainly Catholic nationalists of Ireland, such power was not nearly enough. They argued, and not implausibly, that in reality their homeland was still what it had been for centuries: conquered and oppressed. They wanted their own parliament and government—Home Rule. But for the Ulstermen of northern Ireland, descendants of the Protestants transplanted from Scotland by Oliver Cromwell two and a half centuries earlier when to be a Catholic was a crime, Home Rule meant subjection to the pope in Rome. They—the Unionists—were prepared to fight Home Rule to the death.

By the summer of 1914 the Liberal Party had been in power in London for more than eight years. Its popularity had, inevitably, been worn down by year after year of struggle and crisis and controversy, by the things it had done as well as by those it had failed to do. It was, compared with its Conservative or Tory rivals, a reformist government, the champion of such things as national health insurance and a government system of old age pensions. Governments in Britain fall and are replaced when they can no longer command a majority of the votes in Commons, and by 1914 the Liberals were dependent for their majority on a bloc of thirty Irish nationalists.

The price for this support was Home Rule, and the nationalists, aware of how essential they had become to the government, were demanding to be paid now. Prime Minister Herbert Henry Asquith and his cabinet knew that they had to deliver or be replaced. Thus they were moving a Home Rule bill through Parliament. This bill was passionately opposed by the Conservatives, who were passionately supported by the Unionists. Compromise seemed impossible, so that the struggle became increasingly dangerous. Weapons were being smuggled into northern Ireland, where the Unionists were organizing a hundred thousand Ulstermen into militias with the threat that they would rise in armed rebellion rather than become an impotent minority in an autonomous Ireland.

Tensions rose as the Home Rule bill moved toward passage, and the dangers of the situation were multiplied by the fact that much of the army's leadership was Anglo-Irish, Unionist, and implacably opposed to the Asquith government. As it became clear that implementation of Home Rule was likely to require military suppression of a Unionist rebellion, the crisis began to boil over. In the spring the war office had announced that no British officers whose family homes were in Ireland would be required to participate in putting down a Protestant rebellion. All others would be expected to follow whatever orders they were given. Any who found this policy unacceptable were to state their objections and expect to be discharged.

This sparked what was called the Curragh Mutiny. A number of

Prime Minister
Herbert Henry Asquith
"How one loathes such levity."

the army's senior officers openly declared that they supported the Unionists, that the Unionists' only crime was their loyalty to the United Kingdom, and that portraying the Unionists as disloyal was an outrage. Fifty-seven of the seventy officers of a cavalry brigade based at Curragh in Ireland, their commanding general among them, announced that they would prefer dismissal to waging war against Ulster.

Things rapidly went from bad to worse. The secretary of state for war attempted to defuse the situation by offering assurances that there would be no armed suppression of the Protestants. When the prime minister repudiated these assurances, Field Marshal Sir John French resigned as chief of the imperial general staff. Other senior officers resigned also. The king found it necessary to intervene, and leaders on both sides began to step back gingerly from the edge of chaos. By the end of May it was widely accepted that, in spite of the objections of the nationalists, Ireland was going to have to be partitioned. Some part of the North would be retained as part of the U.K. This situation continued to absorb the government in the weeks following the assassination of Franz Ferdinand. The day when Vienna delivered its ultimatum to Serbia was also the day when a Buckingham Palace conference on how to partition Ireland—a conference called by King George himself—ended in failure. On Sunday, July 26, six days before the French and Germans mobilized, British troops fired on a crowd of demonstrators in Dublin. Civil war seemed imminent.

Meanwhile, and with the public barely noticing, Britain was slowly being drawn into the European crisis. London had long based its foreign policy on maintenance of a balance of power on the continent, its aim being to ensure that no country or alliance could become dominant enough to threaten British security. Throughout all the generations when France was the most powerful nation in Europe, it was also, almost automatically, Britain's enemy. After the fall of Napoleon, when Russia rose for a time to preeminence, relations between it and Britain became so badly strained that in the 1850s the two went to war against each other in the Crimea—with France now on Britain's side. Prussia had often been England's ally, but after 1870 the emergence of the German Empire and the corresponding decline of France changed that too. Suddenly the Germans, who for centuries had been too fragmented and backward to threaten anyone, appeared to have become the leading threat to an evenly divided and therefore (from the British perspective) safe Europe. London's concerns were intensified when Kaiser Wilhelm II made it his goal to build a High Seas Fleet big and modern enough to challenge the Royal Navy. This more than any other factor implanted in many British minds the belief that the next war was likely to be with Germany, and that, in order to keep the Germans from ruling Europe, it was going to be necessary to keep them from overwhelming France.

This kind of thinking was conspicuous at the headquarters of the British army, especially among those Unionist officers who thought (rightly, as it turned out) that British involvement in a European war would mean the death of the Home Rule bill. For years before 1914 British general staff planners had been meeting secretly with their French counterparts to plan a joint war against Germany. (Asquith, it might be noted, got little thanks for allowing these talks.) The chief military liaison to Paris, General Sir Henry Wilson, was an almost violently passionate Unionist. He was heard to say that his loyalty to Ulster transcended his loyalty to Britain. His contempt for Asquith, whom he called "Squiff" in his diary, and for Asquith's "filthy cabinet," was only a somewhat extreme example of the prevailing army attitude.

Wilson's talks with the French led gradually to the development of detailed plans for the movement of a British Expeditionary Force to France in the event of war. Only the "imperialist" minority in the Asquith cabinet was allowed to know the details of this plan-ning, however. When other members asked for information, Grey would assure them that they need not be concerned, that nothing had been done to commit Britain. The skeptical majority was not reassured when, early in the summer, it was revealed (in German newspapers) that British military and naval authorities were now also engaged in secret talks with Russia. Grey publicly denied that any such talks had taken place, but he was lying. Here as in the July crisis that followed the assassination of Franz Ferdinand, his posi-tion was excruciatingly difficult. He had agreed to talks with the Russians only out of fear that without evidence of British interest—of *possible* British support in case of war—the Russians might aban-don their Entente with France. Some influential Russians thought it absurd that the Romanov regime should be allied with republican France. Nor, such men thought, did it make sense for Russia to be allied with Britain, which to protect its overseas interests had consis-tently blocked Russian expansion to the south. More than a few Brit-ish, by the same token, were scornful of a possible alliance with the autocratic, repressive court of St. Petersburg. An agreement worked out with Russia in 1907 was basically, as London saw it, a way of relieving pressure on an empire that had grown too big for even the Royal Navy to defend. It was a quid pro quo affair: a willingness to be friendly toward Russia on the continent of Europe in return for Russia's willingness not to threaten India, Britain's portion of Persia (Iran to us), or Afghanistan.

Only gradually was the attention of Asquith's government drawn from the Irish problem to the worsening crisis in Europe. The cabinet was divided, with a solid majority opposed to involvement in a war that now seemed increasingly likely. The men who made up this majority had varied motives. Some believed that Britain should be allied with Germany, not France or Russia, and that the anti-German bias of the imperialists was irrational and sure to lead to trouble. Some warned that, instead of ensuring a balance of power, the de-feat of Germany would make tsarist Russia dominant in Europe—an unappealing prospect to say the least. Some were simply convinced that there was no justification for going to war, that saving France was not Britain's business, and that the human and material costs would far outweigh any possible gain.

A cabinet meeting on Saturday, July 25, showed plainly that the antiwar majority would resign rather than approve any declaration of war. Such resignations would mean the end of the Asquith government, its near-certain replacement by a Conservative government under the dour Unionist Andrew Bonar Law, and the undoing of everything the Liberals had achieved or expected to achieve in Ireland and at home. It would also mean war, because the Conservatives wanted war, and not incidentally it would mean the loss of every cabinet member's job. Not even the most vociferous members of the majority were eager to bring the government down.

It would be unfair to say that the cabinet's imperialist minority actively wanted war. Such an accusation might have some plausibility if directed at the flamboyantly adventurous young Winston Churchill, who as First Lord of the Admiralty had responsibility for the Royal Navy and admitted to being thrilled by the prospect of a fight. Asquith and Grey were more sober in their views. Both agreed that war, if it came, was likely to be a disaster for winners and losers alike, though they remained convinced that allowing Germany to crush France would be an even more terrible disaster. Russia mattered only as one of the means by which France could be saved. If a successful war increased Russia's size and power, that would be regrettable.

The problem of finding a way through all these complexities fell most heavily on the thin shoulders of Sir Edward Grey, and it presented him with two distinct dilemmas. The first was an immediate one: he had to try to use the influence of the British Empire to avert war while not saying or doing more than the cabinet's majority would tolerate and thereby triggering resignations. In this he failed, though his failure was not his fault. The divisions of the cabinet made it impossible for him to intervene in ways that might have made a difference. Grey's other dilemma had to do with persuading both the cabinet and the House of Commons—it too was mainly against war as August came to an end—to agree to intervention *if* the continental powers went to war. In this he was ultimately successful, but his success like his failure rose out of factors beyond his control. It was made possible by an issue that emerged abruptly, as if out of nowhere (actually it was Kaiser Wilhelm who brought it to light), and ultimately swept the opposition aside.

Grey, fifty-two years old in 1914, was the very model of what an

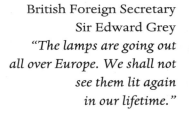

British Foreign Secretary
Sir Edward Grey
*"The lamps are going out
all over Europe. We shall not
see them lit again
in our lifetime."*

Englishman was supposed to be at the zenith of the British Empire. Quiet and refined, intelligent and aristocratic and splendidly well educated, he had the requisite country estate to which he loved to retreat on weekends. He also had the requisite firm belief that Britain was at least one large notch above the Europeans in the realm of morals and ethics, and that in serving the interests of the empire he was serving civilization. He was a lonely man—his wife had been killed when her pony cart overturned on a country lane in 1906, three years before he took charge of the foreign office—whose life was dominated by work. Work was becoming difficult for him because his eyesight was failing.

Prime Minister Asquith was more than content to leave the hard work of diplomacy in Grey's hands. A cautious, cunning lawyer of middle-class origins, Asquith was sixty-one in 1914. He had been in Parliament for three decades and had survived at the head of the Liberal government through six eventful years. Though he was not without principles, he appears to have been dedicated above all other things to staying in power without exerting himself overmuch—without having to give up the pleasures of society, his nightly game of bridge, or the pursuit of desirable women. Staying in power meant holding together his increasingly fragile Liberal majority, a combustible coalition that ranged from the Irish nationalists to the fiery Welsh reformer David Lloyd George, from near-pacifists to the bellicose Churchill. Accomplishing this in July 1914 required skills of the highest order.

From Saturday July 25 on, the cabinet met almost daily, and it remained clear that any attempt to bring a majority around to the support of France could lead to nothing but the end of the government. Asquith and Grey could do little more than hang on and wait. By Monday it was obvious that Grey's proposal for referring the Austro-Serbian dispute to a conference of Britain, France, Germany, and Italy was not going to work. The proposal itself had been naïve, doomed by the fact that the London Conference of 1913 had settled the Second Balkan War in a way that Austria-Hungary and Germany found thoroughly unsatisfactory. By using the London Conference to their own advantage, the other powers had destroyed the potential of conferences generally.

On Wednesday members of the cabinet's majority suggested a resolution by which Britain would declare itself to be unconditionally neutral in case of war. Grey told his fellow ministers that he was not the man to implement such a resolution, and that if it were approved he would resign. When Asquith supported him, the majority drew back. Everything remained unresolved. The pressure on the government—on Grey in particular—was intense and coming from many directions. General Wilson, the Asquith-hating director of military operations, was demanding that the army be mobilized. The French were doing everything possible to persuade the British to support them, while German ambassador Lichnowsky was virtually begging Grey to remain neutral and trying to persuade him that Germany neither wanted war nor had hostile intentions where British interests were concerned. The position that Grey and Asquith had taken with the cabinet might have had a powerful impact if the Germans had learned of it, but it remained secret.

General Wilson began insisting with almost hysterical fervor that the government had a moral obligation to stand with France—that the years of military consultation justified the French in expecting nothing less. He pointed out that France had demonstrated its trust in Britain by agreeing to move its navy to the Mediterranean, leaving the defense of northern waters to the Royal Navy. The antiwar ministers, annoyed, replied that over the years they had repeatedly expressed concern that joint military planning would draw Britain into commitments to France, and that they had been assured that such concerns were unfounded.

Thursday was the day when Tsar Nicholas consented to mobilization. Grey, to his credit, had been urging the Russians to delay, but he and his ambassador in St. Petersburg had less influence there than France's Ambassador Paléologue, who from the start had been urging action. This was also the day when French President Poincaré sent word to Grey that he believed Britain could stop the slide to war if it warned Berlin that it was prepared to support France. Grey, clinging to his pose of impartiality, responded in almost the feeblest way imaginable, saying only that he doubted Britain's ability to make that big a difference. Privately, he now took a step for which he did not have cabinet approval. He told Lichnowsky, whom he knew to regard the prospect of a war between their two countries with horror, that in his opinion a German war with France would mean war with Britain as well.

By Friday, with everyone's options narrowing and the cabinet's majority still against war, Grey pressed upon Lichnowsky his Stop-in-Belgrade idea. When Vienna rejected the proposal despite Kaiser Wilhelm's endorsement, that option too was at an end. It was then that the kaiser, desperate for a way out, instructed Lichnowsky to promise Grey that if Britain would remain neutral, Germany would pledge itself to restore the borders of France and Belgium if war came and Germany won.

Belgium: Germany's raising of this subject introduced an explosive new element into the drama. Even the antiwar ministers saw immediately that this was a momentous question. The cabinet authorized Grey to ask France and Germany for an explicit guarantee of Belgium's neutrality and autonomy. The inability of the Germans to respond said everything.

And so, in a matter of hours, the question of British intervention was cast in an entirely new context. The issue was no longer whether Britain should go to war in support of France and Russia—of whether the British public could possibly be brought to support such a war. Now it was a question of whether Britain would compromise its own interests by allowing a small but strategically important neutral nation, a nation whose neutrality Britain had pledged to uphold, to be invaded. This was something that the public would have no difficulty understanding.

On the last weekend of peace, the weekend when Germany and France both mobilized, the cabinet remained divided with eight members favoring war if Germany invaded Belgium and eleven opposed. Churchill, Grey, and the prime minister were in favor. The most prominent figure on the other side—but careful not to allow himself to be positioned as the leader of the antiwar group, which would destroy his freedom to maneuver—was the chancellor of the exchequer, David Lloyd George. Though the opponents of intervention had maintained their majority, several were no longer firm. Asquith and Grey had deftly softened the ground on which their opponents stood by misleading them into thinking—by allowing them to hope, at a minimum—that Britain's role in the coming war would be a strictly naval one and therefore relatively low in risk and cost. The situation was moving away from the antiwar faction, and few still believed that resignations could make a difference.

Some of the most senior members of the antiwar faction saw the whole matter as a kind of bait-and-switch ruse. Lord John Morley, an aging bulwark of the Liberal Party and one of the small number of cabinet members who in the end did resign rather than assent to war, said "the precipitate and peremptory blaze about Belgium was due less to indignation at the violation of a Treaty than to natural perception of the plea that it would furnish for intervention on behalf of France, for expeditionary force, and all the rest of it." This resentful view would be supported years later by the woman who served as Lloyd George's private secretary (and mistress) in 1914, saw him swing around to support a declaration of war early in August, and later became his wife. "My own opinion," wrote Frances Stevenson Lloyd George more than forty years later, "is that L.G.'s mind was really made up from the first, that he knew we would have to go in, and that the invasion of Belgium was, to be cynical, a heaven-sent excuse for supporting a declaration of war."

On Sunday, August 2, things still hung in the balance. "I suppose," Asquith wrote that day to the young woman with whom he was conducting his own romantic intrigue, "that a good three-fourths of our own party in the House of Commons are for absolute non-interference at any price." But as he wrote, the Germans were moving their army into Luxembourg and launching small raids into France. In the evening Berlin sent its ultimatum to Belgium, lamely stating that it had to invade Belgium before France could do so and demanding unobstructed passage for its troops. The French meanwhile were still holding their forces back from the borders, doing everything possible to make certain that Britain and the world would see the Germans as the aggressors.

Early on Monday King Albert of Belgium issued his refusal of Germany's demands. Later in the day Germany declared war on France. Grey, the eyes of Europe on him, addressed the House of Commons. He spoke for an hour, putting all of his emphasis on the government's efforts to keep the war from happening, on the threat that a violation of Belgium would be to Britain itself, and on his conviction that Britain must respond or surrender its honor. He kept his arguments on a high moral plane, artfully avoiding less lofty subjects such as the continental balance of power.

Not everyone was persuaded. "The Liberals, very few of them, cheered at all," one member of the House noted. But the Conservatives "shouted with delight." In any case a majority of the Commons was won over, and so was the public. The sole remaining questions were whether the Germans were going to pass through only a small corner of Belgium or move into its heartland, and whether the Belgians were going to resist. (The Germans, in demanding free passage through Belgium, had promised to pay for all damage done by their army.)

Tuesday brought the answers. Masses of German troops began crossing the border into Belgium and moved on Liège. King Albert made it clear that he and his countrymen intended to fight.

It was done. Before midnight Britain and Germany were at war. Some members of the cabinet resigned, but only a few, and they knew that no one cared. The pretense that only the Royal Navy would be involved was quickly forgotten. The British army prepared to fight in western Europe for the first time in exactly one hundred years.

Lloyd George, having maneuvered in such a way as to keep his position in the government without seeming to compromise the principles that had long since made him a prominent anti-imperialist, found himself cheered on August 3 as he rode through London. "This is not my crowd," he said to his companions. "I never want to be cheered by a war crowd."

"It is curious," wrote Asquith, "how, going to and from the House, we are now always surrounded and escorted by cheering crowds of loafers and holiday makers. I have never before been a popular character with 'the man in the street,' and in all this dark and dangerous business it gives me scant pleasure. How one loathes such levity."

Chapter 9

A Perfect Balance

"The most terrible August in the history of the world."
—Sir Arthur Conan Doyle

The commander of the British Expeditionary Force, Sir John French, had arrived in France with little knowledge of where the Germans were or what they were doing or even what he was supposed to do when he found them.

French—the same Sir John French who had resigned as chief of the imperial general staff at the time of the Curragh Mutiny—carried with him written instructions from the new secretary of state for war, the formidable Field Marshal Earl Kitchener of Khartoum. These instructions were not, however, what a man in his position might have expected. They did not urge him to pursue and engage the invading Germans with all possible vigor, to remember that England expected victory, or even to support his French allies to the fullest possible extent in their hour of desperate need.

In fact, he found himself under orders to do very nearly the opposite of these things. He was to remember that his little command—a mere five divisions, four of infantry and one of cavalry—included most of Britain's regular army and could not be spared.

"It will be obvious that the greatest care must be exercised towards a minimum of loss and wastage," Kitchener had written. "I wish you to distinctly understand that your force is an entirely independent one and you will in no case come under the orders of any Allied general." In other words, French was not to risk his army and was not to regard himself as subordinate to Joffre or Lanrezac or any other French general. In taking this approach, Kitchener created an abundance of problems.

Certainly the BEF, compared with the vast forces that France and Germany had already sent to the Western Front, seemed so small as to risk being trampled. Kaiser Wilhelm, drawing upon his deep reserves of foolishness in exhorting his troops to victory, had called it Britain's "contemptibly little army." But man for man the BEF was as good as any fighting force in the world: well trained and disciplined, accustomed to being sent out to the far corners of the world whenever the empire's great navy was not enough. The BEF was also an appealingly human, high-spirited army. Even the rank and file were career soldiers for the most part, volunteers drawn mainly from Britain's urban poor and working classes, more loyal to their regiments and to one another than to any sentimental notions of imperial glory, and ready to make a joke of anything. When they learned what the kaiser had said about them, they began to call themselves "the Old Contemptibles." When the first shiploads of them crossed from Southampton to Le Havre, they found the harbor jammed with crowds who burst into the French national anthem, "La Marseillaise." The thousands of British troops—Tommies, they were called at home—responded by bursting spontaneously not into "God Save the King" but into one of the indelicate music hall songs with which they entertained themselves while on the march. The French watched and listened reverently, some with their hands on their hearts, not understanding a word and thinking that this must be the anthem of the United Kingdom.

The BEF moved first to an assembly point just south of Belgium, and on August 20 began moving north to link up with Lanrezac's Fifth Army and extend the French left wing. They were still en route when, on August 21, the units that Lanrezac had positioned near Charleroi on the River Sambre were struck by Bülow's German Second Army. Sir John French, when he learned of this encounter, ordered his First Corps (two divisions commanded by Sir Horace Smith-Dorrien) to move up toward the town of Mons, about eight miles west of Charleroi. From there, it was to cover Lanrezac's flank.

On the next day, with the Germans and French alternately attacking each other on the Sambre (Ludendorff, who happened to be in the area as a member of Bülow's staff, organized the seizure of the bridges across the river), a scouting party of British cavalry encountered German cavalry coming out of the north. The Germans withdrew. The British, savvy veterans that they were, dismounted and began using their trenching tools to throw up earthwork defenses while Smith-Dorrien's infantry came up from behind and joined them. They didn't know what to expect when the sun rose, but they intended to be as ready as it was possible for men armed with little more than rifles to be.

Ahead of them in the darkness was the entire German First Army. Its commander, Kluck (it was a gift to the amateur songwriters of the BEF that his name rhymed with their favorite word), knew nothing except that his scouts had run into armed horsemen, and that they claimed those horsemen were British. It did not sound serious; Kluck's intelligence indicated that the main British force was either not yet in France or, at worst, still a good many miles away. There seemed no need to mount an immediate attack.

Kluck at this point was an angry, frustrated man who didn't want to be where he was and in fact shouldn't have been there. He had recently been put under the orders of the more cautious Bülow, whose army was on his left. The Germans, like the French, were still in the early stages of learning to manage warfare on this scale, and they had not yet seen the value of creating a new level of command to direct forces as large as their right wing. Neither side had yet seen that when two or three armies are operating together and need to be coordinated, the answer is not to put the leader of one of those armies in charge of the others. It is almost inevitable, human nature being what it is, that a commander made first among equals in this way will give too much weight to the objectives and needs of his own army.

This is exactly what happened between the rough-hewn Kluck and the careful, highborn Bülow. Kluck had wanted to swing wide to the right, well clear of the French. Bülow insisted that he stay close, so that their two armies—plus Max von Hausen's Third Army on his left—would be able to deal with Lanrezac together. Kluck protested, but to no effect. Bülow was a solid professional who had long held senior positions in the German army, and a decade earlier he had been a leading candidate to succeed Schlieffen as head of the general staff, losing out to Moltke largely because he favored a direct attack on the French in case of war, rather than envelopment. His approach in August 1914 was conventional military practice; if his army locked head to head with Lanrezac's, Kluck and Hausen would be able to protect his flanks and then try to work around Lanrezac's flanks and surround him. But Bülow's orthodoxy (obviously the war would have opened in an entirely different way if he rather than Moltke had been in charge of planning since 1905) cost the Germans a huge opportunity. Left free to go where he wished, Kluck would have looped around not only the French but also the forward elements of the BEF. He then could have taken Smith-Dorrien's corps in the flank, broken it up, and pushed its disordered fragments into Lanrezac's flank. The possible consequences were incalculable; the destruction of Lanrezac's army—of any of the armies in the long French line—could have led to a quick end to the war in the west. Con-

General Alexander von Kluck
Commander,
German First Army
*An angry, frustrated man—
and eager for a fight.*

General Otto von Bülow
Commander, German Second Army
Favored direct attack rather than encirclement.

tinuing to protest, appealing to Moltke but finding no support there, Kluck had no choice but to follow orders. Doing so caused him to run directly into the head of the British forces, engage them where they were strongest instead of weakest, and give them a night to consolidate their defenses because he didn't know he was faced with anything more dangerous than a roving cavalry detachment.

On the morning of August 23 (a day marked by Japan's declaration of war on Germany), Kluck ordered an artillery bombardment of the enemy positions in his path. When this ended at nine-thirty, thinking that the defenders must now be in disarray, his troops attacked—and were quickly shot to pieces in a field of fire so devastating that many of them thought they must be facing an army of machine guns. They attacked repeatedly and were cut down every time. What they were up against was the fruit of years of emphasis on what the British still called musketry. Every private in the BEF carried a .303 Lee Enfield rifle fitted with easily changed ten-round magazines and had been trained to hit a target fifteen times a minute at a range of three hundred yards. Most could do better than that. Every soldier was routinely given all the ammunition he wanted for practice, and high scores were rewarded with cash. These practices had been put in place after the South African War at the turn of the century, when the Tommies had found themselves outgunned by Boer farmers fighting as guerrillas, and this was the payoff.

But as the day wore on, hour by hour and yard by bloody yard, the persistence of the Germans and the sheer weight of their numbers forced the British back. When the day ended, more than sixteen hundred of Smith-Dorrien's men had been killed, and the Germans had lost at least five thousand. Kluck and his army had been stopped for a full day. In itself, one day meant little. But if the Germans could be stopped for another day and another after that, Moltke's entire campaign would begin to fall to pieces.

After sundown, the BEF's Second Corps under Sir Douglas Haig having come forward to join Smith-Dorrien's, the British again went to work on their defenses. But during the night an English liaison officer arrived at French's headquarters with stunning news: Lanrezac, rather than holding his ground at Charleroi, was pulling back. This exposed the British right and gave them no choice but to pull back as well. French reacted bitterly. He regarded Lanrezac's withdrawal—which probably saved his army and was conducted with great skill under difficult circumstances—as unnecessary. He had entered the war with a very British disdain for the French. That disdain now began to turn into entirely unjustified contempt.

There arose in the aftermath of this battle the strangest and most beautiful legend of the war. It was said that, when the British peril was at its height, a majestic figure had appeared high in the sky with arm upraised. Some said it had been pointing to victory, others that it held back the Germans as the Tommies got away. It came to be known as the Angel of Mons. Even more colorful was the simultaneous legend of the Archers of Agincourt. In the late Middle Ages at Agincourt—not a great distance from Mons—English yeomen armed with longbows had won a great victory over a much bigger force of mounted and armored French knights. Four hundred and ninety-nine years later there were stories of German soldiers found dead at Mons with arrows through their bodies.

It was all nonsense. The disappointing truth, established beyond doubt by postwar investigations, is that the legends were journalistic inventions, and that they first emerged long after the battle. No one ever found a witness who had personally seen an angel, arrows, or anything of the kind.

When the Germans resumed their attack on the morning of August 24, braced this time for tough resistance, they found nothing in front of them but abandoned entrenchments. They got back on the road, caught up with the BEF after two days of hard pursuit, and on August 26 hit Smith-Dorrien's corps at Le Cateau. Under severe pressure, his men exhausted, Smith-Dorrien found it impossible to disengage and resume his retreat when ordered to do so by French. He was the proverbial man with a wolf by the ears, unable to take the initiative and unable to escape. He organized a rear guard that managed by the narrowest of margins to fight off envelopment. Le Cateau turned into a bigger, bloodier fight than the one at Mons, with fifty-five thousand British desperately holding off one hundred and forty thousand Germans. Ultimately, when the Germans found it necessary to pull back and regroup, the British were able to resume their retreat. They had taken some eight thousand casualties (more than Wellington's at Waterloo) and lost thirty-six pieces of artillery. And already-strained relationships within the BEF command were worsened. French, who had disliked Smith-Dorrien for years and had not wanted him in his command, refused to believe that he had not been willfully disobedient. Smith-Dorrien, for his part, thought that Haig had been too slow in entering the fights both at Mons and at Le Cateau. It is a mark of how desperate the British were for something to feed into their propaganda machine that Le Cateau was celebrated, at the time and long afterward, as a British triumph. The only thing to celebrate was that the BEF was still intact when it made its escape.

Elsewhere along the Western Front the Germans were scoring victory after victory. They were turning back French assaults, achieving a high rate of success with their own offensives, and usually losing far fewer men. The reason is not to be found in numbers; as we have seen, the two sides were numerically just about equal. Even the German right wing had no consistent manpower advantage. A French counterattack that marked the climax of the Charleroi fight, for example, ended with three German divisions not only stopping nine of Lanrezac's divisions but ultimately driving them back seven miles—even though the French force included ten regiments of elite colonial troops, veterans akin to the men of the BEF. Clearly the Germans were doing something right, or the French were doing something wrong, or both.

The answer is "both." In the face of repeated bad results, generals throughout the French army threw their infantry against the Germans whatever the circumstances and kept doing so no matter how grisly the results. Lanrezac was a rare exception; he had been reluctant to attack at Charleroi, doing so only because two of his corps commanders insisted. Joffre's other commanders believed that French troops were supposed to charge, not crawl in the earth like worms. They were to win at the point of their bayonets, not by firing steel-clad packets of high explosives into the sky. The Germans, by contrast, quickly became adroit, upon making contact with the enemy, at digging in, waiting to be attacked, and mowing down the attackers with rifle fire, machine guns capable of firing up to six hundred heavy-caliber rounds per minute, and above all artillery. (From the start of the war to the end, cannon would account for most of the killing.) When the attackers fell back, the Germans would continue punishing them with their field artillery, firing shrapnel and high explosives. Then they would come out of their holes and keep the fleeing enemy on the move. From the start they were even better than the British at creating defenses for themselves with the trenching tools every man carried plus picks and shovels brought forward by combat engineers. The difference in the tactics of the two sides explains why, despite the lives they squandered at Mons and Le Cateau and later in other, bigger fights, the Germans had significantly lower casualties on the Western Front in 1914 than the French and British.

But as French casualties climbed without producing a single victory of consequence—it was "the most terrible August in the history of the world," said British author Sir Arthur Conan

Doyle—Joffre found it necessary to conclude that the French army's "cult of the offensive" had to be abandoned. On August 24 he unhappily announced that the armies of France were for the time being "forced to take defensive action based on our fortified positions and on the strong natural obstacles provided by the terrain, so as to hold on as long as possible, taking, meanwhile, all steps to wear down the enemy's strength and resume the offensive in due course." He ordered his left wing—his Third, Fourth, and Fifth Armies—to begin what would come to be known as the Great Retreat. Day after day, in relentless heat, weary French soldiers in their hundreds of thousands trudged farther and farther south. The BEF marched with them, covering more than a hundred and ninety miles in thirteen days. One of its battalions retreated fifty-five miles in thirty-six hours.

Joffre also ordered the creation of a new army to lengthen his left. This Sixth Army was to be "capable of taking up the offensive again while the other armies contained the enemy's effort for the requisite period," Joffre said, but its position near Paris obviously had defensive implications. The Germans' continued pursuit of Lanrezac's army after the defeat at Le Cateau had awakened the government to the fact that Paris was in jeopardy. Minister of War Adolphe Messimy examined the city's defenses and was alarmed by what he found. They were in a sorry state of neglect, at least in part because the army's fixation on the offensive had caused it to give little attention to defenses of any kind.

Messimy turned not to Joffre but to General Joseph Gallieni for help, asking him to become military governor of Paris and offering him near-dictatorial powers to organize a defense of the city. Gallieni, who had been in semiretirement at the start of the war, agreed on one condition. He said he would need not only the garrison forces inside the city walls but a substantial mobile force capable of engaging the Germans as they approached. At least six corps would be needed for this purpose, he said. (A corps was usually made up of two, sometimes three divisions of nearly twenty thousand men each.) Messimy agreed without hesitation, but in fact he had no authority to fulfill his pledge. It was Joffre alone who decided the deployment of troops, and Joffre showed no interest in assisting, or even consulting with, either Gallieni or the government.

Nevertheless, Gallieni set to work immediately to ready Paris for a siege, bringing herds of livestock inside the walls to provide a supply of food, installing new lines of trenches, positioning artillery, and demolishing buildings to give the guns a clear line of fire. As this work proceeded, a political crisis erupted over the city's failure to start preparing earlier, the government fell, and Messimy was displaced (in part, ironically, for refusing to agree to the dismissal of Joffre). He took up his reserve army commission and went off to the front as a major. When Gallieni finally got his mobile force, it came to him in the form of Joffre's new Sixth Army, which was still in the early stages of being assembled. The first elements of this army, many of them brought in by train from stabilizing sectors at the eastern end of the front, were moved inside the Paris defensive perimeter as part of the Great Retreat. They were completely out of touch with Lanrezac and the BEF and not nearly ready for action in any case. Joffre evidently decided that he might as well let Gallieni have them, if only temporarily and if only to quiet the complaints coming from the government.

Behind the retreating French armies, sometimes even beside them in the spreading confusion, marched masses of Germans, tired but energized by the thought that they had the enemy on the run, that victory lay ahead. Joffre's plan was to pull back only as far as a line along the east-west course of the River Somme, call a halt there and, when circumstances were right, counterattack. This plan proved infeasible; when the French got to the Somme, the enemy was still right behind them. They had no choice but to cross the river and keep going.

Nobody, not even the high generals in their headquarters, had a detailed understanding of what was happening along the front. British and French newspapers carried hair-raising but inspiring stories of how the Germans, the Huns, were committing mass suicide in throwing themselves against the guns and bayonets of the valiant defenders of civilization. In the German papers it was civilization's defenders who were advancing victoriously, moving constantly forward on the soil of a nation that had conspired to destroy their homeland. On both sides, anything that wasn't an outright defeat was made a cause for celebration, and every setback was either treated as a canny tactical adjustment or, more commonly, ignored. Journalists were kept far from the action. Even the senior commanders, flooded with reports some of which were accurate and many of which were not, could have little confidence that they knew what the enemy was doing or which side was doing more killing.

With the BEF and Lanrezac's army in almost headlong flight, it seemed to many on Moltke's staff that the Germans had already won in the west; "complete victories" were being declared. Belgium was firmly in hand, and the right wing was in France and staying on Schlieffen's schedule. The German Fourth and Fifth Armies had broken the back of the French offensive in the Ardennes, and in the southeast Crown Prince Rupprecht of Bavaria continued to report that he was gaining ground, taking thousands of prisoners and capturing guns. Rupprecht was also continuing to badger Moltke for more troops with which to press his advantage. Moltke agreed. He also decided to send three infantry corps and a cavalry division to East Prussia. These were fateful moves. Combined with Moltke's earlier adjustments—the use of two corps to besiege Antwerp, and of another to besiege a French stronghold at Maubeuge—they would reduce his right wing from seventeen corps to fewer than twelve. This was a reduction of two hundred and seventy-five thousand men, and it was in addition to the Germans' battlefield losses. The hammer upon which Schlieffen had wanted to bet everything thus shrank by nearly a third. Meanwhile Joffre was doing the opposite, using his rail lines to transfer increasing numbers of troops from his right to his left. Even as the Germans continued their advance, in terms of manpower the balance at the western end of the front was gradually shifting in France's favor.

Moltke's decision to dispatch troops to East Prussia has been much criticized but is easy to understand. He had good reason to be alarmed not only by the situation in East Prussia but by what was happening all across the eastern theater. He knew that the Austrian invasion of Serbia—an invasion he had opposed, arguing rightly that all of the Hapsburg empire's available troops were needed against Russia—had ended in total defeat. He knew too that massive Russian forces were engaging the Austrians on the Galician plain to the north of Serbia, and that if this too ended badly, Conrad's position would become desperate. And his own commander in East Prussia had told Moltke that the German position there was already desperate. That commander, the fat and elderly Max von Prittwitz, an intelligent enough general but one with no combat experience, had at his disposal a single army of some one hundred and thirty-five thousand men—eleven undermanned divisions of infantry and one of cavalry, barely one-tenth of Germany's available total. Moving against this Eighth Army, a small one by the standards of 1914, were two exceptionally large Russian armies that outnumbered it by a huge margin. The Russian First Army, commanded by General Pavel von Rennenkampf (German surnames were not uncommon in the Russian aristocracy and senior officer corps), had been first to cross the border into German territory, approaching from the east. Thereafter it had continued to move forward, capturing towns, burning the farms of the Junkers, and clashing with elements of Prittwitz's army first at Stallupönen and then at Gumbinnen. It was shortly after the Gumbinnen fight, and upon learning that the Russian Second Army under General Alexander Samsonov was entering East Prussia from the south with fourteen and a half infantry divisions, four divisions of cavalry, and 1,160 guns, that Prittwitz had telephoned Moltke and told him that he had to abandon East Prussia. He was afraid that if he stayed where he was, Samsonov would soon be behind him and able to block his escape. The situation was ripe for an encirclement that would end in the destruction of the Eighth Army and leave Germany defenseless in the East. There was no alternative to withdrawing behind the north-south Vistula River, Prittwitz said. Moltke did not demur. Giving up the Prussian homeland was an intolerable thought, but everything being accomplished in France would become meaningless if the Eighth Army were lost.

That Prussian homeland was already involved in the war more directly than any other part of Germany, with the invaders inevitably clashing with the inhabitants and outrages being committed on both sides. An Englishman, John Morse, was serving among the Russian troops, and he later wrote of the brutalities he witnessed. "The Cossack has a strong disinclination to be taken prisoner," he observed, "and I knew of several of them sacrificing their lives rather than fall into the hands of the Germans, who heartily detest these men, and usually murdered such as they succeeded in catching—and murdered them after preliminary tortures, according to reports which reached us. The country people certainly showed no mercy to stragglers falling into their hands. They usually pitch-forked them to death; and this lethal weapon was a favorite with the ladies on both sides of the border, many a fine Teuton meeting his end by thrusts from this implement."

Members of Moltke's staff began telephoning the commanders of the four corps that made up the Eighth Army. The technology of the day made this a laborious process, requiring much waiting for connections, much shouting into receivers, much uncertainty about what the faint and fuzzy voice on the other end of the line was saying. Moltke's men had one question: was a retreat really necessary? The answer was unanimously negative: the Eighth Army need not, must not, fall back. This was reported to Moltke, who concluded that Prittwitz had lost his nerve and could not be left in command.

Prittwitz himself, however, was having his mind changed too. This was accomplished by a new member of his staff, the tall, chubby, hard-drinking, and colorfully un-Prussian Lieutenant Colonel Max Hoffmann, who had been sent from Alsace to join the Eighth Army when mobilization was declared and now took the first of the steps by which he would establish himself as one of the war's master tacticians. Using a map and compass, Hoffmann showed Prittwitz that Samsonov's army was already closer to the Vistula River than the main German force, so that a clean escape was no longer possible. He outlined a plan aimed not only at making withdrawal unnecessary but at defeating both Russian armies. First the Germans would strike again at Rennenkampf, who was still at Gumbinnen, apparently regrouping after the clash there. Finishing off Rennenkampf, Hoffmann calculated, would take only a few days; at a minimum his army could be rendered incapable of pursuit. The Germans would then be free to deal with Samsonov.

His composure restored, Prittwitz agreed that there need be no retreat. He did not, however, accept Hoffmann's plan without amendment. He decided to go after Samsonov without first attacking Rennenkampf. Speed was essential—everything depended on wrecking one of the invading armies before the two of them could combine into a single force too big to be coped with. Expecting his troops to deal with two big armies in just a few days, Prittwitz wisely decided, would be asking too much.

But in the excited rush to prepare, Prittwitz made two mistakes. He neglected to tell Hoffmann or anyone else on his staff of his conversation with Moltke—his announcement of a retreat—and after changing his mind he failed to inform Moltke that he had done so. Moltke continued to believe that the Eighth Army was beginning to withdraw.

Fearful of the consequences if the Eighth Army did not stand and fight, Moltke looked about for a solution. And he thought of Erich Ludendorff, who had been an important member of his planning staff until 1913 and was now the hero of Liège. "I know of no other man in whom I have such absolute trust," Moltke said. He sent orders for Ludendorff to join the Eighth Army not as commanding officer—he was too young for that, too junior in rank, and definitely too much the parvenu commoner—but as chief of staff.

On his way east Ludendorff stopped at Koblenz to confer with Moltke, and the two agreed that the situation in East Prussia was not yet hopeless. When Ludendorff suggested attacking the Russian armies one by one before they could combine, Moltke agreed. That Hoffmann and Ludendorff came up with exactly the same idea, and that they had no difficulty in winning over Prittwitz and Moltke, is not as astonishing as it may seem. The German general staff had given much thought to the defense of East Prussia, had anticipated the arrival of Russian forces from two directions, and had planned accordingly. Ludendorff and Hoffmann were simply drawing upon established doctrine in making their proposals, and in giving their assent Moltke and Prittwitz were simply endorsing that same doctrine.

Before departing Koblenz, Ludendorff was taken to see Kaiser Wilhelm, receiving from him the Pour le Mérite (Germany's highest military honor, higher than the Iron Cross, created and named by the Francophile Frederick the Great) and learning that a new commanding general of the Eighth Army had just been appointed. This was the sixty-seven-year-old Paul von Beneckendorff und von Hindenburg, who was being called out of retirement because of his reputation for steadiness and the fact that he, like Ludendorff, knew the complicated East Prussian terrain. Then Ludendorff was again on his way east, traveling in a special train, stopping along the way to pick up his wife so that she could join him for part of the trip. Hindenburg, dressed in the outdated uniform in which he had ended his long career two years earlier, came aboard at Hanover at four a.m. They talked briefly—Ludendorff outlined the plan he had discussed with Moltke—and retired for a few hours' sleep.

Upon their arrival in East Prussia the next morning, they had much to do. Hindenburg had to tell Prittwitz, who happened to be his wife's cousin, that he was being put on the army's inactive list effective immediately. Ludendorff meanwhile got a staff briefing. When Hoffmann outlined his plan and explained that it was already being put in motion, Ludendorff of course approved it without change. The two knew each other well—had even lived in the same quarters for four years earlier in their careers. Despite being very different kinds of men, they respected each other's abilities. From the start they were able to work together easily.

The situation was challenging in the extreme, requiring the Eighth Army to fight its own two-front war. Its complications began with the landscape of East Prussia, a region pocked with lakes and marshes and studded with woods and low hills, difficult for large armies to maneuver in, especially in the sectors nearest to Russia. Running north-south was a jumble of irregular-shaped bodies of water known as the Masurian Lakes. Rennenkampf's army was north of the lakes, Samsonov's south. They would have to move westward in order to unite. Between them were the Germans, already west of the lakes and in a position from which they could attack in either direction. They also had the advantage of knowing the terrain intimately—it was often the setting for their annual maneuvers. And they had installed the rail lines needed for the execution of their plans.

It was obvious that the Russians should converge without delay. If they did so, the Eighth Army was doomed. It was equally obvious that the Germans must proceed with extreme caution. If they attacked one of the Russian armies, they would have to leave enough troops behind to protect themselves from an advance by the other. It was far from clear that they had enough troops to do both things.

At this point—August 25, the same day on which the British fell back from Mons and Kluck resumed his march toward Paris—there occurred one of those small, strange events that sometimes alter the fates of nations. This one was weirdly like what had happened, in the American Civil War, the first time Robert E. Lee invaded the north: a copy of Lee's orders was found in a Maryland road wrapped around a packet of cigars. The discovery led directly to a stinging Confederate defeat and the end of Lee's offensive. The East Prussian counterpart to this incident was the discovery, on the body of a Russian officer killed in a skirmish, of the plans for both Russian armies. It seemed too good to be true, but the plans' authenticity was soon corroborated by uncoded Russian radio messages intercepted by the Germans.

The intelligence that the Germans now had in their hands indicated that Samsonov intended to continue moving westward, which would increase the distance between the two Russian armies unless Rennenkampf moved too. What the Germans didn't know was that Samsonov was being drawn forward by a glimpse that his troops had caught of the backward movement of a German infantry corps. This move had been nothing more than a minor tactical adjustment: the commander of the corps was shifting to a ridge stronger than his original position. But Samsonov leaped to the conclusion that the Germans were in retreat. He intended to press forward, keep the Germans moving, try to overrun them. A radio message sent from his headquarters, when intercepted, told the Germans exactly what direction he intended to take and what timetable he intended to follow. It stated also, not surprisingly, that he wanted Rennenkampf to come forward to join him.

Rennenkampf's messages indicated that he had other things in mind. He didn't know what had happened to the German force that had attacked him at Gumbinnen, and so, like Rennenkampf, he guessed. His guess was that the Germans had decided to withdraw to the north, toward or even into the coastal fortress of Königsberg ("kingstown," the principal city of East Prussia and the place where the rulers of Prussia had always been crowned). Focusing his attention in that direction, he could see no need to move toward Samsonov; he didn't suspect that the main German force might be between them. If he laid siege to Königsberg and bottled up the Eighth Army inside it, all the rest of East Prussia would be undefended. He was in no hurry, however, because there was no way of being sure how far the Germans had moved. He had no way of knowing (but might have guessed, the reasons being so obvious) that allowing himself to be trapped inside Königsberg was the one thing Moltke had ordered Prittwitz *not* to do.

For the Germans, the situation really did seem too good to be true. By continuing to move forward alone, Samsonov was practically inviting the Germans to lay a trap. By declining to come forward, Rennenkampf was making certain that his army would be unable to rescue Samsonov from that trap. Together they were eliminating the need for the Germans to proceed cautiously. They were freeing the Germans to throw everything into their attack on Samsonov.

Hoffmann had received the Russian messages after his initial meeting with Ludendorff, who had departed by car with Hindenburg. He showed them to the Eighth Army's quartermaster general, a Major General Grünert, offering them as confirmation that the entire Eighth Army could safely be sent against Samsonov. Grünert was skeptical; what seems too good to be true, after all, usually is. It seemed inconceivable to him that the Russian commanders would violate one of the fundamentals of military doctrine by keeping their forces divided in the presence of the enemy.

Max Hoffmann may have been the only man on earth who was junior to Grünert in rank and yet able to win him over at this critical juncture. Hoffmann was one of Germany's experts on the Russian army, and a decade earlier he had been sent as an observer to the Russo-Japanese War. There he had observed Samsonov and Rennenkampf in action. One of the war's minor legends is that, by an astonishing coincidence, Hoffmann had been present when the two Russian generals literally came to blows at a train station in Manchuria. Though it is now regarded as unlikely that anything of the kind actually happened, Hoffmann did know that Rennenkampf and Samsonov belonged to rival factions of the Russian general staff and disliked each other intensely. He was convinced that neither would exert himself to help the other. When he explained this history, Grünert was persuaded. The two got into

General Pavel
von Rennenkampf
Commander,
Russian First Army
*Failed to respond
to Samsonov's
pleas for help.*

a staff car and sped off, catching up with Hindenburg and Luden-dorff and showing them the intercepted messages. All reservations about risking everything were immediately dissolved.

Risking everything meant exactly that: the Germans posted only a single division of cavalry opposite Rennenkampf's army. This was not a serious blocking force but merely a screen; its only function was to keep the Russians from seeing that nothing was behind it. All the rest of the Eighth Army was moved south and west into Samsonov's path. Many of the troops were sent by rail and thus were able to move a hundred miles overnight. Nine divisions were formed into an arc that was open to the southeast and sixty miles across. This arc was intentionally weak in the center but had two strong wings. The idea was for Samsonov, as he continued forward, to strike the center, find himself able to drive it backward, and thus be encouraged to keep moving. When he had gone far enough, the wings would move in on him from both sides.

The very fact that they had two armies inside East Prussia by this date was, for the Russians, a great achievement. The Germans had hoped that Russian mobilization would take six weeks, and they had not given sufficient weight to the fact that two-fifths of Russia's regular army was stationed in Poland when the war began and so was near East Prussia and nearly ready for action. The result had been Rennenkampf's arrival in East Prussia in just over two weeks, with Samsonov close behind. This much speed was also, however, an act of folly: the Russians had begun their advance without adequate provision for supplying their troops, for dealing with the wounded, or for communicating. (Hence the uncoded radio messages that proved such a boon to the Germans.) Some of their soldiers were without shoes, marching with their feet wrapped in rags. Some had no rifles. They were worn out long before making contact with the enemy. Rennenkampf's troops had been on the march for a week by the time they crossed into East Prussia, and their supply system was already failing badly.

These problems were the work of General Yakov Zhilinski, commander of the Russian North-West Front and therefore in charge of the two invading armies. Two years earlier, while serving as chief of the Russian general staff, Zhilinski had promised the French that he could have his forces in the field fifteen days after mobilization. Now he was keeping his promise. Far to the rear—his headquarters were more than one hundred and fifty miles from the showdown that was now taking place—he thought he was masterminding a historic victory.

On August 26, fearing a possible sudden forward lunge by Rennenkampf and unsettled by rumors of substantial Russian forces arriving from Rennenkampf's direction, a nervous Ludendorff tried to spring the trap on Samsonov. When he ordered an attack, however, the usually aggressive General Hermann von François (whose name derived from the fact that his ancestors had migrated to Prussia to escape France's persecution of Protestants in the seventeenth century) curtly refused. His troops were still detraining. They did not yet have their ammunition, their heavy artillery, or all of their field artillery. If they attacked, he said, they would have to do so with bayonets. When Ludendorff repeated his order, François went through the motions of complying but limited himself to occupying an uncontested ridge. In yet another of the odd and unintended twists in this oddest of battles, his failure to strike worked to the Germans' advantage. It allowed Samsonov to continue to believe that he was in contact with a weak enemy force and so to continue pushing forward into the trap. Both of his flanks were encountering German troops and being badly mauled, but his communications were so faulty and he had moved the divisions that formed those flanks so far out from his center that throughout most of the day he knew almost nothing of this. The Germans, meanwhile, were eager to engage him. Much of the Eighth Army was made up of East Prussians, men with personal reasons for wanting to clear the region of invaders. One officer, on August 26, found himself directing artillery fire on his own house after the Russians took possession of it.

Zhilinski continued to prod Samsonov to keep moving and to stay on his present course. When the scanty intelligence reaching Samsonov began to indicate that worrisome numbers of German troops were on his left, he sent a message to Zhilinski suggesting that perhaps he should confront this enemy force—whatever it was—by turning toward it. "I will not allow General Samsonov to play the coward," Zhilinski imperiously replied. "I insist that he continue the offensive."

Samsonov followed orders, but by the end of the day he understood that he was in serious trouble. A cautious withdrawal would have been the right next step. But perhaps because of Zhilinski's rebuke, he decided not to pull back, or even to stay where he was while watching the situation develop, but to continue moving forward. Though his flanks were in increasing disarray, and though his troops had no food and were low on ammunition, his center remained intact. That night he sent plaintive messages asking for confirmation that Rennenkampf was coming to join him. There was no answer.

Rennenkampf's failure to move need not be attributed to any hatred for Samsonov. He had lost seventeen thousand men in the Gumbinnen fight, thousands more before that at Stallupönen. He still thought that much or even most of the Eighth Army was to his north, near Königsberg, and that if he moved westward it could fall on his flank. He feared also that a pursuit of the Germans might hurry them across the Vistula before Samsonov could cut them off. Within the limits of the information available, he was thinking rationally if too cautiously.

At this point Moltke, never having been informed that the situation of the Eighth Army was not nearly as alarming as he and

Ludendorff had believed when they met in Koblenz, had his chief of staff telephone Ludendorff and announce that three infantry corps were being detached from the right wing in France and sent by rail to East Prussia. Ludendorff replied that reinforcements were not needed. He did not, however, state categorically that they should not be sent. Moltke ultimately decided to send two corps instead of three, and Ludendorff would find plenty of use for them after their arrival.

At four a.m. on August 27, ready for action at last, François opened an artillery barrage that devastated Samsonov's left wing. Confused and starving Russian soldiers, exhausted after having marched ten and twelve hours daily for a week, broke and ran. François sent his troops forward in what he intended to be an encircling maneuver, but this was blocked. Samsonov, almost incredibly, then resumed the advance of his center. He advanced so aggressively that Ludendorff began to worry that the Russians were going to break through and out of the trap. He decided to call François's corps back to reinforce the center—a move that would have made an encirclement impossible. Hindenburg gently overruled him.

At dawn on August 28 François again attacked and discovered that the Russian left had evaporated. Its troops had had enough and fled en masse into the nearby woods. Everything began to fall into place for the Germans. François, meeting almost no resistance, swung his corps around to the south and cut off Samsonov's escape. Other elements of the Eighth Army converged from the nooks and crannies of the East Prussian landscape. A corps hit Samsonov from the west. A division emerged from the northwest and attacked the Russians there. When a corps that had been stationed to the northeast in case Rennenkampf showed up finally turned around and also marched toward Samsonov, the trap was complete. Samsonov, saying that he had failed the tsar and could not go home, walked off alone into the woods and shot himself.

It was now just a matter of mopping up. But still Ludendorff was tortured, his judgment distorted by his fears. When he learned that François had spread his corps in a thin line along thirty-five miles of road southeast of the encircled Russians, he ordered him to pull it together more compactly. François ignored him; he had witnessed the disintegration of Samsonov's army and knew that the only remaining need was to intercept the bewildered and demoralized enemy soldiers as they came stumbling toward Poland. In the course of the next three days, François's thin net hauled in sixty thousand prisoners. Overall the Germans captured ninety-two thousand Russians. Total casualties were two hundred and fifty thousand for the Russians, about thirty-seven thousand for the Germans. The Germans decided to call what had just happened the Battle of Tannenberg because a nearby town of that name had been the site of a terrible German defeat at the hands of the Poles hundreds of years before. Hindenburg's ancestors had taken part in that battle.

On the same day that Samsonov's left collapsed, a very different story was unfolding to the south. Conrad's Austro-Hungarian armies, having launched an offensive against superior Russian forces in Galicia, were suffering a defeat even worse than the one inflicted on them earlier by the Serbs. Conrad never should have attacked (the Russians outnumbered him by an immense margin, and he had the Carpathian Mountains in which to stand on the defensive), but the fact that he did was not entirely his fault. Moltke, fearing that if Conrad did not engage the Russians they would send more of their armies into East Prussia, had demanded action. Promising to send help within six weeks, as soon as France had been defeated, he tried to ease Conrad's reservations by assuring him that "the fate of Russia will be decided not on the Bug [a Galician river] but on the Seine." In other words, defeating the Russians was for the moment less important than simply keeping them occupied.

In fact, Conrad's offensive may have contributed to making Tannenberg possible. It not only kept Russia's Galician forces in Galicia but drew out of Poland reserves that otherwise might have gone to East Prussia. But the long-term results would be disastrous. Austria's ability to deal with the Russians, to provide Germany with a strong ally, was going up in flames.

And at that same time, almost within sight of Paris, the war in the west was suddenly and decisively changing. Across Europe a mixture of successes and failures was emerging on both sides, a balance so perfect as to seem almost mysterious. It would make victory impossible for either side and ensure that the terrible carnage of the war's first month was barely the beginning.

THE JUNKERS

IT IS PART OF THE STRANGE DARK POETRY OF THE
Great War that the Battle of Tannenberg, the most dramatic and
complete victory achieved by either side in more than four years of
bloody struggle, was fought in East Prussia.

This was sacred ground. Though the most remote and least developed region of the German federation—so remote that in 1914
it lay north of Russian Poland and today it is part of Poland—East
Prussia was in a sense the heart of the Hohenzollern empire. It was
the ancient home of a collection of families who were neither conspicuously wealthy nor particularly distinguished in any other way
but regarded themselves as Germany's rightful leaders and were regarded as such by their king.

Hindenburg himself was a son of one of those families, which
for him made the victory exquisitely sweet. He had saved the taber-
nacle from violation, overnight turning himself into a national idol.
He had kept alive not only Germany's hopes of winning the war but
his kinsmen's hopes that their privileged place in the life of Germany
would not be lost, and that the weaknesses and contradictions of that
special place—its absurdities, even—could continue to be ignored.

The Germany that Hindenburg and his kind dominated had come
a long way since the Franco-Prussian War. Long regarded as the land
of musicians and dreamy philosophers and Black Forest elves, by
1914 it was the most modern, efficient, innovative, and powerful
economy in Europe. Not only in industrial output but in science,
even in the arts, Germany was a powerhouse. Militarily it was so
strong that Britain, France, and Russia had good reason to fear that
even in combination they might not be able to stand up against it.

Politically, though, Germany was a kind of Rube Goldberg device. Its system of government had not evolved like those of Britain
and France, had not been passed down from time immemorial like
Russia's or gradually improvised like Vienna's. Instead it was the creation of one man, Otto von Bismarck. He had designed it not so

much to help Germany become a modern state as to keep modernity at bay—while, not incidentally, concentrating as much power as possible in his own hands. Its deficiencies had been serious from the start, and they grew more serious as the years passed, the world changed, and the Bismarckian system failed to keep pace. By the second decade of the twentieth century, with Bismarck long dead, those deficiencies had become dangerous. Ultimately they would render the system incapable of functioning under the strain of the Great War.

The root of the problem was that the empire, when it was declared in the Hall of Mirrors at the Palace of Versailles in 1871, was completely dominated by Prussia, the most powerful of the German states and the one that had led the others to victory over France. Prussia's king, Wilhelm I, was proclaimed the first kaiser by a jubilant crowd of sword-brandishing princes and generals. It is not possible to understand the peculiar nature of Prussia, or why Prussia would ultimately not only fail but pass out of existence, without understanding what Wilhelm meant when he said that the creation of the new empire felt like a kind of death—that the day it happened was the most miserable of his life.

What he feared was the disappearance of "the old Prussia," a thing that since the Middle Ages had come to be holy not only to his Hohenzollern ancestors but to the kingdom's landholding gentry. The old Prussia was a place like no other in Europe, and its people were like no other. It arose in what is now northern Poland, east

Otto von Bismarck
Germany's Iron Chancellor
"Preventive war is like committing suicide out of fear of death."

of where the Vistula River runs northward into the Baltic Sea, and originally it was the homeland not of Germans but of Slavs. In the thirteenth century the Teutonic Knights, an order of religious warriors created to participate in the Crusades, were invited to help ambitious German nobles seize the territories around the Vistula. The area east of the river was taken from a Slavic tribe called the Prussians, who disappeared from history but left their name to be picked up by the early Hohenzollerns when they needed something to call the insignificant little quasi-kingdom that the Holy Roman emperor permitted them to establish on the outermost fringe of the German world.

Though the Teutonic Knights tried to recruit Germans to settle east of the Vistula, the soil was too poor and the climate too dank to be powerfully attractive. The Slavs were permitted to remain if they converted to Christianity. Gradually, as the generations passed, German and Slavic families intermarried and gave rise to an ethnically mixed local aristocracy that came to be known as the Junkers. The irony is that when Prussia became dominant in Germany and Prussia's military might made Germany one of the great powers of Europe, the world saw this half-Slavic Junker elite as the most Germanic of Germans. Some of the most Prussian of the Prussians—for example, Karl von Clausewitz, who wrote the classic *On War*—bore names that were Slavic in origin.

The Junkers were not, as a group, rich, and their estates were not large. Life was often almost hardscrabble, requiring much labor and generating barely enough income to sustain a marginally aristocratic way of life. The people who grew up on those estates were, as a rule, neither particularly well educated nor particularly sophisticated. They were pious and provincial Lutherans, upright and sober, hardworking and hardheaded and often hard-hearted, with a deeply ingrained reverence for the law, for property rights, and for the class structure atop which they sat. What came to distinguish them above all was their almost mystic bond not to Prussia as a nation but to the Hohenzollern dynasty. This bond developed slowly, and what made it develop was the advantage it offered the Junkers. In return for their loyalty, they were assured nearly exclusive access to the more coveted positions in the Prussian army and civil service—opportunities for their sons to win a measure of power, snatches of glory, and sometimes, though not commonly, real wealth. The Junkers evolved into Prussia's hereditary military elite. A culture emerged that was unlike any other in Europe, an army, it was said, that happened to have a country attached to it. This arrangement was threatened by the Napoleonic wars at the start of the nineteenth century and by the revolution that shook Europe in 1848. (Prussian king Frederick William IV horrified the Junkers by granting the revolutionaries a constitution, though this was rescinded at the first opportunity.) Having barely survived these upheavals, the Junkers emerged more conservative than ever, their hatred of change in any form deeply ingrained.

Kaiser Wilhelm I was not a man of great intellect, but it was perceptive of him to find little to celebrate in the creation of his empire. In the most visible ways, the empire was a glorious achievement, one that put him at the pinnacle not only of Germany but of Europe and appeared to multiply the opportunities available to the Junker elite. But on a deeper level the new situation was fraught with difficulties, especially for the Junkers. First among the problems was the question of legitimacy. The Junkers were determined to maintain their special connection to the crown and the prerogatives that came with it. The Hohenzollern dynasty wanted much the same thing. But if the Junkers had been a small slice of the population of Prussia, they were an even smaller part of the empire. In the new world of giant industries and great cities, they remained a tribe of provincial farmers without real economic power.

Inevitably, the Junkers came to seem an anachronism to the increasing numbers of Germans who knew how different things were in America, Britain, and France. As agriculture became a less important element in the economy, what little prosperity the Junkers traditionally had came under threat. The richer and more educated the German nation grew, the more prominent among the peoples of the world, the odder it seemed that East Prussia should dominate as it did.

What is most odd is how little resistance to Junker privilege other Germans displayed during the half century that the empire existed. Bismarck, again, made this possible. Though he had deep roots in Junkerdom and for much of his early adulthood had worked a family farm, Bismarck was never entirely trusted or accepted by his own class. (His mother, an outsider from the professional classes, had given young Otto an education that made him more cosmopolitan than was considered quite proper.) He was permitted to create the empire only on the basis of certain understandings. He made it not a centralized country but a federation in which Bavaria, Baden, Württemberg, and other states were allowed semiautonomy under their ruling families while Prussia stood supreme. He fashioned a constitution that concentrated nearly all political power in the hands of the monarch (who remained King of Prussia in addition to being kaiser) and the officials he appointed. He did so with the tacit understanding that the Junkers would continue to be specially favored. And so they were. Though it would have been politically awkward to fill every important chair with Junker bottoms, the Junkers could always be confident of getting more than their statistically fair share. Bismarck's system made ample room for economic liberalism—that was good for revenues and so for the army—but made political liberalism, and above all democracy, impossible.

This was not a system well equipped to deal with the tensions of a modern capitalist and industrial society, and even Bismarck had trouble making it work. After he passed from the scene, his successors were sometimes barely able to keep its wheels turning. In a free market for agricultural products, the Junker estates would have sunk into bankruptcy; to save them, the government enacted so many tariffs on food imports that Germany became what has been described as "a welfare agency for needy landowners." There was a legislature, the Reichstag, but it had little power. As men infected with democratic and even socialist notions became increasingly common within the Reichstag, the Junkers kept them in check by joining forces with industrial interests in what came to be called the alliance of iron and rye. They were greatly helped by an electoral system that gave more votes to people with land and money.

In consequence, thousands of Germans of professional attainment, people with education and talent, had no real voice in public affairs. The political life of the nation remained in an atrophied state. The Reichstag, though it did have a role in budget-making, was otherwise little more than a debating society. In England and France the members of the legislature—the House of Commons and the Chamber of Deputies—chose the prime minister. Thus they, and the people who elected them, had a real connection to the levers of power and could regard themselves as a kind of ultimate authority. Their counterparts in Germany were essentially impotent. Their parties, instead of being contenders for control of the government, were held at arm's length by a government that remained very nearly what it had been in feudal times: a collection of Junkers chosen by their king. The result, in the short term, was widespread public indifference to politics. In tougher times it was a recipe for alienation.

The problem of how the Junkers were going to keep intact what remained of the old Prussia extended into the army. With all their limitations and faults, the Junkers were never expansionist imperialists. They were not even German nationalists; many of them cared little about Germany except as an extension of Prussian power. What they wanted was the little world of their forebears, and every new stage of growth, of expansion, made that world less sustainable. Even the expansion of the army, unavoidable in the arms race that gripped the great powers of Europe at the start of the twentieth century, deeply troubled many traditionalists. Just as for a good Junker the only thoroughly acceptable army officer was an East Prussian of acceptable family background, so too the only dependable recruit was an ignorant and docile East Prussian farm boy. The increasing numbers of alternatives—growing hordes of city dwellers and factory workers, many of them infected with modern notions—were aliens and not to be trusted.

Tensions associated with such questions cost Erich Ludendorff, himself an upstart whose father had sold insurance, his place on Moltke's planning staff just a year before the start of the Great War. He had become convinced that a larger army was essential if the Schlieffen Plan was to remain practicable in the face of increasing French and Russian strength, and he began pressing for the creation of six new army corps. When only half this total was approved, he continued to demand more. After being told to keep silent but refusing, he was banished from the staff. This was a blow; it meant that, in case of war, Ludendorff would not become Moltke's chief of operations. He had brought this punishment down on himself by touching two sets of raw nerves. The government and the army did not want to stir up resistance in the Reichstag by asking for too big an increase in military spending too quickly. And many influential Junkers knew that it would not be possible to find nearly enough young aristocrats to fill the officer billets in six new corps. Outsiders in large numbers would have to be given commissions. The biggest army that Germany was capable of mustering was not likely to be the kind of army that the Junkers could continue to control.

While Ludendorff departed Berlin for Düsseldorf and command of

Erich von Falkenhayn
A model Junker
*Described the German army
as "a broken instrument"
at the end of 1914.*

a nonelite regiment (his not being given a unit of the Prussian Guard was seen as another rebuke), the man who would become his archenemy was rising almost effortlessly. Four years older than Ludendorff, Erich von Falkenhayn had been a favorite of Kaiser Wilhelm's since 1911, the year he had become a regimental commander in the guard. Just a year after that he was made a major general, and in 1913 he was promoted again and made minister of war. Though surprising even to his fellow generals, this rapid ascent (and the still greater promotion that would soon follow) is explicable in terms of Falkenhayn's background. He was very nearly the ideal Junker. Tall and slender, haughtily elegant in bearing, he had been raised on a modest farm in easternmost East Prussia to a family that traced itself back to the twelfth century and the Teutonic Knights and had produced one of Frederick the Great's generals.

He was a pure product of the old Prussia, and Ludendorff's opposite in far too many ways.

Chapter 10

To the Marne

*"We must not deceive ourselves.
We have had successes, but we have not had victory."*
—Chief of Staff Helmuth von Moltke

As big and confused and drawn out as it was, the Battle of Tannenberg was a model of clarity and simplicity compared with the more famous Battle of the Marne, which has come down to us in history as the fight that saved Paris but in fact was settled by one side's decision not to fight.

Far more than Tannenberg, "First Marne" (there would be another huge and crucial encounter in almost exactly the same place four long years later) was not a single great encounter but a weeks-long series of maneuvers punctuated with bursts of ferocious combat. It involved millions rather than mere hundreds of thousands of troops, and they were stretched out over vast expanses of territory. Its starting date is hard to pinpoint; traditionally it has been placed on or about September 5, but events began flowing toward it during the closing days of August, at the time when the Germans were destroying the Russian Second Army in East Prussia.

All the French and German forces, as August ended, were still arranged in the order in which they had begun the war. Kluck's First Army was still the outer edge of the Schlieffen right wing, but now it was well south of Belgium, setting the pace for the rest of the German line as it swung down toward Paris like a great hour hand in counterclockwise motion.

South of Verdun, the German left was also pushing toward Paris but making much slower progress. In place after place there, in woods and fields and on stony hilltops, men were dying by the thousands in savage, obscure fights the names of which are almost completely forgotten today.

Movement had always been most pronounced at the other end of the line, where Lanrezac and the British Expeditionary Force were no longer even attempting to turn and fight. The situation north of Paris had become almost surreal: hundreds of thousands of weary French and British doggedly trudging southward, hundreds of thousands of equally weary Germans following in their tracks, and almost none of them doing any actual fighting. Looming over all was the idea of Paris, the supreme symbolic prize but also a great if dubiously prepared fortress with a sixty-mile perimeter of defensive walls and artillery emplacements. Bülow, when he got there, was supposed to besiege it while Kluck went around. One question was whether Bülow could get there. Another was whether, having arrived, he could take the city. The Germans had encircled Paris in the Franco-Prussian War but failed to get inside.

Schlieffen had predicted that a decisive battle would take place on or about the fortieth day after mobilization. As the twenty-fifth day arrived, then the thirtieth, mounting tension and the increasing exhaustion of the troops as they drew closer to Paris made it seem that a climax of some kind had to be imminent.

The commanders on both sides had little reason to feel that they were in charge of, rather than reacting to, events. At German supreme headquarters, which had been moving westward in cautious steps from Berlin to Koblenz and then on to Luxembourg, the continuing progress of Kluck and Bülow was igniting celebration. Moltke did not join in. As his armies penetrated deeper into France, clashing with or pursuing the French according to what Joffre was ordering his generals to do on any given day, his contact with them became increasingly tenuous. (Radio was still a new and highly unreliable medium.) Keenly aware of his own blindness, under no illusions about his ability to direct the campaign with so little knowledge of what was happening at the front, Moltke became unwilling to issue orders. Expectations became cloudy, prediction impossible, every shred of information precious. Would Kluck, his army worn down and outrunning its lines of supply, really be able to circle all the way around Paris and still remain capable of attacking the French? Or might the best chances now be in Alsace and Lorraine, where the French defenses were reported to be vulnerable?

Joffre, even as he surrendered great expanses of countryside, was accomplishing important things. He was making it impossible for the Germans to close with his left and force it into a fight it had little chance of winning. And he was maintaining good order: his armies remained fully under control in conditions that could easily have produced chaos. They were staying in formation and following routes and timetables worked out by headquarters, their every move planned, coordinated, and carefully directed.

But this couldn't continue. Unless they were going to march past Paris and leave it to the Germans, at some point soon the French, and presumably the British, were going to have to stop and make a stand. When this was going to be possible, or where or even whether, remained unclear. The sphinxlike Joffre was sharing his plans, if at this point he had any, with no one.

Lanrezac was daily more pessimistic. Sir John French, thinking it likely that France had already lost the war, was talking of saving his little army by pulling it out of the line, perhaps even taking it back to England. The only really aggressive commander remaining in the area was Kluck, but his aggressiveness was taking a heavy toll on his troops. They were now advancing an average of more than twenty miles daily, each man burdened with his ten-pound rifle and his sixty or more pounds of gear as the hot dry summer of 1914 blazed on. Often, at the end of a long day on the march, the men had to spread out across the countryside and forage for meat and the vegetables that were, providentially, being harvested in abundance at summer's end. As they moved sixty and then eighty miles beyond the farthest points that their railway support could reach and their horses began to collapse, the problem of supply threatened to become unmanageable.

The German cavalry had difficulty operating in this country; rivers, canals, woods, and other obstructions slowed and complicated every foray. When horsemen closed with enemy troops, they found themselves no match for machine guns and magazine-fed rifles. The labor of constantly moving the artillery, and with it thousands of shells, was terrible and endless.

Things were little better for the French and British, but as they drew closer to Paris they were moving toward rather than away from supplies and reinforcements. They were able to make increased use of the railroad network centered on the capital.

The city was seized with fear. Politicians asked if Joffre intended to retreat forever, got no answer, and called for his dismissal.

On Lanrezac's left the British were retreating so fast—the infantry given only four hours' rest in twenty-four, the cavalry even less—that the Germans no longer knew where they were or if they remained a factor that had to be reckoned with. In his haste, French left Lanrezac's flank once again exposed. But the Germans too were having a hard time keeping their armies aligned. Kluck was outrunning Bülow and beginning to realize that somewhere out in front of him—a juicily tempting target—was Lanrezac's naked flank. On August 27 he had received fresh instructions from Moltke reiterating that his mission continued to be what it had been from the beginning: to march around Paris and proceed from there to the east. By this time, however, Moltke was receiving sketchy reports of a buildup of forces near Paris. The activity being reported was the birth of the French Sixth Army, which Joffre had let General Gallieni have for the defense of the capital. Moltke saw these new forces, correctly, as a threat to his right wing.

Accordingly, on August 28 he sent new instructions. Kluck was to stay not just in line with Bülow but slightly behind him—"in echelon" is the military term. But he neglected to say anything about the new threat from the direction of Paris, thus making it impossible for the First Army's commander to see how these new orders were necessary or even made sense. To put himself in echelon with Bülow, Kluck would have had to stop his advance for a day or more, perhaps even turn around. In doing so he would have thrown away his chance to hit Lanrezac, perhaps to start the unraveling of the French left, and possibly to win the war. He decided that if he continued to move forward but shifted toward the southeast, he could fulfill the letter of his new orders, bring his army closer to where Bülow was heading if not literally to Bülow's side, and continue his pursuit. Destroying Lanrezac's army, or at a minimum pushing it eastward out of Bülow's path and away from Paris, would surely satisfy the spirit of his instructions even if it violated their letter. And so Kluck crossed the River Marne on September 3 and pushed on. He felt free to do so because he was ignorant of one important fact and wrong about another: ignorant of the new French army taking shape to the west, wrong in believing that the mysterious disappearance of the British meant that the BEF was no longer an effective fighting force.

Among Joffre's problems, at this point, was getting the BEF back into the war. He needed the cooperation of Sir John French— something easier said than done, the British commander having decided that his allies were not only unreliable but doomed. Joffre hoped that he could restore French's confidence, and make a try at blocking the German advance in the process, by having Lanrezac attack Bülow's army near the towns of St. Quentin and Guise. Learning that Lanrezac was unwilling, Joffre went to Fifth Army headquarters and confronted his old friend in person. When Lanrezac continued to resist, Joffre threatened to dismiss him. "If you refuse to carry out my orders," Joffre was reported to have said, "I'll have you shot!"

Joffre went next to the BEF's headquarters at Compiègne. There, in the grand château that had become a base of operations for the BEF's staff, he all but begged French to turn his army around, assuring him that in doing so he would be protected by Lanrezac on his right and by the new Sixth Army on his left. French refused. He said that the sorry state of his army left him with no choice but to take it south of Paris for at least ten days of refitting and recuperation.

Lanrezac's attack had begun, meanwhile, and quickly developed into a hard fight. The French were soundly whipped on their left; Lanrezac had again been correct in warning that the German Second Army would overwhelm them there. But on the right, at Guise, the battle seesawed inconclusively and the French were able to hold. At one critical point their position was saved when the dashing General Louis Franchet d'Esperey, a flamboyant character whom the admiring British troops called Desperate Frankie, led an almost theatrical counterattack on horseback, his sword held aloft, accompanied by unfurled regimental banners and a band playing "La Marseillaise." The other side had its moment of glory after the Prussian First Foot Guards, as elite a unit as any in the armies of Germany, was thrown back and seemed in danger of falling apart. Prince Eitel Friedrich, the second of Kaiser Wilhelm's six sons, took command. Beating on a drum, he rallied the troops and led them forward in a successful counterattack. The prince survived, but the son of the commander of the guards corps was killed. Most of the generals on both sides were men in their fifties and sixties, and many had sons in uniform. As the fighting went on and losses continued to be heavy among junior officers responsible for leading attacks and organizing defenses, news that yet another general's son had been killed became almost commonplace.

At Guise, Lanrezac found himself with both flanks so dangerously exposed that he had no choice but to withdraw. Bülow, though he declared victory in reporting to Moltke, had taken heavy casualties. He decided that he had to stop for a day. He asked Kluck to move closer—farther east—to support him. Kluck, hungrier than ever for Lanrezac's flank, agreed. Joffre had had no choice but to accept Lanrezac's decision to resume his retreat. Without the BEF he lacked the manpower to make a stand, as desperately necessary as a stand of some kind was beginning to be.

French, no doubt, was guided in his obstinacy by the instructions he had received from Kitchener before leaving England: to regard his army as independent of the French and to protect it from destruction. Despite his concerns, however, the condition of the BEF was something short of desperate. The corps commanded by Smith-Dorrien, having borne the brunt at Mons and Le Cateau, was indeed no longer fully functional. But the other corps, the one commanded by Haig, had still seen little hard fighting. Haig had, in fact, agreed to an appeal from Lanrezac to move his corps north to join in the fight at Guise, but before he could act he was countermanded by French. This had deepened Lanrezac's sense of betrayal.

In his reports to London, the BEF's commander had much to say about his lack of confidence in the French but little about his own movements and plans. It was only obliquely, from other sources, that the cabinet learned that he had denied Joffre's urgent request for help, that he had decided to move behind Paris, and that he was even considering a withdrawal to the coast. Kitchener sent a wire asking him to explain. When French replied that he was indeed withdrawing south of the River Seine and that "my confidence in the ability of the leaders of the French Army to carry this campaign to a successful conclusion is fast waning," Kitchener shot back another message informing him that he was expected to "as far as possible conform to the plans of General Joffre for the conduct of the campaign." In response, French again gave vent to his disdain for his allies and emphasized how unready the BEF was to withstand further combat. It may have been the haughtiness of his tone—"I think you had better trust me to watch the situation and act according to circumstances"— that prompted Kitchener to don his field marshal's uniform and cross the Channel by destroyer that night.

The next afternoon Kitchener, French, and Joffre met at the British embassy in Paris. Joffre told the Englishmen that with trainloads of troops pouring in from the east, he now had two armies in formation—not only the Sixth at Paris but also a new Eighth, which was to be inserted immediately east of the Fifth. The Germans, he said, were probably unaware of these new units, and almost certainly could not know that a new French army now lay on their right. Thus it might now be possible to turn the tables—*if* the BEF would come forward. French argued, complained, and resisted. As he would acknowledge in his post-war memoir, he not only had no confidence in his allies but was deeply offended by Kitchener's sudden appearance in France. He thought that His Lordship was undercutting him with the impossible French and insulting him by wearing his uniform rather than attire appropriate to what he now was: a representative not of His Majesty's army but of the government. Kitchener took French into a separate room. It is not clear what was said there. French's account states that he put Kitchener in his place in no uncertain terms, but the aftermath of the conversation makes that unlikely. When the two men emerged, there was no further need for discussion. French was prepared to take the BEF north.

Joffre went to Fifth Army headquarters, took his old friend Lanrezac off for a stroll in a nearby schoolyard, and there relieved him of his command. Lanrezac may have saved France by being first to understand what the Germans were planning in Belgium, by putting his army in the path of the Schlieffen right wing, and by being the only army commander unwilling to sacrifice his troops in futile attacks. He had absorbed blow after blow from the invaders, performing well at Charleroi and Guise and keeping his army in good order through its long retreat. But now he had become expendable. Was he, as Joffre would claim, too worn down to remain capable of acting decisively? Or was Joffre unable to forgive subordinates who disagreed with him and turned out to be right? It hardly mattered. What did matter was that Lanrezac hated Sir John French and French hated him. Joffre was determined to do everything possible to satisfy the British. Lanrezac's successor was obvious: Franchet d'Esperey, Desperate Frankie, a particular favorite of the BEF.

Farther to the east, the front was aflame. Moltke was hurling his Third, Fourth, Fifth, Sixth, and Seventh Armies against the French Fourth, Third, Second, and First. The Germans were repulsed, fell back, and were counterattacked in their turn. Joffre by this point was firing generals almost wholesale; by September 6 he would replace the commanders of two of his original five armies, seven corps, and twenty infantry and four cavalry divisions. Other officers were rising to fill the vacancies. Ferdinand Foch, after performing well as a corps commander in Lorraine at the start of the war and heroically during the retreat that followed, was promoted to command of the new Ninth Army. Henri Philippe Pétain, whose brigade had distinguished itself as part of Lanrezac's command in early fighting in Belgium, was given a division.

Uncertainty gave way to panic. The government left Paris for Bordeaux on the Atlantic coast. But in the midst of it all Joffre remained impassive, maddeningly silent, *calm*. No matter how alarming the situation, how terrible the emergency, the tall and rotund generalissimo never seemed disturbed. He became famous for the care he took always to have a good lunch followed by a nap, end the day with a good dinner, and always get a full night's sleep (in bed at nine, back at work at five). Even when things seemed to be at their worst, he made his staff understand that under no circumstances was his rest to be disturbed. But between mealtimes and bedtimes he was steadily on the move, using a big touring car driven by a Grand Prix racing champion to

General Joseph Joffre
"If you refuse to carry out my orders, I'll have you shot!"

make repeated visits to his generals, especially those on the left. Thus he was able to keep himself in touch with events and observe his subordinates in action. He said so little during these visits, had so little to say even when told of shocking events or asked for guidance, that some of the men who dealt with him decided that he was little better than a stately idiot and that his principal contribution was his tranquilizing example. He has also been described as viciously political and self-serving behind his rocklike exterior. He has been accused of dismissing subordinates not so much for failure to perform as for becoming potential rivals or, worst of all, for showing their chief to have been wrong.

But fools rarely succeed under the kinds of circumstances confronting Joffre, and it was not by accident that things began to turn his way. The decision to strip troops from his embattled right wing and send them west by rail was his, and the consequences could not have been more important. The number of divisions facing the German right, seventeen and a half on August 23, rose to forty-one by September 6. In this way, gradually, Joffre gave himself one of the greatest advantages a general can have: superior mass. He magnified the significance of what has to be considered Moltke's most grievous mistake: his incremental removal of nearly a quarter of a million men from the right wing, which was left without enough divisions to do all the things needing to be done. Thus the great strike force that had obsessed Schlieffen literally to his dying breath found itself outnumbered. It was also enfeebled: bone tired, short of supplies, and increasingly without food. It is possible that Moltke's greatest mistake was in sending reinforcements to his left, which was in no danger, and accomplishing little of importance, instead of to Kluck and Bülow, where they might have made all the difference. Apparently he was discouraged from doing so by the Belgians' destruction of key railways.

The French, in contrast to the Germans, were reaping all the benefits of fighting on home ground with interior lines of communication. Every twenty-four hours another thirty-two trains arrived at the capital loaded with troops and guns from the east.

Even now, however, Joffre could find no way of stopping the Great Retreat. He continued to wait and watch. "A natural reluctance to abandon even provisionally more of our national territory," he wrote to the minister of war as late as September 3, "must not make us engage too early in a general battle that might be launched in unpropitious circumstances."

Moltke now made a change of strategy so far-reaching that it amounted to the end of the Schlieffen Plan. Kluck and Bülow were told to halt their advance. They were to stand in place and face west against whatever forces the enemy was mustering near Paris. All the other German armies were to return to the attack. The Third Army was to fight its way southward to the River Seine. The Fourth and Fifth were to advance west of Verdun, the Sixth and Seventh to force a crossing of the Moselle River. The goal of this last two pairs of armies was to break through on their respective fronts, link up, and so encircle the entire French right in the area around Verdun. Never in history had there been an encirclement on such a scale; it would dwarf Tannenberg. There was no way of being confident that such a thing was possible. The irony of this sudden and drastic shift was that its success would depend on the ability of the German left wing to get past the very fortifications whose strength had made the Schlieffen Plan seem necessary in the first place.

It is difficult to judge whether Moltke's change of thinking was rooted in a genuine expectation of success or a desperate sense that his right wing was doomed to failure. It is certain that he did not believe the triumphal reports that continued to arrive at his headquarters and cause his staff to rejoice. "We must not deceive ourselves," he told a member of the German government. "We have had successes, but we have not had victory. Victory means annihilation of the enemy's power of resistance. When armies of millions of men are opposed, the victor has prisoners. Where are ours? . . . The relatively small number of captured guns shows me that the French have withdrawn in good order and according to plan. The hardest work is still to be done."

As remote as he was from the action, as inadequate as knowledge of the situation on the ground was, his intuition was sound.

THE FRENCH COMMANDERS

IT MAY SEEM ODD, AT FIRST, THAT ALMOST NO STUDY of the French army at the start of the Great War fails to discuss Louis Loyzeau de Grandmaison. Though a professional soldier, Grandmaison never achieved high rank, and he did nothing of importance in the war before being killed in combat (a fate his critics could consider poetic justice) in 1915.

Still, he deserves the attention. Three years before the war began, as a lieutenant colonel in the Operations Bureau at army headquarters, Grandmaison delivered a pair of lectures that thrilled the generals in his audience. He heaped scorn on French military doctrine since the Franco-Prussian War, laying out a new approach that soon came to dominate the nation's military thinking.

His doctrine, remembered today as "the cult of the offensive," was rooted in the idea of all-out, nothing-held-back aggressiveness as the key to success in battle. And the word *cult* really does apply; by 1914 any French officer who failed to embrace it would find himself out of favor, suspect, and professionally sidetracked.

The consequences were fateful, almost fatal. Faith in the offensive, in the power of men wielding bayonets to overcome any enemy, caused Joffre's generals to send their troops against German machine guns and artillery again and again in the war's opening months, and to persist even as casualties rose to horrifying levels.

Such thinking had been in the air of France in the prewar years. Philosopher Henri Bergson, later a Nobel Prize winner, was preaching that *élan vital,* the life force, had a mystic power that if harnessed could enable the nation to defeat even the richer, more populous Germany next door. Also preaching was Ferdinand Foch, the gifted strategist and military theorist who in 1908 became director of the War College in Paris. He declared in his books and lectures that "the will to conquer is the first condition of victory." Grandmaison, enrolled at the college during Foch's tenure, became his disciple. Within a few years he was carrying belief in *l'offensive à l'outrance,* in aggressiveness without restraint, far beyond what even Foch had intended. His words were received with relief and gratitude by an officer corps tired of being told that the best France could hope for was to defend itself against the German military machine. Grandmaison's insistence that the generals should expect to *conquer* sounded to them like music.

The triumph of the new doctrine came in 1911. That July, six months after Grandmaison's electrifying lectures, a showdown over strategy erupted in France's Supreme War Council. The newly appointed commander in chief, a certain General Victor Michel, put before the council his ideas on how to prepare for war with Germany. He had based his proposals on a concept called offense-in-defense: if war broke out, he said, France's armies should be arrayed at varying distances from the nation's eastern borders, where they would wait for the Germans to make the first move (impressively, Michel foresaw their invasion of Belgium) before deciding where and how to strike back. There were advantages to such an approach. It would enable the French to know where the enemy forces were situated and where they were going before deciding how best to move against them. It could require the Germans to commit themselves, perhaps overcommit themselves, and wear themselves down on the offensive while all French options remained open. But to the believers in *offensive à l'outrance,* such thinking was heresy and not to be endured. It rejected what Grandmaison had taught them: that "for the attack only two things are necessary. To know where the enemy is and to decide what to do. What the enemy intends to do is of no consequence." Such words imply a willful blindness to the realities of the battlefield, but the beliefs on which they were based prevailed. Michel found it necessary to resign, and the Grandmaisonites became not just popular but the dominant faction in French planning.

It now became necessary to find a replacement for Michel, and the same General Joseph Gallieni who in 1914 would become military governor of Paris emerged as the pivotal figure. He had opposed Michel's proposals, but less on grounds of theory than because of concerns about Michel's personal capabilities and his intention, in case of war, to use reserves as frontline troops (something that the French generals abhorred but the Germans would do with significant success).

Minister of War Adolphe Messimy offered the job to Gallieni himself, who was respected on all sides, and Gallieni declined. Asked to take a few days to reconsider, the general again immediately said no. He explained that he regarded himself as too old; he was sixty-two at the time, in uncertain health, and within two years of retirement. He said also that he had too little experience in the command of large armies, and that—what was most important to Gallieni himself, and most reflective of his integrity—he could not honorably assume an office that he had caused to become vacant by failing to support Michel. Asked to suggest someone else, Gallieni offered the name of Paul-Marie Pau, a respected senior officer who had lost an arm in the Franco-Prussian War. Pau however was politically unacceptable, a practicing Catholic at a time when republican France suspected Catholics of seeking a restoration of the monarchy. (Foch, educated by the Jesuits and brother of a Jesuit priest, carried the same liability.) Gallieni's second suggestion, Joseph Joffre, presented no such difficulties. He was solidly republican but beyond that a man of no politics. Though he enthusiastically accepted the doctrines of Grandmaison, he was no ideologue and in fact displayed little interest in ideas of any kind. He had never attended any of the higher staff schools, had only limited experience in the command of large numbers of troops, and had never attempted to school himself in higher strategy. Because of the gaps in his experience, his appointment surprised many people. Gallieni, however, knew what he was doing—he knew Joffre well.

Gallieni (his family, like the Bonapartes, were of Italian origin and had come to France from Corsica) was twenty-one years old when, on the very day in 1870 that France declared war on the Germans to start the Franco-Prussian War, he graduated from the St. Cyr military academy. He was commissioned in the marine infantry, a branch that destined him for service in the network of colonies that France was establishing around the world. After the war, in which he became a prisoner of the Germans, he went on to assignments in West Africa, the Caribbean, and Tonkin (Vietnam). Responsibility came easily to him, and with responsibility came promotion. By the time he was forty he was governor of French Sudan, and for nine years beginning in 1896 he was governor general and commander in chief of the new colony of Madagascar in the Indian Ocean. After putting down a rebellion there, he introduced an administration that made Madagascar not only peaceful but prosperous.

General Joseph Gallieni
*Prepared the way for the
Battle of the Marne.*

One of the needs at Madagascar was a system of fortifications for the colony's new naval base, and in 1896 an army engineer less than three years younger than Gallieni joined his staff and took charge of construction. This was Joffre, who had started life as the eldest of eleven children of a village barrel-maker in southern France, won a scholarship to Paris's elite École Polytechnique, interrupted his education to participate in the defense of the city when the Germans besieged it, and upon graduation took an army commission after failing to land the civilian job that was his first choice. He married young, but when his wife died he volunteered for foreign assignments. By 1885 he was chief engineer in Hanoi, and in 1893 in Africa he won his first moment of fame and promotion to lieutenant colonel by successfully taking command of an expedition to Timbuktu after his commanding officer was killed by rebellious tribesmen. He was recalled to France in 1900, Gallieni five years later, and by 1911 the two were among the army's highest-ranking generals.

Joffre did not disappoint as commander in chief. He upgraded the army's training and equipment and reformed the promotion system, giving more weight to ability and performance than to political connections or ideological correctness. (He insisted, as a condition of his appointment, on being allowed to select an aristocratic Catholic, the talented General Noël de Castelnau, as his chief of staff.) He was content to leave the Operations Bureau, where strategies were hatched, in possession of Grandmaison and his followers. Under their influence, investment in artillery, especially heavy artillery, was seriously neglected. The reasons were obvious: bayonets, not big guns, were the supreme weapon.

In May 1913 the bureau issued two sets of new field regulations. One was for corps and armies, and the other for units of division size and smaller. Both were saturated with the Grandmaison doctrine. "Battles are beyond everything else struggles of morale," they declared. "Defeat is inevitable as soon as the hope of conquering ceases to exist. Success comes not to him who has suffered the least but to him whose will is firmest and morale strongest." Grandmaison's staff also drafted Plan 17, which discarded the Michel approach and was duly approved by Joffre as the definitive statement of how his armies would be deployed when war came. The French equivalent of the Schlieffen Plan, Plan 17 disregarded even the possibility of a German move into western Belgium, an inexplicable decision in light of what Michel had concluded years earlier. Though Plan 17 was more flexible than the Schlieffen Plan, leaving Joffre free to decide where and when to attack, that he would attack was beyond question.

Adherents of the cult of the offensive did very well during these prewar years. Foch, who could have claimed to be the cult's grandfather, was given command of a division in 1911 and of a corps just one year after that. That at the beginning of the war he was not given an army is surprising; the religious factor is likely the reason. Grandmaison was promoted to brigadier general and did not long survive.

Those deemed to have insufficient faith in the offensive did not prosper. One such officer was Henri Philippe Pétain, who as a lowly assistant professor of infantry tactics at the École de Guerre had attracted unfavorable attention by persistently warning of the vulnerability of flesh and bone when confronted with twentieth-century firepower. In July 1914 he was, as a result, a mere colonel of fifty-eight, an obscure outsider expecting to be retired soon. Even mobilization and the start of the war brought no advancement. When the French Fifth Army assembled (its commander, Lanrezac, was only four years older than Pétain), Pétain commanded a regiment and was still a colonel.

Gallieni had sunk into what appeared likely to be terminal obscurity. Before the start of the war, he had come around to Michel's view that if Germany invaded France, it would do so through Belgium.

He had tried to explain his concerns to Joffre and the deep think-
ers of the Operations Bureau but was ignored. Relieved by Joffre of
responsibility for anything, he retreated to his country home and a
kind of preretirement limbo. In July his wife died, and on the last day
of the month he was informed by Messimy that, in case of mobilization, he would be named Joffre's principal deputy and successor
if the need for succession arose. When mobilization came, he was
given the promised title but no staff, no duties, no information about
what was happening, and no access to the man whose chief support
he was supposed to be. Joffre evidently regarded him as a rival and
wanted to give him no opportunities to be seen or heard. Thus Gallieni, a thin and almost comically homely man with tiny eyeglasses
and a flamboyantly bushy mustache, spent the opening days of the
war alone. He followed the opening movements of the armies on his
maps and worried.

He was unresentful. As the danger to Paris increased and alarmed
members of the government began to complain of Joffre's retreat and
talk of replacing him, it was Gallieni, to whom the politicians would
cheerfully have given the supreme command, who urged patience.

Chapter 11

Back from the Marne

*"Attack, whatever happens! The Germans are at
the extreme limit of their efforts. Victory will come
to the side that outlasts the other."*
—Ferdinand Foch

Fears that war would mean a continent in flames had literally come true by early September. The entire Western Front from Paris to the Alps had turned into a vast bloody slugfest in which more than a dozen armies were fully and simultaneously engaged. In the east, Galicia was the scene of a massive running battle between the Russians and the Austro-Hungarian forces of Field Marshal Conrad. In East Prussia the German Eighth Army was following up its victory at Tannenberg with a pursuit aimed at the destruction of Rennenkampf's Russian Second Army near the Masurian Lakes.

Nothing was more critical than the point where the German right met Joffre's left. Still unaware of the existence of a new French army at Paris, seeing no reason to halt as Moltke had ordered, Kluck continued to plunge southward in search of the French Fifth Army's flank or, failing that, whatever remained of the BEF. But his army was in danger of crumbling even as it advanced. "Our soldiers are worn out," a member of Kluck's staff was recording as early as September 2. "For four days they have been marching forty kilometers a day. The ground is difficult, the roads are torn up, trees felled, the fields pitted by shells like strainers. The soldiers stagger at every step, their faces are plastered with dust, their uniforms are in rags; one might call them living rag-bags. They march with closed eyes, and sing in chorus to keep from falling asleep as they march. The certainty of victory close at hand and of their triumphal entry into Paris sustains them and whips up their enthusiasm. Without this certainty of victory they would fall exhausted. They would lie down where they are, to sleep at last, no matter where, no matter how. And, to give their bodies a drunkenness like that of their souls, they drink enormously. But this drunkenness also helps to keep them up. Today, after an inspection, the General [Kluck] was furiously angry. He wanted to put an end to this collective debauch. We have just persuaded him not to give severe orders. It is better not to be too strict, otherwise the army could not go on at all. For this abnormal weariness abnormal stimulants are needed. In Paris we shall remedy all this."

And Paris still seemed an achievable goal. The British, despite Sir John French's promise to rejoin the fight, were continuing to withdraw. (French would later explain this as an effort to connect as quickly as possible with reinforcements and supplies before turning north.)

Then everything changed. Intercepted German radio messages, some of them not in code, informed the French that Kluck was now heading not toward Paris but southeast. Papers found on a German officer who had taken a wrong turn and been shot dead by a French patrol indicated the same thing—showed not only where the various parts of Kluck's army were but where they had been ordered to go. Joseph Gallieni, quickly grasping the implications, assembled a small group of reconnaissance pilots and told them where he wanted them to fly the next morning and what he wanted them to look for. They returned with the news he wanted: Kluck's army, formed into six thick columns, was indeed moving to the southeast. In doing so it was exposing its right flank to Gallieni's new Sixth Army. The opportunity for a counterattack appeared to have come at last.

Gallieni ordered the Sixth Army, still only half-organized and made up largely of inexperienced reserve troops, to get ready to move. Then he took off by car to visit British headquarters and get Sir John French to join in the attack. French was away when Gallieni arrived, and the staff officers who received this unexpected visitor did so with amused and barely concealed contempt. One of them said later that Gallieni, ungainly and unkempt in his high laced-up black boots and yellow leggings, looked like "a comedian," like somebody "no British officer would be seen talking to."

After three hours of waiting, having extracted from his hosts nothing better than a promise that someone would telephone him after French's return, Gallieni departed. The promised call, when it finally came, informed him that the BEF would be continuing its move to the south; the British had checked with Joffre and received no encouragement to cooperate with Gallieni. Wherever he turned, Gallieni found little cooperation. Joffre, though he approved Gallieni's attack, said he wanted it launched from south rather than north of the Marne. This would blunt its impact, Gallieni thought, and he spent long minutes on the telephone changing Joffre's mind. Worse, Joffre was reluctant to send the additional troops needed for hitting the Germans hard. Worst, when he understood just how rich in opportunity this situation was, how laden with potential glory, Joffre took the Sixth Army back from Gallieni, who then returned to Paris.

Kluck was too good a soldier to offer quite as fat a target as Gallieni hoped. Though he continued his advance, he did not leave his flank uncovered. He moved one corps—two infantry divisions plus artillery—to the River Ourcq to his west, where it took up defensive positions facing Paris and was directly in the path of the French Sixth Army as it began moving eastward. This corps, though made up of reserve units, was commanded by a capable officer, a General von Grönau. Grönau moved his troops onto high ground, had them dig in, and used his artillery to tear at the French as they began arriving on the scene. The result was a battle so singularly uneven that it proved to be the undoing of any hopes for the quick destruction of Kluck's army. On the German side, success gave a last burst of life to Kluck's hopes of breaking the Entente left.

On September 5 France, Great Britain, and Russia entered into the Treaty of London, by which they formalized their Triple Entente and pledged that none of them would enter into a separate peace with Germany. On the same day a member of Moltke's staff, Lieutenant Colonel Richard Hentsch, arrived at Kluck's headquarters to alert him to the existence and probable approach of a French force in the west. While he was there, a report arrived from Grönau stating that he was under attack (by that same French force) and needed help. Kluck was not alarmed. He assumed that this was less a serious French assault than an attempt to trick him into halting the First Army's advance. But he did the prudent thing and detached another corps to go back to support Grönau. He also sent a message to Bülow, asking for the return of two corps that he had earlier made available to the Second Army. Bülow was reluctant to comply, knowing that doing so would weaken his own depleted right wing. If he had known that the BEF was now moving northward in his direction—French had turned around at last—he might not have agreed. But under the circumstances, with Kluck under attack and no one currently attacking him, Bülow had little choice. Though Kluck's reinforcement of Grönau was a turning point, the first backward movement by a sizable unit of the German right wing, it did not mark the end of the offensive. Kluck was still bent on victory.

He was no longer defining victory as Paris, however, and that became a problem in terms of troop morale. For the soldiers of Kluck's army, arrival at Paris meant an end to their long ordeal. This is clear in a German officer's account of an episode on September 3. "One of our battalions was marching wearily forward," he wrote. "All at once, while passing a crossroad, they discovered a signpost, on which they read: Paris, thirty-seven kilometers [twenty-three miles]. It was the first signpost that had not been erased. On seeing it, the battalion was as though shaken up by an electric current. The word Paris, which they have just read, drives them crazy. Some of them embrace the wretched signpost, others dance around it. Cries, yells of enthusiasm, accompany these mad actions. This signpost is their evidence that we are near Paris, that, without doubt, we shall soon be really there. This notice board has had a miraculous effect. Faces light up, weariness seems to disappear, the march is resumed, alert, cadenced, in spite of the abominable ground in this forest. Songs burst forth louder." But now, with Kluck's shift to the southeast and the move back to the Ourcq, the dream of Paris had to be let go.

The Germans were not, however, out of fight. By nightfall on September 5, Grönau's artillery had badly disordered the advance of the French Sixth Army, which was growing rapidly as reinforcements continued to arrive. At one point, when the French appeared to be on the verge of panic, a dashingly aggressive officer named Colonel Robert Nivelle, a man who like Pétain had nearly reached retirement age without achieving the rank of general, led a heroic intervention with field artillery. Rolling his guns through the French infantry to where they could fire point-blank, he drove the Germans back.

After dark, judging correctly that he was badly outnumbered and that his stand had given Kluck sufficient time to adjust, Grönau pulled back from the Ourcq. In doing so he probably saved his corps. The Sixth Army attacked by moonlight but found the Germans gone. Kluck, understanding now that the threat from the west was a serious one, marched his entire army back across the Marne toward the Ourcq. As always, he was thinking aggressively, looking not just to defend himself but to encircle and destroy his enemy.

But by now Kluck was laden with problems. He was no longer engaged with the main line of French armies, no longer in position to contribute to the decision that appeared to be approaching along that line. In pulling back to the Ourcq, he had opened a thirty-five-mile gap between his army and Bülow's, and in the next few days this gap would grow even wider. Between Kluck's and Bülow's armies were only two divisions of cavalry and a few units of light infantry—not nearly enough to hold off a significant enemy advance. The exploitation of such gaps had been the key to many of Napoleon's victories.

"Kluck marched his entire army back across the Marne to the Ourcq" is far too simple a statement to reflect what was happening that day. Every such movement meant yet another long and hurried trek, to be followed by yet another firefight, for men who had been marching and fighting for weeks. Kluck's men had been issued no rations in five days. They rarely got more than a few hours of sleep. Their uniforms were in tatters, and their boots were falling off their feet as they struggled to drag with them the cannon and shells without which they could neither attack nor defend themselves. And they were now outnumbered.

The French Sixth Army, though fresh, was still too raw and unorganized to be a match for Kluck's now-hardened veterans. When it renewed its attack on September 6, it again ran headlong into waiting German artillery. The result was another disaster— not merely a failure to dislodge Kluck's troops from their hastily improvised defenses but a debacle that left the French units shattered. Kluck's hopes of finishing off the Sixth Army began to look more plausible.

Off to the east, the French were falling back in several places. The anchoring strongpoint of their line, the great fortress of Verdun, was in deepening jeopardy. By September 6 it appeared possible that the entire line from Verdun southward might begin to come apart. Moltke's new plan, dual breakthroughs leading to a grand climactic encirclement, also was beginning to seem plausible.

The hour of decision had arrived, and everyone knew it.

The BEF was feeling its way northward in company with a corps of French cavalry and making extremely slow progress. More by happenstance than design, it inched into the gap between Kluck and Bülow. This was a frightening and exciting development. If the two German armies converged, the BEF would be crushed. If the British pushed forward swiftly, on the other hand, they might break through to the German rear and create havoc there.

They did not move swiftly. In part this was because of mistakes: one British division spent an entire day moving in a confused circle, so that at nightfall its lead units ran into the supply train that formed its own tail end. But it was also an understandable reaction to having enormous enemy forces on both of its flanks. What the British didn't know was that neither Kluck nor Bülow was in any position to turn on them. Kluck, on their left, was occupied with the French Sixth Army. Bülow—now at the end of the continuous German line, with his own flank bare— was in a hard fight with Franchet d'Esperey's Fifth Army. Because of his return of two corps to Kluck, Bülow was weak on his right. He was being hammered there by a division commanded by the recently promoted Brigadier General Pétain, and his troops were being pushed back and out of position. Kluck and Bülow were alarmed when they learned that the British were now between them, and both reacted characteristically. Kluck swung some of his troops around to face a possible advance by the British but continued to batter away with his main force at the French. Bülow began to plan a withdrawal in which both his army and Kluck's would pull back at least ten miles and reconnect north of the British.

The fighting intensified all along the line. The French were on the defensive everywhere but on their left; on the right the need was to hold the line against German armies trying to deliver the breakthrough that Moltke had ordered. Gallieni began filling Paris taxicabs with soldiers and sending them out to swell the ranks of the army that Joffre had taken from him. His energy, despite so many reasons to be grudging, caused the Sixth Army to keep growing hour by hour.

The madness rose to its climax on September 8 and 9. The outcome would depend on whether any of the German armies in the east could crack the French line or, alternatively, whether the German First Army or the French Sixth could destroy its opponent. The Battle of the Marne became a series of crises following one after another until finally something broke down.

September 7 had ended with Foch's new army separated from General von Hausen's German Third Army by a treacherously soggy expanse of territory called the Marais (the Marsh) of Saint-Gond. Foch, determined as always to carry the fight to his enemy but naturally assuming that advance across a swamp was not feasible, had launched an attack around both sides. Both wings of this attack ran into strong German defenses and were thrown back with heavy loss of life. Hausen's staff, meanwhile, had been exploring the interior of the Marais and discovering that it was not at all as impassable as its name indicated. Early the next morning the Germans moved across it without the kind of artillery preparation that would have alerted the French, mounted a dawn charge that caught Foch's center unprepared, and forced it out of its defenses. Though this clash was a defeat for the French, it added to Foch's growing reputation. "Attack, whatever happens!" he had said at Saint-Gond. "The Germans are at the extreme limit of their efforts. Victory will come to the side that outlasts the other!" He had been pushed back, but his line had not snapped. The Germans still did not have the breakthrough on which all their hopes depended.

Not only at Saint-Gond but at many places along the front, the French, like the Germans, were near the end of their resources. "For my part I preserve only a confused and burning recollection of the days of 6th and 7th September," a cavalryman would observe afterward. "The heat was suffocating. The exhausted troops, covered with a layer of black dust sticking to their sweat, looked like devils. The tired horses, no longer off-saddled, had large open sores on their backs. The heat was burning, thirst intolerable . . . we knew nothing, and we continued our march as in a dream, under the scorching sun, gnawed by hunger, parched with thirst, and so exhausted by fatigue that I could see my comrades stiffen in the saddle to keep themselves from falling." A French general painted an even darker picture. "What a mess!" he exclaimed. "What a shambles! It was a terrifying sight . . . no order in the ranks . . . straggling along . . . Men emaciated, in rags and tatters, most without haversacks, many without rifles, some marching painfully, leaning on sticks and looking as though they were about to fall asleep."

Moltke, a hundred and seventy miles to the north at his headquarters in Luxembourg, was getting almost no reports from Kluck or Bülow. Kaiser Wilhelm was in Luxembourg also, complete with an enormous staff of his own and advisory groups that also had staffs. This may be one reason why Moltke, unlike Joffre, never ventured out to see for himself what was happening at the front. He had reason to fear that in his absence the kaiser, hungry for a great victory and (as Moltke told his wife in the deeply gloomy letters he sent home every day) incapable of understanding the dangers of the situation, would take personal command and do something disastrous.

While Hausen was attacking Foch across the Marais de Saint-Gond, Moltke again sent Colonel Hentsch, the trusted head of his intelligence staff, off to the front by car. Hentsch's instructions—oral rather than written, so that whether he ultimately exceeded his authority can never be conclusively answered—were to visit the commanders of all but the two southernmost German armies, determine whether they were or were not in trouble, and send reports back to Moltke.

Hentsch worked his way westward along the front, visiting the headquarters of the Fifth Army of Crown Prince Wilhelm, the Fourth Army of Duke Albrecht of Württemberg, and Hausen's Third Army. He found the situation of each of these armies acceptable, with no reason for alarm, and informed Moltke accordingly. It was evening when he got to Bülow's Second Army, and there the picture began to darken. Bülow had Franchet d'Esperey's battered but hard-fighting army in front of him, and between himself and Kluck to the west was a gap that now stretched for as much as fifty miles and had been penetrated by the BEF. A shaken Bülow told Hentsch that only a "voluntary concentric retreat" by his army and Kluck's could avert disaster. This was not a loss of nerve on Bülow's part. His position was dangerously weak. Pétain's attacks had captured tactically important terrain, so that Bülow's right was continuing to be pushed back into an increasingly awkward position.

And this was only one of many emergencies. At the eastern end of the front, the French First and Second Armies were holding high ground near the Alsace border and repelling repeated attacks. The commander of the Second Army, Castelnau, absorbing news of the death in combat of his son (he would lose two more sons before the war ended), reported to Joffre that he had to withdraw from Nancy or risk the loss of his entire force. Joffre told him to hold where he was at all costs for at least another twenty-four hours. To Castelnau's north, around Verdun, the French Third Army was hanging on to rubble that once had been stout French fortifications and slaughtering the oncoming Germans.

Far away in East Prussia, at the Masurian Lakes, Hindenburg's Eighth Army was closing in on Rennenkampf's retreating Russians. Even that wasn't the end of it: in Galicia, the main forces of the Austro-Hungarian army were engaged with more than two million Russian troops in yet another series of battles that were as confusing as they were bloody but in the end would prove little less important than Tannenberg and the Marne.

The only truly fluid sector of the Western Front remained as before the front's western extreme. An incident of September 8 indicates just how confused the situation was, with large and small French, German, and British units in motion all over the landscape. In the afternoon a detachment of French cavalry suddenly came upon a caravan of three German automobiles. When the horsemen started toward them at a gallop, the drivers quickly turned and sped off. In one of the cars was Kluck, moving among the dispersed units of his army. Still tirelessly combative despite his sixty-eight years, Kluck remained confident of his chances. For three days the French had been throwing themselves at his position on the Ourcq. Having withstood these attacks and worn the French down, he now saw an opportunity to finish them off before some other enemy force—possibly the BEF—could fall on him from the rear. He ordered an attack. The goal this time would be an encirclement of the Sixth Army from the north. The assault would be led by a corps of infantry under General Ferdinand von Quast. This was one of the corps that Kluck had lent to Bülow and then taken back. It had crossed Belgium and France with Kluck, had fought at Mons, had been in the thick of things all through the campaign, and was very nearly spent. At the end of the day Kluck said in a message to his army that "the decision will be decided tomorrow by an enveloping attack."

Early on the morning of Wednesday, September 9, Hentsch set out to find Kluck. The roads were jammed with soldiers and equipment moving eastward. This was Kluck's shift of part of his army to positions from which it could protect its rear, along with the usual pathetic streams of refugees. The direction of the flow gave the appearance of an army in retreat. It appeared to support Bülow's appeal for a general pullback. It took Hentsch five hours to cover fifty miles, and during those hours Quast unleashed his attack. The Sixth Army didn't simply retreat—it fell apart. French troops fled in all directions.

In East Prussia, Rennenkampf was still withdrawing, trying to escape destruction at the hands of a German force that was smaller than his but brimming with confidence in the aftermath of Tannenberg. Desperate, he sent two of his divisions in a heroic, suicidal attack on the advancing German center. Both divisions were destroyed, but they accomplished their purpose. The Germans were stopped, and what remained of Rennenkampf's army got away.

On the plains of Galicia, Conrad's long fight with the Russians was ending in disastrous—almost final—defeat. He had moved against the Russians despite being grossly outnumbered, despite learning that the Germans would not be able to support him, and despite the disappointment of learning that Romania with its army of six hundred thousand men would not be joining the Central Powers as hoped. He had sent thirty-one divisions against the Russians' forty-five infantry and eighteen cavalry divisions, and the results were inevitable. The Austrians were driven back a hundred and fifty miles to the Carpathian Mountains. Conrad had lost more than four hundred thousand men—one hundred thousand killed, an equal number taken prisoner, two hundred and twenty thousand wounded—plus 216 pieces of artillery and a thousand locomotives. He had lost more than a fourth of the manpower with which he had begun the war, and among that fourth were insupportably large numbers of Austria-Hungary's commissioned and noncommissioned officers. Less than a month and a half into the war, his capacity for dealing effectively not just with the Russians but even with smaller enemies was nearly exhausted. From now on Vienna would be not so much Berlin's junior partner as a weak and burdensome appendage. The Germans would grow fond of saying that being allied with the Hapsburg empire was like being "shackled to a corpse."

Conrad himself shared in a personal way in the immensity of the tragedy. "I have one of my sons seriously ill," he lamented, "and the son that I idolized in a mound of corpses at Ravaruska."

Around Verdun, where the French were hanging on by such a thin thread that Joffre twice authorized the commander of his Third Army to retreat if necessary, September 9 brought a final, convulsive German assault. The French had no reserves left, no way to seal up any holes in their front. They did, however, have the remains of their immensely strong defenses. In the years leading up to 1914 the main Verdun forts had been greatly improved, with deep sand and loose rock piled onto the original masonry and reinforced concrete as a top shell. Heavy artillery had been installed within armored retractable turrets. As a result, these forts could withstand direct hits even by the kinds of monster guns that had wrecked Liège and Namur, and they could also keep attackers under continuous fire. The rough terrain stiffened French resistance by making retreat almost impossible. At the same time it worked against the Germans by compounding the difficulties of bringing in artillery. The French not only kept their line intact but butchered the attackers as they themselves had been butchered in their earlier offensives. On the night of September 9 the Germans made a last effort to punch through, but in the darkness they ended up blasting away at one another.

When Hentsch arrived at First Army headquarters at last, Kluck was away, keeping a close eye on the victory unfolding at the Ourcq. Hentsch talked with Kluck's chief of staff, explaining that the BEF was now north of the Marne, that Bülow was planning to withdraw, and that there was no alternative to Kluck's withdrawal as well. While they were talking, a message arrived from Bülow reporting that he was starting his retreat. This left nothing to discuss or decide, so Hentsch departed. When Kluck learned of Hentsch's visit and the plans for a retreat, his first reaction was to resist, to insist as always on pushing forward. When he learned that Bülow was already withdrawing, however, he had no choice but to yield. With Bülow moving north, his army was so vulnerable that nothing except retreat could possibly save it.

From the German perspective, the story of the Schlieffen right wing had a melancholy final chapter. At almost the same moment when Kluck was accepting the necessity of retreat, Quast's corps was tearing apart the last of the disintegrating French defenses. Nothing lay between it and Paris but thirty miles of open, undefended ground. It must have been like having an impossible dream come true: all they had to do was keep marching. But then new orders arrived from Kluck: Quast was to call off his attack and turn back. The First Army was retreating.

It was over. Quast's men had more marching to do, but now they would be heading back in the direction from which they had come.

No one felt the melancholy more deeply than Moltke. "I cannot find words to describe the crushing responsibility that has weighed upon my shoulders during the last few days and still weighs on me today," he wrote his wife. "The appalling difficulties of our present situation hang before my eyes like a dark curtain through which I can see nothing."

THE BRITISH COMMANDERS

ON AUGUST 3, 1914, WHEN *THE TIMES* OF LONDON reported that Field Marshal Sir John French had been chosen to lead the British Expeditionary Force to France and the war, it was eager to make its readers understand that this was the best of all possible appointments in the best of all possible armies.

"There was not a moment's hesitation," the newspaper said of French's selection. "No painful canvassing of candidates, no acrimonious discussion, no odious comparison of the merits of respective generals, no hint of favoritism, of Party intrigue."

This happy state of affairs was possible, it explained, because French "surrounds himself with capable leaders and staff officers, and not only brings his troops to a high degree of efficiency, but also makes his officers a band of brothers, and establishes a good comradeship between all arms and all ranks."

As an early exercise in wartime propaganda, in helping the public take pride in its armed forces and the men chosen to lead them, this report was exemplary. As a reflection of the truth, it did not fall far short of absurd. In the art of generalship, French was rarely better than ordinary. An ability to identify and make use of the best available men was not among his talents, and no knowledgeable observer would credit him with displaying, or raising the forces under his command to, impressive levels of efficiency.

As for the officer corps being free of acrimony or favoritism or "party intrigue," *The Times* could hardly have departed more shamelessly from the truth.

The British army of 1914 was a considerably more effective military instrument than it had been at the start of the century, when it experienced great difficulty (and had to resort to savagely brutal methods) in defeating a ragtag collection of guerrilla-farmers in South Africa's Boer War. Since then it had improved its training, started at least to modernize its equipment, and established a general staff on the Prussian model. But in many ways—in its leadership above all—

it remained stubbornly in the past. It was the army of a predemo-
cratic culture in which a majority of the population was poor and
powerless, the benefits of empire were reserved for a tiny elite, and
people at every level of society were expected to accept the status
quo as the natural order of things.

Britain was changing, however, and slowly the army, heels dug
in, was being pulled along. At the start of the 1870s the government
had ended the time-honored system by which officers bought their
commissions and promotions, often paying fortunes to rise to the
senior ranks. Even after this reform, however, only gentlemen were
regarded as suitable candidates for the officer corps. The term *gentleman* applied only to individuals with the right family antecedents,
and not even gentlemen found it possible to survive as junior officers
without private sources of income. Late in the nineteenth century,
when an outstanding young sergeant named William Robertson was
offered the rare opportunity to accept a commission, he was unable
to do so because his expenses as a junior lieutenant (everything from
uniforms to mess fees to a share in supporting the regimental band)
would have been at least four times his salary of £100. When they
did somehow manage to become officers, "rankers" were commonly
shunned and even viciously hazed by gentlemen unwilling to accept
them.

This was the system that had produced Sir John French and the
other generals at the head of the BEF. They were gentlemen almost
to a man, the only exception being the aforementioned William
Robertson, who by then had risen, almost miraculously, to major
general. (He had taken a commission in the Army of India, where
expenses were lower, and his tailor father made his uniforms.) As
gentlemen they adhered to a code that elevated amateurism in all
things to a supreme virtue. Hunting, shooting, polo, and weekend
gatherings at country estates were proper activities. Too much seriousness—for example, too much reading even about military history
and strategy—definitely was not. The kinds of disputes over theory
that racked the French officer corps were unimaginable north of the
Channel, where nobody in uniform cared about theories. The right
connections, and a proper degree of aristocratic insouciance, were
highways to advancement. They made the army an especially attractive career for the less intelligent sons of the very best families.

French himself, sixty-one years old in August 1914, was the son of a naval officer and had begun by entering the Royal Navy at age fourteen. At twenty-two he had switched to the cavalry, the most elite (and expensive) branch of the army, and thereafter he advanced with the help of impressive social skills and his dash as a horseman. In 1899, freshly promoted to major general, he went out to South Africa as commander of a cavalry division, and there he won fame for his boldness while learning to hate, and coming to be hated by, the famous and powerful Lord Horatio Kitchener. In 1912 he reached the summit, becoming chief of the imperial general staff, and though he resigned at the time of the Curragh Mutiny, this was such a respectable, gentlemanly act of disloyalty that it proved no obstacle to his later selection as head of the BEF. By the time he went to France he was a stocky, almost dumpy-looking man in late middle age, stolid, unimaginative, and sour. Kitchener still regarded him as reckless, and so ordered him in writing to do nothing that would put his army at risk.

French's chief of staff in the Boer War had been a young colonel named Douglas Haig, who as a lieutenant general became commanding officer of one of the BEF's two corps. A member of the whiskey-making Haig family of the Scottish borderlands, regarded by the true aristocrats as unworthy of admission to one of the elite

Field Marshal Sir John French
"My confidence in the ability of the leaders of the French Army . . . is fast waning."

cavalry regiments at the start of his career, Haig was not noticeably more intelligent than French but was gifted at acquiring influential patrons. He entered the military academy at Sandhurst at an unusually late age, having first attended Oxford, where he spent the standard three years but failed to earn a degree. Early in his career he failed the examination for entry to the army staff college but was rescued by his connections. His sister, married to a member of the Jameson whiskey dynasty who held the honorary position of keeper of the Prince of Wales's racing yachts, got the Duke of Cambridge (an aged member of the royal family) to have the entry requirements waived on Haig's behalf.

In the Boer War he attracted the favorable attention of Lord Kitchener while building a friendship with French. Haig was handsome and unmarried and outspoken about his disdain for women, and the lifelong bachelor Kitchener always approved of officers of that type. Haig won French's gratitude by lending him the immense sum of £2,000, which French needed to extract himself from woman trouble. After South Africa Haig was made aide-de-camp to King Edward VII, a position that provided visibility in the loftiest circles. In 1905 he married the Honorable Dorothy Vivian, favorite maid of honor to the queen. The Haigs were the first nonroyal couple ever to be married in the chapel at Buckingham Palace; he had proposed seventy-two hours after meeting the lady, and one wonders what his bride thought when he wrote that "I have often made up my mind on more important problems than that of my own marriage in much less time." Within a year of his marriage, when the British army entered the modern world by creating a general staff for the first time, Haig's friends in government and at court campaigned to have him made its chief. This proved impossible, the candidate being only forty-four and never having held a major command, but afterward he never stopped angling for the job. He was still angling even as the BEF prepared for deployment, whispering his doubts about French's abilities to everyone who would listen from his friend King George down, rarely failing to add that of course he was prepared to serve wherever needed. He always got a respectful hearing despite being wrong on a wide range of subjects: before the war he had pontificated that "the role of cavalry on the battlefield will always go on increasing" and "artillery only seems likely to be effective against raw troops." It was typical of Haig that he was able to maintain a good relationship with French while despising him and trying to undermine him. Haig despised almost every one of his brother officers except his own subordinates—so long as those subordinates were sufficiently submissive. Almost paranoid in his belief that he was constantly being conspired against, he responded with endless intrigues of his own.

The other of the two corps with which the BEF began the war was supposed to be headed by James Grierson, but he dropped dead of a heart attack upon arriving in France. This was a stroke of luck for Haig. Grierson was a gifted infantry commander who, in the summer war games of 1912, had defeated Haig so completely, so humiliatingly, that the whole operation was brought to a stop ahead of schedule. Sir John French asked for Herbert Plumer as replacement for Grierson, but Kitchener sent Horace Smith-Dorrien instead. Again Haig was lucky. Plumer, like Grierson, was not only a very senior lieutenant general but an extremely capable one. He would have been a formidable rival, not only because Kitchener liked him but because years earlier, as an examiner at the staff college, he had expressed a scaldingly negative opinion of his student Haig. But he arrived in France under a tremendous handicap: French's intense dislike. He was under a microscope from the start, his every decision questioned.

French's deputy chief of staff was the BEF's archschemer, the wily Henry Wilson, who as director of military operations during the Curragh Mutiny had served as the Unionists' spy inside the general staff and was described by Haig as "such a terrible intriguer, and sure to make mischief." As Britain's primary liaison to the French general staff before the war, Wilson had made important friends in Paris, and almost from the start of the war he was trying to use them to get himself promoted to chief of staff. He and French were united by their hatred of Kitchener, whom Wilson called "as much an enemy of England as Moltke."

When French's chief of staff was replaced, the job went not to Wilson but to "Wully" Robertson, who had performed brilliantly as the BEF's quartermaster general in the opening weeks of the war. He was not French's choice—Kitchener had blocked Wilson's appointment—and not for the first time he paid the price of being up from the ranks. French regularly dined with Wilson while excluding Robertson. Haig was more careful in showing his disdain. "He means well and will succeed, I feel sure," he wrote of Robertson. "How much easier though it is to work with a *gentleman*."

At the top of this dysfunctional brotherhood stood the stern and iron-willed Kitchener. Like Joffre and Gallieni, he had spent most of his life in far-flung colonial outposts. At age twenty he had interrupted his training to serve as a volunteer on the French side in the Franco-Prussian War, and soon thereafter he was sent to the Middle East with the Royal Engineers. From then on his career was the stuff of legend. By 1886, when he was thirty-six, he was governor of Britain's Red Sea territories. He became commander of the Egyptian army in 1892, a baron after putting down a rebellion in the Sudan in 1898, and Viscount Kitchener of Khartoum after leading the British forces to victory in the South African War (burning the farms of the Boers and herding their wives and children into concentration camps, where they died by the thousands). He was commander in chief in India from 1902 to 1909, battling endlessly with the viceroy, and from 1911 he ruled Egypt and the Sudan as British proconsul. By 1914 he had little knowledge of English society or politics and was so accustomed to being in charge of everyone and everything around him that he had virtually lost the ability to cooperate or delegate.

He happened to be in England during the crisis of August 1914. (He had been invited to come home to be made an earl.) When the

Lord Kitchener of Khartoum
"This is not war!"

war began, he was on a ship preparing to return to Egypt. Asquith called him back to London, asking him to join the cabinet as secretary of state for war. He agreed but without enthusiasm; his sole remaining ambition was to become Viceroy of India, and until that became possible, he preferred to remain in Cairo. In his new post (he did not relinquish his commission as the army's senior field marshal, or the salary that went with it) he was the first serving officer to hold a British cabinet post since the 1600s. He was a hard and shrewd man and a living legend, as familiar a symbol of the empire as the King. Other members of the government and the army were skeptical when he predicted that the main German invasion force would cross Belgium before entering France, incredulous when he warned that the war was going to last three years at least and that Britain would have to build an army of a million men. He was right on all points. In the end not a million but five and a half million men would serve in His Majesty's armed forces.

Chapter 12

Flanders Fields

"The enemy fought desperately for
every heap of stones and every pile of bricks."
—Official German account of First Ypres

The French and British, though jubilant at and in many cases astonished by the German withdrawal from the Marne, were badly battered, worn out, and running low on essential equipment. Many were almost too exhausted to move. "After five days and nights of fighting," one English soldier wrote, "decimated, spent and hungry, we are lying on the bare earth, with only one desire in our hearts—to get ourselves killed." And they were short of shells for their artillery. It is one measure of the sustained intensity of this new kind of warfare that the French faced critical shortages of ammunition for the 75mm cannon, their most effective field artillery piece, because only ten thousand rounds were being produced per *day*. This was barely 20 percent of the need.

For any number of such reasons, the armies of the Entente failed to close with the retreating Germans or exploit the huge gap that had prompted their withdrawal. They did not attack in force until after the German First, Second, and Third Armies had settled into fortified positions on high ground north of the Aisne, the next east-west river north of the Marne. By then it was too late. The fighting was ferocious, with the British especially taking heavy losses in trying to force the Germans out of their defenses, but it accomplished essentially nothing. "Three days ago our division took possession of these heights and dug itself in," a German officer wrote his parents. "Two days ago, early in the morning, we were attacked by an immensely superior English force, one brigade and two battalions, and were turned out of our positions. The fellows took five guns from us. It was a tremendous hand-to-hand fight. How I escaped myself I am not clear. I then had to bring up supports on foot . . . and with the help of the artillery we drove the fellows out of the position again. Our machine guns did excellent work; the English fell in heaps . . . During the first two days of the battle I had only one piece of bread and no water. I spent the night in the rain without my overcoat. The rest of my kit was on the horses which had been left behind with the baggage and which cannot come up into the battle because as soon as you put your nose up from behind cover the bullets whistle. War is terrible. We are all hoping that a decisive battle will end the war."

The fighting was anything but decisive, however, and the British and French had lost whatever opportunity they might have had to force the Germans into a Great Retreat of their own. Some of France's richest mining and industrial areas remained in German hands.

The Germans made a final unsuccessful effort to capture Verdun, which if taken would have given them an anchoring strongpoint from which to keep their armies on the Marne. Without Verdun, the Marne line was untenable. In pulling back, the Germans had to abandon valuable real estate—notably the rail junctions of Reims, Amiens, and Arras.

British and French headquarters bubbled with optimism, with Sir John French predicting that his troops would be in Berlin within six weeks. Erich von Falkenhayn, the fifty-three-year-old general and former war minister who replaced a bitterly disappointed Moltke as head of the German general staff (illness was given as the excuse for Moltke's reassignment), was quicker to see that the war was now likely to be a long one. He encouraged Chancellor Bethmann Hollweg to pursue a negotiated settlement on either the Eastern or Western Front—perhaps a negotiated peace with Russia that would persuade the French too to come to terms. Woodrow Wilson's government in Washington had already offered its services as a mediator, and soon Denmark would do the same. It was already too late, however, for such overtures to bear fruit. None of the warring governments thought they could possibly accept a settlement in which they did not *win* something that would justify all the deaths. The war had become self-perpetuating and self-justifying.

Though not as ebullient as French and Joffre, Falkenhayn believed that a decision in the field was still possible. Within days of taking command he was developing plans for a fresh offensive, and before the end of September he was putting those plans in motion. He had two primary aims: The first was to correct the Germans' single greatest vulnerability, their exposed right wing, which came to an unprotected end north of Paris. The other was to capture Antwerp, the last stronghold of the Belgian army, the greatest port on the north coast and, so long as it remained in enemy hands, a redoubt from which the Belgians and British could strike at Germany's lines of supply.

Falkenhayn could have solved the problem of his exposed right wing by pulling back still farther—by withdrawing, for example, to a line running from the Aisne to Brussels or even east of Antwerp. But this would have surrendered most of the gains of Moltke's offensive, demoralizing the armies and outraging all of Germany. Instead, he took an aggressive approach, deciding to extend his line westward along the River Somme all the way to the Atlantic. Such a move was feasible only if the French failed to defend the region northwest of Paris, but if it succeeded the Germans would control all of northern France, the ports on the English Channel included. They would be positioned to resume the move on Paris from both the east and the west.

Like Kluck and Moltke before him, however, Falkenhayn was trying to do too much with the resources at hand. To strengthen his right, he ordered the transfer of the Sixth and Seventh Armies from Alsace and Lorraine (where they would be replaced by two of the several new armies now being formed). This was not easily accomplished; the movement of a single army required 140 trains, and only one rail line connected the German right more or less directly with the left. Partly because of the resulting delays, Falkenhayn's offensive westward along the Somme was not as strong as it should have been; it ran into a new French Tenth Army and was stopped. That left Antwerp, which though more strongly fortified than even Liège (it was surrounded by nineteen large, state-of-the-art, powerfully armed forts plus a number of smaller ones, and defended by nearly a hundred thousand troops) seemed a more achievable objective.

Before the Germans began hauling their siege guns to Antwerp, General Sir Henry Wilson, the BEF's deputy chief of staff, suggested transferring the BEF from France, where it was tucked between two French armies on the Aisne, to its original position beyond the end of the French left. This meant, as the line now stood, moving the British troops to the Flanders region of western Belgium. Such a change, Wilson said, would put the BEF where it logically ought to be: close to the ports from which it drew its supplies, reinforcements, and communications. Sir John French was reluctant at first, thinking no doubt of the advantages of having one of Joffre's armies on each of his flanks. But when Winston Churchill pointed out that, if the BEF were in Flanders, the guns of the Royal Navy would be able to support it from the Channel, he changed his mind. A career cavalryman, French began to see the flat terrain of Flanders as a place where his mounted troops could prove their value at last, spearheading a plunge eastward into central Belgium and from there to Germany.

Now it was Joffre's turn to be reluctant. He feared that if the BEF again got into trouble, and if French started thinking again of taking his army back to England, a position on the coast would make withdrawal all too easy. When French announced that he was moving north with or without Joffre's assent, Joffre urged him to proceed slowly and cautiously. French instead moved so swiftly that soon Joffre was blaming his haste for the success of German attacks along the Aisne and blaming his commandeering of scarce railcars for the Germans' capture of the industrial city of Lille. Falkenhayn's movement of troops and guns toward Antwerp had by this time awakened Joffre to the danger on his left. He moved his Second Army, which Foch now commanded, north into Flanders along with the British. The BEF's destination was west of Ypres, a lace-manufacturing center endowed with treasures of medieval architecture and suddenly important as the nexus of roads leading eastward into central Belgium and westward toward France and the Channel ports.

When the Germans began systematically crushing Antwerp's fortresses with their artillery, the British were more alarmed than the French. For a major port so close to England to fall into the hands of an enemy possessing a navy as substantial as Germany's would be no trivial matter. Winston Churchill hurried a small force of marines—all that were available—to help with the Belgians' defense. Churchill himself went with it, met with Belgium's king and queen, conferred with the Belgian commanders, and involved himself in the search for some way to hold the Germans off. He sent a telegram to the government in London, proposing that he be appointed British military commander in Antwerp and replaced as First Lord of the Admiralty. Members of the cabinet were said to have laughed when they read this message; it seemed typical Winston, too eager for adventure, constantly hatching wild ideas, always thinking himself capable of anything. Kitchener, not only the secretary of state for war but the living symbol of the British military (it was his face that fiercely told young Englishmen that "Your Country Wants You!" on the recruiting posters), did not regard Churchill's suggestion as ridiculous at all. He knew the first lord fairly well and had apparently been impressed. He knew that Churchill had been almost alone in recognizing the importance of the Channel ports even before the turnaround at the Marne and in urging that something be done to secure them. (Nothing had been.) Kitchener proposed that Churchill be made a lieutenant general on the spot. The prime minister did not agree.

By October 6 the Belgians themselves, staggered by round-the-clock German shelling, decided that Antwerp could not be saved and that giving it up was the only way to save their army. Churchill departed for home, and a day later sixty thousand Belgian troops under the command of their king left the city. Demoralized, nerves stretched, they hurried west until they were almost in France, arranging themselves in a defensive line north of Ypres behind the barrier that the River Yser forms as it flows to the sea. There they waited while Foch's army began to extend their line to the south and British troops filed into Ypres from the west. The Germans, meanwhile, took possession of Antwerp. The end of resistance there freed four German corps, most of an army, for other uses. Whole corps of new, barely trained reserves, many of them student volunteers, were arriving in Belgium from Germany.

As commander of all German forces, Falkenhayn faced far

broader problems than did French or even Joffre. He had the vast war in the east to deal with—a war that now stretched across five hundred miles of front and in which his forces and those of the Austrians continued to be outnumbered by frightening margins. The heroes of Tannenberg—Hindenburg and Ludendorff—were scrambling to cope with the Russian threat not only to East Prussia but to Silesia to its south and, farther south still, to the badly shaken armies of Vienna. Two things were imperative. The Germans had to move south to connect with the Austrian left, shoring up Conrad's armies before they were overrun. And, not having enough troops to defend at every threatened point, they had to go on the offensive. They had to strike a blow that would stop the Russian juggernaut before it became unstoppable.

Hindenburg, Ludendorff, and their operations chief, Max Hoffmann, decided that they could satisfy both imperatives simultaneously by taking a newly formed Ninth Army south by rail to the vicinity of Warsaw, a key base of operations for the Russians. There they could link up with the Austrian left and join it in a move against the four armies that the commander in chief of the Russian forces, the tsar's cousin Grand Duke Nicholas Romanov, was sending toward Silesia. The Eighth Army would remain behind to guard East Prussia. Ludendorff, bold as usual, wanted to take part of it south too, but Falkenhayn rejected this proposal as too risky.

These movements set the stage for the First Battle of Warsaw, in which eighteen German and Austrian divisions found themselves in the path of sixty Russian divisions advancing on a 250-mile front. Conrad's assignment was to break the Russian line in the south by moving forward across the River San in Galicia, but his attempts to do so failed. Farther north, the German right and center made swift progress at first but then were slowed by days of torrential rain. "From Czestochowa we advanced in forced marches," an officer in charge of munitions transport wrote. "During the first two days roads were passable, but after that they became terrible, as it rained every day. In some places there were no roads left, nothing but mud and swamps. Once it took us a full hour to move one wagon, loaded with munitions and drawn by fifteen horses, a distance of only fifteen yards . . . Horses sank into the mud up to their bodies and wagons up to their axles . . . One night we reached a spot which was absolutely impassable. The only way to get around it was through a dense forest, but before we could get through there it was necessary to cut an opening through the trees. For the next few hours we felled trees for a distance of over five hundred yards . . . For the past eight days we have been on the go almost every night, and once I stayed in my saddle for thirty consecutive hours. During all that time we had no real rest. Either we did not reach our quarters until early in the morning or late at night. We consider ourselves lucky if we have one room and straw on the floor for the seven of us. For ten days I have not been out of my clothes. And when we do get a little sleep it is almost invariably necessary to start off again at once . . . Long ago we saw the last of butter, sausages, or similar delicacies. We are glad if we have bread and some lard."

As the Germans struggled forward, the Russians had time to assemble a mass of forces and counterattack. The German left was gradually bent back under the weight of repeated assaults until it faced northward instead of eastward and appeared to be on the verge of disintegrating.

By October 17 the Germans saw that they had to withdraw or be destroyed. The Ninth Army retreated sixty miles in six days, and by the time it was free of the Russians, it had lost forty thousand men. Overall the campaign had cost Germany a hundred thousand casualties, including thirty-six thousand men killed, the Austrians between forty and fifty thousand. The Russians pulled their guns out of the slime, and Grand Duke Nicholas began reassembling his sodden forces for a resumption of their advance.

By the start of the German retreat from Warsaw, Sir John French was beginning to move some of his forces eastward in Flanders. Falkenhayn, at almost exactly the same time, was setting in motion a westward offensive over adjacent ground. Until hours before their armies crashed into each other, neither was expecting to encounter an enemy in force. Both commanders were after territory: French's goal was Brussels by way of Ghent, while Falkenhayn wanted the area directly west of Belgium and the port towns that would come with it. Each was eagerly aware that, if he could advance far enough, he might then be in position to turn away from the sea and encircle his enemy. Glory seemed just over the horizon.

Almost immediately, both sides encountered immovable resistance. A joint French-British thrust toward Ghent ran into Falkenhayn's main force and was thrown back. The Germans tried to tear through the Belgian line at the Yser, but they too were stopped. Thus was set in motion the month of carnage called the First Battle of Ypres.

The nightmare was nowhere more hellish than where the Germans met the remains of the Belgian army. The suffering was magnified for the Belgians by the impossibility of digging in the waterlogged ground of the Flemish lowlands; for the Germans by the terrors of trying to cross a river under infantry fire while British navy shells screamed down on them from the nearby Channel; for both sides by the approach of winter and the new experience of being not only wet but half-frozen day after day and night after night.

King Albert rallied the Belgian troops. He was a competent soldier and a young man of considerable courage. He was also motivated: Foch had sternly warned him that if he failed to hold this last sliver of Belgium, he could not expect to retain his throne after the war. His Majesty positioned noncommissioned officers behind his line with orders to shoot any man who tried to retreat.

After days of murderous German shellfire that killed or wounded more than a third of the Belgians and effectively ended their ability to stand their ground, Albert played his last trump card. He ordered the opening (in some places the process required dynamite) of sluice gates in the dikes holding back the sea. The Germans, who were getting more and more men across the Yser and sensed that victory was near, could not understand what was happening. In the morning the ground was covered with ankle-deep water. Assuming that this was the result of the continuing rains, the Germans slogged on. By midnight, the water was knee-deep and still rising. The Germans not only had to give up any hope of continuing their offensive but spent a difficult night getting their troops back to dry land. Soon they were separated from the Belgians by a five-mile-wide, shoulder-deep lake, and that part of the fight was at an end. The German troops who had been attacking across the Yser were sent south to join in the fight around Ypres. They found themselves in a terrible struggle, often hand to hand, for the villages atop the low ridge that circled

around Ypres to the north, east, and south. The German objective
was to break through the Entente line on that ridge and close in
on Ypres itself.

At one of the villages, Wytschaete, there was hard fighting a
day after the opening of the dikes. A unit of Bavarians had tried
to take Wytschaete and failed, and in the aftermath of the attack
a captain named Hoffman lay badly wounded between his troops
and the French defenders. One of Hoffman's men moved out of a
protected position and, under enemy fire, picked him up and carried him to safety. The rescue accomplished nothing—the captain
soon died of his wounds. But his rescuer would claim years later,
in a notorious book, that his escape without a scratch was his first
intimation that he was being spared for some great future. In the
nearer term he was decorated for bravery. It was just a few days
after Adolf Hitler's exploit that Kaiser Wilhelm pinned the Iron
Cross Second Class on his tunic.

The Germans found progress against the British and French as
hard as it had been against the Belgians. But when the BEF and
Foch launched their own attacks, they too were quickly thwarted.
Along this part of the line, however, there were no dikes to be
opened, so that the opposing forces could be separated and their
misery brought to an end. The fighting continued day and night,
the two sides taking turns on the offensive, and as the casualties
mounted companies were reduced to the size of platoons and the
tattered remnants of units were mixed together helter-skelter. Officers were all but annihilated, so that young lieutenants found
themselves in command of what remained of battalions and regiments.

The rain continued, the nights grew colder, men lay on the
surface of the earth because any holes they dug immediately filled
with water, and still somehow the fighting went on. The landscape, though almost uniformly flat, was broken by villages and
patches of woodland and by rivers and canals and hedgerows and
fences extending in every direction. This was far better for defense
than offense, and practically impossible for cavalry (which in any
case was proving to be helpless against machine guns). The British were often outnumbered, sometimes by margins that seemed
impossible, but time after time they held off attacks or came back
to recapture lost ground. One thing that saved them was the skill

of their cavalry, acquired in the guerrilla fighting of the Boer War, in dismounting and fighting as infantry. What ultimately saved them, at Ypres as earlier at Mons and Le Cateau, was the accuracy and speed (and of course the courage) of the ordinary British rifleman. Here again the fire laid down by the Tommies was often intense enough to convince the Germans that they were advancing not against rifles but against machine guns.

The devastating effectiveness of the British fire, coupled with the inexperience of some of the German reserves thrown into the Ypres meat-grinder, led to perhaps the most poignant of the many butcheries of late 1914. Thousands of schoolboy recruits, many of them as young as sixteen, followed almost equally inexperienced reserve sergeants and officers in heavily massed formations directly at the waiting BEF. They formed a wall of flesh—British soldiers recalled them advancing arm in arm, singing as they came, wearing their fraternity caps and carrying flowers—that blind men could hardly have missed. They were mowed down in rows. Where they somehow succeeded in driving back their enemies, they often didn't know what to do next and so milled around aimlessly until hit with a counterattack. Many thousands of these youngsters lie in a single mass grave a short distance north of Ypres. At the site is a sculpture, the figures of a pair of parents kneeling in grief, created after the war by the mother of one of them.

Flanders was disaster after disaster for both sides, and horror after horror. One evening, at the end of a day of murderous infantry gunfights under constant artillery fire, one of the German reserve units managed at tremendous cost to drive the British out of the village of Bixshoote. Later they received word that they were to be relieved overnight. In their lack of experience they assembled and marched away before their relief arrived. Observing this, the British moved in and again took possession. In the following two weeks the Germans would try again and again to retake what they had given away, failing repeatedly and always with even more casualties than before.

Losses were no less shocking on the other side. When Scotland's Second Highland Light Infantry Battalion was taken out of action, only about thirty men remained of the thousand-plus who had come to France at the start of the war. The BEF was moving toward annihilation. In some places along the line the British were stretched so thin that the Germans, observing, outsmarted themselves. They decided not to attack at those points, thinking that such a tempting target must be a decoy behind which lay masses of British or French reserves. There were no such reserves.

Somehow, the Germans and British again launched simultaneous attacks on October 30, and again they ran head-on into each other and grappled in a struggle in which the losses were almost insupportable on both sides. The next day the Germans alone were still attacking, and this time, at the village of Gheluvelt, another of their green reserve units broke through the defensive ring. Nothing lay between them and Ypres, but this sudden success after so much failure apparently was more than they could believe. While they waited for instructions, a British brigadier general found the only troops in the vicinity, the seven officers and 357 enlisted men who remained of the Second Worcester Regiment, and ordered them to retake Gheluvelt. To get to the village, these men had to cross a thousand yards of open ground, and during the crossing a hundred of them were cut down. The survivors, when they reached the edge of the village, darted into a grove of trees, fixed their bayonets, and attacked. Twelve hundred confused and frightened German soldiers, thinking that this ragged little gang must be the advance of some powerful force, ran for their lives. The Worcesters, with nothing between them and Ypres but open country, had sealed the hole.

That night Falkenhayn called a halt. He had no idea that the BEF was at the point of breakdown—out of reserves, nearly out of ammunition, at the limits of endurance. He still thought that a breakthrough was possible, but he wanted to assemble more trained and experienced troops before trying again.

Things became briefly quiet both in Flanders and in Poland in the early days of November, but almost daily the war continued to grow in size and change in shape. The first Canadian troops were in England now, being readied to cross the Channel and link up with the British. An entire corps of Indian troops, tough Gurkha units among them, was with the BEF in Flanders, and black troops from France's African colonies were arriving at the front as well. In the east, Hindenburg was named commander in chief of all German forces on the Russian front. Ludendorff continued as his chief of staff, and Hoffmann stayed with him as well. When word came from Istanbul that the Ottoman Empire was entering the war on the side of the Central Powers, in Berlin and Vienna it must have sounded like a gift from heaven.

Before November was a week old, the Eastern and Western Fronts were heating up again. Grand Duke Nicholas put two armies on the march through Poland toward Silesia, and other Russian armies were moving southwestward to the Carpathians. And Falkenhayn was almost ready to try again to take Ypres. The kaiser was still at Supreme Headquarters, and his presence was as big a headache for Falkenhayn as it had been for Moltke. Wilhelm was constantly demanding a victory, a reason to don one of his most gorgeous uniforms and be paraded in triumph through some conquered city. In his protracted disappointment he was like a petulant adolescent, and no more useful.

During the lull in the Flanders struggle, Falkenhayn received a hurried visit from Ludendorff. As usual, and with Hoffmann's help as always, Ludendorff had an ambitious plan ready for execution. Also as usual, his plan was aimed not just at stopping the Russian armies advancing into Poland but at destroying them. He proposed to do this by allowing the Russians to advance beyond the railheads that were their source of support until they ran out of momentum. Then the Germans would descend on them from the north, taking them in the flank and rear, cutting them off from Warsaw and safety. But more troops were needed. This was what Ludendorff had come for: reinforcements. Falkenhayn refused; he had been assembling all the divisions he could find for the new attack in Flanders, and the kaiser was hounding him. Ludendorff departed in a fury. Another war, this one within the German general staff, began at about this time. It was between Falkenhayn and the Hindenburg-Ludendorff team, and it was over the question of whether the Germans' best hope of victory lay in the west or the east.

Denied the manpower their original plan required, Hindenburg, Ludendorff, and Hoffmann did not give up. They moved their Ninth Army, the one that had had such a narrow escape from the Russians near Warsaw, back into East Prussia by train. There they combined it with the Eighth Army to form a mass of

troops extending across seventy miles. They then waited as the
Russians moved across Poland toward the west. When, as expected, the advance began to show signs of bogging down under its
own tremendous weight and the difficulties of resupply, they sent
their two armies down on it like a hammer. At the main point
of contact the Germans actually had a numerical advantage, and
the Russians were staggered. After four days of hard fighting they
began to retreat. The Germans pursued, hitting at the Russians
repeatedly.

Falkenhayn was attacking again in Flanders, this time using
more experienced troops and limiting himself to a narrower
front. What he got was not victory but another series of inconclusive battles all along the ridge outside Ypres, which was slowly
being destroyed as the Germans shelled the ancient towers being used by the defenders as observation posts. Large and small
groups of soldiers dashed from village to woodland, from canal to
hedgerow, settling into firefights, advancing with bayonets, being thrown back and counterattacking while artillery from both
sides rained shrapnel and high explosives down on every target
their spotters could find. The nature of the struggle is captured in
the official account of First Ypres later prepared for the German
general staff:

> The enemy turned every house, every wood and every wall
> into a strong point, and each of them had to be stormed by
> our men with heavy loss. Even when the first line of these
> fortifications had been taken they were confronted by a sec-
> ond one immediately behind it; for the enemy showed great
> skill in taking every advantage of the ground, unfavorable in
> any case to the attacker. To the east and south-east of Ypres,
> even more developed than in the north, there were thick
> hedges, wire fences and broad dikes. Numerous woods
> also of all sizes with dense undergrowth made the country
> almost impassable and most difficult for observation pur-
> poses. Our movements were constantly being limited to
> the roads which were swept by the enemy's machine-guns.
> Owing to the preparatory artillery bombardments the vil-
> lages were mostly in ruins by the time the infantry reached
> them, but the enemy fought desperately for every heap of

stones and every pile of bricks before abandoning them. In the few village streets that remained worthy of the name the fighting generally developed into isolated individual combats, and no description can do adequate justice to the bravery of the German troops on such occasions.

Nor, of course, is it possible to do justice to—perhaps even to understand—the bravery of the British and French troops who were defending those piles of stones and bricks. Even the barest chronology of how the villages near Ypres were taken and surrendered and taken again is enough to show why, in the end, hardly a stone was left standing upon a stone. Lombartzyde was captured by the Germans on October 23, retaken by the French a day later, recaptured by the Germans on October 28, taken yet again by the British and French on November 4, recaptured by the Germans on November 7, only to change hands twice more before finally and permanently ending up in the possession of the Germans.

Gradually, village by village, the Germans managed to inch forward and tighten their grip on the Ypres Salient, the semicircle held by the French and British east of the town. But time after time they failed to break through. On several occasions various French and British generals suggested that a retreat might be in order. Always it was Foch who refused. Before the war he had written that an army is never defeated until it believes itself to be defeated. Now, with considerable help from the Tommies, he appeared to be proving his point.

The German offensive crested on November 11 when the most elite unit in the entire German army, the First Guards Regiment led by the kaiser's son Prince Eitel Friedrich, drove the British troops out of Nonnebosschen. It was a repeat of Gheluvelt. Once again nothing separated the Germans from Ypres, and once again a ragtag assortment of the only British soldiers in the neighborhood (not combat troops at all but cooks, drivers, staff officers—anyone who could pick up a rifle) mounted a seemingly hopeless counterattack. Once again the Germans thought that the mysteriously absent Entente reserves must be moving into action at last and fled. That turned out to be the last time the Germans came close to breaking through.

The fighting went on until November 22, with more attacks, but increasingly it was an obviously futile struggle in rain and cold mud by half-crazed and hungry men desperate for rest. Even the old lion Kitchener was horrified. "This," he exclaimed, "is not war!" Whatever it was, it finally came to an end when the rains turned to snow and the mud froze hard and the impossibility of achieving anything became too obvious to be ignored. Both sides claimed victory, the Entente because they had held on to Ypres and kept the Germans from reaching the Channel ports, the Germans not only because they had kept the enemy from breaking through but because by the end they had captured so many of the strongpoints around the destroyed town that the British and French no longer had an adequate base from which to launch new offensives.

By the time the Flanders front shut down for the winter, the British had taken fifty thousand casualties there. More than half of the one hundred and sixty thousand men that Britain had by then sent to France were dead or wounded. France's Ypres losses are believed to exceed fifty thousand, Germany's at least one hundred thousand. *Burke's Peerage,* the registry of Britain's noble families, had to postpone publication of its latest edition to make the editorial changes required by the death in combat of sixty-six peers, ninety-five sons of peers, sixteen baronets, eighty-two sons of baronets, and six knights.

The Russian retreat across Poland continued, with the Germans in pursuit. First the Russians tried to withdraw behind an expanse of wet lowland marshes, but the Germans drove them out. Then they tried to make a stand at the city of Lodz, but on December 6 they were again forced to move on. They had lost another ninety thousand men at Lodz, the Germans thirty-five thousand. The Germans were thirty miles east of Lodz, and in possession of a hundred and thirty-six thousand Russian prisoners, when their drive finally came to a stop. Winter made the stop necessary—the killing Russian winter. "Only about half had overcoats," an English war correspondent observed of German soldiers captured in a Russian counterattack. "And these were made of a thin, shoddy material that is about as much protection as paper against the Russian wind. When you know that the prison camps are all in Siberia, try and think of the lot of prisoners. Yet for the moment the Germans were content. They were allowed to sleep. This is the boon that the man fresh from the trenches asks above all things. His days and nights have been one constant strain of alertness. His brain has been racked with the roar of cannon and his nerves frayed by the irregular bursting of shell. His mind is chaos . . . But when a soldier is once captured he feels that this responsibility of holding back the enemy is no longer his. He has failed. Well, he can sleep in peace now."

Both sides settled down to hacking makeshift defenses out of the frozen earth. The Germans had lost a hundred thousand men in this last 1914 campaign while inflicting the astounding total of five hundred and thirty thousand casualties on the Russians. Their success, however, was of discouragingly limited value. As winter arrived, the Russians had 120 divisions on the front, and each division included twelve battalions. The Germans and Austrians together could muster only sixty divisions of eight battalions each.

For Conrad and his armies, December was a month of high drama, of brief glory followed by final humiliation. As it opened, one of the Russian armies advancing against the Carpathians had taken possession of a mountain pass that gave it a gateway into Hungary. The commander of this Russian Eighth Army, a talented general named Alexei Brusilov, was in position to advance on Budapest and begin the conquest of the Hapsburg homeland. But at just this moment Conrad tried something that worked. He learned of a gap between Brusilov and the Russian army on its right, assembled an attack force, and on December 3 drove it into the gap. The Russians were thrown off balance. In four days Conrad drove them back forty miles. Though the masses of reinforcements sent forward out of the Russian reserve brought him to a halt by December 10, the victory was an important one. It spoiled the Russians' hopes of crossing the Carpathians. It also rendered them incapable of executing a newly hatched plan to send a force from Krakow toward Germany. In combination with Hindenburg's and Ludendorff's November successes in Poland, it left the Russians bogged for the winter far from Berlin, Budapest, and Vienna.

Conrad poisoned his own hour of triumph by launching a year-end invasion of Serbia, his third since the start of the war. This newest incursion started as promisingly as the others, with the Austrians quickly taking possession of much of the Serbian interior along with Belgrade. Just one day after the fall of Belgrade, however, in a moment of Balkan high drama, the mustachioed King Peter of Serbia, rifle in hand, announced to his soldiers that he was releasing them from their pledge to fight for him and the homeland but that he for one was going to the front, alone if necessary. This gesture rallied every doubting patriot to the cause. A counterattack organized by Serbian General Radomir Putnik—the same old soldier who had been caught vacationing in Austrian territory when the war began but was allowed to return home in an act of almost medieval courtesy by Emperor Franz Joseph—sent two hundred thousand Serb troops down on the overextended Austrians. The Austrians, who had gone days without food and were freezing in summer uniforms, fled back across the border. Again their losses were outlandish: twenty-eight thousand dead, a hundred and twenty thousand wounded, seventy-six thousand taken prisoner. The Serbs too had been badly hurt, with twenty-two thousand killed, ninety-two thousand wounded, nine thousand captured or missing, and the survivors ravaged by dysentery and cholera.

Never again, in the years of fighting that lay ahead, would the Austro-Hungarians be involved in a major offensive as anything more than adjuncts to the Germans. Never again would they win a major victory they could call their own. With the war scarcely begun, they were a spent force. With almost four years of war remaining, nearly two hundred thousand of Vienna's best troops—including ruinous numbers of its experienced officers and noncoms—were dead. Almost half a million had been wounded, and some one hundred and eighty thousand were prisoners of the Russians.

There was fighting elsewhere as the year drew to a close. Even after the last assault at Ypres, the Western Front was never entirely quiet. Joffre kept ordering attacks wherever he thought the enemy wall might be weak. "Nibbling," he called it, but its cost in lives was high. By March it would add another hundred thousand casualties to the French total.

People were becoming accustomed to the term *world war*. Since August there had been naval battles, some of them high in drama but none terribly important, all around the globe. There was bloodshed in Africa as the police and small military forces of the various European colonies jockeyed for advantage and the indigenous populations became involved, and in the Far East Japan helped itself to Germany's scattered holdings.

The Middle East was being drawn in as well. The newest member of the Central Powers, Turkey, sent troops based in Syria into Persia. After so many years of watching the Europeans feast on its crumbling empire, the government in Constantinople was eager to recover some of its losses at last.

The British, in particular, were disturbed. When Russia suggested that a show of force near Constantinople might frighten the Turks and cause them to pull back from Persia, London found the idea attractive. A battleship was dispatched to the mouth of the Dardanelles, the narrow channel leading from the northeastern Mediterranean to Constantinople, the Black Sea, and Russia beyond.

Upon arrival, the ship began shelling one of the outermost forts guarding the Dardanelles. Within half an hour the fort was totally wrecked, incapable of defending itself or the sea route to Constantinople.

The battleship, never threatened while it did its work, steamed serenely away. The whole thing had been so *easy*. First Lord of the Admiralty Churchill began to wonder: might the entire passage up to Constantinople be that easily taken?

In Flanders, where there had been so much horror, 1914 ended with a strange spontaneous eruption of fellow feeling. On Christmas morning, in their trenches opposite the British near Ypres, German troops began singing carols and displaying bits of evergreen decorated in observance of the occasion. The Tommies too began to sing. Cautiously, unarmed Germans began showing themselves atop their defenses. Some of the British did the same. Step by step this led to a gathering in no-man's-land of soldiers from both sides, to exchanges of food and cigarettes, even to games of soccer.

This was the Christmas Truce of 1914, and in places it continued for more than a day. The generals, indignant when they learned of it, made certain that nothing of the kind would happen again.

PART THREE

1915

A Zero-Sum Game

The new face of war: a German Uhlan, or lancer, could seem a figure out of ancient legend except for the mask that protects him from poison gas.

Chapter 13

The Search for Elsewhere

"I can only love and hate,
and I hate General Falkenhayn."
—Erich von Ludendorff

Nineteen-fifteen opened repetitiously and prophetically, which is to say that it opened with lethal violence on the grand scale. On New Year's Day, in the English Channel, a German submarine fired a torpedo into the hull of the British battleship *Formidable* and sent 546 seamen to their deaths. On the continent the French were on the offensive, or trying to be, all along their long front: in Flanders, the Argonne, Alsace and, most bloodily of all, the Champagne region west of Verdun. In the east, under appalling winter conditions that were causing hundreds of men nightly to freeze to death in their sleep, the Russians were slowly forcing the armies of Austria-Hungary back into the Carpathian passes that separated the plains of Galicia from the Hapsburg homeland. Beyond Europe, on the ice-packed heights of the Caucasus Mountains, the Russians and the weather together were destroying a badly led and ill-equipped army of Turks. There was bloodshed in Africa, in Asia, in the South Pacific, and in the South Atlantic—in improbable places all around the world.

All the belligerents were locked in a situation for which they were woefully unprepared. In the last five months of 1914 more than eight hundred thousand Germans had become casualties, and more than a hundred thousand of them were dead. French and Austro-Hungarian casualties were in the million-man range, Russia's total approached twice that, hundreds of thousands of Frenchmen were listed as dead or missing, and more than half of the Tommies who had come over in August were dead or injured. In every country the shock was numbing. A monument in a single Parisian church, Notre Dame des Victoires, displays the names of eighty parishioners killed in battle between August and December.

The worst of it was that this carnage had not come close to producing a decision. In every country shattered armies had to be rebuilt and expanded and sent out to do it all again. Some of the leaders—none more than Joffre of France and Britain's Sir John French—continued to believe that victory lay just ahead and could be achieved with one or two more effusions of sacrificial blood. Others—Falkenhayn in Germany, Kitchener in Britain— were able to see that a long and terrible struggle lay ahead. For all of them, optimists and pessimists alike, one question had become paramount:

What do we do now?

All the camps but two, France and Austria-Hungary, were deeply divided over how to answer. In Paris the dominating fact was German occupation of a huge expanse of the French homeland: regions that included 14 percent of the nation's industrial workforce, two-thirds of its steel production, 90 percent of its iron mines, and 40 percent of its sugar refineries, along with substantial parts of its coal, wool, and chemical output. This made it easy for the French to agree on one great goal: to drive the Germans out, blast them out, burn them out, break their defensive line by any means possible and throw them back across the Rhine. More than in any of the other warring nations, only one man's opinion mattered. That man was "Papa" Joffre. Exclusive authority over questions of strategy had been in Joffre's hands from the start. If some were skeptical about the wisdom of trusting Joffre to such an extent, if calls for his removal had erupted during the weeks when his armies were in seemingly endless retreat, the Marne had silenced the doubters even if it had not entirely removed their doubts. Ambiguous as the victory may have been in terms of who had actually made it possible and what it meant for the long term, the simple fact that Joffre had been in command elevated his prestige to a level at which it was, and would long remain, above challenge. As shocking as Joffre's losses continued to be, his appetite for more of the same was undiminished. He remained certain that the war could still be a fairly short and glorious one, and he was determined to make it so.

A similar absence of disagreement pervaded official Vienna, but not because of any such high expectations. Austria-Hungary was forced into near-unanimity by sheer desperation. Its losses were particularly serious because the dual monarchy had less than a third of Russia's manpower to draw upon in trying to make whole its ravaged armies. Field Marshal Conrad's offensives into Galicia and Serbia had literally wiped out some of his most elite units, demoralized many of the survivors, and multiplied the difficulties of maintaining the enthusiasm of the empire's non-German majority. With Serbia unbeaten, with Russia continuing to advance, and with Italy's possible entry into the war on the side of the Entente, Austria-Hungary had only one possible first priority: to somehow keep the Russians from getting through the Carpathians. Achieving this goal was almost certain to require help from the Germans. The Austrians were already incapable of accomplishing anything of consequence without Berlin's assistance.

Conrad, rarely reluctant to engage the enemy, announced plans for a winter campaign aimed at driving the Russians back from the Carpathians and relieving the besieged fortress of Przemysl. He hoped, through a persuasive show of force, to discourage Italy, Romania, and Bulgaria (all of which were eager for a share in the spoils of war but uncertain of which side could make the best offer) from joining the Entente. He asked the Germans to contribute four divisions—upward of sixty thousand troops—to this offensive. In doing so he put his allies on the spot. Nobody in the German high command supposed that Conrad was capable of moving effectively against the Russians without assistance, and nobody was confident that he could succeed even if his request was granted. On the other hand his plan was far from pointless; if he did nothing but wait for the Russians to attack, the results could be disastrous. Falkenhayn had at his disposal four new corps, more than a hundred thousand well-equipped recruits led by experienced officers and noncoms. A struggle immediately erupted over how and where to use them.

What to do about Austria—the question that was, as Ludendorff told Falkenhayn, Germany's "great incalculable"—was only one of the puzzles facing the Germans as the winter deepened. They had not only the entire Western Front to deal with, the relentlessly growing French and British armies, but also a Russian steamroller that despite its huge losses continued to outnumber the German and Austrian forces in the east by overwhelming margins and was obviously preparing to resume the offensive. The Germans had no simple or obviously right way to balance these dangers and distribute the available resources—no clear way to victory on either front, never mind both. Nor were the leaders of the government or army agreed on what should be done. Their differences were so fundamental that they threatened the entire German war effort with paralysis.

Falkenhayn, the handsomely youthful-looking Junker who was now both chief of the general staff and war minister, appeared to have all the power needed to decide questions of strategy. And he knew what he wanted to do. Alarmed by the losses of 1914—he described his army as "a broken instrument"—he was convinced that Germany had no chance of defeating all the forces arrayed against it. A negotiated peace on one front or the other was therefore necessary. In the west, Falkenhayn believed, an acceptable peace could never be achieved without British acquiescence; the English Channel made Britain unconquerable, and the only way to bring it around was to take one of its allies out of the war. As for the east, the size of the front and of the Russian armies made victory improbable within a tolerable period of time. The answer, Falkenhayn thought, was to punish the Russians enough to make them receptive to an eventual settlement while focusing all possible force on the defeat of the French, whom he described as a sword in the hand of the British. "If we succeed in bringing Russia to terms," he said, "we could then deal France and England so crushing a blow that we could dictate peace terms."

He was unwilling to send to the east any troops that might usefully be used in the west, and he was similarly unwilling to thin his forces in East Prussia for the benefit of Conrad. This put him at odds with Hindenburg and Ludendorff. Both men—Ludendorff most importantly, because he and Max Hoffmann were the brains of the team—saw opportunities to crush the Russians. Whether out of strategic conviction or jealousy or some mixture of the two, both were contemptuous of Falkenhayn. And though Falkenhayn's two offices made him doubly the superior of Hindenburg and Ludendorff and every other member of the German high command, his credibility had been damaged by his failure to break through at Ypres even after expending so many lives. Tannenberg and the Masurian Lakes had raised Hindenburg to heights of popular adulation comparable to those occupied by Joffre in France. He was not inclined to use his prestige to help or support Falkenhayn. Prodded by Ludendorff, he undercut Falkenhayn at every opportunity, spoke openly of Falkenhayn's unfitness for the positions he occupied, and encouraged his admirers at court and in the government to do likewise. Falkenhayn, not surprisingly, responded in kind.

Things should have been simpler for the Russians because they, like the French and British, had only one truly dangerous enemy to contend with. But they too were divided and uncertain. The chief of the Russian general staff, the tsar's six-foot-six and stick-figure-thin cousin and namesake the Grand Duke Nicholas Romanov, was a competent commander. He was also aggressive and determined to use the massive forces at his disposal to invade Germany and win the war in the east. But his political position was not strong. He despised the monk Rasputin, once informing him that if he visited army headquarters he would be hanged on the spot, and partly for this reason he was distrusted and feared by Tsarina Alexandra, who had convinced herself that the grand duke coveted the imperial throne. Though Russia could have only one prime objective in 1915—to throw the Germans into terminal disarray—the question of how to accomplish this was anything but settled. Powerful members of the general staff wanted to strike directly at central Germany. Another faction wanted to complete the penetration of the Carpathians and finish off Austria-Hungary as a prelude to Germany's destruction. The grand duke, lacking clear guidance or firm support from Tsar Nicholas, was not well positioned to resolve such questions and lacked firm convictions. His inclination was to try to satisfy everyone.

Field Marshal Paul von Hindenburg
*Germany's national idol—but increasingly
a mere figurehead as the war continued.*

A new reality facing all the combatants was Turkey's entry into the war—a strange and unnecessary development. Backward and corrupt, economically and militarily feeble, the Ottoman Empire of 1914 was in no position to compete effectively with the great powers of Europe or even to function as a true partner of any of them. And it had much to lose by going to war with any of them. But to the Young Turks who had seized control in Constantinople in 1908 and clung to power in spite of their country's losses in the Balkan wars, Europe's August crisis had the appearance of a heaven-sent opportunity. Suddenly the Europeans coveted the Turks as potential allies. This change was as surprising as it was abrupt.

For years—for generations, actually—none of the great powers had wanted a formal connection with Constantinople. Turkey was "the sick man of Europe," slowly disintegrating, relentlessly dying. Its demise had been averted only by jealous disagreements among the powers over who should reap the benefits when it finally collapsed. Russia was prevented from taking possession of Constantinople only by Britain's and France's insistence that such a conquest would not be tolerated—that they would fight rather than let it happen. But becoming Turkey's actual *ally* was a different matter. To do that would be to incur obligations to an empire that had little to offer in return. And no ally of Turkey's would be free, precisely because it was an ally, to snatch up fragments of the empire as opportunities arose. So Turkey remained alone as Greece and Serbia and Bulgaria and Romania all broke away, as Britain grabbed Egypt and Cyprus, France took Algeria, Greece took Crete, and Austria-Hungary absorbed Bosnia-Herzegovina.

Turkey and its rulers lived in a state of apparently irreversible fear and humiliation.

The two powers with which Turkey had the closest relationships were Britain, its chief protector against Russian expansion, and Germany, which had increasingly substantial economic interests in the Middle East, including a Berlin-to-Baghdad railway. Prussia had been given responsibility for training the Turkish army as early as 1822. In 1913, when German General Otto Liman von Sanders arrived in Constantinople as head of his country's military mission, he found himself also named inspector of the Turkish army—chief of staff, in effect. As a balancing measure, the Young Turks invited Britain to take charge of upgrading their navy. They placed an order for two new dreadnoughts to be built in England at the cost of £11 million—a colossal sum for an empire that had been financially ruined by the Balkan wars. This purchase was so popular with the people of Turkey that much of the necessary money was raised through public fund-raising drives.

The outbreak of the war meant the end of Turkey's long isolation—if Turkey chose to end it. What was not at all clear was which side it would embrace, or whether it should embrace either. It came down, in the end, to a matter of ships, and of British blundering, and of German bullying. When the summer crisis of 1914 rose to its climax, a crew of Turkish seamen was in Britain, ready to take possession of the first of the new dreadnoughts. First Lord of the Admiralty Winston Churchill announced that his country was confiscating both ships. He did so on July 28, the day Austria-Hungary declared war on Serbia, and his act was understandable as a way of assuring that two of the world's newest and most potent warships would not fall into enemy hands. The matter could have been handled more delicately, however. It appears not to have occurred to the British government to negotiate with Turkey—to offer to release the ships in return for an alliance that at least some of the Young Turks would have welcomed. Churchill's announcement provoked outrage in Constantinople. At the beginning of August, with the start of the war only hours away, the Turkish government proposed a formal alliance with Germany.

Berlin, as it happened, already had a draft of such an alliance ready for use and eagerly wired it to Constantinople. It would

require Turkey to enter any war in which Germany became involved. The Young Turks, unprepared for such a drastic commitment, made excuses for not signing. Meanwhile they were secretly approaching Russia about a possible alliance in that direction.
The Russians, confident at this early stage of the Entente's ability
to overwhelm the Central Powers, brushed this overture aside.
To them it seemed little more than a pathetic request that they
refrain from seizing Constantinople.

While the Turks dawdled, two swift and powerful German
warships, the *Göben* and the *Breslau,* were playing a game of hide-
and-seek across the Mediterranean with the British and French
fleets. On August 10, pursued by their enemies after shelling the
coast of Algeria, the two vessels arrived at the entrance to the
Dardanelles and requested permission to enter. Enver Pasha,
Turkey's thirty-four-year-old minister of war and a dominant
figure among the Young Turks, found himself under intense pressure from all sides. His German advisers insisted that he admit
the ships. British and French diplomats demanded a refusal. He
tried to delay, but when the Germans insisted on an immediate
decision, he yielded. The *Göben* and the *Breslau* were allowed
to steam north to Constantinople. Later, when their pursuers
arrived at the straits, they were turned away. The Dardanelles
were thus sealed, with three hundred and fifty thousand tons
of Russian exports suddenly unable to reach the Mediterranean
from the Black Sea.

Even that did not settle the matter. Even when the Germans
presented the *Göben* and *Breslau* as a gift to the Turkish government (it was an empty gesture: the ships were given Turkish names but retained their German crews and continued to
take their orders from Berlin), the Turks declined to commit.
Everything remained unresolved until the end of September,
when, for the precise purpose of precipitating a crisis, the two
German ships steamed up the Bosporus strait into the Black
Sea. Flying the Turkish flag, they shelled the Russian cities of Feo-
dosiya, Odessa, and Sebastopol. The Young Turks, as alarmed as
the Russians by news of this attack, hastened to assure St. Petersburg that they remained neutral, that the attack had been a *German* act. The Russians replied that the Turks could prove their
good faith by expelling the Germans. This they were powerless

to do. On November 30, after an Entente ultimatum went unanswered, Russia declared war on Turkey. Britain and France did the same a few days later.

Though Turkey's alliance with the Central Powers was a serious setback for the Entente, some of Britain's leaders thought it opened new options. Being invulnerable to invasion, the British—unlike the French and Russians—had never been required to commit themselves to any theater of operations. By early 1915, thanks to the arrival of units of the regular army from distant parts of the empire and of colonial forces from India, Canada, Australia, and New Zealand, Sir John French had more than three hundred thousand troops under his command. Hundreds of thousands more, the "Kitchener's armies" made up of men who had flocked to recruiting centers at the start of the war, were in training back in England. The question was what to *do* with all this power. The answer was obvious to many senior members of the army and the cabinet, but they were far from united on exactly what they thought was so obvious.

French himself, despite the horrors of Ypres, was as convinced as Joffre that the German defenses could be cracked open, and he was as eager as Joffre to prove it. Consistent exaggeration of German casualties had helped to persuade him that the enemy must be approaching exhaustion. Entente propagandists depicted almost every fight in the West as a slaughter of Germans mounting robotlike suicide attacks, when in fact German losses were often markedly lower than those of the Entente. Back in London, the army's director of military operations produced an analysis supposedly demonstrating that Germany was going to run out of men "a few months hence." (This hopeful myth was slow to die. Before June 1915 another operations director would predict that if Britain would "keep hammering away . . . we shall wear Germany out and the war will be over in six months.") Though French like Joffre wanted to stay on the offensive, he remained unwilling to do so under Joffre and even reluctant to do so *with* Joffre. He continued to demand the freedom to operate independently. There was one final point, however, on which Joffre and French were in complete agreement: every available British soldier, they insisted, should be sent to the Western Front at the earliest possible moment.

Early in January, French went to London and met with the British War Council, a new planning body whose seven members included Asquith, Kitchener, Churchill, Grey, and Chancellor of the Exchequer David Lloyd George. He proposed a new offensive that would follow the coast and be aimed at recapturing the Belgian Channel ports. Churchill supported this idea, seeing in it a way to bring neutral Holland into the war on the Entente side and, by drawing more German troops to the west, to prepare the way for a landing of troops on Germany's Baltic coast. At first the council turned French's proposal down. Most members regarded it as too risky to justify the possible gains and also as contrary to the wishes of Joffre, who wanted the British to attack not along the coast but, again, near Ypres. Days later the idea was brought back to life, not as an approved plan but as a possibility to be kept under consideration. Asquith was unfriendly to the idea. Kitchener was absolutely opposed. What he wanted—it was not a thing to be talked about openly—was to keep Britain's new armies at home until the French and Germans had exhausted each other. Then London could send masses of fresh troops across the Channel and decisively tip the scales. "The German armies in France may be looked upon as a fortress that cannot be carried by assault," Kitchener told French. The British lines, he added, "may be held by an investing force while operations proceed elsewhere."

Elsewhere. For Kitchener and Churchill and others, that became a kind of dream. Shaken by the destruction of the BEF's first divisions and hoping to avoid a repeat, they began looking for less painful ways to prosecute the war. Grand Duke Nicholas was encouraging their search by sending telegrams to Kitchener, asking him to make a show of force in the Middle East and thereby oblige the Turks to suspend their offensives in Persia and the Caucasus. A campaign in Syria was one idea; by drawing the Turks from the north, it could free Russian troops for the Eastern Front. A Baltic landing was another option; the navy was building a fleet of six hundred motor barges and other craft for an invasion (by *Russian* troops, though St. Petersburg had not been informed) of Germany's Pomeranian coast. Still another possibility, one less fraught with risk than the Baltic scheme, was the landing of an Entente force at the port of Salonika, in northwestern Greece. Greece was not even in the war (it was one of the several neutral states being courted by both sides), but the council hoped that the injection of Entente troops into the southern Balkans might win over not only Greece but Romania, Bulgaria, and Italy. An army moving northward out of Salonika could secure Serbia. Then, reinforced, it might be able to invade Austria-Hungary. Kitchener liked this idea. So did Lloyd George, who as chancellor of the exchequer was not necessarily a central figure in Britain's military planning but was making himself one by sheer force of will.

Finally there were the Dardanelles, which had already been briefly attacked by a British ship at the end of 1914 and had demonstrated no ability to resist. Renewed action there in greater force could create problems for all the Central Powers. Churchill sent a telegram asking the commander of the British fleet in the eastern Mediterranean if a naval force could fight its way through the Dardanelles to Constantinople. When the admiral replied that this might be accomplished "by extended operations with a large number of ships," Churchill was satisfied. He instructed the admiral to submit a detailed plan for such an operation.

The Dardanelles were becoming *elsewhere.*

Just a week into the new year, two offensives that Joffre had put in motion in France's Champagne and Artois regions were essentially at an end. The French advanced only five hundred yards in three weeks and by January 8, with the Germans launching counterattacks, had added tens of thousands of casualties to their dizzily rising total. The Champagne operation alone, by the time it was shut down, had cost ninety thousand French casualties. Even then Joffre did not give up. He would try again in February and yet again in March, continuing to think that he was on the verge of a breakthrough. The British War Council felt confirmed in its skepticism about the Western Front and about Sir John French's promises of success.

The Germans, while successful in holding their line against this endless hammering, were still divided on strategy. No mechanism existed by which Germany's competing strategists could discuss their differences in any systematic way. The kaiser, the "All-High Warlord," rarely attempted to bring them together, and as a result the rivalries within the high command could only fester. Clear policy formulation was replaced by backstabbing and bickering. Those who wanted to concentrate on the Western

Front tried in childish ways to undercut and discredit their rivals. (Falkenhayn, for example, deleted the names of Hindenburg and Ludendorff from reports of success in the east.) The "easterners" not only responded in kind but plotted to have Falkenhayn dismissed. The kaiser, meanwhile, neither led nor allowed anyone else to do so. A crisis was inevitable. But instead of experiencing *a* leadership crisis, the high command went through a series of such crises that lasted a year and a half.

Falkenhayn's position remained ambiguous in the extreme. He wanted to win the war in the west, but also to make the Russians willing to negotiate. When he refused Conrad's request for help in a winter offensive, then refused again when Hindenburg demanded that his unassigned new corps be sent to the east, Hindenburg and Ludendorff announced that they were detaching three and a half divisions from their own Ninth Army and sending them to Conrad. In any army this would have bordered on insubordination. By the traditions and standards of the Prussian army, it was little short of shocking. Falkenhayn protested to the kaiser. Hindenburg responded with an appeal of his own for the kaiser's support. The battle for control over German strategy was joined.

Falkenhayn's next move was clever but certain to enrage his rivals. He used his double-barreled authority as head of the general staff and war minister to declare that the troops being sent from Hindenburg's army to Conrad would become the core of a new Army of the South. This army would be commanded by General Alexander von Linsingen, a protégé of Falkenhayn's, who would report not to Hindenburg but to Falkenhayn himself. Ludendorff was named Linsingen's chief of staff. With this move, Falkenhayn dissolved the team that had given Germany its only victories and diminished the authority of its leading members.

Refusal to obey was out of the question, and Ludendorff prepared to go south. Before departing, he joined Hindenburg in drafting—essentially dictated for the old man's signature—a telegram to the kaiser. "I have grown into close union with my Chief of Staff," it said. "He has become to me a true helper and friend, irreplaceable by any other, one on whom I bestow my fullest confidence. Your majesty knows from the history of war how important such a happy relationship is for the conduct of affairs and the well-being of the troops." Edging closer to direct criticism of what Falkenhayn was doing, the telegram added that Ludendorff's "new and so much smaller sphere of action does not do justice to the General's comprehensive ability and great capacity." It ended on a groveling note: "I venture most respectfully to beg that my war comrade may graciously be restored to me as soon as the operation in the south is under way."

The telegram sent, Ludendorff departed. Within hours he was in the south, involved with Linsingen and Conrad in finalizing arrangements for an advance out of the Carpathians. Even when he was deeply embroiled in military politics at their most vicious, even when he was using every trick at his disposal against his rivals, Ludendorff remained a resourceful, focused, and indefatigable strategist. He had added a team of talented code-breakers to his staff, and thanks to their work he knew what Grand Duke Nicholas was planning. Conrad had been right in expecting a new Russian attack through the Carpathians, but decoded messages showed that this was not all the Russians had in mind. Simultaneously they were planning to renew operations in East Prussia, and still other Russian armies were to drive through Poland into the German heartland. Ludendorff's response was exactly as it had been when he was faced with apparently overwhelming odds in 1914. Instead of allowing the enemy to take the initiative, he would strike first. Again he saw an opportunity not just to hold off the Russians but, with coordinated attacks in the north and south, to cripple them.

Falkenhayn, in the aftermath of his restructuring of German forces in the east, was drawn into the planning of this campaign. On January 11 he met with Conrad, Linsingen, and Ludendorff at Breslau. Their talks were polite if not cordial. Falkenhayn thought it was little better than madness to launch an offensive against superior forces in mountain country in midwinter, and he said so. Conrad replied coolly that he knew the country in question and knew what he was doing. On the following day, at Posen, Falkenhayn met with the old Tannenberg team of Hindenburg, Ludendorff, and Hoffmann. This more private gathering was not a happy one; the pent-up resentments of the past months boiled over. By all accounts, Hindenburg and his lieutenants treated their commanding general with open contempt. Hindenburg told Falkenhayn that he did not have the confidence of the men

under his command and should resign. After Falkenhayn's departure, Ludendorff and Hoffmann talked Hindenburg into sending
another telegram to the kaiser. This one was not at all groveling.
It demanded the dismissal of Falkenhayn, the dispatch of the
four new corps to the east, and the return of Ludendorff to Hindenburg's staff. Behind it lay the unmistakable threat that Hindenburg was prepared to resign.

The showdown appeared to be at hand. The kaiser, offended by Hindenburg's presumption and regarding Ludendorff
as "a dubious character devoured by personal ambition," declared that he wanted them both court-martialed. Chancellor Bethmann Hollweg, ordinarily all too willing to stay out
of military affairs, was horrified. He replied that public punishment of the hero of Tannenberg was unthinkable, that it
was Falkenhayn who should be dismissed. Almost the entire
imperial court was drawn into the struggle. Falkenhayn's enemies, influenced negatively by his warnings of a long war
and positively by Hindenburg's and Ludendorff's assurances that
the war need not be long at all, were numerous and influential.
The kaiser's wife, Empress Augusta Victoria, was active among
them. So was Crown Prince Wilhelm. Even Moltke, encouraged
by Bethmann to hope that Falkenhayn's fall might restore him to
leadership, said Falkenhayn must go. But Falkenhayn retained the
support that at this point still mattered most: that of Kaiser Wilhelm, who acted at last. Falkenhayn would remain at the head of
the general staff, the kaiser announced, but would give up the war
ministry. The contested army corps would be sent to the east,
which the kaiser now declared the "theater of decision." Ludendorff, as soon as he could be spared in the south, would return to
Hindenburg's staff.

Not nearly enough had been settled, and much damage had
been done. Falkenhayn's authority had been irretrievably compromised: his subordinates had defied him and won much of
what they demanded. Falkenhayn's removal from the war ministry was in all likelihood a mistake: he had proved to be a
capable administrator, doing much to prepare not only the army
but the German economy for a long struggle. The kaiser too had
been damaged; his credibility as a commander, never strong,
was wearing thin. Wilhelm was showing increasing signs of psy-

chological fragility. Almost completely withdrawn from the real work of planning and conducting the war, he would relieve himself of nervous energy by cutting wood for hours. Unable to sleep, he would pass his nights reading popular novels. In the end he had to beg Hindenburg to accept the new arrangement rather than resign.

The confusion seemed boundless. At one point it was suggested that Falkenhayn should leave the army and replace Bethmann Hollweg as chancellor. Falkenhayn refused out of fear it would leave Ludendorff in effective charge of the army. Yet somehow these men were supposed to work together to save their country from destruction. The prospects were not encouraging. "I can only love and hate, and I hate General Falkenhayn," Ludendorff declared. "It is impossible for me to work together with him." Even Hoffmann, whose temperament was far better balanced than Ludendorff's, told his staff that Falkenhayn was "the fatherland's evil angel."

But for now, for all of them, it was back to the war that was fought with guns. Conrad's offensive began on January 23, when the forty-one divisions of a combined Austro-Hungarian and German force set out to expel forty-two Russian divisions from the Carpathians and proceed to the recovery of Galicia and the relief of Przemysl. This last objective was crucial to the Austrians both strategically and symbolically. Przemysl was the biggest, stoutest fortress in the Austro-Hungarian Empire, the center from which Vienna had long dominated Galicia and its Polish-Ukrainian population. The Russian advance of 1914 had left it surrounded, with a hundred and fifty thousand troops and civilians trapped inside and running out of food and supplies. Conrad was desperate to break through before its surrender became unavoidable.

The campaign stalled almost as soon as it began. The problem was less the Russian defenders than the nightmarish difficulties of mountain warfare in winter—the need not just to attack but to climb up ice-bound passes. There were successes, but they were more than balanced by the failures. While one Austrian army captured the city of Czernowitz and sixty thousand Russians with it, another lost eighty-nine thousand men in two weeks. The morning discovery that entire encampments had frozen to death in their sleep became commonplace. Conrad, meanwhile, remained at his headquarters far from the action—an exceptionally comfortable headquarters where the generals lived with their wives in private villas.

Five days after the start of this offensive, Ludendorff, once again at Hindenburg's headquarters, kicked off an attack in the north. In doing so he introduced something new in warfare: gas. The Germans began their assault by opening eighteen thousand canisters of xylyl bromide, a kind of tear gas that was supposed to be carried by the wind into the Russian lines and incapacitate the defenders without killing them. They had not understood, however, that xylyl bromide is ineffective in freezing temperatures. Thus it had so little impact that the Russians scarcely noticed it—never told the British and French of having encountered it. The advance by the German infantry, when it came, made modest initial gains and then was stopped by stiff resistance. Ludendorff, sensibly, called it off. He had accomplished his objective, which was simply to keep the Russians engaged while preparations were finalized for a more important effort on another part of the northeastern front. Engaged they certainly

The Eastern Front in winter
The cold ruined plans and took countless lives.

were. Counterattacks by eleven Russian divisions took back all the ground that Ludendorff's offensive had gained—ground of no importance—at a cost of forty thousand casualties in three days. German losses were light: their infantry conducted an orderly retreat while the artillery tore chunks out of the tightly massed Russian formations.

In a month of struggle Conrad barely managed to take the objectives he had planned to reach the first day. Przemysl remained out of reach. Soon it was the Russians who were advancing, managing for a while to push back the Austrians and Germans but at last being stopped by the same impossible weather that had ruined Conrad's plans. But Ludendorff, in the north, was just getting started. He had positioned the German Tenth Army north of the Masurian Lakes, the Eighth to the south, and on February 5 he was ready to unleash a campaign aimed at encircling and destroying virtually all the Russian forces in the region. Though exceedingly ambitious, this plan was rendered almost feasible by the way Grand Duke Nicholas, under conflicting pressures from the   generals commanding his northern and southern sectors, had deployed the Russian armies. Russia, at this time, had approximately a hundred divisions on the Eastern Front with others moving forward to join them. They also had, as the failure of Conrad's offensive showed, a strong defensive position in Galicia. The Central Powers, by contrast, had only eighty-three divisions in the east, half of them Austro-Hungarian, many of those of questionable reliability. It is at least possible that the grand duke, by concentrating most of his forces in the north, could have overwhelmed Hindenburg and Ludendorff. But such an approach would have required forcing the generals in the south to spare troops for the fight in the north. This the grand duke would not or could not do.

Just as Ludendorff was ready to move, heavy snow began to fall. It fell for two days, accumulating to a depth of five feet as temperatures fell to forty degrees below zero. The Germans attacked anyway. Even more incredibly, they made good progress, taking the Russians by surprise and driving them out of their defenses. Again, winter gave the fighting a specially hellish quality, made all the worse by a sudden thaw that on February 14 turned ice to ice water and frozen earth to mud. Earlier the Germans had needed as many as eighteen horses to move each of their guns forward through the snow. Now, with the guns sinking into the ground, no number of horses could move them. Soldiers became drenched with snowmelt and their own sweat, and as night fell their clothing froze hard. As in the Carpathians, men froze to death almost as often as they were shot. The battle turned into a race in which all the competitors were painfully handicapped, the Germans struggling forward to get around the Russians and encircle them, the Russians struggling to escape and abandoning trainloads of supplies.

Things moved to a climax on February 18, when a German corps managed to fight its way through deep snow around the Forest of Augustow and seal a Russian corps inside it. The trapped Russians put up a heroic defense through three long days, allowing other units to escape, but finally they were forced to surrender. The day after that some of the escaped Russian forces, having caught their breath, managed to mount a counterattack that captured no ground of consequence but brought the German advance to an end.

The German propagandists declared Augustow a great victory, one of Tannenbergian proportions. Ludendorff claimed that a hundred thousand soldiers and three hundred pieces of artillery had been captured. Though Russian casualties of all kinds were actually about fifty-six thousand and the number of guns taken was 185, this was a substantial success all the same. The Russians had been pushed back seventy miles. What mattered more, Grand Duke Nicholas's plans for a springtime attack in the northeast had been wrecked beyond possibility of recovery. Hindenburg was once again Germany's hero. The Berlin press declared him a genius, invincible, an almost godlike figure.

But the Russian forces in the north had not been destroyed as Ludendorff had said they would be. And although in the west a penetration of seventy miles would have been an immense achievement, in the vast reaches of the east it had little importance. Even Hindenburg admitted that "we failed strategically." In the south there was no basis upon which even to pretend that anything had been accomplished. On February 17 Conrad had tried to restart his offensive, and the result was more pointless carnage. The winter campaign, by the time it ended, added eight hundred thousand Austrian casualties to the million of 1914. In attempting to relieve Przemysl, Conrad had lost six or more times the number of men trapped there. By April, even after rushing the recruits of 1914 into the field, Austria would have only about half a million men available for the front. It was a pathetically small number for an army at war with Russia.

Aside from all the lives lost or ruined, very little had changed. For Falkenhayn, Conrad's campaign and the Second Battle of the Masurian Lakes (the name given to Ludendorff's offensive) seemed a vindication. As far as he was concerned, the two ventures had proved him right not only about the folly of winter offensives but about the impossibility of defeating Russia. Every one of his warnings had turned out to be well founded. Understandably, he decided that his western strategy too would turn out to be the right one.

THE MACHINERY OF DEATH

THE GREAT WAR DID NOT END IN 1914—OR IN 1915, 1916, or 1917 for that matter—in large part because of the state of technology in the second decade of the twentieth century. The war had broken out at the end of almost a century of dizzily accelerating advances in metallurgy, chemistry, and high-precision mass production, at a moment in history when weaponry was immeasurably more advanced than it had been a few generations before. And the war itself accelerated everything still further. The nations involved were not only the world's military giants but its industrial leaders as well. They rolled out one innovation after another year after year; whenever one side produced an implement of destruction that promised to tip the scales, the other came up with a way to preserve the deadlock.

The armies that mustered after Sarajevo did not understand the potential of the weapons they already possessed, did not know that the tactics they had learned in school were obsolete. The stalemate could not be broken until two things happened: the generals figured out what to do with the power that the industrial revolution had placed in their hands, and they found solutions to such innovations as the machine gun and the submarine.

It takes effort to recall, after a century that included both Kitty Hawk and men on the moon, just how slowly military technology evolved through most of human history. There was no such a thing as an effective sword until the first production of iron implements around 1200 B.C. (weaponry was pretty much a matter of clubs and spears until then), horsemen didn't have the stirrup or the bit until the seventh century A.D., and only in the ninth century did some tinkerer in China learn to combine saltpeter, charcoal, and sulfur in proportions that turned it into a substance that exploded when touched by fire. Gunpowder didn't reach Europe until the thirteenth century—it was brought by Mongol invaders—and the process by which it came to be used effectively was glacially slow. The first muskets were markedly inferior to the longbow in range, in rapidity of fire, and in accuracy and killing power. They replaced the bow only because they required much less strength and skill and so could be used by almost anyone after hours instead of years of training. Napoleon's cannons fired balls of solid iron that were not fundamentally different from the rounded chunks of stone used by Europe's first gunners centuries before. Rifled artillery—big guns with enough range and accuracy to render obsolete the kinds of fortresses that soldiers had been building for millennia—did not appear on the scene until the time of the American Civil War.

That—the middle of the nineteenth century—was when everything really began to change. New machine tools and new ways of casting metal made possible the manufacture of identical parts in practically infinite numbers, and so the way was cleared for the locomotive, truly modern firearms, and the internal combustion engine—for total war. The chemical industry was being born too, its pioneers discovering things that further changed the face of war. They learned that when cotton is soaked in nitric acid and allowed to dry, the result is a smokeless gunpowder far cleaner and three times more powerful than the Chinese concoction. That when nitroglycerin is mixed with absorbent earth, dynamite results. That some of the gases being synthesized for peaceful purposes were deadly when inhaled.

From the start of hostilities in 1914, it became obvious that the very nature of combat had forever changed. The new artillery, equipped with hydraulic mechanisms for absorbing recoil, no longer had to be repositioned after every round. The "shells" fed into it, combining propellant, warhead, and a timing device in a single easily handled cylinder, could be rained down on the enemy more rapidly, more accurately, at greater range, and for longer periods of time than anything seen before. For the first time in history, and from the beginning of the war to the end, artillery dominated. It did more killing between 1914 and 1918 than any other weapon.

But it was an entirely new weapon, the machine gun, that turned the Western Front into a prolonged siege. It was invented in 1884 by an American named Hiram Maxim, whose key achievement was using the force that smokeless powder puts into a gun's recoil and gas discharge to eject spent cartridges, reload the empty chamber, and fire again in potentially endless sequence. Maxim's gun could pour out six hundred rounds per minute. It was a simple, sturdy mechanism that, with its barrel cooled by water, could fire at that rate for hours. Batteries of machine guns could and did turn infantry attacks into mass suicides. Their weight made the early models impractical as offensive weapons (those in use at the start of the war required crews of from three to six men), which gave an almost insuperable advantage to the defense.

Even the rifles carried by the soldiers of the Great War were astonishing weapons in comparison with anything previously available. They varied little from country to country: the German Mauser, French Lebel, British Lee-Enfield, Austrian Männlicher, and Italian Männlicher-Carcano all were about four feet long, weighed less than ten pounds, were equipped with bolt actions, and fired metal cartridges of approximately thirty caliber fed from magazines containing between five and ten rounds. All were capable of putting bullet after bullet into a bull's-eye at a range of hundreds of yards. In the hands of a platoon of well-trained infantry, they could put up a field of fire as lethal as any produced by a machine gun.

Simpler innovations, some of them almost crude in technological terms, also proved to be important. Barbed wire, developed in the United States to keep cattle from breaking through fences, became an essential. On the Western Front especially, every trenchline was protected with coils of barbed wire strung between wooden uprights. Unless cleared away in advance of infantry attacks (shrapnel was the standard way of destroying wire), these coils became traps, entangling their victims within point-blank range of enemy guns.

Rudimentary methods of underground tunneling—methods brought to the war by the coal miners of every country, and by the builders of big-city subway systems—added another dimension. Eventually scores of thousands of men on both sides would be engaged in digging under enemy defenses, either to create passageways for sneak attacks or to blow up the men, weapons, and fortifications on the surface above. Inevitably the diggers on one side, accidentally or by design, would sometimes break into the tunnels of their foes. The resulting battles under the earth, often illuminated by nothing but the flash of gunfire, were as ugly and terrifying and secret as the aircraft engagements above the earth were visible, romantic, and admired.

Humblest of all was the lowly mortar. A kind of simple miniature howitzer capable of throwing a charge of explosives a short distance on a high trajectory, the mortar had fallen out of favor in the years before the war. The Germans had a version they called the *Minenwerfer* (mine thrower), but the other armies had few and the British began with none. Mortars proved to be effective in the static fighting of the Western Front—a way of lobbing an unpleasant surprise into an enemy trench—and soon the Tommies were fashioning them out of empty shells. In 1915 an Englishman named Frederick Stokes developed a more sophisticated production model, one whose teardrop-shaped projectile was equipped with stabilizing fins. In short order the "Stokes bomb" became an integral element in every company's inventory of weapons.

Some new things were more horrifying than effective. Poison gas, introduced by the Germans early in 1915 and thereafter used by both sides, killed thousands and left thousands disabled. It was "improved" as the war went on, chlorine being succeeded by phosgene and phosgene by mustard, but it never produced or even contributed significantly to a major victory on any front. Its deficiencies came to be so universally recognized that not even the Nazis would use it in World War II. Much the same happened with the flamethrower, introduced experimentally in 1914 and soon a standard weapon. Using pressurized gas from one tank to propel an ignited jet of oil from a second tank outward in a plume of fire as much as forty yards long, the

Flamethrowers: terrifying, but of limited effectiveness

flamethrower was terrifying in combat but otherwise of limited effectiveness. It was almost useless when used at any distance against entrenchments. And it was dangerous for its users. Operators would be engulfed in fire if a bullet penetrated both of the tanks strapped to their backs. Caught in an agonized dance of death, they might then helplessly spray fire in all directions, incinerating their own comrades.

A war that introduced so many new weapons naturally brought others to an end. It reduced the bayonet, long the infantry's signature weapon, to being a nearly obsolete romantic symbol. The foot soldiers of the Great War often did affix bayonets to their rifles before attacking, even to the end of the war. But they did so because they had been trained to do so and were ordered to do so; it became a largely ceremonial gesture. Men equipped with repeating rifles and face-to-face with armed enemies preferred to shoot before they got close enough to use their bayonets. They also preferred to throw grenades. When it came down to hand-to-hand combat in its most brutish form, they were more likely to use the handmade clubs they had learned to carry with them, or trenching tools with sharpened edges, or even blackjacks or brass knuckles. The number of men killed by bayonets in the war was, on the whole, very small.

Most dramatically, the Great War brought the end of cavalry. Mounted soldiers had been a central element in offensive warfare since before the time of Alexander the Great. As a way of delivering a decisive shock to an enemy, they dominated European battlefields from the Middle Ages to the nineteenth century. All the armies that went to war in 1914 included huge numbers of troops on horseback—the Russians put more than a million in the field, many of them Cossacks—despite the fact that the decline in their value had begun to be apparent as early as the Civil War. On the Western Front especially, the cavalry were from the start more a burden than an asset, difficult to support and transport, and helpless when confronted with modern gunnery.

What is shocking is the persistence with which the British general staff, far more than the Germans or the French, refused to reduce the size of their cavalry. Right through to the end of the war, Douglas Haig clung to the conviction that horsemen were going to be the key to exploiting infantry breakthroughs (whenever they were achieved) and that under the right circumstances (whatever they might be) his cavalry would prove a match for machine guns. It never happened.

Chapter 14

The Dardanelles

"To attack Turkey would be to play the German game,
and to bring about the end which Germany had in
mind when she induced Turkey to join the war."
—Field Marshal Sir John French

In February the Twenty-ninth Infantry Division became the most important unit in the British army, not because it was the last of the prewar regular divisions to have escaped being sent to the war and wrecked there—though it was that—but because it was still in England, not committed to any theater of operations, and therefore *available*. It became the symbol of, and the immediate prize in, an epic tug-of-war over the direction of Britain's war strategy.

The struggle began with the fact that Sir John French, though his command continued to grow, was not satisfied. His certainty that the German lines opposite the BEF had to be ripe for conquest made him urgently hungry for more men. He wanted the Twenty-ninth, wanted it without delay, and could see no reason why he should be denied. He was supported by Joffre, who agreed with French about everything except how the British forces on the Western Front should be used and who should make the decision.

Authority for the deployment of British troops lay not with French but with the war minister, Lord Kitchener. Kitchener had severely narrow ideas about what kinds of divisions should be fed into the meat-grinder of the Western Front. The so-called territorial units, which before the war had made up a kind of national guard, he regarded as third rate and parted with more or less willingly. It was the same with the colonials arriving from distant parts of the empire: Indians, Canadians, Australians, and the like. Kitchener was fiercely protective, however, of the new, still-raw divisions formed out of the men and boys who had volunteered in the first months of the conflict, and he was no less protective of the Twenty-ninth. After six months of war a division that was both intact and made up of experienced professional soldiers was a rare and precious asset. More than enough such divisions had been ravaged at Mons, Le Cateau, and Ypres, and on the Aisne.

The Twenty-ninth could become especially important if Britain opened a theater of operations somewhere other than in western Europe, and by February the search for such an opportunity was far along. It appeared, in fact, that the choice had been made: the new theater would be Salonika, the Greek port city that lay, like the Dardanelles but west of them, on the north coast of the Aegean Sea, which separates Greece from Turkey. Salonika was the recommendation of a committee that the War Council had created in January to evaluate possible new fronts. Because of its potential as a base from which to inject troops into the Balkans, thereby threatening both Turkey and Austria-Hungary, it quickly received enthusiastic support, especially from David Lloyd George. The government of Greece, though still officially neutral, was indicating that it would not be unfriendly to a landing in Salonika. Support for the project grew stronger when, early in February, an attack force of five thousand Turks led by a German lieutenant colonel crossed the Sinai Desert and reached the Suez Canal in British-controlled Egypt before being driven back. This alarming development threatened Britain's connection to India. Taking some kind of action in response to Grand Duke Nicholas's appeals for support in the Middle East seemed increasingly necessary. It also dovetailed nicely with the wish for a way to use Britain's manpower more productively than in Flanders.

Early in February, when Lloyd George traveled to Paris for a meeting on financial matters, he brought the idea of a Salonika expedition to the attention of the French. Though Joffre replied, predictably, that he had no troops to spare for such an adventure, Minister of War Alexandre Millerand was more receptive. Days later, it was learned that Bulgaria, one of the neutral Balkan states that both sides were courting, had accepted a large loan from Germany and appeared likely to throw in with the Central Powers. That settled the question: the War Council approved the Salonika proposal. Kitchener, among the strongest supporters of the idea, thereupon ordered the Twenty-ninth Division to move to the Aegean island of Lemnos. The Greeks had agreed to make the island available to Britain. From there, as soon as everything was in readiness, the Twenty-ninth could be quickly transferred to Salonika.

Sir John French, when he learned of this development, declared that without the Twenty-ninth he was not going to be able to fulfill a promise made earlier to take over part of the French line near Ypres and launch an attack in support of Joffre's next offensive. Nor was Joffre pleased. He joined French in protesting, and together the two brought so much pressure to bear on London that Kitchener called off the Twenty-ninth's deployment. The division would, for the time being, remain in England. Green Australian and New Zealand troops being trained in Egypt were ordered to Lemnos in its stead.

Many of the British leaders who supported the Salonika landing looked favorably also on the preparations being made for a naval incursion against the Dardanelles. There seemed no reason why both ventures could not be undertaken at the same time. Both were made possible by Britain's naval superiority, which was all the more overwhelming in the Mediterranean because France's naval forces were concentrated there as well. The two ventures would not compete for the same resources. Salonika was to be an excursion of ground troops; ships would be needed only to ferry those forces to their starting point and keep them supplied. The Dardanelles initiative, by contrast, was to be a naval operation exclusively. A fleet made up of some of the biggest warships that Britain and France had available—and the two countries had plenty—would blast its way northward to Constantinople. Churchill's enthusiasm for the project was rooted in what the commander of the British naval squadron in the eastern Mediterranean had reported at the start of the year. With a fleet of warships and enough minesweepers to clear the way, Vice Admiral Sackville Carden said, he could reach Constantinople in thirty days. Substantial army involvement would not be required.

Little was necessary except to assemble ships that were already in the Mediterranean and send them into action. On February 19, when Carden steamed up to the entry to the strait and began shelling the forts there, he had under his command the most potent fleet ever assembled in that part of the world. It included twelve British and four French battleships (second only to dreadnoughts among the world's biggest, most heavily armed vessels), fourteen British and six French destroyers (much smaller, unarmored vessels, built for speed and firepower), an assortment of cruisers (midway in size between battleships and destroyers), plus—rather an oddity—thirty-five fishing trawlers that had been brought from the North Sea with their civilian crews for use as minesweepers. Most of the battleships were old to the point of being obsolete, but they carried heavy guns capable of doing tremendous damage at long range. And among them was the crown jewel of the Royal Navy: His Majesty's Ship *Queen Elizabeth*, the newest of Britain's state-of-the-art superdreadnoughts. She had just been launched and happened to be in the Mediterranean for her sea trials when orders went out for the Dardanelles task force to be assembled.

The key to success was obvious: the fleet had to attack quickly, clearing away the mines that the Turks were known to have laid in the Dardanelles, using shellfire to destroy the artillery on the high ground on both sides of the strait, and then pushing through into the open waters of the Sea of Marmara, at the far end of which lay Constantinople. The Turks, and their German military advisers, had been expecting an attempt of this kind. Their defenses, however, were woefully thin; they had only about a hundred pieces of artillery on the heights and very few troops with which to fend off landing parties. The Germans calculated that if the invaders were prepared to lose ten ships, it would be impossible to stop them. The Turkish government was so pessimistic that it began preparations to flee Constantinople for the interior.

Naval commanders, however, are not easily persuaded to risk ships and their crews. On this first foray Carden never seriously tested the strength of the defenses. A cautious man with no experience commanding large forces, he made no effort to move his ships into or even near the two-and-a-half-mile-wide entry to the strait. Instead he stood off in the distance, shelling the forts from three miles away, and at sunset he brought the attack to an end. His second in command, Vice Admiral John de Robeck, asked permission to continue firing but was refused. Carden intended to resume the next day, but the weather turned foul and spoiled visibility. The fleet waited far offshore while the defenders, having been alerted to the fact that a major assault was imminent, hurried to fortify their positions.

The ships returned on February 25 with De Robeck commanding, possibly because Carden's health was not good. Again they brought the forts under fire, and this time they put ashore raiding parties that encountered almost no resistance. Within twenty-four hours all the outer forts were neutralized, their garrisons either dead or in flight. Some of the big ships moved just inside the entry to the Dardanelles, but they dared not venture farther. To the north were other forts, most menacingly at a point where the channel was only a mile wide. Even worse, the strait was known to be heavily mined.

Clearing away the mines had turned into the navy's first major headache. The civilian crews of the improvised minesweepers had refused to proceed when they came under fire. The navy crews who replaced them proved to be inexperienced in handling both the trawlers and their complicated minesweeping gear. When a miniature flotilla of seven trawlers made its most aggressive probe, moving beyond the entry to the strait after dark, the Turks turned spotlights on them, brought them under heavy fire, sank one and put the others to flight. That was not the only problem. The British and French lacked adequate aerial reconnaissance, and the Turks' howitzers, lobbing shells from behind the ridges that lined the strait, could not be reached by the flat trajectories of the naval guns. And so De Robeck, like Carden before him, thought it imprudent to proceed. He withdrew, the days began to slip by, and the Germans and Turks continued to build their defenses. Churchill, too far away to appreciate the difficulties of the situation, sent message after message demanding that Carden *move*.

An interesting sidelight, considering that the campaign had been undertaken largely to help the Russians, is Russia's non-involvement. Russia had substantial forces not a great distance to the north (including warships in the Black Sea), and the campaign's ultimate target was the city, Constantinople, that the tsars had been coveting for centuries. Sergei Sazonov, foreign minister at the St. Petersburg court, was unenthusiastic about the naval assault for much the same reason that, the previous August, he had spurned an offer of alliance from Turkey. With Turkey as her ally, Russia would have been barred from seizing Constantinople and other pieces of the Ottoman Empire. Similarly, it was improbable that Britain and France, having taken possession of Constantinople, would then hand it over to their ally. If the city could not be captured by Russia alone, it should not be captured at all. "I intensely disliked the thought that the Straits and Constantinople might be taken by our Allies," Sazonov said later. "When the Gallipoli expedition was finally decided upon by our Allies . . . I had difficulty in concealing from them how painfully the news had affected me."

Russian nonparticipation was not the worst of it. On March 1, in what should have been a triumphant achievement for the Entente, the same Greek government that was encouraging Britain and France to send troops to Salonika and Lemnos offered three divisions of infantry for use at the Dardanelles—thereby proposing to end its neutrality. Italy, Bulgaria, Romania—all might be influenced to follow Greece's lead to get their share of the booty as Austria-Hungary and Turkey went down to defeat. The possible benefits of landing troops at the Dardanelles were brought into high relief: by clearing out the Turkish forts, they could reduce the dangers to the naval force to the vanishing point. And Joffre and Sir John French would have no reason to object.

But Samsonov was unwilling to allow Greek involvement. A British-French move on Constantinople was deplorable enough; involvement by Greece, a potential challenger to Russia's postwar dominance of the Balkans, was out of the question. And so the Russian government said no. In a message to Athens, Sazonov declared that "in no circumstances can we allow Greek forces to participate in the Allied attack on Constantinople." Sir Edward Grey intervened in an effort to save the situation, promising the

Russians that at war's end they could have Constantinople and territories around it. He was too late. News of the Greek offer and Russia's rejection, when it became widely known, threw Athens into turmoil. The Greeks amended their offer, making it contingent upon Bulgaria too joining the Dardanelles operation. The Greeks feared, the Balkans being the Balkans, that if they sent a substantial part of their army to the other side of the Aegean, the Bulgarians would attack them. There was no possibility of drawing Bulgaria in, and so the negotiations limped to a sorry end.

The consequences were far-reaching. Three Greek divisions could have been invaluable at a time when (as the Turkish army's history of the Dardanelles campaign would state) "it would have been possible to effect a landing successfully at any point on the peninsula, and the capture of the straits by land forces would have been comparatively easy." Instead, the Greek government fell. It was replaced by a government friendly to the Germans, which did not displease the King of Greece, whose wife was Kaiser Wilhelm's sister.

As the political complexities multiplied and Admiral Carden waited for the strait to be cleared of mines, fissures appeared among the leadership in London. Churchill, emerging as the principal advocate of the Dardanelles incursion, demanded that Carden and De Robeck proceed. Admiral John Fisher, as lofty a symbol of the Royal Navy as Kitchener was of the army and a close ally of Churchill's since the latter had brought him out of retirement at the start of the war, was skeptical. He continued to favor what was undoubtedly the riskiest idea that anyone had come up with thus far, the landing of troops on Germany's Baltic coast. He saw the Dardanelles as a threat to that venture and insisted that an attack there could not succeed without the landing of as many as a hundred thousand troops. He and Churchill began to draw apart.

Sir John French, to complicate things further, continued to complain that a commitment of troops anywhere except on the Western Front would be a monumental mistake. "To attack Turkey," he said, "would be to play the German game, and to bring about the end which Germany had in mind when she induced Turkey to join the war—namely, to draw off troops from the decisive spot, which is Germany herself."

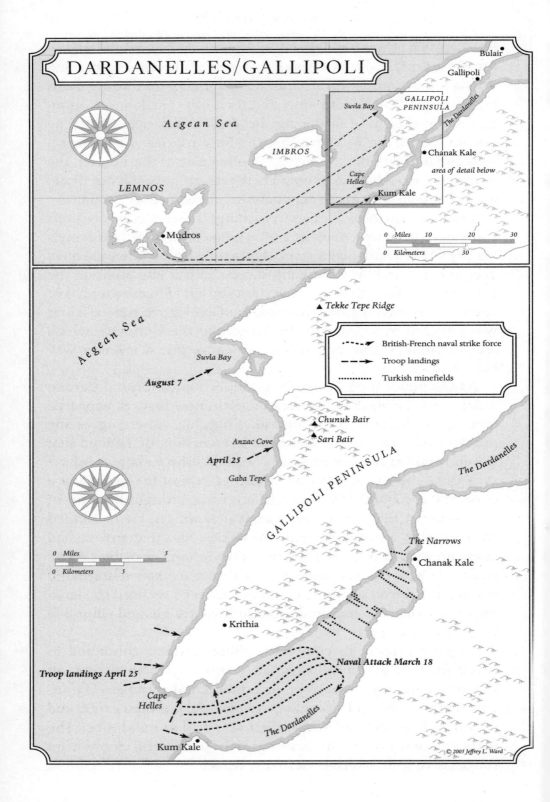

DARDANELLES/GALLIPOLI

Bulair

Gallipoli

Aegean Sea

IMBROS

GALLIPOLI PENINSULA

Suvla Bay

The Dardanelles

Chanak Kale

area of detail below

Cape Helles

Kum Kale

LEMNOS

Mudros

| 0 | Miles | 10 | 20 | 30 |
| 0 | Kilometers | | 30 | |

Tekke Tepe Ridge

- - - - ► British-French naval strike force

——► Troop landings

········· Turkish minefields

Aegean Sea

Suvla Bay

August 7 ►

Chunuk Bair

Sari Bair

Anzac Cove

April 25 ►

Gaba Tepe

The Dardanelles

GALLIPOLI PENINSULA

The Narrows

Chanak Kale

| 0 | Miles | 5 |
| 0 | Kilometers | 5 |

Krithia

Naval Attack March 18

Troop landings April 25 ►

Cape Helles

The Dardanelles

Kum Kale

© 2005 Jeffrey L. Ward

Churchill, seeing no need for troops and therefore not in conflict with French, impressed upon Carden that a successful assault would justify even serious costs. "The unavoidable losses must be accepted," he declared by telegram. "The enemy is harassed and anxious now. The time is precious." Kitchener was firmly with Churchill, saying that Britain "having entered on the project of forcing the straits, there can be no idea of abandoning the scheme." (Lloyd George, though without military experience, observed that continuing an offensive that has already proved unsuccessful has rarely in history turned out to be a good idea.)

Again Kitchener released the Twenty-ninth Division for service in the Aegean. This time, however, it was to be used—if needed—not at Salonika but at the Dardanelles. It was to become part of a new expeditionary force along with the Australian and New Zealand troops being transferred from Egypt. This force was put under the command of a longtime friend and protégé of Kitchener's, General Sir Ian Hamilton, a lanky sixty-two-year-old veteran who had served with distinction in India and the Boer War, had been a British observer in the Russo-Japanese War, and had a reputation for fearlessness under fire. Hamilton left England immediately, without specific orders and without a staff appropriate to his new responsibilities. He was to be rushed to the Mediterranean by train, put aboard a fast ship, and delivered to the Aegean in a matter of a few days. Once there, he was to take stock of the situation and decide what should be done. The French, meanwhile, had assembled a new infantry division for service in the Dardanelles and, in spite of Joffre's reluctance, started it for the Aegean. What was still supposed to be a naval operation, therefore, had by now come to involve almost eighty thousand troops. Russia too, Sazonov's concerns having been put to rest by Grey's grandiose offer of Constantinople, was promising a corps. It would go into action as soon as—no small condition—the British and French broke through to the Sea of Marmara.

Carden and De Robeck continued their preparations. Progress was being made in clearing the mines beyond the mouth of the strait. Weather permitting, the attack was only days away. Carden, however, was finding it impossible to eat or sleep. On March 13 he suddenly declared that he was unable to continue and would have to resign. De Robeck attempted to dissuade him—surrender of the Dardanelles command would mean the end of Carden's career—but was unsuccessful. A doctor examined Carden, declared him to be on the verge of nervous collapse, and advised him to start for home without delay. De Robeck took command.

Neither De Robeck nor anyone in his fleet knew of something that had happened on the night of March 8 inside the strait in waters that the British had earlier cleared of mines. The *Nousret,* a little steamer that the Turks had converted into a minelayer, had slipped past the destroyers guarding the cleared sector. There, parallel to the shore, it had silently deposited a line of twenty mines. It had then made its escape undetected. The mines hung motionless just beneath the surface of the water.

On March 10, the same day that Kitchener released the Twenty-ninth Division for the Dardanelles, Sir John French began at the Belgian village of Neuve Chapelle his first offensive since the onset of stalemate on the Western Front. It is perhaps no coincidence that the two things happened simultaneously. French was motivated, in part at least, by a determination to demonstrate that Britain's available troops would be better

Vice Admiral Sackville Carden
Said a British and French naval force could reach Constantinople in thirty days.

used on the Western Front than in some distant corner of the Mediterranean. It would not be strange if Kitchener had decided to get the Twenty-ninth away from Europe before the pressure to send it to Flanders became irresistible.

Just as French had been angling to have the Twenty-ninth added to the BEF, Joffre had been angling to get the British to take over the portions of the front that his troops were manning north of Ypres. What he wanted was reasonable: the patchwork character of the front, French then British then French again, created endless logistical problems. Joffre also wanted to free his troops for fresh offensives he was planning in Artois and Champagne. In mid-February, when Kitchener made the first of his decisions to send off the Twenty-ninth and French retaliated by announcing that this would leave him without the resources to do as Joffre wished—extend his line or support Joffre's latest offensive with an attack of his own—Joffre had called off the part of his plans that was to have been conducted in coordination with the British. He had begun complaining both to London and to his own government in Paris.

French and Douglas Haig feared that if Joffre got his way, the BEF would be consigned permanently to a supportive role. They wanted a different kind of role—they wanted *British* victories, and with them a full share of the glory. As it happened, Haig had a plan for producing victory: an artillery barrage of unprecedented ferocity to be followed by an infantry advance onto the ground cleared by the guns. He chose Neuve Chapelle because the Germans, who were thinning out their defenses in order to send troops to the more turbulent east, were known to have made especially severe cuts there. His objectives were to capture the Aubers Ridge, a long stretch of high ground a mile east of Neuve Chapelle, threaten Lille, and cut the rail line on which the Germans were shuttling troops and guns between Antwerp and Alsace-Lorraine.

French assented to Haig's plan. He wanted the attack to happen as soon as possible, before the politicians decided to give the BEF piecemeal to Joffre and independent action became impossible. March 10 became the chosen date despite the fact that the ground at Neuve Chapelle was always waterlogged in springtime and would not be suitable for infantry operations until April at the earliest. Joffre, asked to mount a supporting attack at Arras on the same date, waited until March 7 to take his revenge by replying that the British failure to take over his line near the coast had left him without enough manpower to help. The British decided to proceed anyway.

Weather aside, Haig had chosen his battleground well. The sector that he had targeted was a bulge in the German line, a salient exposed to fire from three directions. It was defended by only fourteen hundred Germans equipped with only a dozen machine guns, with few reserves nearby. The wetness of the ground made entrenchment impossible, so that the Germans were up on the surface, behind sandbag barriers that provided scant protection against artillery. Haig had forty thousand men, many of them Indian colonials, to throw into the attack. Their way would be cleared by fire from a concentration of artillery that would not be equaled until 1917: one field gun for every five yards of front, one heavier piece for every nineteen.

All these weapons opened fire at seven-thirty a.m., and for thirty-five minutes they turned the German line and the areas immediately behind it into an inferno where almost nothing could survive. Then they stopped, and the infantry, bayonets fixed, began their advance. Taught by experience to expect the worst, the troops at the center of the British line instead found almost no resistance. The defenders, everywhere except on the outer edges of the barrage, had been virtually annihilated. What was supposed to be the second line of defense was unoccupied and, when the British reached it, gave no evidence of having been occupied in months. When the Tommies moved through wrecked and abandoned Neuve Chapelle to yet another German line, it too proved to be empty. Only an hour and a half after setting out, they had reached their objective for the day. Ahead was empty territory, open and undefended. Haig had broken completely through—the first of only three times in the entire war that the German line would be torn open in this way. And only about a thousand German reserves were near enough to join the survivors within the next twelve hours. The gate to a tremendous victory stood wide open.

The story of how this triumphant beginning came to nothing is a chronology of mistakes, confusion, and leadership so deficient that it explains why Max Hoffmann, when Ludendorff later in the war exclaimed that British soldiers fought like lions, replied that fortunately for Germany they were "led by donkeys." Haig had limited his attack to a front only two thousand yards wide. This was not only unnecessary in light of the thinness of the German defenses—which the British were aware of—but too narrow an opening for such a large force to pass through efficiently. But when questions had been raised by Edmund Allenby, a cavalry commander who later would win fame in the Arabian Desert, Haig swept them aside with the observation that Allenby knew nothing about handling such large numbers of troops. Another difficulty was that a four-hundred-yard-wide sector at the northern end of the German line had not been shelled according to plan and was still intact when the advance came. Although the guns responsible for bombarding the sector in question had not arrived until the night of March 9 and therefore could not be ready for action the next morning (platforms had to be built, telephone lines installed), nothing was done to assign the sector to other batteries. The result was a pocket of German defenders who, untouched by the bombardment, were able to bring machine-gun fire to bear on the attackers both directly ahead of them and to their south. This fire need not have been enough to stop the main offensive, but it and a similar problem at the other end of the attack zone caused the officers on the scene to order a halt until the machine guns could be dealt with.

There followed a series of almost inexplicable delays, most painfully at the center, the point of breakthrough, where the colonel in charge requested permission to continue his advance but received no answer. Behind him tens of thousands of troops and support units found themselves jammed together at the too-narrow hole in the line, barely able to move and not knowing what they were expected to do. Meanwhile small German units began to arrive from all directions, and though they were pitifully few they brought machine guns and light artillery with them and quickly threw together new defenses. When the attack finally resumed at the end of the afternoon, the opportunity was gone.

Haig tried again the next day and yet again on March 12, but the Germans were growing stronger by the hour and soon were counterattacking. When Haig finally gave up, his gains included little beyond the ghost town of Neuve Chapelle. He had lost 11,600 men, the Germans 8,600—the numbers being mere abstractions that, as always, veil thousands of stories of lives lost and wrecked. The recollections of one British veteran of Neuve Chapelle provides a peek behind the veil. "I was wounded in the battle and taken to a casualty clearing station," said Cavalryman Walter Becklade. "I was beside a fellow who had got his arms bandaged up—I'd simply got my right arm bandaged. He was trying to light his pipe but couldn't get on very well so I offered to fill and light it for him. But when I'd lit it I suddenly realized he had nowhere to put it, as he'd had his lower jaw blown away. So I smoked the pipe and he smelt the tobacco, that was all the poor chap could have."

Lessons had been learned on both sides. The Germans acquired new confidence in their ability to hold off attacks even when outnumbered, and Falkenhayn became less reluctant to spare troops for the east. The British, on the other hand, learned a tragically false lesson. French and Haig concluded that Neuve Chapelle had failed because the opening artillery barrage had been too short. Henceforth they would insist on whole days of bombardment at the start of any offensive.

On March 13, the day after Haig ended his attacks, General Sir Ian Hamilton left London to take command of the not-yet-existent Mediterranean Expeditionary Force (which Kitchener had been calling the Constantinople Expeditionary Force until Hamilton suggested such a name might tempt the fates). He arrived in the northern Aegean just hours before the start of Admiral De Robeck's March 18 attempt to force the Dardanelles and was able to witness its climax.

The fleet that De Robeck took into the strait that morning was awesome: sixteen battleships—four French and the rest British— most of them old but every one of them enormous, heavily armored, massively armed. At the head of the formation, steaming abreast, were De Robeck's flagship *Queen Elizabeth* (which carried a dozen guns that fired shells fifteen inches in diameter) and three British battleships. About a mile astern of this vanguard, also abreast, were the four French vessels, commanded by a French admiral eager for combat and cheerful about following the orders of the British. Four other battleships guarded the flanks of these two groups while the others waited outside the mouth of the strait.

The only Turkish guns heavy enough to penetrate battleship armor were more than ten miles north at a place called the Narrows, where the sea-lane is only a mile wide. If these guns could be silenced, and if the mines that were known to lie in the Narrows could be removed, nothing could stop De Robeck from reaching the Sea of Marmara.

Once inside the strait De Robeck stopped the *Queen Elizabeth* and her three sister ships at a point where their biggest guns could fire on the Narrows. They were out of range of the Turks' heaviest guns (which were manned by both Turkish and German crews), and the guns that could reach them were too light to be more than a nuisance. For half an hour the four lead ships poured high explosives on the gun emplacements at the Narrows, knowing they had to be doing tremendous damage but unable to tell if their targets were being destroyed. Then De Robeck began the second phase of his attack, signaling for the four French ships to move past him deeper into the strait. This was a courtesy to the French commander, who had requested the honor of a prominent part in the offensive, and once his ships were north of De Robeck's line, they too began firing and coming under fire themselves. The clash continued for another two hours, with the fire from the Turks growing noticeably less frequent and less accurate, until De Robeck ordered the French ships to retire to the south and the ships that had not yet been engaged to come forward. Up to this point everything had gone perfectly.

Having completed U-turns to starboard, the French battleships were moving toward the rear in single file when suddenly the second vessel in line, the *Bouvet,* blew up. She sank with stunning speed, disappearing in less than two minutes and taking almost her entire crew of more than six hundred with her. No one knew what had happened; the general assumption was that either a lucky Turkish shell had somehow penetrated one of the *Bouvet*'s shell storage compartments or an enemy submarine had entered the strait. It was in any case an isolated disaster, and otherwise everything continued to go well. The surviving French ships completed their withdrawal and were replaced by six British battleships that had not yet seen action; they moved even farther north

Rear Admiral John De Robeck
*Changed his mind about naval assault,
dashing Churchill's hopes.*

than had the French, and for another two hours all the ships continued to fire. By late afternoon the return fire from the Narrows had almost ended. De Robeck, moving to the next phase of his plan, called the minesweepers into action.

The trawler-minesweepers came under heavy fire from the howitzers in the hills and soon turned and fled. Minutes later the battleship *Inflexible,* which had been firing her guns all afternoon despite substantial damage to her superstructure and was now near the place where the *Bouvet* had sunk, was seen to heel over sharply to starboard. Her captain sent up signal flags indicating that she had hit a mine and began steering for the exit from the strait. Minutes later exactly the same thing happened to HMS *Irresistible,* which was so completely disabled that De Robeck dispatched a destroyer to take off her crew. In the disorder that followed, as De Robeck withdrew his gunships and sent destroyers back into the strait to tow the *Irresistible* to safety or sink her if necessary to keep her from falling into Turkish hands, yet another British battleship was hit and went to the bottom.

This sudden turn of fortune had been costly—two battleships lost, two gravely damaged—but not ruinous. De Robeck at first was despondent, certain that his losses would prompt his dismissal. Instead, he received word from Churchill that four British battleships and a French replacement for the *Bouvet* were already on their way to join him. The minesweeping problem was quickly if belatedly remedied: the trawlers were replaced with destroyers fitted with minesweeping equipment. De Robeck, his confidence restored, telegraphed his eagerness to return to the strait and finish the job. Back in London, Churchill was delighted. Even "Jackie" Fisher, his doubts temporarily dissolved by De Robeck's expressions of confidence, was pleased.

But then, slowly, the tide of opinion began to turn. General Hamilton, troubled by what he had witnessed, wired Kitchener as he had been instructed to do. His message was not optimistic. "I am being most reluctantly driven towards the conclusion that the Dardanelles are less likely to be forced by battleships than at one time seemed probable," he reported, "and that if the Army is to participate, its operations will not assume the subsidiary form anticipated." In other words, troops were likely to be essential— troops in large numbers. An army was going to have to be landed, Hamilton said, and this "must be a deliberate and prepared military operation, carried out at full strength, so as to open a passage for the Navy." Kitchener agreed, declaring that it was now his opinion that the next phase "must be a deliberate and prepared military operation"—not, that is, an assault by ships alone.

By March 22, four days after the loss of the ships, De Robeck was brought around to Hamilton's way of thinking. When he reported to London that he too was now skeptical of clearing the strait with his battleships, even the navy and army staffs became internally divided. No one, however, suggested calling the whole thing off. The fruits of success were too tempting: Turkey out of the war, Bulgaria, Greece, and Romania all in on the Entente side. Failure, on the other hand, might induce the Balkan states not only to remain neutral but possibly to join the Central Powers.

At the center of the struggle, still determined to resume the naval attack, stood Churchill. He prepared a telegram ordering De Robeck to take his fleet back into the strait at the first opportunity. But when he showed his draft to several senior admirals, most of them—Fisher included—refused to endorse it. They told Churchill that it was unthinkable for London to insist on an action that the responsible admiral on the scene did not himself support. Churchill tried again to get De Robeck to change his mind—De Robeck's own chief of staff was also arguing that a resumption of the attack was certain to succeed—but could not do so. The prime minister thought Churchill was probably right but found

General Ian Hamilton
*"The Dardanelles are less likely
to be forced by battleships than
at one time seemed probable."*

it impossible to countermand Fisher and so many other admirals. Finally Churchill had to accept that he was beaten.

It is entirely possible that De Robeck would have succeeded if he had promptly returned to the strait. The Turkish and German defenders were amazed when he failed to do so, and they were not hopeful of stopping him if he did. Though most of their guns remained operable and the worst damage at the Narrows was soon repaired, their stocks of ammunition were dangerously low (a fact that was known to the British), and they had no way of resupplying. All along the strait, they had fewer than thirty armor-piercing shells. Their supplies of mines were likewise nearly exhausted. Officials in Constantinople were hurrying their families out of the city and preparing the government for flight.

The Turks were no better prepared to deal with a military landing, but the British and French were unprepared to land. Ian Hamilton was still waiting for most of his troops, and those that had arrived were not at all ready to undertake a vastly complicated amphibious operation. Lemnos, the island being used as the British base, lacked enough fresh water for all the troops pouring in. Hamilton decided that he was going to have to transfer the troopships to Egypt, where they could be unloaded and then re-loaded in proper fashion. He would have to decide where to land his forces, and how.

In one sense at least, Hamilton now seemed to have time to spare. The Russians, with the Eastern Front stabilized, were no longer quite so desperate for relief. Their defeat at Second Masurian Lakes was now weeks in the past and had done little lasting damage. In the south, in and around the Carpathians, they were by late March again on the attack. On March 22, Przemysl had fallen after a siege of 194 days. The siege had been a nightmare for most of the starving people sealed up inside—a nightmare made all the more intolerable by the fact that the fortress's top military officers and their mistresses had lived in luxury throughout the ordeal, waxing fat on secretly hoarded foodstuffs. In the hours before surrendering to the Russians outside, the Austrian commanders blew up their remaining supplies of shells. "The first ammunition dump exploded with a terrifying boom, the ground shook and the glass fell out of all the windows," a Polish woman who had gone to Przemysl in an effort to save her family's house wrote. "Clouds of ash cascaded from chimneys and stoves, and chunks of plaster fell from the walls and ceilings. There was soon a second boom. As the day dawned the town looked like a glowing, smoking crater with pink flames glowing from below and morning mist floating above—an amazing, menacing sight. These hours were perhaps the only hours like this in the whole history of the world. Countless people died of nervous convulsions last night, without any physical injuries or illnesses. By the time the sun climbed into the sky everything was still. Soldiers knelt on their balconies, praying . . . There is a corpse in our house, on the floor above the Litwinskis'. The man seems to have died of fear. I have to do something about him, but nobody wants to get involved, they are all leaving it to me. I persuaded one of the workmen to go down to the army hospital to ask what to do . . . he was told they would deal with it tomorrow, they've got too many corpses today as it is, littering the streets awaiting collection."

With Przemysl the Russians had captured a hundred and twenty thousand troops, nine generals, and hundreds of guns—all of which reduced Emperor Franz Joseph to fits of weeping. The surrender of Przemysl freed three Russian army corps to join a spring offensive that looked increasingly promising.

The Russians still were unable to move their accumulating surplus grain from the Black Sea to the Mediterranean and so get urgently needed currency for it. Nor could the British and French send supplies to the Russians via the Black Sea ports. But the Dardanelles campaign, if successful, would solve that problem permanently.

The suspension of the naval offensive at the Dardanelles, and the delay in getting an army offensive under way, were a huge boon to the Turks and their German advisers. They were still badly equipped and widely dispersed, but gradually, ever so slowly, they were managing to pull together a defense that just might, with much luck, be adequate to fend off Hamilton's attack whenever it came.

THE SEA WAR

THE DARDANELLES EXPEDITION WAS BY NO MEANS the Great War's first demonstration of British naval power. From the start of the conflict, under the aggressive leadership of Winston Churchill, the Royal Navy had asserted control of sea-lanes around the world and denied the Central Powers access to them. But not until 1915, when the likelihood of a long war had become clear to everyone, did the importance of sea power grow equally clear.

In a short war, one in which the Schlieffen Plan succeeded and was followed by the defeat of Russia, the United Kingdom's great navy would have mattered even less than its little prewar army. But in the siege that the Western Front became, all the combatant powers desperately needed access to the outside world. Few of them, the island nation of Britain least of all, produced enough food to support their populations. None could keep their war machines in operation without imported raw materials.

Britain, by 1914, had enjoyed unchallenged naval supremacy for a century. The Royal Navy provided the sinews that held the empire together. The government in London adhered to a policy of spending whatever was needed to keep the navy bigger and more potent than any other two navies in the world.

This policy was no great burden for the United Kingdom, and it posed no great problem for the other Great Powers, from Lord Nelson's destruction of the French and Spanish fleets at Trafalgar in 1805 on through the rest of the nineteenth century. But in the 1890s the young Kaiser Wilhelm II, eager to make his empire not only a continental but a global power, was persuaded by the ambitious Admiral Alfred von Tirpitz that Germany's growing world trade and colonial possessions required a first-class navy. By the start of the new century Berlin was expending enormous sums to build warships that rivaled Britain's.

The consequences were profound. Until the kaiser began his shipbuilding program, Britain and Germany had seemed designed by destiny not to conflict. Britain had the world's greatest collection of colonies and greatest fleet of warships, but only a small and widely dispersed army and no ambitions on the European mainland. Germany's overseas possessions were small by comparison, and it had no navy at all beyond a tiny coastal defense force. Both nations were focused on France, which for generations had been the most powerful country on the continent (it had taken Britain, Prussia, Russia, Austria, and Spain together to bring Napoleon down) and Britain's great rival in North America and the Caribbean, Africa, the Middle East, and elsewhere.

Even after the Franco-Prussian War, which established the newly unified Germany as Europe's leading power, Britain saw little reason to be concerned. She and Germany continued to regard each other as natural allies and old and good friends—a relationship personalized in the happy marriage of Queen Victoria's daughter and the first kaiser's son and heir. After 1890, when Russia and France became allies, whatever worries London might have had about Germany disrupting the European balance of power were temporarily put to rest.

But when Wilhelm II and Tirpitz embarked upon the building of a navy that they hoped to make as powerful as Britain's, they threatened the foundations of British security. From the perspective of London, Germany was no longer a friend but a rival at best and a serious danger at worst. (The kaiser neither intended nor foresaw this change. At once jealous and admiring of a United Kingdom ruled in succession by his grandmother, his uncle, and his cousin, he entertained fantasies in which Britain would embrace Germany as its equal on a world stage that the two would govern to the benefit of everyone, including the "natives" of backward and faraway lands.)

The German navy was born in 1898, when legislation financed the construction of seven state-of-the-art battleships immediately and fourteen more over the next five years. This ignited an enormously costly arms race. Britain was able to pay for its shipbuilding with tax revenues, but the Germans, already spending heavily to keep their army competitive with those of France and Russia combined, had to borrow heavily. (Members of the Reichstag objected, but they had no authority over the naval budget.) Further naval construction bills were enacted in Berlin in 1900, 1906, 1908, and 1912, each one more costly than the last. In 1898 Germany's annual naval spending had been barely one-fifth of the army budget. By 1911, with the army much bigger and more expensively equipped, the navy was costing more than half as much.

The result, for a nation with little in the way of a maritime tradition, was a surprisingly excellent navy, one whose ships and crews were by every measure at least equal in quality to those of the British. But London had done, and spent, still more. Admiral Sir John Arbuthnot Fisher—"Jacky" Fisher, the brilliant, dynamic, and strangely Asian-looking little first sea lord—radically reformed and upgraded the Royal Navy to trump the German challenge. Thanks largely to Fisher, in 1906 Britain launched a monster ship that revolutionized naval warfare: HMS *Dreadnought*, which at 21,845 tons was more than a fourth bigger than any battleship then in service, was sheathed in eleven inches of steel armor, carried ten twelve-inch guns capable of firing huge projectiles more than ten miles, and in spite of its size and weight could achieve a speed of twenty-one knots. When the Germans then built dreadnoughts of their own, the British responded by building still more, making them even bigger and arming them with fifteen-inch guns. It was a race the Germans could not win, but it went on.

Germany began the war with fifteen *Dreadnought*-class warships, each fitted with a suite of luxury quarters for the exclusive use of the kaiser, and five under construction. The British had twenty-nine and were building another thirteen. With France's ten heaviest warships added to the equation, the Entente had an insuperable advantage. Neither side was willing to risk its best ships in all-out battle, the Germans because they were outgunned and the British because the loss

Admiral Lord John Fisher
"Damn the Dardanelles—
they will be our grave!"

of their fleet would mean ruin. And so the first months of war saw a distinctly limited naval conflict in which no dreadnoughts were involved.

That war was a costly one despite its limits. It showed the Germans that their High Seas Fleet was not big enough to compete, and the British that they could keep that fleet bottled up in port but not destroy it. On August 28 a British foray at Helgoland Bight in the North Sea turned into the war's first naval battle; three German cruisers and one destroyer were sunk. On September 3, north of Holland, a single German submarine sank three antiquated British cruisers, fourteen hundred of whose crewmen were lost. On November 1 five German cruisers commanded by Admiral Maximilian von Spee met and defeated the Royal Navy's South American squadron off the coast of Chile, sinking two cruisers and badly damaging a third. Fisher, retired in 1910, had been called back to active duty by Churchill after war hysteria forced Prince Louis Battenberg to retire as first sea lord because of his German antecedents. (The family soon changed its name to Mountbatten.) Dispatching a task force of two battle cruisers (smaller than dreadnoughts and battleships), three armored cruisers (smaller still), and two light cruisers to South America, Fisher ordered Admiral Sir Frederick Sturdee not to return until Spee and his ships had been destroyed. On December 8 Spee raided Port Stanley in the Falkland Islands and was surprised to find Sturdee already there, taking on coal. Spee fled and Sturdee pursued, catching up with the slower German ships and sinking all but one. Spee went to the bottom with his flagship and his two sons.

Later that month German battle cruisers shelled three towns on England's east coast, killing a number of civilians. In January British and German ships clashed inconclusively—there were no sinkings—at Dogger Bank in the North Sea. Surface combat then came to an end, the British satisfied to keep the Germans in port and Kaiser Wilhelm, in the face of protests from Tirpitz, unwilling to send his fleet out to engage them.

The Royal Navy had by this time clamped down a naval blockade that cut off most of Germany's imports. In violation of international agreements, the Asquith government declared that the entire North Sea was a war zone in which not only German but neutral ships would be boarded, searched, and prevented from delivering cargo of any kind (food and medicine included) to places from which it might be forwarded to the Central Powers. Even neutral ports were block-aded, with most of Germany's merchant fleet interned therein. The British and French, meanwhile, were using their control of the world's oceans to move troops and supplies wherever they chose—to Europe from India, Africa, Australia, Canada, and the Middle East, and from Europe to the Mediterranean.

Berlin responded with a new and still-primitive weapon that was the only kind of ship it could send into open waters with any hope of survival. On February 4, though they had fewer than twenty sea-worthy submarines (Britain and France each had more, Fisher having insisted on adding them to the Royal Navy during his first tenure as sea lord), Germany declared that the waters around Britain and Ireland were to be regarded as a war zone in which all ships, merchantmen included, would be fair game.

Like poison gas and the machine gun, like the airplane and the tank, the submarine was something new in warfare. Both sides needed time to adapt to it. Only the Germans went after commercial shipping, because there was no German commercial shipping for the Entente's submarines to sink. At first they observed traditional "prize rules," ac-cording to which naval vessels were supposed to identify themselves (which in the case of the submarines meant surfacing) before attack-ing nonmilitary ships and allow passengers and crews to depart by lifeboat before torpedoes were fired. Such practices proved dangerous for the tiny, fragile, slow-moving and slow-submerging U-boats. They became suicidal when the British began not only to mount guns on merchantmen but to disguise warships as cargo vessels in order to lure submarines to the surface. The prize rules were soon abandoned.

The U-boats (*Unterseebooten*) sank hundreds of thousand of tons of British shipping, suffering heavy losses themselves in the process. They were, however, of little real value. At its peak their campaign was stopping less than 4 percent of British traffic but was arousing a ferociously negative response not only in Britain but in the United States. The German foreign office, fearful of American intervention, tried to persuade the kaiser that the U-boats' successes were not nearly worth the risk. Most leaders of the German army and navy demanded that the campaign continue.

On May 1 the German consulate in New York ran newspaper advertisements warning readers of the dangers of sailing on the *Lusitania,* a British Cunard steamship famous as the biggest, fastest

The "auxiliary cruiser" *Lusitania* embarking from
New York Harbor on her last Atlantic crossing

liner in Atlantic service. Less known was the *Lusitania*'s status as
an "auxiliary cruiser" of the Royal Navy. Its construction had been
subsidized by the government, which equipped it with concealed
guns, and it almost certainly had American-manufactured guns and
ammunition as part of its cargo for the May crossing.

On May 7, passing close to Ireland as it neared the end of its
voyage, the *Lusitania* turned directly into the path of the patrolling
submarine *U-20* and was torpedoed. It sank in twenty minutes after
a massive second explosion that soon would be attributed to the
German commander's gratuitous firing of a second torpedo into the
mortally wounded ship but has since been traced to an ignition of
coal dust in empty fuel bunkers. Some twelve hundred passengers
and crew drowned, 124 Americans among them, and the United
States erupted in indignation. German diplomats warned with new
urgency that the U-boat attacks must stop, and on June 5 an order
went out from Berlin calling a halt to the torpedoing of passenger
liners on sight.

Chapter 15

Ypres Again

"Out of approximately 19,500 square miles
of France and Belgium in German hands,
we have recovered about eight."
—Winston Churchill

As March turned to April the leaders of the Entente had reason to be satisfied with how the war was going for them in the East. The Russian offensive against Austria-Hungary in Galicia and the Carpathians—the same offensive that had taken Przemysl—continued to make headway despite lingering winter weather and chronic shortages of weapons and ammunition. (Ludendorff wrote admiringly of how the Russian soldiers, attacking uphill and armed only with bayonets, displayed a "supreme contempt for death.") The Russian Eighth Army, commanded by the able and aggressive General Alexei Brusilov, was capturing miles of the Carpathian crest and the passes leading to the Danube River valley. Russian control of Galicia was so secure that the tsar himself visited the conquered city of Lemberg (Lvov to the Russians, now Lviv in Ukraine), where he had the satisfaction of sleeping in the suite that until then only Emperor Franz Joseph had been allowed to use. A massive Russian move beyond the Carpathians seemed inevitable by spring or early summer. The Austrians, frightened, knew that they had little hope of fending it off. The Russians were so confident of their prospects that they no longer saw any need to offer a rich share of their anticipated postwar spoils in order to draw Italy into the war. And they were being successful enough against the

Turks in the Caucasus to make a Dardanelles campaign seem no longer imperative or even particularly desirable except in connection with a Russian advance on Constantinople.

On the other side, Conrad saw that his armies were on the verge of collapse and was begging the Germans for more help. Falkenhayn remained reluctant to comply, though increasingly he was of two minds on the question. His reluctance was fortified by the obvious intention of the French and British to continue their attacks on the Western Front, and by his belief that the war was going to have to be decided there. A complicating factor was the willingness of the Italian government, which until August 1914 had been joined to Germany and Austria-Hungary in what was called the Triple Alliance, to put itself on the auction block and see which side could offer the best terms.

Rome had been excluded from the July 1914 crisis by its putative but distrustful allies in Vienna and Berlin. This suited Italy's astute foreign minister, Antonio di San Giuliano, who wanted nothing to do with any of it. He saw Austria's behavior toward Serbia as aggressive and provocative, and he accused Germany and Austria of violating the terms of the alliance by failing to confer. Their actions, he said, relieved Italy of any obligation to go to war.

San Giuliano died in October, and Italy's foreign affairs were taken over by the prime minister, Antonio Salandra, a future fascist who regarded his country's neutrality not as a gift to be treasured but as a negotiable asset to be sold to the highest bidder. He put Italy up for sale, and because he claimed to have a ready army of almost a million men, the bidding was intense. The Entente and the Central Powers both thought it likely that the war would be decided by what Italy did. By spring, with the situation of the Entente so promising overall, it seemed almost impossible that the Central Powers would not collapse if a million fresh troops were thrown into the scales against them.

Britain made extravagant offers. It enjoyed the advantage of not having to promise anything that it, or France, possessed or wanted. Everything to be given to Italy (the port city of Trieste, lands from the crest of the Alps southward, islands in the Aegean, pieces of the Balkans and Asia Minor and Africa) could be extracted from the Austro-Hungarian and Ottoman Empires at the end of the war. The Russians were less forthcoming. Confident at this

Antonio Salandra
Prime Minister of Italy
Put his nation and its army
on the auction block.

point of defeating Austria, they wanted to promise nothing that might compromise their postwar dominance in the Balkans and points farther east. To win the acquiescence of the Russians, Sir Edward Grey promised them Constantinople and other parts of the Ottoman Empire—thus reversing what had long been an essential element of Britain's Middle East policy.

The ability of the Central Powers to bargain was limited: much of what Italy wanted belonged to or was coveted by Vienna. The Germans, accordingly, hoped for nothing more than to keep Italy neutral, but they were willing to pay a high price to achieve this goal. Chancellor Bethmann Hollweg went so far as to float the idea of giving part of Silesia to Austria-Hungary in compensation for its concessions to Italy. The proposal was shunned in Berlin; Silesia had been the single most highly prized conquest of Frederick the Great of Prussia.

The intrigues were endless. In Vienna the desperate Conrad and Berchtold came up with a scheme for getting Italy to mediate a general eastern settlement. Italy's reward would be the South Tyrol, part of Austria-Hungary's Alpine domain. Russia would be won over with offers of part of Galicia, Constantinople, and the whole chain of waterways from the Dardanelles to the Black Sea. That these plans would have been a flagrant betrayal of the Turks and likely would have been seen as a betrayal of the Germans as well appears to have been of no concern to either Conrad or Berchtold. Emperor Franz Joseph, when he learned of the idea, dismissed Berchtold. Thus the man most responsible for the war departed the stage before the conflict was a year old.

To Salandra, the bargaining appears to have been a game in which he had nothing to lose. It was obvious that he could do best by siding with the Entente. He merely went through the motions of bargaining with Germany to force the Entente partners to improve their offer. A decision could not be delayed indefinitely, however. If the Russians broke through the Carpathians, Italy's market value would plummet.

Meanwhile the French general staff had turned its attention to the St. Mihiel salient, a forward bulge in the German line south of Verdun (which was itself a French salient extending like a spear point into German-held territory). The plan was typical: by breaking the line on both sides of St. Mihiel, the French could either cut the Germans off or force them to withdraw. In so doing they would straighten and shorten their line and reduce Verdun's vulnerability. If fully successful, they would capture the railway lines extending westward from the German-held city of Metz and force an even more extensive withdrawal. These goals were, as always, deliciously attractive. The only question was, as always, their feasibility.

The offensive began on April 5. Fourteen French divisions supported by three hundred and sixty heavy guns—fully half of the total number of such guns possessed by the French army—attacked on a front almost fifty miles wide. The weather was terrible, the ground muddy, and visibility spoiled by fog, rain, and snow. French security was so lax, with French officers talking of what was coming in the cafés of Paris and towns nearer the front, that the Germans knew of the attack well before it began. Though most of the defenders were reservists, German combat engineers had been installing strong defenses since the capture of St. Mihiel in the fall, and the salient was rich in artillery. The fight quickly degenerated into prototypical Western Front warfare: bloody and sterile French assaults across the Woëvre plateau on the north side of the salient, withering fire from German machine guns and cannon. When Joffre finally allowed what came to be called the Battle of the Woëvre to gutter out, it had cost him sixty-two thousand men. But the relentless commander in chief, convinced yet again that he had come tantalizingly close to success, immediately set his staff to work on plans for another, bigger, two-pronged offensive north of St. Mihiel and in the Artois region to the west. All Europe settled down to a brief period of relative quiet. Even the Russians, their troops and supplies exhausted, had found it necessary to suspend—temporarily, they expected—their attacks in the Carpathians.

No one on the Entente side was comfortable with the lull. Joffre wanted another attack by the British, to keep the Germans occupied in Belgium. Sir John French, eager as ever to demonstrate that London should let him have more troops, was willing to cooperate. Falkenhayn meanwhile, unable to ignore a cacophony of warnings about danger in the east, continued to thin his lines in Belgium and France. He wanted, naturally, to keep these withdrawals secret from the French and British. To this end he was preparing a series of diversionary offensives. The first and most important would be at Ypres, where France too was preparing to take the initiative.

The Second Battle of Ypres, which introduced a horrifying new element into the history of warfare, had a suitably novel and horrendous prologue. For weeks British miners operating crude foot-powered devices called "clay-kickers" had been digging a tunnel from behind their lines into German territory. Their destination was Hill 60, the highest point on the Messines Ridge that overlooked much of the Ypres salient. The hill had been a key strongpoint and artillery observation post for the Germans since the autumn, when they first captured it. Once under Hill 60 (so named because it was sixty meters high, having been created years before with earth removed for construction of a railway), the tunnelers scooped out an underground chamber and packed it with explosives. When this cache was detonated at seven p.m. on April 17, it blew much of the hill hundreds of feet into the air, the German defenders and their weaponry and bunkers with it. The explosion was followed by an infantry attack that captured what

remained of the hill at a cost of exactly seven casualties. An estimated one thousand Germans had died, with perhaps a hundred
surviving. Hill 60 proved to be an uncomfortable prize, however,
exposed as it was to German fire from three directions. Its possession was not enough to prevent the Germans from moving up
an awesome array of their biggest siege mortars in preparation
for Falkenhayn's coming offensive and the experiment to be conducted in conjunction with it.

Second Ypres began late on the afternoon of April 22 after
forty-eight hours of the kind of intense artillery bombardment
that everyone now knew to be the preamble to an infantry attack. This time, however, when the guns fell silent, they were followed not by waves of charging riflemen but by the opening of six
thousand metal cylinders containing 168 tons of chlorine, a lethal
heavier-than-air gas that stayed close to the ground as it was carried on the evening breeze toward the French lines. Chlorine had
been chosen because it was readily available—the German chemical industry produced 85 percent of the world's supply—and
because of its effects: it destroys the ability of the lungs to absorb
oxygen and causes its victims to drown, generally with excruciat-
ing slowness, in their own fluids. No one on the French side knew
what the gas was. It first appeared in the distance as a white mist,
turning yellow-green as it drew closer. Its effects were immediate
and terrifying. Every man still capable of moving ran for his life.
With astonishing speed a four-mile expanse of the French front
line was totally cleared. Nothing stood between the Germans and
the shattered ruins of the little city of Ypres, which they had
spent so many lives trying to take in 1914. In minutes, and without losing a man, they had achieved a breakthrough even more
complete than the one the British had won and squandered at
Neuve Chapelle five weeks before.

The introduction of gas need not have come as such a surprise.
A French divisional commander, a General Ferry, had learned of
the German plans to use chlorine weeks before from a captured
soldier. He had informed both the French high command and the
British, suggesting that the canisters of which the prisoner had spo-
ken should be located by aerial reconnaissance and destroyed with
artillery. The only action taken in response to this warning was
directed at Ferry himself. First he was reprimanded for commu-

nicating directly with the British rather than going through channels. After the battle, when the importance of Ferry's warning was beyond question, he was sacked.

The success of the new weapon was as big a surprise to the Germans as the weapon itself was to the French. The only earlier use of gas, on the Eastern Front in the depths of winter, had been such a failure that the Russians hadn't bothered to report it to their allies. Though this new attempt, unlike the first, involved a deadly chemical, the Germans regarded it as a mere experiment, a peripheral element in an operation intended only to persuade the French and British that the Germans remained strong in the west. Not enough reserves were on hand to push through and occupy Ypres, in part because so many troops had been sent to the east. And though protective breathing devices had been developed years before for industrial purposes, none had been provided to the attacking troops.

The advancing Germans were shocked by what they found: five thousand enemy soldiers on their backs, struggling for breath, suffocating in agony and terror. The Germans became so afraid of catching up with the gas as it rolled on before them that they advanced only two miles and stopped. By the time their commanders understood the scope of the opportunity that had been created, a congeries of British, French, and colonial troops had been sent forward into the gap and the opportunity was gone. From now on all the armies of the Great War would expect gas and be more or less prepared for it. And though both sides would use it extensively, never again would it disable enough men to decide the outcome of a battle. Even at Ypres the British and French needed only hours to understand what they were faced with and find ways to deal with it. First it was noticed that the brass buttons on the soldiers' uniforms had turned green. Someone deduced from this phenomenon that the mysterious cloud must be chlorine and knew of a quick preventive: by breathing through a cloth on which they had urinated (a spare sock, for example), the troops could neutralize the poison before it reached their lungs. The first improvised gas masks thus emerged almost immediately after the first use of chlorine.

It was not necessary to be exposed to the gas or in direct contact with the enemy to experience the horror of Second Ypres.

Canadian Sergeant S. V. Britten tasted his share when, just hours after the start of the attack, he and his unit were assigned to strengthen defensive positions not used since the fighting of late 1914. "Left at 6:30 p.m. for reserve trenches and reached our reserve dugouts via St. Julien," he recorded. "Just rat holes! One hell of accommodation! Got to the trenches as a fatigue party with stake & sandbags, and though they were reserve trenches, they were so rotten. No trenches at all in parts, just isolated mounds. Found German's feet sticking up through the ground. The Gurkhas had actually used human bodies instead of sandbags. Right beside the stream where we were working were the bodies of two dead, since November last, one face downward in full marching order, with his kit on his back. He died game! Stench something awful and dead all round. Water rats had made a home of their decomposed bodies. Visited the barbed wire with Rae—ordinary wire strung across. Quit about 1 a.m., came back to our dugouts and found them on fire. Had to march out to St. Julien, & put up in a roofless house—not a roof left on anything in the whole place. Found our sack of food had been stolen and we were famished. Certainly a most unlucky day, for I lost my cherished pipe. Bed at 4 a.m."

After the first day Second Ypres too turned into a standard Western Front slaughterhouse. The Germans, never having intended to capture anything, settled into defensive positions as usual while the French and British launched counterattacks that accomplished nothing.

On the evening of April 24 General Sir Horace Smith-Dorrien, who had been one of the BEF's senior commanders from the start of the war and had repeatedly demonstrated his steadiness and courage, visited French at his headquarters and asked him to cancel an attack planned for the following morning. French refused, the attack went ahead, and the result was as Smith-Dorrien had predicted: a loss of thousands more British, Canadian, and Indian troops, with a gain of no ground. A division of Indian troops freshly arrived in Europe was almost annihilated while crossing a mile of open ground; the few who reached the enemy line alive were promptly gassed. Nearby a regiment of Senegalese troops—Africans transported to Europe by their French colonial masters—panicked after being ordered to follow the Indians and en-

Lt. Gen. Horace Smith-Dorrien
*Removed from command for
trying to do the right thing.*

countering chlorine. They turned on their heels, shot the officers who ordered them to stop, and kept running until they reached a supply area in the rear, where they ran amok. A corps of British cavalry had to be dispatched to bring the rampage to an end. The next day Smith-Dorrien sent a message to BEF headquarters, asking Chief of Staff Robertson to explain to French the hopelessness of further attacks. He also suggested a withdrawal to a shorter, stronger line nearer the city of Ypres. Upon receiving a curt reply, he sent another message suggesting that, if his resignation was wanted, he was prepared to submit it. Smith-Dorrien soon found himself ordered home.

Day after day, assured by Foch that Joffre would soon be sending reinforcements, French continued his offensive. The casualty lists grew longer. Not until May 1 did Foch confess that no French troops were coming—that exactly the opposite was happening; Joffre was removing troops from Ypres and sending them south for an entirely separate offensive. Finally French gave up. He ordered a pullback of three miles to precisely the position that Smith-Dorrien had been dismissed for suggesting.

The battle dragged on into late May, not ending until the Germans ran low on shells. They had taken forty thousand casualties, the British sixty thousand. "The profitless slaughter pit of Ypres," as Churchill would call it, had injected two new elements into the war: mining and gas. By introducing the latter, the Germans further damaged themselves in the eyes of the world—in American eyes most importantly. Intellectually, it was perhaps not easy to draw a moral distinction between piercing men's bodies with bullets and bayonets, blowing them apart with high explosives, and killing them with gas. On some deeper level, however, people sensed that warfare had been made monstrous in a new way, that another step had been taken toward barbarism. Not for the first time and not for the last, it was the Germans who looked most barbaric.

TROGLODYTES

THERE IS NOTHING MORE BIZARRE ABOUT THE GREAT War than the way in which, for four years, millions of citizens of Europe's most advanced nations lived in holes in the ground. The Western Front was unlike anything the world had seen before or has seen since.

In trying to visualize the front, the easiest mistake is to imagine a pair of ditches running parallel from the North Sea to Switzerland. The whole setup was much more complicated than that. Each side had five thousand men per mile of front on average, and this manpower was used to construct elaborate defensive *systems,* usually miles deep, that were zigzagging mazes fortified in all the ways that the latest technology made possible.

Though the methods of the three armies differed in their details, the basics were similar everywhere. First came the true front line, a trench six or more feet deep and about that wide, generally heavily manned. A mile or so to the rear was a support trench with a second concentration of troops. Farther back still, beyond the range of all but the biggest enemy artillery, was a third line for the reserves. All but the lightest guns were behind this reserve line, unreachable except by the most successful offensives.

Even this description is too simple. Trenches were often impossible to dig in the waterlogged soil of Flanders, where walls of sandbags had to be erected instead, and maintaining a continuous line could be difficult in the rough hills north of Switzerland. The German front "line" often included three parallel trenches, the first for sentries, another for the main force, the third for backup troops. However many such rows there were in any particular place, they were connected by perpendicular communications trenches, shielded by fields of barbed wire as much as thirty feet deep, and, more and more as the war wore on, studded with machine-gun nests. The trenches were less often straight than broken by dogleg turns, so that any enemy troops who got into them would have a limited field of fire.

Life in this maze embodied a cliché about war: that it is tedium punctuated by eruptions of sheer terror. The food was loathsome: bread that was a week old by the time it reached the front, canned meat when meat was available, overcooked vegetables that invariably arrived cold. Alcohol was issued daily: wine for the French (half a liter at first, then a full liter), brandy for the Germans, and rum for the British first thing every morning. Latrines, six-foot-deep pits at the end of short side-trenches, were unspeakably foul, and the traffic made them a magnet for enemy artillery. With dysentery widespread, the men often preferred to use buckets, old food containers, or the nearest shell hole.

Discipline was harsh and not infrequently arbitrary. British officers made wide use of Field Punishment Number One. Men deemed guilty of minor infractions would be lashed to a post or spread-eagled on an upright wagon wheel two hours daily (one in the morning, another in the afternoon) for as long as three months, often within range of enemy guns. And the punishments inflicted by the environment were often even worse.

There was trench foot, a fungal infection caused by prolonged exposure to cold and wet. It could lead to gangrene, then to amputation. Twenty thousand British troops were afflicted with it in the first winter of the war. Until someone discovered that daily rubbings with whale oil were an effective preventive, men crawling to the rear were a common sight and were often accused of malingering.

And there was trench mouth, which diseased the gums and caused teeth to fall out.

And when the weather was warm, trench fever erupted, caused by the excretions of lice. It began with a tingling in the shins and led to something akin to a bad case of flu. It was rarely fatal but put thousands out of action.

Lice were universal, their bites leaving red marks on the skin of every soldier. The men spent hours searching out the lice in their clothing and killing them with their fingernails or a candle flame. It was hardly worth the effort; the eggs remained in the seams and would hatch in a few hours.

The rats were even worse. A single pair can produce more than eight hundred offspring in a year. The front, with its garbage and decaying human bodies, turned into rat heaven. Soldiers wrote home of rats everywhere, rats almost as big as cats, rats eating the eyes out of corpses. Rats would chew through a sleeping man's clothes to get at the food in his pockets.

To all this was added a stench that rose to heaven, the impossibility when it rained of finding a place to lie down, and artillery fire that never quite stopped even when the front was supposedly quiet. Historians note that the armies of the Great War were made up largely of industrial and farm workers who were inured to hard labor, bad treatment, and minimal creature comforts. Even the generals most inclined to regard them as cannon fodder, however, understood that no one could endure much of this life.

And so the men were rotated. After no more than a week at the front, they would be pulled back to the support line, then to the reserve line, and finally to the rear. Even there, however, conditions were primitive. Shells still came roaring in, and exhausted, nerve-shattered troops would be drilled and harassed by officers eager to demonstrate their diligence.

The men were supposed to be given regular leave—a week every four months, in the case of the French—but often it didn't happen. When it did, the congestion of the railways and the low priority given to soldiers traveling alone could make it impossible for them to get home. Men returned to duty with venereal disease, contracted by eighty of every thousand men in the BEF. (The German rate was worse, the French somewhat lower.)

A trench culture emerged, with its own hierarchy, language, and rituals. Stretcher-bearers, many of them conscientious objectors, were admired for the courage with which they went out to rescue the wounded. Runners (Adolf Hitler was one of them, and he ended the war with two Iron Crosses) were constantly exposed to fire as they delivered messages and scouted ahead when their units prepared to move.

The setting was ideal for snipers, who became a professional elite. Sniper schools were established. Their products worked in pairs, a rifleman and an observer, firing high-powered rifles equipped with telescopic sights through holes in sheets of steel. Antisniper snipers came next. They were not always welcomed by the other troops, however; when snipers' positions became known, they drew enemy artillery fire.

Out beyond the lines lay no-man's-land. (The term has been traced back to medieval England, where it applied to disputed ground between two jurisdictions.) Pocked with shell holes, littered with debris and dead bodies, no-man's-land was sometimes half a mile or more in depth, sometimes only yards. Entering it meant death in the daytime, but at night it came to life. Raiding parties went out at sunset and returned at dawn, trying to see what enemy units were opposite, trying to capture prisoners to be questioned in the rear, sometimes just hoping for a few quick kills. For the most adventurous soldiers, this became a form of sport.

Wounds that allowed a man to go home without causing permanent damage were prized and envied. For the British these were "Blighty wounds"; for the Germans they were *Heimatschüsse*—"home shots." Veterans developed respect, even something akin to affection, for the soldiers on the other side. The enemy was suffering in the same way, after all, and was doing so with courage. Temporary truces were arranged for the bringing in of dead and injured, and some sectors came to be dominated by a live-and-let-live attitude with no one trying to make things difficult. The Bavarians were known to be particularly good-natured. When they were about to be replaced at the front by Prussians, they would warn the men opposite to expect more difficult days.

The British troops were "Tommies" to the Germans. The British called the Germans "Fritz" at first, then "Jerry." Names like "Hun" belonged to the patriots back home, from whom the men on the front felt increasingly alienated.

Officers could become objects of resentment. Even the most junior of them, often teenagers just out of the best schools, had personal servants. They lived in comparative comfort with better food and luxuries brought from home, and they never had to lift anything heavier than a swagger stick. Most despised of all were the staff officers, billeted in private homes far to the rear and rarely exposed to gunfire.

All this put officers in a different universe from the Tommies, the poilus, and the German *Frontschwein*. These common soldiers, whenever they moved, even when sent off on long marches or across no-man's-land in daylight assaults, carried a ten-pound rifle, at least 150 rounds of ammunition, bottles of water, an overcoat, a blanket with ground cloth, a trenching tool, days of rations that were not to be opened without an officer's permission, a "pocket primus" miniature stove with fuel, a mess kit with mug and cutlery, and whatever else they could manage, from socks and underwear to shaving gear, toothpaste, bandages, and books.

Chapter 16

Gallipoli

"I don't order you to attack. I order you to die."
—Mustafa Kemal

The Dardanelles have always been regarded as part of the line that separates Europe from what is broadly known as Asia. They are, in the most strictly literal sense, the stuff of legend. Before the dawn of history a maiden named Helle was said to have drowned there while fleeing with the Golden Fleece, and so until modern times the Dardanelles were known as the Hellespont. Leander swam the Hellespont nightly to visit his lover, the priestess Hero, and ultimately they too drowned. Jason and his Argonauts sailed through the Hellespont. Since the nineteenth century it has been accepted as fact that the city of Troy stood on the Asian side of the Hellespont, and a mound of earth there has since time immemorial been said to contain the bones of Achilles. The Persian ruler Xerxes took his great army across the strait when he set out to conquer the Greeks in 480 b.c., and Alexander the Great crossed in the other direction a century and a half later. The poet Byron swam the Hellespont for no better reason than that doing so was the most romantic act imaginable.

The importance of the Dardanelles derives from their position at the southern end of one of the most remarkable waterways on earth, one that connects the Aegean Sea and therefore the entire Mediterranean world with the Black Sea, with the Balkan states of Bulgaria and Romania, and with nations (Ukraine,

Georgia) that at the time of the Great War were parts of the Russian Empire. Entering the Dardanelles at their southern or Aegean end (the end attacked in 1915), a ship must pass through a deepwater strait forty-five miles in length before reaching the great open expanse of the Sea of Marmara, 170 miles long and fifty wide. At the northeastern end of this sea is Istanbul—Byzantium to the ancient Greeks, Constantinople from the early Christian era. It was a great city from ancient times because of its position at the entrance to a second navigable channel, the Bosporus, which is twenty miles long and leads to the immensity of the Black Sea. Even today, standing on the heights overlooking the point where the Bosporus opens onto the Black Sea, one sees an unending stream of freighters moving between the heart of easternmost Europe and the world beyond, carrying oil and grain and other riches. Nothing could be more understandable than Russia's centuries-old hunger to possess this passage, or the British belief that by wresting it from the Turks in 1915 they could win the war.

The Dardanelles owe their existence to an arid, ruggedly hilly peninsula that reaches some fifty miles southward from the Balkan mainland into the Aegean. The eastern coast of this Gallipoli Peninsula parallels the coast of Asian Turkey and is separated from it by only a few miles; it is within this gap that the Dardanelles channel lies, with steep ridges looming over it on both sides. From the peninsula's highest peaks everything is visible: the Aegean to the west and south, the entire length of the Dardanelles to the east, and the hills of Asian Turkey beyond, all of it controllable, in the years before bomber aircraft, by anyone who could get artillery onto those peaks. Once it was decided that the British and French ships would not be able to break through the narrows and that troops must be landed, the next step became obvious: to seize the heights of Gallipoli and take control of everything below. Once that was accomplished, everything else— the fall of Constantinople, the opening of the sea-lane to Russia, the winning of Greece and Bulgaria and Romania to the Entente cause—could be expected to follow.

As of March 18, the day De Robeck's battleships tried to force their way through the strait and ran into mines, the Turks had only a single ill-equipped, unprepared, and badly deployed division of infantry on the entire peninsula. Luckily for the Turks, however, the newly arrived British army commander in the Aegean, General Ian Hamilton, found his troops completely unprepared for anything as demanding as a landing on hostile shores. Everything was in disarray; the gun crews were not even on the same ships with their cannon or ammunition. Everything was going to have to be taken across the Mediterranean, unloaded, and reorganized. Accordingly, on March 22 Hamilton led his task force off to the Egyptian port of Alexandria. On that same day, in another stroke of good fortune for the Turks, Enver Pasha, who dominated the Constantinople government, had the good sense to put aside his faith in his own military brilliance. Instead of taking personal command (as he had done earlier, with disastrous results, in Turkey's winter offensive in the Caucasus), Enver created a new army for the defense of the Dardanelles and appointed as its commander General Otto Liman von Sanders, head of the German military mission in Constantinople. Sanders understood that the British, not having renewed their naval assault, must be preparing an infantry invasion. "If the English will leave me alone for eight days!" he implored the heavens when he saw the sorry state of the Turkish defenses. In the event, the British left him alone for four weeks, and he made use of every hour, pouring in troops, building fortifications, even improving the peninsula's primitive roads. The urgency of the work was increased by reports of the size of the force being assembled at Alexandria. Hamilton's command was far too big, Egypt far too thick with spies, for there to be any possibility of secrecy.

Not until April 25 did the invasion force steam over the horizon from the south and approach Gallipoli. It was the most powerful force ever to have attempted an amphibious landing in the face of an armed enemy. Two hundred transport ships were accompanied by eighteen battleships, a dozen cruisers, twenty-nine destroyers, and eight submarines. On those transports were twenty-seven thousand British soldiers, including the crack Twenty-ninth Division that before leaving England had been such a bone of contention, thirty thousand "Anzac" troops from Australia and New Zealand, and sixteen thousand Frenchmen. They had all the guns of De Robeck's great flotilla to support them and an abundance of their own artillery to take ashore. The Gallipoli expedition having been made a high priority in London and Paris, it was magnificently well equipped in virtually every way that mattered except two: hand grenades and trench mortars were in short supply. This deficiency would prove a serious handicap in the broken and hilly ground on which the troops would soon be grappling with the Turks.

Sanders by now had six Turkish divisions on the peninsula, eighty-four thousand men. But he had more than a hundred miles of shoreline to defend, much of it nearly inaccessible, and he could only guess where his enemies intended to come ashore. As it happened, his guesses were so wrong that their consequences should have been fatal. Hamilton had decided to divide his force and send it to three places. The French would be landed—only temporarily and solely as a diversion—at a place called Kum Kale, on the Asian shore south of the tip of the Gallipoli Peninsula. Correctly anticipating this deployment, Sanders had placed two divisions not far from Kum Kale, which was vulnerable because within easy reach of naval gunfire. What he couldn't know was that Hamilton had no intention of accomplishing anything substantial at Kum Kale; Kitchener had ordered him to avoid trying to establish a permanent position on the eastern side of the strait.

Otto Limon von Sanders
"If the English will leave me alone for eight days!"

The British were to be put ashore on five separate beaches at Cape Helles, the toe of the peninsula. This Sanders did not expect at all. With good reason, he thought it improbable that the invaders would land at the point of maximum distance from what was presumably their destination, the Sea of Marmara. He decided that Hamilton was most likely to send most of his troops by ship to the area around the town of Bulair, at the narrow northern neck of the peninsula. There, if successful, the invaders would be almost at the Sea of Marmara and positioned to cut communications between the Turkish forces on Gallipoli and their home base to the north. He placed two divisions at Bulair and made it his headquarters.

The Anzacs, the biggest part of the Allied force, were to be taken up Gallipoli's Aegean coast but less than halfway to Bulair. Their destination was a promisingly easy-looking beach leading to flat terrain at a point called Gaba Tepe. Air reconnaissance had found few Turkish troops in the area, and no reserves were nearby. Sanders therefore had a third of his troops on the wrong side of the strait and another third much too far north. Of the remaining third, half—a single undersize division—was sent to Cape Helles, where it would find itself trying to hold off the entire British landing force. The remaining one-sixth of Sanders's force, his last division, was sent to the middle of the peninsula, to a position from which it could move wherever needed. The only substantial Turkish force within a day's march of the Anzac landing, it was under the command of a strange, eccentric young lieutenant colonel who was so disliked and distrusted by the cabal that governed the Ottoman Empire that before the outbreak of war he had been consigned to inactive status. This was Mustafa Kemal, the future Atatürk.

The invasion should have been a triumph. The British, when they came ashore at Cape Helles, outnumbered the Turks there by six to one and met resistance at only two of their five landing beaches. Those beaches were, however, defended ferociously. At one of them, 700 of the first thousand troops to land were mowed down by machine-gun fire; at the end of the day only four hundred British were both on dry land and alive. At the other beach the Twenty-ninth Division, in action at last, fought its way through barbed wire and heavy fire, took control of the immediate area, and hunkered down to await instructions. None came, and so they did nothing. With a terrible absurdity, the same thing happened at the three undefended beaches. The British could have moved inland effortlessly and taken the crucial high ground that lay before them. They also, after advancing, could have swung around and taken from behind the Turks at the defended beaches. But no one had told their commanders what to do after getting ashore, and they stayed, uselessly, where they were.

At one of the undefended beaches, after standing by idly all day, the British spent a long hard night fighting off an enemy force that had at last come forward to meet them. In the morning, thinking their position hopeless, they returned to their landing craft and were taken away. At exactly the same time their Turkish adversaries, also having had enough, were themselves withdrawing. By then half the Turks at Cape Helles had become casualties, with barely a thousand still alive and unwounded. If the British had attacked, the sheer weight of their numbers would have been enough to sweep all resistance aside. But no orders came, and so again there was no move inland. Instead the British braced for a counterattack that the Turks were utterly incapable of attempting. Hamilton, on the battleship *Queen Elizabeth* well out to sea, had almost no idea of what was happening ashore and was able to issue no orders. By the end of the second day the French had disembarked from Kum Kale and were on their way to Cape Helles. It was too late. Sanders, having seen that there would be no landing in the north, was hurrying the Bulair divisions southward.

The landing of the Anzac force was also a disaster but of a markedly different kind. The Australians and New Zealanders, when they went ashore, encountered relatively light resistance but found themselves in a landscape far different from what they had been told to expect. Instead of the flat and easy ground that supposedly lay beyond Gaba Tepe, they found themselves having to clamber up into steep craggy hills and rock-lined ravines in the face of gunfire from Turkish riflemen concealed in the nearby hills. "A galling fire rained on us from the left where there were high cliffs," an Australian corporal would recall. "One man dropped down alongside me laughing. I broke the news to him gently: 'You've got yourself into the hottest corner you'll ever strike.' I had shown him where the enemy were, he fired a few shots. And again I heard the sickening thud of a bullet. I looked at him in horror. The bullet had fearfully mashed his face and gone down his throat, rendering him dumb. But his eyes were dreadful to behold. How he squirmed in agony. There was nothing I could do for him, but pray that he might die swiftly. It took him about twenty minutes to accomplish this and by that time he had tangled his legs in pain and stiffened. I saw the waxy color creep over his cheek and breathed easier."

Eventually it would become clear that the Anzacs had been landed not at Gaba Tepe but, probably because of a misreading of the tidal currents, a full mile north of their destination. They were on a piece of coast so harsh and inaccessible that not even the Turks knew their way through it. Twelve thousand Anzacs got ashore in less than twelve hours, however, and almost immediately their advance units began pushing on into the hills. Soon they stood unchallenged on the ultimate prize: peaks from which they could look back to the Aegean and eastward to the Dardanelles. From here, once artillery was in place, they would command everything that mattered on land and sea.

But just then, before enough Anzac troops could be brought up to consolidate what had been gained, Mustafa Kemal arrived with a single ragged battalion at his heels. Compass in one hand and map in the other, he had been leading a forced march to the shore since getting word of the landing. As soon as he saw the enemy troops, he led his men in an attack that cleared the crest. He then ordered his men to lie down, rifles at the ready, and sent back word for the rest of the battalion to hurry forward. An epic fight for the high points called Chunuk Bair and Sari Bair was on, and what followed was a day of desperate close-quarters fighting, much of it hand to hand, with both sides constantly bringing forward more troops and launching one assault after another. Kemal, ordering his men to make yet another charge in which no one seemed likely to survive, uttered the words that would forever form the core of his legend. "I don't order you to attack," he said. "I order you to die. In the time which passes until we die, other troops and commanders can take our place."

Slowly, at terrible cost, the Turks forced the Anzacs backward down the hill toward their landing place. That night, unaware that the Turks too had reached the end of their strength, the general commanding the landing force sent a message reporting failure and asking to have his men taken off. Hamilton, after much agonizing, replied that the Anzacs must stay where they were and "dig, dig, dig."

Three days later nineteen thousand British troops attacked at Cape Helles, briefly taking the high ground overlooking the end of the peninsula. Then they were driven back, suffering three thousand casualties in the process. On May 26 twenty-five thousand British and French attacked again, made no progress, and gave up after nearly a third of them had been killed or wounded. The Australians and New Zealanders remained crowded into, and unable to break out of, the wretched toehold that they had named Anzac Cove. Gallipoli was turning into something almost worse than outright defeat: a stalemate as tightly locked as the one on the Western Front.

As in Europe, both sides were soon mounting sterile attacks followed by equally sterile counterattacks. As in Europe, the sol-

Mustafa Kemal
*Saved Gallipoli
for the Turks.*

diers on both sides developed the familiar mixture of fear and respect, of hatred and admiration, for the men they were fighting. The Turks "came over in two great waves from their trenches, in great hulking mass," an Australian private observed of one attack. "They were rather big men, the Turks, fine body of men. As they came over, they were shouting 'Allah!' and blowing their trumpets and whistling and shouting like schoolboys. As they got closer, within nice rifle range, we had the order to fire and opened up with rapid fire and brought them down in hundreds, hundreds of them fell, and in front of our trenches." A corporal at Anzac Cove took a less admiring view: "The Turks suffer severely in their half-hearted bayonet attacks, usually delivered at night. They approach calling on Allah. We hold our fire until they are within twenty paces. Then they get a couple of stunning volleys and we hop out and bayonet anyone who cannot run away quick enough. I have not been lucky enough to catch one yet."

By May 8 the British and French had taken twenty thousand casualties. They had no uncommitted reserves to throw into the fight, and their supplies of shells were low. Desperation was deepening not only at Gallipoli but in London. With two more divisions, Hamilton wired Kitchener, "I could push on with great hope of success. Otherwise I am afraid we shall degenerate into trench warfare." Not everyone was even that hopeful. "Damn the Dardanelles" was Fisher's judgment—"they will be our grave."

AN INFINITE APPETITE FOR SHELLS

THE GREAT WAR IS REMEMBERED AS THE WAR OF the machine gun. Its defining image is of doomed foot soldiers, bayonets fixed, climbing doggedly out of their trenches and being mowed down like so many stalks of corn by gun crews dispensing instant death at the industrially admirable rate of ten rounds per second. And of course that image is no mere phantasm. It happened again and again from the summer of 1914 until the autumn of 1918. The machine gun was one of the war's essential elements, a prime reason why so many offensives failed so miserably, a puzzle that the generals had to solve before they could begin to succeed.

But in fact it was artillery that dominated the battlefields. World War I was the first major war, and it would also be the last, in which more men were killed by artillery than by small arms or aerial bombardment or any other method of destruction. Until late in the war artillery was the only weapon that, when used to maximum advantage, could neutralize the machine gun. It was the one weapon without which infantry, both when attacking and when defending, had almost no chance. Armies could and did misunderstand and misuse the machine gun and survive. There was less room for error where the big guns were concerned. Huge numbers of such guns proved to be indispensable from the start, as did astronomical numbers of shells. Where this need was not met, empires tottered.

The Boer, Russo-Japanese, and Baltic Wars had all given warning of what would happen if the armies of the great powers of Europe met in battle armed with thousands of the latest rifled, breech-loading, rapid-firing cannon. No one came close to imagining, however, how great the hunger for shells was going to be when such a war came. In the years leading up to 1914 all the powers had spent heavily on artillery (in addition to its heavy artillery, Germany began the war with more than five thousand smaller field guns and twelve hundred field howitzers), and all entered the conflict with what they thought were immense quantities of ammunition. All were stunned by the speed with which their supplies were exhausted. When 1915 arrived with both fronts deadlocked, all the belligerents found themselves desperately short not just of shells but of production capacity. No amount ever seemed to be enough.

The French, who thought they had a three-month supply on hand at the end of July 1914, were rationing the number of shells given to each battery within six weeks; the Battle of the Marne nearly cleaned them out. The British, believing that they were going to war with a six-month supply, were running short before the end of October. The Russians, proud of having stockpiled a thousand rounds for every gun in their army, were likewise soon baffled by a conflict in which a single artillery piece might be called upon to fire a thousand times every couple of days.

When Grand Duke Nicholas told the Petrograd government that he needed two and a half, then three and a half *million* shells per *month,* these were numbers that Russian industry could not begin to provide. And so the Russians began placing huge orders overseas, first with British suppliers (who cheerfully accepted them and the advance payments that came with them in spite of being unable to meet their own army's needs), then with the United States. Being essentially bankrupt by early 1915, Russia was able to pay only by drawing on a line of credit of £25 million per month grudgingly extended by a British government fearful of collapse in the east. The systemic corruption and profiteering of the Russian procurement system assured that much of the money simply disappeared. Much of what was ordered was never delivered, and much of what was delivered piled up uselessly at Russia's only functioning (and woefully inadequate) ports of entry, Vladivostok at the eastern end of Siberia and Archangel in the Arctic.

Though the shortage was severe for all the belligerents, its nature varied from country to country. Austria was plagued by the need to produce ammunition for a ridiculously large number of different *kinds* of guns, many of them antiques long since discarded by armies that had done a better job of modernizing and standardizing. But even the most modern armies encountered problems not only of quantity but of shell type. All of them, before the war, had given priority to the production and accumulation of shrapnel, an antipersonnel projectile that, upon exploding in midair, showers lethal lead pellets over a wide area. The early months of the war showed

A British munitions plant, pouring out shells for the armies of the Entente

that, though shrapnel was effective in cutting away barbed wire, it was useless for destroying fortifications and killing the men inside. Only high explosives such as dynamite and nitroglycerin did the job. The consumption of high-explosive shells—much more complicated and costly than shrapnel—increased exponentially.

France and Germany adapted best. In Paris an able and energetic young socialist politician named Albert Thomas was named under-secretary for armaments in the ministry of war and hurried to make changes. He got three hundred and fifty thousand skilled industrial workers—eventually half a million—released from military service and assigned to munitions factories and coal mines. He brought tens of thousands of women onto the payrolls of private and government plants. He thereby started a gender revolution that would change European society; by the end of the war women would fill more than a third of all industrial jobs in Britain and France, and more than half of such jobs in Germany. Prisoners of war were put to work as well, and refugees. With remarkable speed France was soon coming close to meeting the needs of its army.

Germany's situation was especially perilous in the first year of the war. Moltke, uniquely among Europe's prewar military planners, had insisted on the development of industrial facilities capable of achieving and sustaining high rates of munitions production. These facilities provided a basis for rapid expansion, but they were not nearly enough. The Germans had used more ammunition in the Battle of the Marne than in the Franco-Prussian War; First Ypres and the war in the east further drained supplies; and the naval blockade put in place by Britain cut Germany off from sources of essential commodities.

To attack the problem Falkenhayn, in his capacity as minister of war, recruited a dynamic young Jewish industrialist named Walter Rathenau. Rathenau got almost miraculous results out of Germany's chemical and engineering industries. Soon camphor, essential in the production of gunpowder, was being extracted from turpentine rather than imported from Japan. Nitrogen was being drawn from the atmosphere rather than from the guano deposits of Chile, and wood products were replacing American cotton and also providing the acetone needed for making nitroglycerin. In Germany as in France, skilled workers were exempted from military duty and women went into the factories. By the summer of 1915 Germany was manufacturing upward of four million shells per month. That was sufficient, though barely.

Historians who have examined the question argue persuasively that the shell crises of 1914 and 1915 need not have been as serious as they were and in fact were sometimes not as serious as the generals claimed. In many battles, especially when bad weather turned roads to muck, the problem was not so much a lack of ammunition as an inability to get the necessary tons of it to the waiting guns. In Serbia in 1914 horse-drawn Austrian wagons laden with shells were able to move only twelve miles in four days of hard labor. Gunners were often profligate, opening fire, for example, upon seeing just one or two distant soldiers. The Russians made especially bad use of their supplies, stockpiling mountains of shells in fortresses that usually had little military value and eventually fell to the Germans.

Generals on both sides became adept at blaming a shortage of shells for their failure to produce the results they had promised. In Russia, Minister of War Sukhomlinov was so convinced that his rivals were using such complaints to undercut him politically that he withheld urgently needed ammunition. At the end of First Ypres, Sir Douglas Haig complained to a journalist that his troops could simply have walked through the German lines unopposed "as soon as we were supplied with ample artillery ammunition of high explosives."

Haig's failures in later offensives, when his supplies of ammunition were practically infinite, make this complaint dubious at best. But it was not the last such complaint to be made—and made publicly—by a senior commander of the BEF. The result, before 1915 was half finished, would be a crisis that brought down Asquith's Liberal government and led to a radical redistribution of power among Britain's political leaders.

Chapter 17

The Ground Shifts

*"Success will come in the final analysis to
the side which has the last man."*
—Henri-Philippe Pétain

By the end of April the Germans had scraped together enough troops to form yet another new eastern army, the Eleventh. They accomplished this through a general reorganization in which the number of battalions per division was reduced from twelve to nine, compensating for the reduction in manpower by giving every division more machine guns. Command of the Eleventh was given to August von Mackensen, a ferocious-looking general who had figured importantly in the Tannenberg victory and offered Falkenhayn the advantage of being no friend of Hindenburg and Ludendorff.

The question facing Falkenhayn would have seemed familiar in London: how should the new army be used? Giving it to Hindenburg was out of the question. Transferring it to the Western Front was impossible because contrary to the wishes of Kaiser Wilhelm, who though declining in influence remained hereditary All-High Warlord with the power to set strategy. The fact that not a single offensive on the Western Front had achieved its intended results reinforced the kaiser's belief that victory could be achieved only in the east.

Falkenhayn had to do *something*, he was going to have to do it in the east, and he strongly preferred that it not happen in the northern sectors where Hindenburg was in command. A simple process of elimination pointed him toward the southeast—toward the Austrians and their endless problems. And though he still had powerful political enemies, Falkenhayn also had a new ally: Crown Prince Wilhelm, the kaiser's heir. This far-from-incapable young officer, now developing into a seasoned army commander, suggested how Falkenhayn might satisfy the skeptics and at the same time prepare the way for the Western Front offensive that he wanted. The prince's idea was simple and sensible. Germany's prime objective should be not to defeat the Russians conclusively—an unrealistic goal, in light of the enemy's manpower and the vast distances of the eastern theater—but to damage them so badly that in 1916 the Germans would be free to turn their attention to the west.

Falkenhayn was thus disposed to pay heed when Conrad reported from Vienna that he saw an opportunity to break through the momentarily static Russian line between the Galician towns of Gorlice and Tarnow, and thereby preempt the inevitable resumption of Russia's Carpathian offensive. Conrad, however, remained desperately short of troops and shells, and so he added that he would be incapable of executing his plan without the assistance of at least four German divisions. Falkenhayn's answer was surprising from a man who had so long been incapable of enthusiasm where the east was concerned. He told Conrad that he was sending not just the four requested divisions but twice that many: all four of the corps that made up Mackensen's new army. Conrad, formally in charge of the campaign, was required to promise that he would do nothing without the approval of Falkenhayn or, in Falkenhayn's absence, of Mackensen. Mackensen, along with the Army of the South that was already operating with Conrad under the command of General von Linsingen, would be reporting not to the two giants of the north but to Falkenhayn himself.

Over a ten-day period Mackensen's army was moved into place, surreptitiously so as not to alert the Russians, behind a thirty-mile expanse of front facing Gorlice and Tarnow. Falkenhayn himself went east to oversee the deployment, while Hindenburg and Ludendorff remained on the sidelines. Pointedly declining to give them any direct role in the impending offensive, Falkenhayn asked them to undertake a diversionary action to draw as many Russians as possible away from Galicia. Ludendorff, interested not in diversions but in conquest, took Falkenhayn's request as justification for sending a large cavalry force into Russian-controlled territory on the far northern Baltic coast, a remote and desolate region called Courland that the war had not yet reached. At first this probe did not produce the result that Falkenhayn, at least, was hoping for: the Russians didn't regard it as important enough to require a strong response.

The southern offensive, with Conrad and his troops in a distinctly subordinate role, began on May 2 with a brief but fantastically intense artillery barrage and almost immediately turned into a success unlike anything seen in the west. In four hours fifteen hundred German and Austrian gun crews dropped seven hundred thousand rounds of high explosives, shrapnel, and poison gas onto a twenty-eight-mile front occupied by the Russian Third Army, which had not troubled to construct strong defenses and was short not only of artillery but even of rifles. Worse, the Russians' five and a half divisions—sixty thousand men—had been worn down by the winter fighting in the Carpathians and had been left in an isolated position that no other Russian force would be able to reach quickly. When the bombardment ended and Mackensen's ten divisions and Conrad's eight moved forward, the Third Army collapsed. The attackers pushed it back beyond Gorlice in less than twenty-four hours. They advanced eight miles in forty-eight hours, Tarnow fell on the fifth day, and within a week a hundred and forty thousand Russians and two hundred guns had been captured. Two other Russian armies came forward to rescue the Third, but their movements were poorly coordinated and accomplished little beyond feeding more bodies to the German gunners. General Radko Dimitriev, commander of the Third Army, was begging for approval to begin—so far as his troops were still capable of such a thing—a retreat across Galicia to the River San. This would have required abandoning the great prize of Przemysl. Grand Duke Nicholas, unable to accept the surrender of everything he had won, refused. He ordered Dimitriev to do what the German artillery made an impossibility: to stand his ground.

With winter finished, the war was heating up everywhere. A week after the start of the Gorlice-Tarnow offensive, Joffre and French launched in the Artois region directly south of Ypres (where the fighting had never entirely died down) a massive attack that both men expected to produce great results—that Joffre said could "finish the war in three months." The thinning of the German line had gone too far to remain secret. Knowledge of it helped make Joffre and French as confident as ever that the eternally hoped-for great breakthrough was at hand.

The bloody mess called the Second Battle of Artois began on May 9. After only forty-six minutes of shelling (the brevity of this bombardment was made necessary by a scarcity of high-explosive shells), three corps of Haig's recently formed British First Army hit two sectors of line defended by only two German regiments. The Germans had constructed parallel lines of defense, including dugouts reinforced with timbers that, when topped with layers of dirt-filled sandbags, could not be penetrated even by high explosives. Only 8 percent of the British shells had contained high explosives, and their shrapnel hadn't been sufficient even to cut away the barbed wire in front of the trenches.

The defenders emerged from the barrage almost untouched, their machine guns so positioned as to be able to direct a heavy fire into the flanks of the two formations of British attackers. The target of the offensive was Aubers Ridge, which rose up abruptly behind the Germans' first line. Once there, the attackers were to move southeast along a line of ridges until they linked up with French troops who, according to the plan, would by then be on the march toward the town of Lens. Beyond Lens lay a flatland called the Douai plain, the wrecked Belgian fortress of Namur, and (so Joffre hoped) victory.

On that first day British casualties totaled 11,600, more than four hundred and fifty officers included, with so little result that the offensive was brought to a halt. The stop was temporary; three more divisions were thrown at the Germans May 16 through 18, suffering seventeen thousand additional casualties while gaining no ground.

The French had much greater initial success, in part because their attack was preceded by six *days* of bombardment during which twelve hundred guns poured seven hundred thousand shells onto the Bavarians of Crown Prince Rupprecht's Sixth Army. In the four hours before the infantry's advance, the gunners fired enough rounds to put eighteen high-explosive shells on every yard of front; most of their guns were 75mm field pieces with low trajectories ill suited to the shelling of trenches, but the cumulative effect was devastating. Though both flanks of the attack force were butchered by machine-gun fire, the center quickly penetrated three miles into enemy territory. For three days the center continued its advance, taking possession of three German lines.

Then heavy rain began to fall, turning the ground to a gluey mud that made further progress impossible. In the end the early success of this assault led to losses so severe that it would have been better for the French if they had been checked at the beginning as completely as the British. The attackers made no breakthrough, finally, just an impressive but temporary bending-back of the German line. Ultimately they found themselves blocked by a last-ditch line of machine-gun nests that alone stood between them and the German artillery. As usual, the fight went on long after any chance of success had evaporated, with repeated French and British attacks neutralized by German counterattacks, casualties piling up, and nothing of importance accomplished. When the battle came to its end on June 18, the French had lost more more than a hundred thousand men, the Germans just under fifty thousand.

Joffre remained undaunted. He was already making plans not only to restart the Artois offensive in the fall but to combine it with a simultaneous, even bigger attack in Champagne, thereby swamping the ability of the Germans to respond. If only in numerical terms, Joffre's optimism had a rational basis: by early summer the British and French outnumbered the Germans on the Western Front by fully half a million men. Sir John French was as confident of success as Joffre and as eager for more offensives.

But the costs of Artois did affect people whose minds were not impervious to reality. Across France this latest torrent of death produced shock, though complaint was muted by Joffre's assurances that German losses had been immensely greater. The government in Paris was deeply troubled, all the more so as some of Joffre's subordinate generals grew restive, and the humble poilus, the "hairy ones," were beginning to display an unwillingness to participate in the most suicidally hopeless assaults. Joffre was still the savior of France, but the ground under his feet was no longer quite so solid.

At the same time the prestige of Henri-Philippe Pétain, who less than a year earlier had been an obscure colonel preparing a country home for retirement, was rising rapidly. It was a corps under Pétain's command that had made all the early gains in the Artois offensive, its advance units getting to the top of Vimy Ridge before being driven off by arriving German reserves. Pétain's painstaking preparations and efficient execution had been essential to this success, limited and temporary as it was. He was a hard disciplinarian but nearly unique among the high-ranking generals of the time in the concern he showed for the living conditions of his troops and his willingness to share their risks. (He would move forward into the combat zone when his men were under bombardment.) The disdain for the cult of the offensive that had crippled his peacetime career was beginning to look like wisdom. In the crucible of combat he was emerging as a model of professional competence and common sense. Above all he was a commander who got results, and so in the immediate aftermath of the Artois campaign he was promoted to command of the French Second Army.

Plainspoken as always, he produced a report on Second Artois in which he declared that this war was not going to be won by some breakthrough, some great and brilliantly executed conclusive battle. This, he said, was a war of attrition, and it required keeping casualties at tolerable levels. "Success will come in the final analysis," he said, "to the side which has the last man." In this regard he was much closer in his thinking to Falkenhayn than to Joffre, French, and Haig. He was also ahead of his fellow French generals, and almost abreast of the best German thinking, in his understanding of how to use artillery and infantry together. It was the big guns that took enemy ground, he said. The infantry's job was to occupy what the artillery had conquered.

In London too the ground was shifting. Kitchener, as potent a national symbol in Britain as Joffre was south of the Channel, was as baffled as his French counterpart by this terrible new kind of warfare and far more prepared to admit that no solutions were at hand. Behind the scenes he was losing the iron-hard self-assurance that had for so long been an essential element of his public persona. He had lost faith in the Gallipoli campaign, where the British and French were bogged down on their landing beaches and were beginning to be ravaged by dysentery and the fly-plagued miseries of the Turkish summer. But he could see no way of extracting Hamilton's force without losing tens of thousands of men in the process. He could see no alternative to pushing ahead to victory (one of his fears was that defeat in Turkey would provoke a revolt by Britain's Muslim subjects in Egypt) and seemed prepared to pay almost any price in doing so. Early in May there had been talk of trying again to use the Entente's Mediterranean fleet to force the Dardanelles, but all such planning came to an end with the sinking at Gallipoli of the British battleship *Goliath*. The mighty *Queen Elizabeth,* crown jewel of the Dardanelles task force, was withdrawn to safer waters. Three days later, on learning that Churchill was sending still more warships to the Dardanelles, Admiral John Fisher resigned as first sea lord and sent a wildly emotional letter to the leader of the Tory opposition. Calling Churchill "a real danger," he warned that "a very great national disaster is very near us in the Dardanelles!" On May 25 the first U-boat to reach the Aegean torpedoed and sank the battleship *Triumph*. A day later it sank the *Majestic,* at which point the six British battleships remaining near the Dardanelles were sent away. With that, even the possibility of a naval attempt on the strait disappeared.

Kitchener remained skeptical about the prospects of success on the Western Front but was finding it increasingly difficult to act in accordance with his doubts. The enormous prestige that had prompted his appointment as secretary of state for war had by now shriveled considerably, at least in the eyes of his fellow cabinet members, and his hold on power was slipping. Kitchener had always been better suited to the role of satrap, to ruling distant parts of the empire, than to the compromises and collaboration of party politics, and his political skills had not improved since the start of the war. He remained secretive, autocratic, and unwilling to cooperate or delegate. "It is repugnant to me," he had said after getting a taste of cabinet government, "to have to reveal military secrets to twenty-three gentlemen with whom I am hardly acquainted." By the spring of 1915 he was sorely disliked and resented by many ministers and by the Tories as well.

In mid-May, with the bloodletting of Second Artois at its height and Haig's attack on Aubers Ridge having come to its disastrous conclusion, Kitchener canceled an order that would have sent the first of Britain's new divisions to the Western Front. Sir John French, driven half mad with frustration by news that three of the divisions were going to Gallipoli, fired off a wire to Kitchener announcing that he was so low on shells that he would not be able to resume his offensive unless immediately resupplied. When Kitchener's reply arrived—it was, to French's shock, an order to release 20,000 artillery rounds for shipment to Gallipoli—something inside the commander of the BEF snapped. Possibly too angry to notice that the message also said that the diverted shells would be replaced within twenty-four hours (a promise that was kept), French decided to make war on Kitchener. He called in an old friend and former army colleague, the London *Times* military correspondent Charles à Court Repington, and told him, not for attribution, that the British offensives were failing because of a lack of artillery ammunition and that the fault lay with Kitchener. A few days later a series of articles based on French's accusation began appearing, with sensational impact, in London. Coupled with Fisher's resignation, these articles created the impression of a government in chaos. The situation was worsened by two staff officers dispatched to London to explain French's complaints. They found receptive listeners in Andrew Bonar Law, the leader of the Conservative Party, and David Lloyd George, who was becoming increasingly outspoken in criticizing Kitchener's dominance over military policy.

Lloyd George, long one of the most brilliant stars in Britain's political firmament, was emerging as a dominant figure. Paying a visit to Asquith, he warned the prime minister that he himself would make further public disclosures about mismanagement of armaments production unless drastic action was taken without delay. Asquith, being if nothing else skilled at self-preservation, reacted quickly. The government was dissolved and replaced with a coalition cabinet—the first wartime coalition in British history. Asquith held on to his job, but Conservative members became a major element in the cabinet and Lloyd George was the leader of the surviving Liberals. Parliament passed a Munitions War Act that established a new ministry of munitions, thereby taking responsibility for armaments out of Kitchener's hands. The prime minister ordered him to start submitting frequent and detailed reports on his actions and plans, ending his freedom to operate in as much secrecy as he wished. Eventually, as a final humiliation, responsibility for strategy would be shifted from Kitchener to the chief of the imperial general staff.

Lloyd George moved into the new munitions ministry and took drastic action. He outlawed strikes in the weapons industry and sharply increased the production of heavy artillery and high-explosive shells. Trying to come to grips with a problem plaguing all the belligerent nations, he took steps aimed at controlling profiteering by arms manufacturers.

French, in launching his press campaign, had hoped to destroy Kitchener. But Kitchener survived, albeit with his authority diminished. The only politician destroyed was one whom French liked and admired: Winston Churchill. The Conservatives had old scores to settle with Churchill, who a decade earlier had deserted them to join the Liberals. One of their conditions in joining the coalition was that Churchill could not continue as First Lord of the Admiralty. Asquith was not a man to endanger his own position in order to defend anyone else, and so Churchill was out. He departed the Admiralty in tears, certain that his career was at an end.

Kitchener retained, along with his job title, the power to decide where to send the volunteer armies that were now fully trained and ready for active service. Weakened as he was, he finally consented to send most of these units where he did not think them likely to accomplish much—to the Western Front. He also continued to feed troops to Gallipoli, where victory seemed at once imperative and unachievable. With one of these deployments went a request that Hamilton tell him how many troops he thought he would need to take control of the peninsula.

Falkenhayn too was affected by the French and British spring offensives, if not so conspicuously as Asquith, Lloyd George, and Churchill. He understood that Second Artois had been a near thing—Pétain would have held Vimy Ridge if the reserves he needed had not been too far to the rear—and had no doubt that the Entente would be attacking again within a few months. This prospect worsened his uneasiness about German weakness in the west, increased his anxiety about moving troops back from the east, and made him more unwilling than ever to commit to the kinds of grand Napoleonic schemes that Ludendorff never tired of putting forward. He was haunted by the ruin that had come to Napoleon in 1812 as a result of his movement deep into Russia. His fears ensured that there could be no resolution of his rivalry with the Hindenburg-Ludendorff team.

The Western Front remained quiet through the rest of the summer—"quiet" being a relative term indicating a state of affairs in which only scores or hundreds of men were killed daily in obscure forays, skirmishes, limited attacks, and routinely murderous sniper and artillery fire. A letter that Private Jack Mackenzie sent to his wife in Scotland on July 3 illuminates life on the line at a time of little action. "We relieved our fourth battalion in here, these are the trenches which they lost so many men in capturing, & is just one vast deadhouse, the stench in some places is something awful, the first thing we had to do was dig the trenches deeper & otherwise repair them & we came across bodies all over the place, you know the Germans occupied these trenches nearly the whole winter and have been losing heavily & has had to bury their killed in the trenches, there were legs and arms sticking out all over the place when we arrived but we have buried the most of them properly now. The ground behind us us [sic] is covered yet by dead Camerons and Germans who fell on the seventeenth of May & we go out at night & bury them, it is a very rotten job as they are very decomposed, but it has to be done." Mackenzie (who would be killed in action in 1916) goes on to thank his "own darling wife" for sending food and clothing by mail, regretting only that a recently received pair of pants was not some color other than white. "But many thanks dearest for sending them," he added, "they will do fine."

In the east, by contrast, the summer was a prolonged crisis. On May 10 the Russian Third Army, bleeding to death under the pressure of the Gorlice-Tarnow offensive, was at last given permission to fall back to the River San, where it was to make a stand. The Germans were hard on its heels and by May 16 were breaking through its new line (which was badly equipped, the Russians having sold to local entrepreneurs the mountains of supplies that had fallen into their hands with the capture of

Przemysl earlier in the year). Soon the Germans were across the San, but then their offensive began to run down, encumbered by supply and transport problems in a region where good roads and railways were scarce. A Russian counterattack against the Austro-Hungarian part of the attacking force was initially successful, taking another huge batch of Conrad's troops as prisoners. But it was not successful enough to balance the German gains, and within a week it too came to a stop. The Russian government, which earlier had been indicating a willingness to send troops to Gallipoli, announced that doing so was no longer possible. Its armies, in disorderly retreat in the southeast and threatened in Poland as well, had taken more than four hundred thousand casualties in May alone (bringing their total for ten months of war to almost four million). In the south they were barely able to pull back fast enough to keep the Germans from cutting off their escape.

Fearing catastrophe, the government in St. Petersburg developed new interest in getting Italy into the war. Prime Minister Salandra, sensing that this was the moment to extract maximum concessions from the Entente and willing to gamble on the eventual defeat of the Central Powers, made Italy a party to the Treaty of London. In return for a promise to enter the war within thirty days, he was given almost everything he wanted. The matter was not settled, however. Powerful groups in Italy were opposed to war, among them the Catholic Church and the socialists, who agreed on little else. When they learned what Salandra had done, these groups protested and the government fell. Salandra's deal appeared to have died with it. But there followed a kind of protofascist coup d'état that foreshadowed the Mussolini era and led on May 23 to Italy's declaration of war on Austria-Hungary. The government did not declare war on Germany, fatuously thinking that with this omission it could avoid unnecessary trouble.

The Gorlice-Tarnow offensive, though a triumph for the German high command, set the stage for further bitter disputes. Falkenhayn had wanted to stop when Mackensen's army reached the San, but Conrad persuaded him to continue. As soon as he learned of Italy's declaration of war, Conrad urged an attack into the north Italian plain. Falkenhayn wanted to subdue Serbia—a land route through the Balkans to Turkey was badly needed. On June 3 all the major players including the kaiser met at German headquarters. Falkenhayn, warning that fresh British troops were arriving on the continent in alarming numbers, said it was time to move at least four divisions to the West. Conrad pressed his case for an invasion of Italy and was taken seriously by no one. Ludendorff laid out his latest grand plan: a move from the north (where he and Hindenburg were in command) aimed at encircling whole Russian armies. Falkenhayn argued that not enough troops were available for such an operation. Ludendorff replied that nothing less could produce lasting results—that it was futile to keep pushing the Russians back without destroying their ability to make war.

Once again the kaiser ordered a compromise that left the heart of the conflict unresolved. Mackensen's army would be reinforced with troops provided by Hindenburg and Ludendorff. (How the two must have seethed at that.) It and the Austro-Hungarian troops on its flanks would resume the Gorlice-Tarnow offensive as soon as possible. The rest of the Austrian army would move south, not to attack Italy but to prepare for a possible Italian attack.

Two weeks later, when Mackensen went into action, he was again startlingly successful. The Germans took possession of Lemberg on June 22 and crossed yet another river, the Dniester, as the Russians stumbled back to the River Bug. The Russians had been pushed completely out of Galicia, giving up everything they had gained since the start of the war, and their ability to fend off further attacks was questionable. In Courland in the far north, at the same time, Ludendorff's supposedly diversionary action was posing an increasing threat to the cities of Russia's Baltic coast. The dangers of the Courland campaign—if it continued, it could even threaten St. Petersburg—were becoming apparent to the Russians. Grand Duke Nicholas, visited at his headquarters by the tsar and trying to report on all the disasters coming down on his armies, collapsed in grief. "Poor Nikolasha, while telling me this, wept in my private room and even asked whether I thought of replacing him by a more capable man," Tsar Nicholas wrote his wife, perhaps hoping to make her less hostile to the grand duke. "He kept thanking me for staying here, because my presence here

August von Mackensen
His offensives drove the
Russians out of Galicia.

supported him personally." Riots broke out in Moscow. Houses and businesses owned by people with German names were looted and destroyed, but the rage was not directed at Germany only. At a huge demonstration in Red Square, people called for the tsar to be deposed, for the German-born tsarina to be confined to a convent, and for Rasputin to be hanged. The unraveling of the Romanov regime was beginning.

But even now the German generals were unable to agree on strategy. The leaders of Berlin's eastern forces met again at the end of June. Ludendorff arrived with a new plan even more ambitious than the one rejected at the start of the month. It was Hoffmann's work, and Ludendorff had accepted it only when, after an all-night debate, all four of the army commanders who would be responsible for its execution gave it their endorsement. It called for the armies in the north to move east to cut key rail lines, then swing south to trap the Russians in Poland. Encircled, the Russians would have to surrender or perish. Having been won over, Ludendorff was enthusiastic. He instructed Hoffmann to stand by at northern headquarters for a phone call announcing the kaiser's approval. When Hoffmann's phone finally rang hours later than expected, a furious Ludendorff told him that Falkenhayn had again rejected their proposal and had received the support of the kaiser for an alternative, less ambitious offensive.

What Falkenhayn had first proposed was not an alternative offensive but an end to the attacks coupled with an attempt to open negotiations with the Russians. The kaiser was taken aback by this idea and would not discuss it. But he was inclined to agree when Falkenhayn said "The Russians can retreat into the vastness of their country; we cannot go chasing them forever and ever." Another compromise emerged, a plan for a three-pronged offensive that, if not as grandiose as what Ludendorff wanted, nonetheless had a lofty objective: to force the Russians out of Poland.

Russian Poland, wedged between East Prussia and the Hapsburg domains to the south, was thus exposed on three sides. The new campaign began on July 12 with one German army group driving southward to east of Warsaw, another attacking west of the city, and Mackensen moving north toward Lublin and Brest-Litovsk. When the Russian commander in Poland sensibly suggested withdrawal, Grand Duke Nicholas refused, much as he had at first refused to permit his Third Army to pull out of Galicia. His reasons were more political than military. Some in St. Petersburg—called Petrograd now, to erase the taint of Germanism—feared that if Russia abandoned Poland while the British and French achieved a great victory at Gallipoli, Russia's claim to Constantinople might be compromised. They feared too that if Russian reverses continued while Italy was inflicting defeat on Austria-Hungary (that too was still widely expected), Italy would move into the Balkans. The Russians had strong fortresses in Poland, recently updated at tremendous expense and generously supplied with guns and ammunition that were badly needed elsewhere; the grand duke, in believing that they could hold out, ignored the lessons of Liège and Namur.

At first the German advance on Poland was slow. The emphasis was not on infantry attacks but on colossal artillery bombardments—hundreds of thousands of shells day after day—that had a ruinous effect on Russian numbers and morale. Gradually the pace accelerated. Town after town was abandoned to the Germans, and soon Warsaw, which had been in Russian hands for exactly one hundred years, was in grave danger. Townsfolk and peasants fled in all directions, leaving behind almost all their possessions and finding safety nowhere. "They are in despair, and protest bitterly," a Russian soldier wrote. "At eight in the evening we are on the march again. We come out onto the road. It is dark. But what's that noise? Oh my God, what's happening on the road ahead? It is blocked by carts, full of kids and household stuff. The cows are bellowing, the dogs are barking and yelping. The poor people are going God knows where, anywhere to get away from the fighting. But the old nags don't have the strength to pull the loads; the air is filled with the sound of horses being whipped and the Polish 'tso,' and still the carts won't move. We don't have the heart just to drive through them. It's such a heartbreaking scene, we drag one cart after another out of the mud, get them onto the main road and then onto the bridge over the river Narew. I pity them all, particularly the little children, sitting in the carts or in their mothers' arms. They don't understand what is happening around them. My thoughts turn to my own family, I feel depressed and before I know it tears run down my cheeks."

By any measure, the German achievement in the east had been tremendous. Russian resistance was crumbling everywhere. But Hindenburg, Ludendorff, and Hoffmann were contemptuous. The Germans were merely forcing the Russians to move. They were not annihilating them.

The French and British were troubled. Something big had to be done to turn the tide—to ease the danger of Russia making a separate peace. For Joffre and French, only one thing could suffice: a fall offensive big enough and successful enough to neutralize everything that had happened in the east. For others, it meant that Gallipoli had to be carried to a victorious conclusion. For still others, Kitchener among them, *both* aims now seemed imperative.

GENOCIDE

THE HOPE WITH WHICH MANY OF CONSTANTINOPLE'S Young Turks had begun the war—a hope of regaining lost territories, of taking revenge on old enemies (on Russia above all), and of restoring their empire's faded glory—soon turned to fear. A December 1914 invasion of the Caucasus, led personally by War Minister Enver Pasha, had aimed at driving the Russians out of a region whose population was overwhelmingly Muslim, but it ended in failure and the death of more than a hundred thousand Turkish troops. Then came the Entente assaults on the Dardanelles and Gallipoli—and a panicky realization that Constantinople itself was threatened. By the time the war was six months old, everything that remained of what Suleiman the Magnificent and his forebears had built was in danger of falling into ruin.

These disasters, coming hard on the heels of the Turkish expulsion from the Balkans in 1912 and a century of other humiliating concessions to the Europeans, inflamed the worst tendencies of the Turkish leadership. For more than a generation before the war, nationalist Turks and Islamic extremists had been saying that the Ottoman Empire, in order to be saved, must first be purified—must above all be purged of non-Muslim elements. By the spring of 1915 this idea was policy. The government of Turkey embarked upon the first true genocide of the twentieth century, the modern era's first effort to eliminate a whole people. The target was Armenia, which the loss of Bosnia, Bulgaria, Greece, Montenegro, Romania, and Serbia had left as the last large Christian population still inside the Turkish empire.

History had long been unkind to Armenia, which in ancient times was the most powerful independent kingdom on the eastern border of the Roman Empire and in the fourth century became the first nation to make Christianity its official religion. In the fourteenth and fifteenth centuries the northward advance of the Turks and the collapse of the Byzantine Empire reduced the Armenians, like the Christian kingdoms of the Balkans, to a persecuted subject people.

In the centuries that followed they became entangled in the conflict between the Turks and the Russians, who were by then advancing southward. By the late nineteenth century Armenia was divided, upward of a million and a half of its people still subject to the Turks but another million living in areas annexed by Russia.

This division—the Armenian homeland occupying a contested borderland between two bitterly hostile empires—eventually brought disaster. Russia justified its expansion by claiming to be the champion, and where possible the liberator, of the Turks' Christian subjects. The Turks, brutish in their management of non-Islamic populations, responded by electing to deal with the Armenians as hostile aliens. They raised taxes to ruinous levels and encouraged the Kurds to enrich themselves, by force, at the expense of their Armenian neighbors. Inevitably such actions gave rise to Armenian radical groups demanding autonomy and to further Turkish suppression.

In the last two decades of the nineteenth century Constantinople's treatment of Turkish Armenia was so atrocious that it became an international cause célèbre and an early focus of the American Red Cross. Constantinople saw the attention it was receiving as interference in its internal affairs. When Armenians living in Constantinople raised a disturbance, the Turks responded with a savagery that was remarkable even by Ottoman standards. Tens of thousands of Armenians were slaughtered, many others were driven from their homes, and whole towns were leveled.

Among the Young Turks who took power in 1908 were men who wanted the Ottoman Empire to become a multicultural enterprise in which the rights of religious and ethnic minorities were respected. Such men were eventually pushed aside, however, and the government came to be dominated by fanatical nationalists who found in the Armenians a convenient object for their hatred. When a counterrevolution against the Young Turks failed in 1909, the Armenians again became scapegoats. At least fifteen thousand were butchered at the city of Adana amid grotesque scenes of rape, mutilation, and destruction of property.

When the Balkan wars sent a flood of displaced Muslims into Turkey, many were sent to Armenia (where Christians had no legal rights and were under the heel of Kurdish tribal chieftains) with license to take what they wanted and kill anyone who tried to interfere. Against this background it is remarkable that a hundred thousand Armenian men joined the Ottoman army when Constantinople entered the Great War. Rather naturally, however, loyalties were divided, and the situation became hopelessly confused. Armenians on the Russian side of the border were joining the tsar's army, and they encouraged their cousins on the other side to join in the fight against a regime that had done nothing to earn their loyalty. In December 1914 an Armenian division organized by the Russians crossed the border and killed one hundred and twenty thousand non-Armenians (most of them Turks and Kurds).

The Young Turks found here all the justification they needed for actions that in peacetime probably would have been unimaginable. They began in comparatively innocuous fashion, disarming their Armenian soldiers and assigning them to labor battalions. Then they proceeded to work, and starve, those battalions to death. Next, having eliminated the part of the population most capable of defending itself, they sent an army onto the plateau that had long been home to most of Turkey's Armenians. In town after town and city after city, all males over the age of twelve were gathered up and shot or hacked to death en masse. Women were raped and mutilated, and those who were not killed were sold into slavery. Hundreds of thousands of civilians were marched off to the deserts of Syria and Mesopotamia. Many died of exposure, starvation, or exhaustion along the way, and others were murdered by their Kurdish escorts. The pogrom spread across all of Turkey. In Constantinople thousands of convicted criminals were organized into death squads whose only assignment was to kill every Armenian they could find, giving first priority to those intellectuals, professionals, and religious and political leaders who might have the potential to serve as leaders. The families of Turkish officials took the choicest booty; the death squads and rabble took the rest.

It is estimated that more than half a million Armenians were killed in 1915, and that was far from the end of it. The massacre would continue through 1916, with further death marches in Syria. Still later, when the Russian armies withdrew from the Caucasus, the Armenians whose shield they had been fell prey to the Turks in their turn. The final convulsion would not come until 1922, when a new Turkish government took possession of Smyrna, set the city afire, and systematically slaughtered its tens of thousands of Armenian and Greek inhabitants.

No one would ever be punished. In the years after the war the United States found it more advantageous to come to terms with the Muslims of the Middle East with their oil riches than to redress the wrongs done to an Armenian nation described by the American high commissioner in Istanbul as "a race like the Jews; they have little or no national spirit and have poor moral character."

Successive Turkish governments continued into the twenty-first century not only to deny that an Armenian genocide ever occurred but to prosecute any Turk who dared to write of it.

Chapter 18

Gallipoli Again, and Poland, and . . .

"Perhaps a scapegoat is needed to save Russia.
I mean to be the victim."
—Tsar Nicholas II

As the first faint hint of dawn began to glow in the eastern sky beyond Gallipoli on August 9, the men of the British Thirty-second Brigade were crouched in readiness just below the crest of Tekke Tepe Ridge, a high point dominating the center of the peninsula. These were untested but well-trained troops, some of the hundreds of thousands who had volunteered in the first days of the war, and they had landed at Gallipoli scarcely more than fifty hours before. They were also very tired troops, having spent the night clawing their way through the dark up the steep and rugged hillside. But the great prize, the heights that men from Britain, France, Australia, and New Zealand had for more than three months been trying and failing to reach, was now just yards away. And it was undefended: just the previous afternoon air reconnaissance had found no sign of Turkish forces anywhere in the neighborhood. Best of all, at the backs of the battalion, down on the beach at Suvla Bay less than three miles to the rear, were another twenty thousand newly arrived and well-equipped Tommies. They would be more than enough, once the ridge was in hand, to free the Anzacs from the nearby beachhead where they had been bottled up since July, cut off the Turkish units defending the lower peninsula, and crush them against the British and French at Cape Helles.

With the darkness fading to a predawn gray and the details of the landscape becoming visible, the order came to move. Silently, rifles in hand, the men started for the top. As they climbed, there suddenly appeared on the skyline above them, as if out of nowhere, the backlighted outlines of human beings. In another instant the silhouettes turned into a mass of shouting, shooting, bayonet-waving Turks, and the mass became a downrushing wave. Defense was impossible; those British who didn't flee were overrun and killed. The survivors were chased all the way down to the coastal flats. What they could not know was that their pursuers too had just arrived at Tekke Tepe. They had reached the crest at the end of a thirty-six-hour forced march and had been immediately sent into their attack by Mustafa Kemal, who himself had just spent three sleepless days and nights in desperate combat at Anzac Cove. Thus it had all come down to a question of minutes.

The August 6 landing at Suvla Bay had delivered to Gallipoli the four divisions that Ian Hamilton, in response to inquiries from Kitchener, had said back in May that he would need to break the stalemate. In London there had been much disagreement over whether to send those divisions—disagreement heightened by the collapse of the Liberal government and its replacement with a coalition. But when Kitchener threatened to resign if they were not sent, the opposition relented. From that point forward, events both in Europe and at Gallipoli made victory seem more imperative than ever. Repeated attempts to break out at Cape Helles and Anzac Cove had ended in bloody failure, the Turks had begun mounting attacks of their own, and the beachheads had turned into stinking pits of disease.

Back in Europe, Italy had shown itself to be unprepared for war. Its army was ill-equipped, untrained, ineptly led, and incapable of the kind of impact the Entente had hoped for and the Central Powers had feared. The Italian commander in chief, Luigi Cadorna, had marched more than six hundred thousand troops north to the Isonzo River between Vienna and Trieste, where they greatly outnumbered the Austrian defenders. They had attacked in June, losing fifteen thousand men, and again in late July, when their casualties totaled forty-two thousand. These attacks had accomplished nothing. There would be two more before the end of the year, gaining no ground of significance and producing another one hundred and sixteen thousand casualties.

The Italian failures and Russian setbacks up and down the Eastern Front had been carefully watched in the Balkans. Bulgaria now seemed closer to joining the Central Powers; Romania and Greece were less inclined to throw in with the Entente. On August 4 the Russians were pulling out of Warsaw, and British and French fears that they were giving up rose almost to the level of panic. Joffre was well along with his planning of a new offensive, but it could not be ready until autumn and British cooperation was not assured. On all the many fronts of this increasingly immense war, there remained only one place where the Entente could act immediately to end the sequence of calamities. That place was Gallipoli.

The August 6 assault had been given the highest priority and all the support that any commander could have wished in terms of manpower, weaponry, and naval and air support. Its centerpiece, the nighttime landing at Suvla Bay, was well planned and took the defenders by surprise. Sanders, the German commander, knew in advance that another invasion was coming but had no idea where. Hamilton opened the operation with attacks by the thirty-five thousand men already ashore at Cape Helles and the fifty-seven thousand at Anzac Cove, tying up the Turks in both places. To avoid drawing attention to Suvla, he had ordered no naval bombardment there before the landing.

Everything went as well as anyone could have expected when putting masses of inexperienced troops ashore on a wild and unfamiliar coast on a moonless night. By the morning of August 7 more than twenty thousand men had been landed, meeting almost no resistance and suffering practically no losses. The troops moved two miles inland and stopped to secure a perimeter. A wealth of munitions and supplies was quickly piled up on the beach. Fewer than fifteen hundred Turkish troops, armed with little more than rifles, stood between Suvla and Tekke Tepe Ridge—the key to everything beyond, the whole point of the landing. When attacked, they fled, many of them throwing down their weapons. The nearest reinforcements were at least a day and a half away. The only thing remaining to be done was for some substantial part of the invading force to move the few miles uphill to Tekke Tepe and establish a defensible position there. Rugged as those few miles were, rocky and overgrown and broken by Gallipoli's maze of ravines, they could have been traversed by noon on the first day.

All through that first day the troops ashore were marched back and forth in confusion, their officers having been given no clear instructions as to what they were supposed to do. Hamilton himself remained miles away at his headquarters on the island of Lemnos. The commander of the landing force—a sixty-one-year-old lieutenant general named Sir Frederick Stopford, who had been given the assignment by Kitchener because Hamilton's choices supposedly were needed on the Western Front—had never in his career commanded troops in combat. Satisfied that all was going well, believing that nothing more needed to be done until his artillery was put ashore, he remained aboard the ship that he had made his headquarters.

Late on the morning of August 8, half mad with frustration because of the absence of any indication that Stopford was trying to take the heights, Hamilton decided to go to Suvla himself. For a long time he was unable to find a ship to take him. It was late afternoon when he finally arrived, and when he did the senior officer ashore told him, absurdly, that no troops would be available to advance into the interior until morning. Hamilton's air spotters had reported that, although Tekke Tepe remained empty,

British troops and supplies on the beach at Suvla Bay

Lt. Gen. Sir Frederick Stopford
in his prewar finery
*Remained far from the action
while the opportunity was lost.*

a Turkish force was marching toward it from the north. When
he insisted that morning would be too late, the Thirty-second
Brigade suddenly became available. But the climb to the ridge
now had to be made in darkness. The brigade repeatedly lost its
way in the confusing terrain and so took seven hours to finally
reach the point from which, as the night ended, it began its final
ascent and was met just short of its goal by the troops of Mustafa
Kemal.

The fight for Tekke Tepe Ridge had followed two days of terrible combat at Anzac Cove (where Kemal had yet again saved
the day for the Turks and been vaulted by Sanders to command of
all the troops in the area) and at Cape Helles. A day afterward, still
without sleep, able to stay on his feet only with the aid of stimulants administered by a doctor who followed him everwhere, Kemal was shot through the wrist while driving the Anzacs from the
high point of Chunuk Bair. This was the final crisis; if the Anzacs
had been able to hold Chunuk Bair, it might have compensated
for the failure at Tekke Tepe. When they were driven off, the
second invasion of Gallipoli was essentially finished. The hapless
Stopford launched additional attacks on August 12, 15, and 21,
the last being the biggest battle of the Gallipoli campaign. It all
but wrecked the Twenty-ninth Division that had arrived on the

peninsula amid such high hopes in April. These anticlimactic offensives managed to connect the beachheads at Suvla and Anzac Cove but not to take any of the high ground on which the Turks were now positioned in strength. Both sides settled down to more stalemate. Hamilton sent a telegram to London reporting that Suvla Bay was a failure and stating that to regain the initiative he was going to need another ninety-five thousand troops. His August casualties totaled forty-five thousand, eight thousand of them at Suvla.

When Hamilton's grim news reached its destination, Kitchener was in France attending the last of a series of meetings called for the purpose of deciding what should be done next on the Western Front. The first of these conferences, at Calais on July 6, had been attended not only by the army leadership but by Prime Minister Asquith and French War Minister Millerand. It had exposed continued disagreement as to priorities and had made plain that the lines of division extended in many directions. Joffre had outlined his plan for a fall offensive. Kitchener had reacted with something close to scorn, as had Arthur Balfour, a former prime minister who had recently replaced Churchill as First Lord of the Admiralty. The next day, Kitchener and the civilians having departed, Joffre and French met at Chantilly and quietly agreed that the preparations for their offensive should proceed regardless of what the politicians thought. At a larger meeting of French and British generals on July 17, it was Haig who raised objections. He had examined the area where Joffre, Foch, and French wanted his army to attack. He declared it to be unsuitable and himself to be unwilling. The ground was too open, he said; his troops would be too exposed. And he did not have nearly enough artillery. Joffre was unmoved.

Kitchener was back in France in mid-August not only because details of the offensive needed to be settled but because of mounting trouble in the east. The fall of Warsaw—and so of all Poland—had been followed by continued German advances and increasing evidence that the Russian armies were on the verge of disintegration. The Russian retreat was turning into not just an alarming mess but a wave of crimes against humanity.

For generations most of Russia's Jews had been forcibly confined to eastern Poland, where they were required to live in

ghettos and shtetls and almost entirely barred both from farm-
ing and from the learned professions. In late 1914, claiming to be
addressing security concerns, the Russians had driven more than
half a million of these people out of their homes and left them to
the tender mercies of the long central European winter. In the
first months of 1915 another eight hundred thousand of them
were put out onto the roads of Poland, Lithuania, and Courland
by the tsar's Cossacks, who often did not even permit them to
take whatever possessions they might have been able to carry or
cart away.

The Russians' final withdrawal from Poland was directed by
General Nikolai Yanushkevich, a protégé of one of the tsar's
favorites, the corrupt War Minister Vladimir Sukhomlinov.
Yanushkevich, whom the tsar had forced a reluctant Grand
Duke Nicholas to accept as his chief of staff early in the war, adopted a scorched-earth policy in which all the region's inhabitants, Jews and Gentiles alike, were put to flight. Stores of grain
and other foodstuffs were destroyed; machinery was loaded onto
wagons and railcars and moved east. Four million head of cattle
were gratuitously slaughtered, ushering in a meat shortage that
would persist in Russia beyond the end of the war. The refugees
were ravaged by starvation, cholera, typhus, and typhoid. The
number of lives lost will never be known.

The scale of the war in the east was breathtaking. Not long
after taking Warsaw, the Germans captured the fortress city of
Novo Georgievsk, taking ninety thousand soldiers, thirty generals, and seven hundred guns with it. Days later they took the
equally important city of Kovno and another thirteen hundred
guns. By now the Germans had taken more than seven hundred
thousand Russian prisoners, the Austrians nearly that many, and
their armies were still marching eastward. The Russian general
staff was so alarmed by the rate at which its men were surrendering that it issued draconian decrees. Families of soldiers taken
prisoner would receive no government assistance. Soldiers who
surrendered would be sent to Siberia after the war.

As reports of what was happening arrived in the west, General
Sir Henry Wilson, the British officer closest to the French high
command and a masterful if sometimes too obvious manipulator,
found ways to use them to the advantage of his friends. He be-

gan warning London that failure to give full support to France's next offensive could lead to the fall of Joffre and Millerand—and to *France* making a separate peace. Not surprisingly, Kitchener informed Hamilton that he should expect no more troops at Gallipoli and gave the BEF unambiguous new orders for the autumn. Britain must support Joffre's offensive to the utmost, he said, "even though, by doing so, we suffer very heavy losses indeed." What is striking is that Kitchener at no point, privately or otherwise, expressed the smallest hope that the coming offensive might be a success. Its purpose, for him, was not to achieve victory but to hold the Entente together. His fears were eased though not ended when, in the closing days of August, Tsar Nicholas removed Grand Duke Nicholas as head of the Russian armies and, to the entirely appropriate horror of his ministers, appointed himself to the position. Nicholas was the soul of gentleness in dismissing his cousin, explaining in a letter that he believed it to be his "duty to the country which God has committed to my keeping" to "share the burdens and toils of war with my army and help it protect Russian soil against the onslaught of the foe." The grand duke, when he got the news, was more succinct. "God be praised," he said. "The Emperor releases me from a task which was wearing me out."

The decision to take command was characteristic of the tsar: it was courageous, even selfless, and deeply foolish. It was the last and by far the worst in a series of command changes that Nicholas made that summer. Late in June the tsar at last faced up to the incompetence of War Minister Sukhomlinov, who had rendered himself indefensible with his cavalier disregard of the most urgent problems. (When the army's chief of artillery came begging for shells, claiming that without them Russia would have to make peace, Sukhomlinov told him to "go to the devil and shut up.") The war ministry was given to Alexei Polivanov, an able and energetic general who immediately undertook a program of reforms. He made radical improvements in the supply system; created committees to take responsibility for munitions, food, fuel, transport, and refugees; and showed himself willing to work constructively with the Duma, the national assembly. Other such appointments had been similarly productive and were welcomed by almost everyone except Tsarina Alexandra, who believed that the only answer to Russia's problems was for Nicholas to become more the autocrat, less willing to tolerate reformers and liberals. "You are about to write a glorious page in the history of your reign and Russia," she wrote to her husband after persuading him to ignore the many ministers who had begged him not to become commander in chief. In her warped view, those ministers had questioned not just the wisdom of the tsar's decision but his authority as autocrat. All of them were, she decided, enemies of the crown; all should be dismissed.

It was not hard to win Alexandra's enmity, and she had a long memory. She had never forgiven Grand Duke Nicholas for refusing, during the failed revolution of 1905, to accept the leadership of a military dictatorship. In the wake of this refusal, the tsar had been left with no choice but to agree to a constitution and the creation of a national assembly. Both concessions compromised the autocracy. By making them necessary, the grand duke had shown himself too to be an enemy of the crown. Or so Alexandra thought. The possibility that the grand duke's refusal and the tsar's acquiescence had saved the regime is unlikely to have occurred to her.

Tsar Nicholas understood that from now on, as commander in chief, he would be blamed directly and personally for whatever happened to the army. "Perhaps a scapegoat is needed to save Russia," he said in explaining himself to French Ambassador Paléologue. "I mean to be the victim. May the will of God be done." Nicholas does not appear to have understood that, by keeping him far from the capital, his new responsibilities would encourage the increasingly widespread (and not mistaken) belief that the government was under the control of the tsarina and her beloved Rasputin. In any case, the British and French welcomed the change of command as evidence of Nicholas's commitment to the war. They were pleased by the tsar's choice of General Mikhail Alexeyev, a seasoned commander and a strategist of proven competence, as his chief of staff. The Germans too welcomed the change. They had learned to respect—though it is not always easy to understand why—Grand Duke Nicholas's abilities.

As before, success in the east was not giving the Germans as much comfort as might have been expected. By early September, having abandoned the cities of Brest-Litovsk and Bialystok, the

Russians had withdrawn to a remote, treacherous, and largely un-charted region called the Pripet Marshes. Falkenhayn, refusing to follow them into such a morass, ordered all the commanders in the east to cease offensive operations. He began making arrangements to transfer several army corps back to the west and, at the same time, to get Bulgaria into the war by helping it to conquer Serbia. His instructions were disregarded by Conrad and Ludendorff alike; both would later claim to have misunderstood.

On August 31, apparently swept up in one of his periodic fan-tasies about duplicating the triumphs of the Germans, Conrad had launched his tattered forces on a sweeping offensive aimed at encircling twenty-five Russian divisions and, after defeating them, driving eastward into Ukraine. This effort started out well enough but ended badly. One of the Austrian armies, after cap-turing the city of Lutsk, was taken in the flank by a Russian force that had concealed itself in marshland grasses. Disaster followed upon disaster. Ultimately Falkenhayn had to detach two of the di-visions preparing to invade Serbia and send them to the rescue. Conrad lost three hundred thousand men in September. Luden-dorff meanwhile, continuing his Courland campaign, had taken the Lithuanian capital of Vilna. In doing so he provoked a panic in Petrograd, which though hundreds of miles from the Courland front became the scene of hasty preparations for flight. The cap-ture of Vilna had come at such a cost, however—fifty thousand German casualties—that Ludendorff soon abandoned his hopes of taking the Russian city of Riga. He settled down to a busy winter of organizing and administering his conquests.

Max Hoffmann, unquestionably one of the most brilliant gen-erals on either side, was by now also one of the most frustrated. He continued to blame Falkenhayn for failing to pursue a decision in the east, but now he blamed Ludendorff too, for attacking too directly at Vilna and thereby making that victory such a painful one. As for Hindenburg, Hoffmann regarded him as so passive, so utterly a figurehead, as to be little short of contemptible. "On the whole Hindenburg no longer bothers himself with military mat-ters," Hoffmann wrote at this time. "He hunts a good deal and otherwise comes for five minutes in the morning and evening to see how things are going. He no longer has the slightest interest in military matters." Another general on Ludendorff's staff confided at about this time that "Hindenburg himself is becoming increasingly a mere stooge." The aged hero spent many hours having numerous portraits of himself painted and writing to his wife.

As for Ludendorff and Falkenhayn, all the successes of 1915 had done nothing to cool their mutual hatred. When they met at Kovno late in the year to join in the kaiser's ceremonial celebration of their conquests, Falkenhayn used the occasion to throw down the gauntlet.

"Now are you convinced," he demanded of Ludendorff, "that my operation was correct?"

"On the contrary!" Ludendorff replied. Russia had not surrendered. Russia had not sued for peace. How could anyone be satisfied? Falkenhayn was heard to say that when the war ended it was going to be necessary to court-martial Ludendorff.

The next bloodstorm broke in the west on September 25 with the opening of Joffre's fall offensive. And a very great storm it was: three distinct offensives in three places. In the Second Battle of Champagne, west of Verdun where the front ran east-west, twenty-seven French divisions backed by nine hundred heavy and sixteen hundred light guns that Joffre had stripped from his border fortresses attacked seven German divisions stretched thin across thirty-six miles of front. The Third Battle of Artois saw seventeen divisions commanded by Ferdinand Foch set out against a north-south line defended by only two German divisions. A little farther north, at Loos, the British had a comparably overwhelming advantage: six British divisions against one German. It was the spring offensive repeated on an even larger scale. The objective was to cut off the Noyon salient, break the rail line that connected the two ends of the German front, and force a general withdrawal.

Even in the spring, however, the Germans had demonstrated prodigious defensive capabilities in the face of superior numbers, and throughout the summer they had been installing new lines far to the rear beyond the reach of enemy artillery and connecting them with perpendicular trenches and tunnels. They were well equipped with heavy artillery and adept at its use, and they were learning to place their machine guns so as to neutralize any attackers who survived their artillery. All this helps to explain the lack of optimism on the British side. Kitchener, in insisting on full British participation despite not believing it could succeed, may have been motivated in part by talk of putting all Entente forces under a single commander, and by fear that a refusal to cooperate might cost him the appointment. Sir John French, though usually eager to attack, warned that in this case he had less than a third of the divisions needed for success, and that the ground over which his men were asked to advance was dangerously devoid of cover. But he too had political reasons for not complaining too vehemently: he believed that only the support of Joffre and Foch was preventing his own government from removing him from command, and that his future depended on keeping that support. General Sir Henry Rawlinson, commander of the corps that would lead the British attack, predicted before starting out that "it will cost us dearly, and we will not get very far." French General Pétain, who would be in direct charge of the Champagne offensive, was similarly skeptical.

The only optimist, oddly, was Haig, who in the beginning had been opposed to Joffre's scheme. His early gloom had been rooted in the fact that the BEF would have only 117 heavy guns to prepare its advance on a five-mile-wide front—fewer than half the number of guns per mile that Joffre was putting in place in Champagne—and in the same lack of protective cover that troubled French. His spirits had begun to lift when it was decided to precede the attack with a release of chlorine. He was so encouraged by this idea that he had a tower constructed from which to observe his troops as they rolled over the German defenses.

Haig's high spirits were briefly dampened when King George V visited BEF headquarters and borrowed one of the general's horses for a review of the troops. A corporal in the Sherwood Foresters regiment left a record of what happened when the men lined up to be inspected: "The King rode along the first three or four ranks, then crossed the road to the other three or four ranks on the other side, speaking to an officer here and there. Our instructions had been that at the conclusion of the parade we were to put our caps on the points of our fixed bayonets and wave and cheer. So that's what we did—'Hip, hip, hooray.' Well, the King's horse reared and he fell off. He just seemed to slide off and so of course the second 'Hip, hip' fizzled out. It was quite a fiasco and you should have seen the confusion as these other high-ranking officers rushed to dismount and go to the King's assistance. They got him up and the last we saw of him he was being hurriedly driven away."

The attack was preceded in the French sectors by four days and nights of shelling. This had the advantage of obliterating the German first line and many of the men in it, the disadvantage of making it obvious to the Germans that something big was coming. When the morning of the attack arrived, operations began smoothly everywhere except in the British sector, where uncertain winds made it difficult for Haig to decide whether to allow the release of the gas. His men meanwhile were huddled in the frontline trenches—"some chaps were crying, some praying," one of them would recall—and being given all the rum they could drink while waiting for the order to advance. At five-fifteen a.m., when the wind seemed favorable at last, Haig gave his approval and climbed his tower. Soon afterward, however, the wind shifted. The gas began drifting back into the faces of the British troops. When it had dissipated, the Tommies who had not been disabled began to advance. Like the French to their north and east, they were soon making rapid progress.

And then, in place after place and in an absurdly wide variety of ways, everything started to go wrong. In Champagne the French ran through the wreckage of the first German line and reached the second much sooner than anyone had expected—so much sooner that they entered the trenches just as a French artillery barrage timed to prepare the way for them came down on their heads. The survivors of this terrifying stroke of bad luck had to retreat to escape being destroyed. By the time a resumption of the attack became possible, the opportunity was gone. German reserves had come forward and, being rich in machine guns, quickly took possession of what the French had had to give up. Among these reserves were two of the corps that Falkenhayn had recently rushed to the west. Falkenhayn himself was on the scene—such was his worry about the Germans' lack of manpower—and took a hand in keeping the defenses intact. Early on, when the French were moving forward strongly, he arrived at the headquarters of the German Third Army only to discover that its chief of staff was preparing to order a retreat. Falkenhayn relieved the man on the spot and ordered that the army hold its ground at all costs while waiting for the reinforcements that he knew would soon arrive.

At Artois too, after making excellent progress and for the second time that year briefly occupying the crest of Vimy Ridge, the French were stopped by an intact German second line and ultimately driven back. Joffre, who from the start had regarded Champagne as the key to the offensive and Artois as relatively unimportant, at this point began to play what can only be regarded as an underhanded game. He wanted the British, whose attack at Loos was supposedly intended merely to support the bigger French force at Artois, to remain on the offensive. But he also now wanted to end the Artois attack, having concluded that it had no chance of accomplishing anything. Therefore he suspended operations at Artois while pretending, for the benefit of the British, that he was doing nothing of the kind. Even alone, however, the British did well at first. Like the French, they passed easily through the pulverized German first line. Unlike the French, they also broke through the second line, though with heavy losses. The ground ahead was clear, and if reserves had been available, the long-yearned-for push into open country might have been possible. French, however, had positioned the BEF's general reserves as many as ten miles to the rear, and Haig had departed from sound military practice by failing to hold part of his own army back in reserve. Getting the general reserve to the front line ended up taking many hours; by the time it arrived, the Germans had filled the hole and were hammering away with their machine guns. When the British tried to resume their advance, the result was the most one-sided slaughter of the war: 7,861 troops and 385 officers were killed or wounded in a few hours, while German casualties totaled exactly zero. As the British finally began to withdraw, the Germans stopped firing and let them go. The machine-gunners were "nauseated by the sight," a German history of the fight would state, "of the massacre of the field of corpses."

"Coming back over the ground that had been captured that day," one Tommy wrote, "the sight that met our eyes was quite unbelievable. If you can imagine a flock of sheep lying down sleeping in a field, the bodies were as thick as that. Some of them were still alive, and they were crying out, begging for water and plucking at our legs as we went by. One hefty chap grabbed me around both knees and held me. 'Water, water,' he cried. I was just going to take the cork out of my water-bottle—I had a little left—but I was immediately hustled on by the man behind me. 'Get on, get on, we are going to get lost in no man's land, come on.' So it was a case where compassion had to give way to discipline and I had to break away."

Joffre continued to batter away in Champagne into November, not giving up until Pétain began ignoring orders to continue. In the end the casualties of Second Champagne totaled a hundred and forty-three thousand for the French, eighty-five thousand (including twenty thousand men taken prisoner) for the Germans. The Loos and Third Artois offensives cost the British sixty-one thousand casualties (two generals and twenty-eight battalion commanders among them), the Germans fifty-six thousand, and the French forty-eight thousand. Again France was stunned. On the whole, however, Joffre was believed when he told the Paris newspapers that his losses had been dwarfed by the enemy's and that the campaign had been a great success. The truth was that the Germans, though almost overwhelmingly outnumbered, had inflicted huge losses on the Entente armies while preventing them from accomplishing anything. In the process they had done more than Joffre or French to demonstrate that the Entente truly did have no troops to spare for Gallipoli or other distant theaters. Joffre's credibility was freshly damaged, if only among those insiders who knew what was actually happening at the front, but Joffre himself survived.

Sir John French did not survive. Even as the Loos offensive was still in progress, Haig began to complain to his many well-placed friends that only French's incompetence had prevented it from being a success. "If there had been even one division in reserve close up," he later declared, "we could have walked right through." Haig's own position was far from unassailable—his failure to provide a reserve from his own forces was just one of his mistakes at Loos. But French, frightened and almost desperate to defend himself, made a fatal error. Foolishly, he falsified the official record of orders issued during the battle. When Haig learned of this, he made sure it was brought to the attention of King George, who intervened with the prime minister. When Asquith gave French the opportunity to resign, he yielded to what had become inevitable and agreed. Haig, to no one's surprise, was appointed to the position for which he had been angling since before the start of the war. French returned to England and was made Viscount Ypres.

As the fighting wound down in the west and the exhausted armies of the east settled in for another winter, attention swung back to the Balkans and the Aegean, where intertwined events were once again unfolding rapidly. During the summer Bulgaria had become the centerpiece of an auction much like the one that had earlier brought Italy into the war. The Bulgarian government, like Italy's, was motivated solely by considerations of which side could help it to grab the most territory from its neighbors, and early in September it opted to join the Central Powers. Even before the start of the fall campaign on the Western Front, it became clear that Germany and Bulgaria were preparing to invade Serbia. It was equally clear that, in the wake of the failures at Gallipoli, the fall of Serbia would endanger what little toehold the Entente still had in Europe's southeastern corner. Sir Edward Grey had tried desperately to win the Bulgarians over, offering them many concessions. Because Serbia was Britain's ally, however, Grey was unable to offer what Germany could: territory that Serbia had taken from Bulgaria in the Second Balkan War. Now Serbia had to be saved or Russia would be further demoralized and Greece and Romania might follow Bulgaria in joining the Central Powers. Saving Serbia meant getting Entente troops to Serbia. With the Russians gone from Galicia, there was only one possible way to accomplish that: through Salonika, the Greek port that early in the year had been an alternative to the Dardanelles as the focus of an Aegean offensive.

Before the end of September the French had several divisions, including one removed from Gallipoli, en route to Salonika. They were led by General Maurice Sarrail, who despite having been removed from command on the Western Front retained such potent political connections that the government had been obliged to find an assignment for him somewhere. Britain, unwilling to leave the Balkans to the French, ordered its Tenth Division from Suvla Bay to Salonika. For a time there were hopes of persuading the Russians to send troops as well, but on October 3 Foreign

Minister Sazonov declared that this was impossible. His explanation was stark and indisputable: Russia was losing men at a rate of two hundred and thirty-five thousand a month. Its prewar professional armies had been essentially wiped out. Many of the armies that remained were wrecks.

Sarrail and the French and British divisions were ashore at Salonika on October 5. Two days later German and Austro-Hungarian troops under Mackensen entered Serbia from the north. After another two days two Bulgarian armies arrived from the east, one trying to push the Serbs toward Mackensen, the other cutting the rail lines connecting Salonika to Serbia. Sarrail, when he tried to advance, found himself blocked. The Serb army, trapped between overwhelming enemy forces approaching from two directions, decided to run for the sea. Masses of civilians fled with it; the entire nation seemed to be in flight. Exhausted, without food or other supplies, a mass of humanity tried to cross the snowbound mountains of Albania and was set upon by tribal enemies eager to settle old scores. "I remember things scattered all around," a Serb officer named Milorad Markovic would recall. "Horses and men stumbling into the abyss; Albanian attacks; hosts of women and children. A doctor would not dress an officer's wound; soldiers would not bother to pull out a wounded comrade or officer. Belongings abandoned; starvation; wading across rivers clutching onto horses' tails; old men, women and children climbing up the rocks; dying people on the road; a smashed human skull by the road; a corpse all skin and bones, robbed, stripped naked, mangled; soldiers, police officers, civilians, women, captives. Vlasta's cousin, naked under his overcoat with a collar and cuffs, shattered, gone mad. Soldiers like ghosts, skinny, pale, worn out, sunken eyes, their hair and beards long, their clothes in rags, almost naked, barefoot. Ghosts of people begging for bread, walking with sticks, their feet covered in wounds, staggering. Chaos; women in soldiers' clothes; the desperate mothers of those who are too exhausted to go on." Markovic would survive and become the father of a daughter named Mirjana. She would marry Slobodan Milošević, the Serbian strongman, who, nine decades later, was put on trial for war crimes after a later round of Balkan atrocities.

Serbia lost some two hundred thousand troops in this disaster. Of the hundred and fifty thousand who reached the Adriatic coast, only half were found to be fit for further service and transported on British ships to dismal camps on the island of Corfu.

Sarrail's failure to prevent the conquest of Serbia, coming on the heels of so many other calamities, caused the French government to fall. Premier Viviani was succeeded by Aristide Briand. Minister of War Millerand was succeeded by—of all people— General Joseph Gallieni, Joffre's unheralded partner in the saving of France a year before. Joffre found himself reporting to the man who had been responsible for his elevation to the commander in chief's post years before, and whom he had tried so jealously to keep in the shadows before and after the Battle of the Marne. Joffre's critics, increasingly numerous, hoped that Gallieni would dismiss him. Instead he once again defended and shielded him.

On October 11 Kitchener cabled Hamilton to ask his opinion of how many troops would be lost in a withdrawal from the Gallipoli beachheads. After replying that such a move would cost the British and French at least half the men they still had on the peninsula, Hamilton was relieved of command, his part in the war finished. Grey promised to give the island of Cyprus to Greece if it would join the Entente. The Greek government, intimidated by events at Gallipoli and in Serbia, declined.

In mid-November Kitchener traveled to Gallipoli, took a quick look, and said that the peninsula should be evacuated. When he returned to London, he discovered that Asquith had used his absence as an opportunity to further reduce his authority. The prime minister had reconstituted the committee responsible for war strategy, reducing it to five members with Kitchener, shockingly, no longer included. General Sir William Robertson, the onetime sergeant, was brought from France to become chief of the imperial general staff, the new War Committee's chief adviser on military operations, and the channel through whom the government's instructions were to be issued to the BEF. When Kitchener learned of this development, he went to Asquith and offered his resignation, which was refused. He still had much value as a figurehead, a symbol in the propaganda wars.

Also excluded from the new committee was Winston Churchill, who since losing his post as First Lord of the Admiralty had been left with no office except the essentially meaningless one of

Chancellor of the Duchy of Lancaster (where his only duty was to appoint county magistrates). Angry and hurt, Churchill resigned from the government and entered the army as a major (he had hoped to become a brigadier general) on the Western Front. Far from an ordinary field-grade officer, he arrived in France with a servant, a black stallion with groom, mountains of luggage, and a bathtub equipped with its own boiler. He was met by a limousine and sped off to elegant accommodations at a château. By January, however, he would be serving on the front and proving to be a competent battalion commander.

One drama remained to be played out in the closing days of the year: getting the troops away from Gallipoli without incurring serious—and politically insupportable—casualties. On November 23 the War Committee approved a detailed withdrawal plan prepared by Hamilton's successor. Over the next month, though an ignominious retreat, the escape from the peninsula proved to be the closest thing to a genuine military achievement by the Entente since the Marne. Working together night after night, the soldiers on the beaches and the Royal Navy steadily and stealthily got more and more men away under cover of darkness without letting the Turks and Germans know that anything of the kind was happening. The longer the evacuation continued, the more outnumbered the remaining men were—and the more vulnerable to being overrun and wiped out. The force at Cape Helles was down to nineteen thousand men when, on January 7, 1916, General Liman von Sanders launched an assault.

Here the entire Gallipoli fiasco came to the strangest possible end. Faced with British rifle and machine-gun fire, the Turkish troops for the first time since the start of the campaign simply and absolutely refused to attack. Even when threatened by their officers, even when shoved and slapped, they would not advance. Perhaps the problem was the absence of Mustafa Kemal; his health broken, he had been sent away in December. Perhaps the Turks had just had enough. "I'm twenty-one years old," one of their lieutenants had written in November. "My hair and beard are already gray. My mustache is white. My face is wrinkled and my body is rotting. I can't bear these hardships and privations any more."

Thirty-six hours after this mutiny, the last Australian troops on Gallipoli were carried safely off to sea and it was all over. The campaign had taken the lives of at least eighty-seven thousand Turks. (That is the official number, but it is widely regarded as too low.) Forty-six thousand British, French, Australians, and New Zealanders had either been killed or died of wounds or disease. Total casualties on both sides were in the neighborhood of half a million.

Nineteen-fifteen was finished at last.

Notes

PART ONE
July 1914: *Into the Abyss*

The causes of the First World War, and the culpability of the
nations and individuals involved, have been controversial
through nine decades and appear likely to remain so forever. The
relevant literature is almost infinite in quantity and in the variety
of conclusions offered. The author, having attempted to consult as
much of this literature as possible, found many works to be helpful but four to be particularly so: Immanuel Geiss's *July 1914, The
Outbreak of the First World War, Selected Documents*, William Jannen,
Jr.'s *The Lions of July, Prelude to War, 1914*, Eugenia V. Nomikos and
Robert C. North's *International Crisis: The Outbreak of World War I*,
and the second volume of Gerhard Ritter's *The Sword and the Scepter:
The Problem of Militarism in Germany*. Geiss's book is an invaluable
collection of diplomatic communications and government records
during the July crisis, though the interpretation that Geiss puts on
these communications is itself controversial to the point of being
generally discredited. Jannen's day-by-day, hour-by-hour recounting
of the crisis is unparalleled in the amount of detail provided, and
Ritter offers a uniquely thorough analysis of what was happening on
the German (and Austro-Hungarian) side and why.

Page

8   "For heaven's sake!" and "Sophie dear": Taylor, *Fall of the Dynasties*, 13.

8   "It's nothing": Fromkin, 136.

9   "A higher power": Remak, 160.

10   "My purpose . . . was to plant": Millis, 23.

10   "the imperative duty": the quotes from Bryan, the *Review of Reviews*, and Elihu Root are in Millis, 9–14.

16   "some young Serb might put": Marshall, 25.

17   "he only wanted to die": Z.A.B. Zeman, "The Balkans and the

Coming of War," in Evans and Strandmann, *Coming of the First World War*, 20.

18   "In 1908–1909 we would": Ritter, 2:235.

19   In the course of 1913: Conrad's 1913 calls for war are in Strachan, *First World War*, 69.

20   "a final and fundamental": Ibid., 71.

21   "a man . . . the monarchy needed": Jannen, 3.

22   He had at his disposal: Austria's and Serbia's 1913 manpower figures are in Herrmann, 123.

23   People who knew Franz Ferdinand: The archduke's views on trialism are in, among other sources, Strachan, *First World War*, 68.

28   *Bella gerant alii:* Taylor, *Dynasties*, 75.

31   "Yes, yes, but one is": Remak, 162.

32   Gangs of hooligans: Details about disturbances in Sarajevo and Belgrade are in Jannen, 10; Marshall, 24; and Remak, 147.

32   "into one another's arms": Jannen, 10.

32   "behaving shamefully": Fromkin, 143.

33   "The event almost failed": Ibid.

34   Either of the Austro-Hungarian: Austria-Hungary's mobilization plans are described in Strachan, *First World War*, 291.

35   "Then he's a false rascal!": Geiss, 346.

35   "Who authorized him to act that way?": Jannen, 21.

35   "How often have I asked myself": Ibid., 18.

36   "It was his opinion": Geiss, 77.

36   "did not succeed in convincing me": Ibid., 78.

37   "I don't believe we are headed": MacDonogh, 354.

37   At the July 5–6 meetings: Berchtold's scheme for using Bulgaria to separate Romania from Russia is in Jannen, 30.

38   "put an end to Serbia's intrigues": Ibid., 41.

39   "Our exactions may be hard": An Austro-Hungarian government summary of the council's proceedings, and the quotes in this and the following paragraphs, are in Geiss, 80.

40   "would, as far as can humanly be": Berghahn, 194.

44   "You are setting fire to Europe": Lincoln, 428.

52   "The most brilliant example": Fay, 2:340.

52   "The Royal Government cannot accept": Geiss, 203.

53   The Austrian mobilization that followed: The numbers of divisions are in L.C.F. Turner, "The Russian Mobilization in 1914," in Kennedy, 262.

54   They involved the mustering: troop numbers are in Fay, 298.

57	"I would like to call your attention": Geiss, 206.
57	"a question of the balance": Ibid., 209.
59	"in the most decided way": Ibid., 236.
60	"He was always lecturing me": Jannen, 37.
61	"Nothing has helped": Ibid., 56.
61	"This was more than one could have expected": Ibid., 147.
62	"a capitulation of the most humiliating": Ibid.
62	"Orientals . . . therefore liars": Fay, 420.
63	"Austria has declared war on us": Jannen, 138.
63	"has left us in the dark concerning": Geiss, 259.
64	He wanted to discuss a number of ideas: The content of the conversation, and the nature of the misunderstanding to which it gave rise, are detailed in Jannen, 133.
65	"complete readiness of France to fulfill": Turner, "Russian Mobilization," in Kennedy, 252.
70	"faith in the power": Massie, *Nicholas and Alexandra*, 16.
71	"Among the falsest": Ibid., 14.
71	"What am I going to do?": Ibid., 43.
72	"ignoble war has been declared": The words of the telegrams, and the kaiser's marginal notes, are in Geiss, 260.
73	One ordered the mobilization: The numbers of army corps and divisions are in Ritter, 2:253.
74	Crowds were gathering in Vienna: The anecdotes about reactions to the impending war, including the words of Russell, Grey, and Churchill, are in Ferguson, 176ff.
75	"the leading nations of Europe": Ritter, 2:253.
75	"kindly impress upon M. Sazonov": Turner, "Russian Mobilization," in Kennedy, 265.
76	In one of his middle-of-the-night: this exchange is in ibid., 263.
76	"Think of the responsibility": Fay, 2:265.
77	Russia's general mobilization: Nomikos and North, 6.
78	"Let Papa . . . not plan war": Taylor, *Dynasties*, 243.
78	"unless Austria is willing": Geiss, 286.
79	"serious error": Jannen, 223.
79	"We are of course, ready": Geiss, 293.
80	"how difficult it would be": Ibid., 317.
80	"What a joke!": Fromkin, 229.
82	"Fear is a bad counselor": The words of Ambassador Nikolaus von Temerin Szécsen are in Jannen, 186.
83	"You must inform German Chancellor": Grey's message to Ambassador Sir Edward Goschen is in Geiss, 315.

84   "must follow in case Russia": The double ultimatum is dealt with in Jannen, 256.

84   "If France had actually": Renouvin, 224.

84   "the peace of Europe": Geiss, 324.

84   "technically impossible": Ibid., 323.

85   "the same guarantee from you": Ibid., 344.

90   "Wherever the Sultan went": Barber, 85.

95   "France will have to regard": Mayeur and Reberieux, 350.

95   An hour later the French government: Joffre's warning is in Fay, 531.

95   Their conversation turned into: An exceptionally thorough and lucid account of the dispute between Germany's military and diplomatic leaders over whether and how to mobilize and declare war is in Ritter, 2:267.

96   "if I thought I could assure": Geiss, 343.

96   "We shall simply march": Jannen, 298.

97   "I assured His Majesty": Strachan, *First World War,* 90.

98   "This pained me a good deal": Renouvin, 251.

99   "it is understandable that each increase": Röhl, 43.

99   "would make it difficult": Geiss, 346.

100   "My impression": Ibid., 347.

101   "I have no other reply": Samsonov and Pourtalès each left an account of their last meeting. Not surprisingly, these accounts are not identical in their details, but they do not conflict substantially. Elements of their accounts have been taken from Gilbert, *First World War,* 30, and Jannen, 311.

PART TWO
August–December 1914: *Racing to Deadlock*

Entering upon August 1914 and the opening of hostilities, the student of the Great War encounters problems having to do with the number of casualties suffered by the various belligerent nations in specific battles and in specific time periods shorter than the war as a whole. Years of research that included visits to the Imperial War Museum in London, the Library of Congress, and a variety of archives in and near Paris brought the author to the conclusion that there is no single, simple, or absolutely authoritative solution to such problems. Many of such numbers must be taken as approximations, especially in the case of countries whose record-keeping was never meticulous or whose records have been lost since the war. The best approximations are at a minimum useful as measures of the scale of the fighting and of the comparative effectiveness of the various armies, and they are used for this purpose in the present work. The number of published sources on the Battles of the Marne, Tannenberg, and First Ypres is of course immense. Different authors shed light on these subjects from different angles, and many of the resulting works are valuable. The author found the following works to be notably helpful as guides to these contests: Robert Asprey's *The First Battle of the Marne* and *The German High Command at War*, Georges Blond's *The Marne*, Holger H. Herwig's *The First World War: Germany and Austria*, Henri Isselin's *The Battle of the Marne*, and the first volume of Hew Strachan's epic work of scholarship, *The First World War*.

Page

105   "If the iron dice roll:" Tuchman, *Guns of August,* 74.

106   "a long weary struggle": Barnett, 40.

106   "too reflective, too scrupulous": Ibid., 23.

107   "Art is the only thing": Blond, 30.

108   The so-called Grand Program: Strachan, *First World War,* 62.

108   By 1914, 1.4 million Russian troops: Rutherford, 20.

108   "We should exploit in the West": L.C.F. Turner, "The Significance of the Schlieffen Plan," in Kennedy, 200.

108   His commentaries, which he continued to produce: The weaknesses of the Schlieffen Plan, and Schlieffen's recognition of those weaknesses, are described briefly in Stevenson, *Cataclysm,* 38, and in vastly greater detail in Ritter, 2:193–216.

109   Bismarck had joked: Bismarck, 134: The kaiser said that this quip was Bismarck's "pet motto."

109   As late as 1913: France's alertness to British sensitivities on the subject of Belgium, and Britain's role in discouraging France from planning to violate Belgian neutrality, is described in Asprey, *Marne,* 24.

110   "for the civilian side to have": Ritter, 2:206.

110   "If we were to": Ibid., 2:195.

111   The infantry would have to do this: Herwig, 60.

111   Schlieffen calculated: Schlieffen's estimates of the number of divisions required for executing his plan are in Farrar-Hockley, 6.

111   "Before the Germans reach the Somme": Turner, "Schlieffen Plan," in Kennedy, 202.

111   "It must come to a fight": Asprey, *Marne,* 11.

111   The most challenging aspect: Herwig, 60.

112   "will hardly be possible": Turner, "Schlieffen Plan," in Kennedy, 212.

112   As the years passed: Moltke's changes in the proportions of troops assigned to the German right and left wings are in Stevenson, *Cataclysm,* 39.

112   In its 1914 iteration: Turner, "Schlieffen Plan," in Kennedy, 212.

113   In the thirty days following: The troop and division numbers given here and in the next paragraph are in Ferguson, 92.

115   This measure was a requirement: French and German conscription percentages are in Stevenson, *Cataclysm,* 161.

116   "the most hated man in France": Berenson, 71.

117   Though his enemies accused him: Caillaux's handling of the Morocco crisis is detailed in ibid., 76.

117   "bring Jaurès's pacifist dream": Ibid., 71.

118   "comic interlude": Ibid., 22.

119   "Do not touch me": Ibid., 2.

121   Joffre was demanding: Joffre's demands, and Poincaré's restraining influence, are in Herwig, 58.

122   "The danger is great": Jackson, *Jean Jaurès,* 181.

122   "We have no wish to incite" and "if on the eve of war": Ibid., 176.

123   "everything is finished": Goldberg, 471.

124   His little army: The size of King Albert's force is in Ferguson, 92.

124   Each of these forts contained: Information about the defensive forces at Liège is in Mosier, 58.

125   The Germans, as part: The Liège assault force is described in Herwig, 96.

126   His First Army: The size of Kluck's army is in Stevenson, *Cataclysm,* 43.

127   The first three of these armies: Ibid.

127   This was war on a truly new scale: The size of Wellington's Waterloo force is in Herwig, 48.

131   An advancing army's worst: Strachan, 237.

132   "In such a case": The Joffre-Lanrezac exchange is in Blond, 57.

133   The day after that: Herwig, 88.

134   On August 13, after taking: Belgian casualties at Fort Chaudfontaine are in Mosier, 60.

135   "I ask you to bear witness": Keegan, *Illustrated History,* 78.

136   More than five hundred trains: rail transport data are in Asprey, *German High Command,* 52.

136   Kluck's First Army alone: The German First Army's requirements are in Herwig, 100.

136   August 17: A collision: Russian prisoner totals are in Gilbert, *First World War,* 28.

137   "We cannot ask our Bavarian": Isselin, 33.

137   On this same day: Austrian casualties are in Gilbert, *First World War,* 50.

139   "Our advance in Belgium": Moltke's words are in Keegan, *Illustrated History,* 71.

140   "Do you already hold me": Ritter, 3:14.

140   His intelligence bureau: French estimates of German strength are in Blond, 22.

141   The fourteen French divisions: Numbers of divisions are in Bruce I. Gudmundsen, "Unexpected Encounter at Bertrix," in Cowley, 25.

141   The fight at the town of Rossignol: Casualty totals are in Mosier, 71.

142   French casualties for the war's first month: The numbers are in Stevenson, *Cataclysm*, 45.

142   Among the dead: The ten percent figure is in Asprey, *Marne*, 59.

142   "In a moment it is clear": in Lacouture, 30.

142   The Germans, except on their right: Germany's combat death figure is in Mosier, 72.

146   "Squiff" and "filthy cabinet": Jannen, 325.

150   Grey told his fellow ministers: In later years, criticized for not acting more forcefully during the July crisis, Grey would state that "the idea that one individual sitting in a room in the Foreign Office could pledge a great democracy definitely by his word, in advance, either to take part in a great war or to abstain from taking part in it, is absurd." See Hazelhurst, 51.

152   "the precipitate and peremptory": Ibid., 67.

152   "My own opinion . . . is that L.G.'s mind": Ibid., 68.

152   "I suppose . . . that a good three-fourths": Ibid., 32.

153   "The Liberals, very few of them": Ibid., 44.

153   "This is not my crowd": Ibid., 117.

154   "It is curious . . . how": Jenkins, 328.

155   "It will be obvious that the greatest care": Terraine, *Western Front*, 38.

158   "Bülow was a solid professional": Bülow's background is Mombauer, 68.

160   Every private in the BEF: The capabilities of British riflemen are in Pound, 46.

160   When the day ended: Mons casualties are in Keegan, *Illustrated History*, 86.

161   It was all nonsense: The origins of the Mons legends are in Hayward, 46.

161   Le Cateau turned into a bigger: Casualty figures are in Stevenson, *Cataclysm*, 47.

161   They had taken some eight thousand: Casualty figures are in Keegan, *Illustrated History*, 90.

162   A French counterattack that marked: Ibid., 86.

162   "the most terrible August": Marshall, 58.

163   "forced to take defensive action": Blond, 19.

163   The BEF marched: Strachan, *First World War*, 225.

163   "capable of taking up the offensive": Isselin, 37.

165   "complete victories": Asprey, *Marne,* 64.

165   He also decided to send: Marshall, 63.

165   Combined with Moltke's earlier adjustments: Details about Moltke's troop dispositions are in Asprey, *German High Command,* 100; and *Marne,* 65, 103; Herwig, 99; and Strachan, *First World War,* 241.

166   That commander, the fat and elderly: Prittwitz's manpower is in Stevenson, *Cataclysm,* 52.

166   Moving against this Eighth Army: The Russian manpower advantage is in Strachan, *First World War,* 316.

168   "I know of no other man": Asprey, *German High Command,* 69.

172   Nine divisions were formed into an arc: The troop dispositions are in Marshall, 61.

173   Rennenkampf's troops had been on the march: Strachan, *First World War,* 320.

174   "I will not allow General Samsonov": Marshall, 61.

174   He had lost seventeen thousand: Asprey, *German High Command,* 58.

176   In the course of the next three days: Prisoner and casualty figures are in ibid., 80.

176   "the fate of Russia will be decided": "Moltke and Conrad," in Kennedy, 224.

187   On Lanrezac's left: The hours spent retreating daily are in Strachan, *First World War,* 259.

188   "If you refuse": Blond, 62.

190   "my confidence in the ability": The French-Kitchener exchange is in Magnus, 293.

190   "I think you had better trust me": Asprey, *Marne,* 81.

190   French's account states: French's memoir of the conversation is in Magnus, 68.

191   Joffre by this point: The number of general officers removed by Joffre is in Asprey, *German High Command,* 103.

193   The number of divisions facing: The increase in the strength of Joffre's left is in Strachan, *First World War,* 243.

193   Apparently he was discouraged: the effect of railroad damage on Moltke's thinking is in Mombauer, 243.

193   The French, in contrast to the Germans, were reaping: Information about Joffre's rail system is in Strachan, 243.

193   "A natural reluctance to abandon": Blond, 90.

194   "We must not deceive ourselves": Asprey, *Marne,* 94.

195   "the will to conquer is the first": Tuchman, *Guns of August,* 32.

196   "for the attack only two": Ibid., 34.

199   "Battles are beyond everything": Ibid., 32.

201   But his army was in danger: Austin, 2:232.

203   "a comedian" . . . "no British": Liddell Hart, *Reputations*, 85.

203   "One of our battalions": Austin, 2:272.

205   In pulling back to the Ourcq: The size of the gap is in Keegan, *Illustrated History*, 31.

207   "Attack, whatever happens!": Tuchman, *Guns of August*, 435.

208   "For my part I preserve": Asprey, *Marne*, 120.

208   "What a mess!" Isselin, 156.

209   "voluntary concentric retreat": Keegan, *Illustrated History*, 107.

210   "the decision will be": Ibid., 101.

211   He had sent thirty-one: Numbers of Austrian and Russian divisions are in Stevenson, *Cataclysm*, 58.

211   Conrad had lost more: Austrian losses are in ibid., 58.

211   "shackled to a corpse": Falls, 54.

211   "I have one of my sons": Herwig, 96.

212   "I cannot find words": Blond, 215.

213   "There was not a moment's hesitation": Clark, *Donkeys*, 21.

214   Late in the nineteenth century: Robertson's first opportunity to become an officer is in Bonham-Carter, 29.

216   "I have often made up my mind": Winter, *Haig's Command*, 33.

216   "the role of cavalry on the battlefield": Clark, *Donkeys*, 22.

217   "such a terrible intriguer": Ibid., 32.

217   "as much an enemy": Tuchman, *Guns of August*, 201.

217   "He means well and will succeed": Winter, *Haig's Command*, 25.

220   "After five days and nights": Isselin, 228.

220   It is one measure: French munitions production figures are in Marshall, 73.

220   "Three days ago our division": Austin, 2: 293.

221   British and French headquarters: French's prediction is in ibid.

222   To strengthen his right: Falkenhayn's troop movements are in Herwig, 114.

222   That left Antwerp, which was already: The Antwerp defenses are in Mosier, 116.

224   Members of the cabinet were said: The varying responses of Kitchener and other cabinet members are in Marshall, 74.

225   These movements set the stage: the forces engaged in the Battle of Warsaw are in ibid., 80.

225   "From Czestochowa we advanced": [Story], 193.

226   The Ninth Army retreated sixty miles: Ibid., 82.

226   Overall the campaign had cost: German losses are in Stevenson, *Cataclysm*, 64.

229   When Scotland's Second Highland Light Infantry: The unit's losses

are in Farrar-Hockley, 180.

232   The enemy turned every house: Schwink, 65.

233   Lombartzyde was captured: A chronology of the times Lombartzyde changed hands is in Gleichen, 30–38.

234   "This . . . is not war!": Marshall, 77.

234   By the time the Flanders front: Casualty totals are in Asprey, *German High Command*, 124.

234   *Burke's Peerage*, the registry: The losses to England's titled families are in Pound, 77.

234   They had lost another ninety thousand: The numbers in this paragraph are from Herwig, 109–10.

234   "Only about half had overcoats": Austin, 2:421.

236   A counterattack organized by Serbian: The Austrian and Serbian troop numbers are in Herwig, 112.

236   Again their losses were outlandish: Casualty totals are in Stevenson, *Cataclysm*, 65.

236   With almost four years of war remaining: Vienna's losses are in Herwig, 120.

236   By March it would add another hundred thousand: This number is in Stevenson, *Cataclysm*, 75.

PART THREE
1915: *A Zero-Sum Game*

The first full calendar year of the Great War was dominated by two epic struggles: the fight for mastery on the Eastern Front, and the Dardanelles-Gallipoli campaign. In connection with the former, particularly helpful works include *The Eastern Front, 1914–1917* by Norman Stone and (a little-known gem that proved to be indispensable) *The Russian Army in World War I* by Ward Rutherford. Trumbell Higgins's *Winston Churchill and the Dardanelles*, Robert Rhodes James's *Gallipoli* of 1965, and Alan Moorehead's more recent *Gallipoli* all provide useful guidance to their subject.

Page

241   On New Year's Day: Gilbert, *First World War*, 124.

241   In the last five months of 1914: The casualty figures in this paragraph are from Stevenson, *Cataclysm*, 75.

242   In Paris the dominating fact: Data on French resources lost to Germany are from Ferguson, 250, and Marshall, 73.

244   "great incalculable": Stone, 122.

244   "a broken instrument": Asprey, *German High Command*, 152.

244   "If we succeed in bringing Russia to terms": Zeman, 83.

249   "a few months hence" and "keep hammering away": Ferguson, 292.

250   "The German armies in France": Magnus, 311.

251   "by extended operations": James, 28.

251   The Champagne operation alone: Keegan, *Illustrated History,* 159.

252   "I have grown into close union": Churchill, *The Unknown War,* 279.

254   "a dubious character": Asprey, *German High Command,* 153.

254   "theater of decision": Churchill, *Unknown War,* 280.

255   "I can only love and hate" and "the fatherland's evil angel": Herwig, 132.

255   Conrad's offensive began: Stone, 113.

255   While one Austrian army captured: Herwig, 137.

256   The Germans began their assault: Asprey, *German High Command,* 162.

257   Counterattacks by eleven Russian divisions: Stone, 112.

257   Russia, at this time, had approximately: The numbers of Russian and Central Powers divisions are in Stone, 112.

258   Ludendorff claimed that a hundred thousand soldiers: Ibid., 118.

258   "we failed strategically": Churchill, *Unknown War,* 299.

259   The winter campaign, by the time it ended: Stone, 122.

261   It was invented in 1884: Ellis, 36.

262   Rudimentary methods of underground tunneling: This matter is the sole subject of Barrie, *War Underground.*

264   A war that introduced so many: Buehr, 5.

268   The Germans calculated: Marshall, 85.

270   "I intensely disliked the thought": Rutherford, 115.

270   "in no circumstances can we": Ibid., 116.

271   "it would have been possible": Liddell Hart, *Real War,* 147.

271   "To attack Turkey . . . would be": Higgins, 104.

273   "The unavoidable losses must be accepted": Magnus, 323.

273   "having entered on the project": Ibid., 325.

276   It was defended by only: Figures on German and British troop strength are in Clark, *Donkeys,* 49.

276   Their way would be cleared: Winter, *Haig's Command,* 37.

277   "led by donkeys": Clark, *Donkeys,* frontispiece.

278   He had lost 11,600 men: Keegan, *Illustrated History,* 174.

278   "I was wounded": Arthur, 76.

281   "I am being most reluctantly driven": Higgins, 164.

281   "must be a deliberate": James, 65.

282   All along the strait: Moorehead, 67.

283   "The first ammunition dump": Arthur, 83.

283   With Przemysl the Russians had captured: Herwig, 139.

291   "Out of approximately 19,500 square miles": Asprey, *German High Command,* 180.

291   "supreme contempt for death": Tschuppik, 121.

294   The offensive began on April 5: French data are in Mosier, 145.

295   When Joffre finally allowed: Ibid., 148.

295   The explosion was followed: Casualty figures are in Groom, 97.

296   This time, however, when the guns: Data on chlorine gas are in Barrie, 62.

297   The advancing Germans were shocked: Groom, 102.

298   "Left at 6:30 p.m. for reserve": Lewis, 83.

299   They had taken forty thousand: Asprey, *German High Command,* 180.

299   "The profitless slaughter pit": Gilbert, *Churchill,* 3:516.

307   "If the English will leave me alone": Marshall, 110.

307   Two hundred transport ships: Ship and troop numbers are in Moorehead, 107.

308   Sanders by now had six Turkish divisions: Keegan, *Illustrated History,* 219.

309   The British, when they came ashore: Moorehead, 140.

310   By then half the Turks: Ibid., 141.

310   "A galling fire rained on us": Palmer and Wallis, 125.

311   Twelve thousand Anzacs got ashore: James, 111.

311   "I don't order you to attack": Moorehead, 131.

312   "dig, dig, dig": James, 130.

312   Three days later nineteen thousand: Ibid., 141.

312   On May 26 twenty-five thousand: Ibid., 150.

313   "came over in two great waves": Arthur, 114.

313   A corporal at Anzac Cove: Palmer and Wallis, 127.

313   By May 8 the British and French: Casualty figures and the quotes by Hamilton and Fisher are in Moorehead, 156.

314   In the years leading: German figures are in Strachan, *First World War,* 995.

315   The French, who thought they had: British, French, and German consumption data are in ibid., 998.

315   When Grand Duke Nicholas told: Stone, 144.

315   Being essentially bankrupt: Ibid., 153.

316   He got three hundred and fifty thousand skilled industrial workers: Stevenson, *Cataclysm,* 189.

316   He thereby started a gender revolution: Ferguson, 268.

317   Historians who have examined: Uses of shell shortages for political advantage are explored at length in Stone, 144–63, and Strachan, *First World War,* 993–1005.

317   "as soon as we were supplied": Strachan, *First World War*, 1001.

320   Conrad, however, remained desperately short: Churchill, *Unknown War*, 308.

321   In four hours fifteen hundred: details of this bombardment are in Falls, 122; Gilbert, *First World War*, 154; and Rutherford, 121.

321   Worse, the Russians' five and a half: Austro-Hungarian, German, and Russian troop and division totals are in Stone, 130.

321   They advanced eight miles: Ibid., 139.

322   "finish the war in three months": Marshall, 123.

322   After only forty-six minutes: Clark, *Donkeys*, 106.

322   Only eight percent of the British shells: Douglas Porch, "Artois 1915," in Cowley, 76.

322   On that first day: Asprey, *German High Command*, 179.

322   The French had much greater initial success: Porch, "Artois," in Cowley, 76.

323   When the battle came to its end: Evans, *Battles*, 23.

323   If only in numerical terms: Asprey, *German High Command*, 194.

324   "Success will come in the final analysis": Gilbert, *First World War*, 173.

325   "a real danger . . . a very great national disaster": Higgins, 196.

325   "It is repugnant to me": Woodward, 48.

328   "We relieved our fourth": Lewis, 112.

329   Its armies, in disorderly retreat: Casualty figures are in Herwig, 144, and Rutherford, 133.

330   "Poor Nikolasha, while telling me this": Massie, *Nicholas and Alexandra*, 313.

332   "They are in despair": Palmer and Wallis, 107.

336   It is estimated that: Death totals for Armenians in 1915 are in Balakian, 179.

337   In the years after the war: U.S. high commissioner Mark Bristol is quoted in ibid., 367.

343   Hamilton sent a telegram: Hamilton's troop request is in James, 307.

343   His August casualties totaled forty-five thousand: Casualty figures for Suvla and Gallipoli are in James, 297 and 301, and Marshall, 118.

344   In late 1914, claiming: Numbers of Polish Jews displaced in 1914 and 1915 are in Rutherford, 152.

344   Four million head of cattle: Ibid.

344   Not long after taking Warsaw: Data on what was captured at Novo Georgievsk are in Gilbert, *First World War*, 180, and Rutherford, 153.

344   By now the Germans: Prisoner of war totals are in Stone, 165.

345   "even though, by doing so, we suffer": Stevenson, *Cataclysm*, 129.

345   "duty to the country which God": Massie, *Nicholas and Alexandra*,

320.

345   "God be praised . . . The Emperor releases me": Rutherford, 155.

346   "You are about to write a glorious page": Ibid., 156.

346   "Perhaps a scapegoat is needed": Ibid., 156.

347   The capture of Vilna had come: Asprey, *German High Command*, 190.

347   "On the whole Hindenburg no longer bothers" and "Hindenburg himself is becoming": Ibid., 204.

348   "Now are you convinced" and "On the contrary!": Ibid., 188.

348   In the Second Battle of Champagne: Troop numbers are in ibid., 197, and artillery totals are in Keegan, *Illustrated History*, 185.

348   The Third Battle of Artois: The number of divisions at Artois and Loos are in Liddell Hart, *Real War*, 188.

349   "it will cost us dearly": Ibid., 187.

349   His early gloom: BEF data are in ibid., 190.

349   A corporal in the Sherwood: Arthur, 104.

350   His men meanwhile were huddled: Liddell Horta, 101.

351   When the British tried to resume: Casualty figures are in Clark, *Donkeys*, 173.

351   "nauseated by the sight": Winter, *Haig's Command*, 41.

351   "Coming back over the ground": Arthur, 421.

352   In the end the casualties: Casualty numbers for Second Champagne, Third Artois, and Loos are in Evans, *Battles*, 25.

352   "If there had been even one division": Liddell Hart, *Real War*, 195.

352   Haig's own position was far from unassailable: Haig's duplicity is examined in detail in Winter, *Haig's Command*, 38–41.

354   His explanation was stark: Rutherford, 168.

354   "I remember things scattered": Arthur, 116.

355   Serbia lost some two hundred thousand troops: James, 348.

356   "I'm twenty-one years old": Palmer and Wallis, 141.

Bibliography

Allen, Kenneth. *Big Guns of the Twentieth Century and Their Part in Great Battles.* Hove, England: Firefly, 1976.

Angell, Norman. *The Great Illusion.* London: William Heinemann, 1910.

Arthur, Max. *Forgotten Voices of the Great War.* Guilford, Conn.: Lyons Press, 2002.

Asprey, Robert B. *The First Battle of the Marne.* Philadelphia and New York: J. B. Lippincott, 1962.

————. *The German High Command at War.* New York: William Morrow, 1991.

Audoin-Rouzeau, Stephane, and Annette Becker. *1914–1918: Understanding the Great War.* New York: Hill and Wang, 2000.

Austin, Walter F., ed. *Source Records of the Great War.* [no city given]: National Alumni, 1923.

Bach, H. I. *The German Jew.* London: Oxford University Press, 1984.

Balakian, Peter. *The Burning Tigris.* New York: HarperCollins, 2003.

Banks, Arthur. *A Military Atlas of the First World War.* Barnsley, South Yorkshire: Leo Cooper, 1997.

Barber, Noel. *The Sultans.* News York: Simon and Schuster, 1973.

Barnett, Corelli. *The Swordbearers.* New York: Signet, 1965.

Barrie, Alexander. *War Underground: The Tunnelers of the Great War.* Staplehurst, Kent: Spellmount, 2000.

Berenson, Edward. *The Trial of Madame Caillaux.* Berkeley: University of California Press, 1992.

Berghahn, V. R. *Germany and the Approach of War in 1914.* New York: St. Martin's Press, 1973.

Bismarck, Otto von. *The Kaiser vs. Bismarck: Suppressed Letters.* New York: Harper & Brothers, 1920.

Blond, Georges. *The Marne.* Harrisburg, Pa.: Stackpole Books, 1965.

Bonham-Carter, Victor. *The Strategy of Victory, 1914–1918.* New York: Holt, Rinehart and Winston, 1964.

Brandenburg, Erich. *From Bismarck to the World War.* London: Oxford

University Press, 1933.

Bruce, Anthony. *The Last Crusade: The Palestine Campaign in the First World War.* London: John Murray, 2002.

Bruun, Geoffrey. *Clemenceau.* Cambridge, Mass.: Harvard University Press, 1943.

Buchan, John. *The Battle of the Somme.* New York: George H. Doran, 1917.

Buehr, Walter. *Firearms.* New York: Thomas Y. Crowell, 1967.

Caffrey, Kate. *Farewell, Leicester Square: The Old Contemptibles 12 August–20 November 1914.* London: André Deutsch, 1980.

Cameron, James. *1914.* New York: Rinehart & Co., 1959.

Carew, Tim. *The Vanished Army: The British Expeditionary Force 1914–1915.* London: William Kimber, 1914.

Carsten, F. L. *The Origins of Prussia.* Oxford: Clarendon, 1954.

Cassels, Lavender. *The Archduke and the Assassin.* New York: Stein & Day, 1985.

Chickering, Roger. *Imperial Germany and the Great War, 1914–1918.* Cambridge: Cambridge University Press, 1999.

Churchill, Winston S. *The Unknown War, The Eastern Front.* New York: Scribner's, 1931.

———. *The World Crisis, 1916–1918.* New York: Charles Scribner's Sons, 1927.

Clark, Alan. *The Donkeys.* London: Pimlico, 1998.

Clark, Christopher M. *Kaiser Wilhelm II.* London: Longman, 2000.

Clayton, Anthony. *Paths of Glory: The French Army 1914–1918.* London: Cassell, 2003.

Coetzee, Frans, and Marilyn Shevin-Coetzee, eds. *Authority, Identity and Social History of the Great War.* Providence, R.I.: Berghahn, 1995.

Coffman, Edward M. *The War to End All Wars.* New York: Oxford University Press, 1968.

Cooper, Bryan. *The Ironclads of Cambrai.* London: Cassell, 1967.

Cowles, Virginia. *The Kaiser.* New York: Harper & Row, 1963.

Cowley, Robert, ed. *The Great War.* New York: Random House, 2003.

Craig, Gordon A. *The Politics of the Prussian Army 1640–1945.* New York: Oxford University Press, 1972.

Crankshaw, Edward. *The Shadow of the Winter Palace.* New York: Viking, 1976.

Cruttwell, C.R.M.F. *A History of the Great War 1914–1918.* 2nd ed. Chicago: Academy Chicago Publishers, 1991.

Dallas, Gregor. *At the Heart of a Tiger: Clemenceau and His World 1841–1929.* New York: Carroll & Graf, 1993.

———. *1918: War and Peace.* London: Pimlico, 2002.

Dancocks, Daniel G. *Sir Arthur Currie.* Toronto: Methuen, 1985.

Darrow, Margaret H. *French Women and the First World War.* Oxford: Berg, 2000.

David, Daniel. *The 1914 Campaign.* New York: Military Press, 1987.

Dedijer, Vladimir. *The Road to Sarajevo.* New York: Simon & Schuster, 1966.

De Groot, Gerard J. *Blighty: British Society in the Era of the Great War.* London: Longman, 1996.

Dupuy, Trevor N., Curt Johnson, and David L. Bongard. *The Harper Encyclopedia of Military Biography.* Edison, N.J.: Castle Books, 1995.

Edwards, Cecil. *John Monash.* Melbourne: State Electricity Commission of Victoria, 1970.

Eisenhower, John S. D. *Yanks.* New York: Free Press, 2001.

Eksteins, Modris. *Rites of Spring: The Great War and the Birth of the Modern Age.* New York: Doubleday, 1990.

Ellis, John. *The Social History of the Machine Gun.* Baltimore: Johns Hopkins University Press, 1975.

Enock, Arthur Guy. *This War Business.* London: Bodley Head, 1951.

Essame, H. *The Battle for Europe 1918.* New York: Charles Scribner's Sons, 1972.

Eubank, Keith. *The Summit Conferences 1919–1960.* Norman: University of Oklahoma Press, 1966.

Evans, Martin Marix. *Battles of World War I.* Marlborough, Wiltshire: Airlife, 2004.

Evans, R. J. W., and Pogge von Strandmann, eds. *The Coming of the First World War.* Oxford: Clarendon Press, 1988.

Eversley, Lord. *The Turkish Empire from 1288 to 1914.* New York: Howard Fertig, 1969.

Falls, Cyril. *The Great War, 1914–1918.* New York: Putnam's, 1959.

Farrar, L. L., Jr. *Arrogance and Anxiety: The Ambivalence of German Power, 1848–1914.* Iowa City: University of Iowa Press, 1981.

———. *Divide and Conquer: German Efforts to Conclude a Separate Peace, 1914–1918.* Boulder, Colo.: East European Quarterly, 1978.

Farrar-Hockley, Anthony. *Death of an Army.* Ware, Hertfordshire: Wordsworth Editions, 1998.

Farwell, Byron. *Over There: The United States in the Great War.* New York: W. W. Norton, 1999.

Fay, Sidney Bradshaw. *After Sarajevo: The Origins of the World War.* New York: Free Press, 1966.

Feldman, Gerald D., ed. *German Imperialism, 1914–1918.* New York: John Wiley & Sons, 1972.

Ferguson, Niall. *The Pity of War.* New York: Basic Books, 1999.

Ferrell, Robert H. *Woodrow Wilson and World War I.* New York: Harper &

Row, 1985.

Ferro, Marc. *The Great War 1914–1918*. Boston: Routledge & Kegan Paul, 1982.

Fleming, Thomas. *The Illusion of Victory: America in World War I*. New York: Basic Books, 2003.

Ford, Roger. *The Grim Reaper: Machine Guns and Machine Gunners*. New York: Sarpedon, 1996.

Freidel, Frank. *Over There: The American Experience in World War I*. Short Hills, N.J.: Burford Books, 1964.

French, John Denton Pinkstone. *1914*. Boston: Houghton Mifflin, 1919.

Friedrich, Otto. *Blood and Iron*. New York: HarperCollins, 1995.

Fromkin, David. *Europe's Last Summer*. New York: Alfred A. Knopf, 2004.

Fussell, Paul. *The Great War and Modern Memory*. New York: Oxford University Press, 1975.

Geiss, Imanuel, ed. *July 1914: The Outbreak of the First World War: Selected Documents*. New York: Charles Scribner's Sons, 1967.

Gies, Joseph. *Crisis 1918*. New York: W. W. Norton, 1974.

Gilbert, Martin. *The First World War*. New York: Henry Holt, 1994.

———. *Winston S. Churchill*. Boston: Houghton Mifflin, 1971.

Gleichen, Lord Edward, ed. *Chronology of the Great War, 1914–1918*. London: Greenhill Books, 2000.

Goemans, H. E. *War and Punishment: The Causes of War Termination and the First World War*. Princeton, N.J.: Princeton University Press, 2000.

Goerlitz, Walter. *History of the German General Staff, 1657–1945*. New York: Frederick A. Praeger, 1960.

Goldberg, Harvey. *The Life of Jean Jaurès*. Madison: University of Wisconsin Press, 1968.

Goodspeed, D. J. *Ludendorff: Genius of World War I*. Boston: Houghton Mifflin, 1966.

Griffiths, Richard. *Pétain*. Garden City, N.Y.: Doubleday, 1972.

Groom, Winston. *A Storm in Flanders: The Ypres Salient, 1914–1918*. New York: Atlantic Monthly Press, 2002.

Guinn, Paul. *British Strategy and Politics, 1914–1918*. Oxford: Oxford University Press, 1965.

Haber, L. F. *The Poisonous Cloud: Chemical Warfare in the First World War*. Oxford: Clarendon, 1986.

Hall, Richard C. *The Balkan Wars 1912–1913*. London: Routledge, 2002.

Halperin, John. *Eminent Georgians*. New York: St. Martin's, 1995.

Haste, Cate. *Keep the Home Fires Burning: Propaganda in the First World War*. London: Penguin, 1977.

Hayward, James. *Myths and Legends of the First World War*. Stroud, Gloucestershire: Sutton, 2002.

Hazelhurst, Cameron. *Politicians at War, July 1914 to May 1915.* New York: Alfred A. Knopf, 1971.

Herrmann, David G. *The Arming of Europe and the Making of the First World War.* Princeton, N.J.: Princeton University Press, 1996.

Herwig, Holger H. *The First World War: Germany and Austria 1914–1918.* London: Arnold, 1997.

Heyman, Neil M. *Daily Life During World War I.* Westport, Conn: Greenwood Press, 2002.

Higgins, Trumbull. *Winston Churchill and the Dardanelles.* New York: Macmillan, 1963.

Higonnet, Margaret Randolph et al., eds. *Behind the Lines: Gender and the Two World Wars.* New Haven, Conn.: Yale University Press, 1987.

Hoehling, A. A. *The Great War at Sea.* New York: Barnes & Noble, 1965.

Horne, Alistair. *The Price of Glory: Verdun 1916.* New York: St. Martin's, 1963.

Horne, John, ed. *State, Society and Mobilization in Europe During the First World War.* Cambridge: Cambridge University Press, 1997.

Hough, Richard. *The Great War at Sea.* Oxford: Oxford University Press, 1983.

Hynes, Samuel. *A War Imagined: The First World War and English Culture.* New York: Atheneum, 1991.

Isselin, Henri. *The Battle of the Marne.* Garden City, N.J.: Doubleday, 1966.

Jackson, J. Hampden. *Clemenceau and the Third Republic.* New York: Collier, 1962.

———. *Jean Jaurès.* London: George Allen & Unwin, 1943.

James, Robert Rhodes. *Gallipoli.* New York: Macmillan, 1965.

Jannen, Jr., William. *The Lions of July.* Novato, Calif.: Presidio Press, 1997.

Jenkins, Roy. *Asquith.* New York: Chilmark, 1964.

Johnson, J. H. *Stalemate! Great Trench Warfare Battles.* London: Rigel, 2004.

Joll, James. *The Origins of the First World War.* London: Longman, 1984.

Keegan, John. *A History of Warfare.* New York: Vintage Books, 1994.

———. *An Illustrated History of the First World War.* New York: Alfred A. Knopf, 2001.

Keiger, John F. V. *France and the Origins of the First World War.* New York: St. Martin's, 1983.

Kennedy, Paul M., ed. *The War Plans of the Great Powers, 1880–1914.* Boston: Allen & Unwin, 1979.

Kent, George O. *Bismarck and His Times.* Carbondale, Ill.: Southern Illinois Press, 1978.

King, Jere Clemens, ed. *The First World War: Selected Documents.* London: Macmillan, 1972.

———. *Generals and Politicians.* Berkeley: University of California Press,

1951.

Kitchen, Martin. *The German Offensives of 1918.* Stroud, Gloucestershire: Tempus, 2001.

Kluck, Alexander von. *The March on Paris and the Battle of the Marne.* London: Edward Arnold, 1920.

Kohut, Thomas A. *Wilhelm II and the Germans.* New York: Oxford University Press, 1991.

Kraft, Barbara S. *The Peace Ship.* New York: Macmillan, 1978.

Lacouture, Jean. *De Gaulle: The Rebel 1890–1944.* New York: W. W. Norton, 1990.

Lafore, Laurence. *The Long Fuse.* Prospect Heights, Ill.: Waveland Press, 1971.

Lauret, René. *France and Germany.* Chicago: Henry Regnery, 1964.

Lederer, Ivo J., ed. *The Versailles Settlement.* Boston: D. C. Heath, 1960.

Leed, Eric J. *No Man's Land: Combat and Identity in World War I.* Cambridge: Cambridge University Press, 1979.

Leese, Peter. *Shell Shock: Traumatic Neurosis and the British Soldiers of the First World War.* New York: Palgrave Macmillan, 2002.

Lewis, Jon E., ed. *The Mammoth Book of Eyewitness World War I.* New York: Carroll & Graf, 2003.

Liddell Hart, B. H. *The Real War 1914–1918.* Boston: Little, Brown, 1930.

———. *Reputations. Ten Years After.* Boston: Little, Brown, 1928.

Lincoln, W. Bruce. *In War's Dark Shadow.* New York: Oxford University Press, 1994.

Listowel, Judith. *A Hapsburg Tragedy.* New York: Dorset, 1986.

Lomas, David. *First Ypres 1914.* New York: St. Martin's, 1963.

Ludendorff, Erich von. *Ludendorff's Own Story.* New York: Harper & Brothers, 1919.

Lutz, Ralph Haswell, ed. *The Causes of the German Collapse in 1918.* Archon Books, 1969.

Macdonald, Lyn. *1914.* New York: Atheneum, 1988.

———. *1915, The Death of Innocence.* New York: Henry Holt, 1993.

———. *Somme.* London: Michael Joseph, 1983.

MacDonogh, Giles. *The Last Kaiser.* New York: St. Martin's, 2000.

Macdougall, A. K., ed. *War Letters of General Monash.* Sydney: Duffy & Snellgrove, 2002.

Macmillian, Margaret. *Paris 1919.* New York: Random House, 2002.

Magnus, Philip. *Kitchener.* New York: Dutton, 1968.

Mann, Golo. *The History of Germany Since 1789.* New York: Frederick A. Praeger, 1968.

Marshall, S. L. A. *The American Heritage History of World War I.* [no city given]: American Heritage, 1964.

Marwick, Arthur, ed. *Total War and Social Change.* New York: St. Martin's, 1988.

Massie, Robert K. *Castles of Steel.* New York: Random House, 2003.

———. *Nicholas and Alexandra.* New York: Atheneum, 1967.

May, Arthur. *The Passing of the Hapsburg Monarchy 1914–1918.* Philadelphia: University of Pennsylvania Press, 1966.

Mayeur, Jean-Marie, and Madeleine Reberieux. *The Third Republic from Its Origins to the Great War, 1871–1914.* Cambridge: Cambridge University Press, 1987.

McDougall, Walter A. *France's Rhineland Diplomacy, 1914–1924.* Princeton, N.J.: Princeton University Press, 1978.

Middlebrook, Martin. *The First Day on the Somme.* New York: W. W. Norton, 1972.

Miller, Steven E., Sean M. Lynn-Jones, and Stephan Van Evera, eds. *Military Strategy and the Origins of the First World War.* Princeton, N.J.: Princeton University Press, 1991.

Millis, Walter. *Road to War, America 1914–1917.* Boston: Houghton Mifflin, 1935.

Mitchell, David. *Monstrous Regiment: The Story of the Women of the First World War.* New York: Macmillan, 1965.

Mombauer, Annika. *Helmuth von Moltke and the Origins of the First World War.* Cambridge: Cambridge University Press, 2001.

Mommsen, Wolfgang J. *Imperial Germany, 1867–1918.* London: Arnold, 1990.

Moore, William. *The Thin Yellow Line.* Ware, Hertfordshire: Wordsworth, 1974.

Moorehead, Alan. *Gallipoli.* New York: Perennial Classics, 2002.

Mosier, John. *The Myth of the Great War.* New York: HarperCollins, 2001.

Muncy, Lysbeth Walker. *The Junker in the Prussian Administration under Wilhelm II, 1888–1914.* New York: Howard Fertig, 1970.

Neiberg, Michael S. *Fighting the Great War.* Cambridge: Harvard University Press, 2005.

Neillands, Robin. *Attrition: The Great War on the Western Front, 1916.* London: Robson, 2001.

Nomikos, Eugenia, and Robert C. North. *International Crisis: The Outbreak of World War I.* Montreal: McGill–Queen's University Press, 1976.

Ousby, Ian. *The Road to Verdun.* New York: Anchor, 2003.

Palmer, Alan. *The Gardeners of Salonika.* New York: Simon & Schuster, 1965.

———. *Twilight of the Hapsburgs.* New York: Grove, 1995.

———. *Victory 1918.* New York: Atlantic Monthly Press, 1998.

Palmer, Svetlana, and Sarah Wallis. *Intimate Voices from the First World War.* New York: Perennial, 2005.

Panichas, George A., ed. *Promise of Greatness: The War of 1914–1918.* New

York: John Day, 1968.

Parkinson, Roger. *Tormented Warrior: Ludendorff and the Supreme Command.* New York: Stein & Day, 1979.

Paschall, Rod. *The Defeat of Imperial Germany, 1917–1918.* Chapel Hill, N.C.: Algonquin Books, 1989.

Passingham, Ian. *All the Kaiser's Men.* Stroud, Gloucestershire: Sutton, 2003.

Pedersen, P. A. *Monash as Military Commander.* Carlton, Victoria: Melbourne University Press, 1985.

Perry, Roland. *Monash: The Outsider Who Won a War.* Sydney: Random House Australia, 2004.

Philpott, William James. *Anglo-French Relations and Strategy on the Western Front, 1914–1918.* New York: St. Martin's, 1996.

Pitt, Barrie. *1918: The Last Act.* New York: Norton, 1963.

Ponsonby, Frederick, ed. *The Letters of Empress Frederick.* London: Macmillan, 1929.

Pontig, Clive. *Thirteen Days: The Road to the First World War.* London: Chatto & Windus, 2002.

Pope, Stephen, and Elizabeth-Anne Wheal. *The Macmillan Dictionary of the First World War.* London: Macmillan, 1997.

Pound, Reginald. *The Lost Generation of 1914.* New York: Coward-McCann, 1964.

Preston, Diana. *Lusitania.* New York: Walker, 2002.

Rachamimov, Alon. *POWs and the Great War: Captivity on the Eastern Front.* Oxford: Berg, 2002.

Radzinsky, Edvard. *The Last Tsar.* New York: Doubleday, 1992.

Read, James Morgan. *Atrocity Propaganda 1914–1919.* New Haven: Yale University Press, 1941.

Remak, Joachim. *Sarajevo.* New York: Criterion Books, 1959.

Renouvin, Pierre. *The Immediate Origins of the War.* New York: Howard Fertig, 1969.

Reynolds, Francis J. *The Story of the Great War.* New York: P. F. Collier & Son, 1916.

Ripley, Tim. *Bayonet Battle: Bayonet Warfare in the Twentieth Century.* London: Sidgwick & Jackson, 1999.

Ritter, Gerhard. *The Sword and the Scepter; The Problem of Militarism in Germany.* Coral Gables, Fla.: University of Miami Press, 1970.

Röhl, John. *1914—Delusion or Design?* New York: St. Martin's, 1973.

Rutherford, Ward. *The Russian Army in World War I.* London: Gordon Cremonesi, 1975.

Schmitt, Bernadotte E., and Harold C. Vedeler. *The World in the Crucible, 1914–1919.* New York: Harper & Row, 1984.

Schulz, Gerhard. *Revolutions and Peace Treaties 1917–1920.* London: Methuen, 1967.

Schwink, Otto. *Ypres 1914* [An Official Account Published by Order of the German General Staff]. London: Constable & Co., 1919.

Serle, Geoffrey. *John Monash.* Melbourne: Melbourne University Press, 1982.

Seton-Watson, R. W. *Sarajevo.* London: Hutchinson, 1926.

Sharp, Alan. *The Versailles Settlement.* New York: St. Martin's, 1991.

Sheehan, James J., ed. *Imperial Germany.* New York: New Viewpoints, 1976.

Shephard, Ben. *A War of Nerves.* Cambridge, Mass.: Harvard, 2001.

Silkin, Jon. *The Penguin Book of First World War Poetry.* London: Penguin, 1996.

Simpson, Andy. *Hot Blood and Cold Steel.* London: Tom Donovan, 1993.

Sked, Alan. *The Decline and Fall of the Hapsburg Empire 1815–1918.* London: Longman, 2001.

Smithers, A. J. *Sir John Monash.* London: Leo Cooper, 1973.

Spears, Major General Sir Edward. *Liaison 1914.* New York: Stein and Day, 1968.

Steinberg, Jonathan. *Yesterday's Deterrent: Tirpitz and the Birth of the German Battle Fleet.* London: Ashgate, 1965.

Stevenson, David. *Cataclysm: The First World War as Political Tragedy.* New York: Basic Books, 2004.

———. *The First World War and International Politics.* New York: Oxford University Press, 1988.

———. *French War Aims Against Germany.* Oxford: Clarendon Press, 1982.

Stone, Norman. *The Eastern Front, 1914–1917.* New York: Scribner's, 1975.

Strachan, Hew. *The First World War,* vol. 1, *To Arms.* Oxford: Oxford University Press, 2001.

Strachan, Hew, ed. *World War I, A History.* Oxford: Oxford University Press, 1998.

Sweetman, John. *Tannenberg 1914.* London: Cassell, 2002.

Swettenham, John. *To Seize the Victory: The Canadian Corps in World War I.* Toronto: Ryerson, 1965.

Taylor, A.J.P. *The First World War: An Illustrated History.* New York: Penguin, 1972.

Taylor, Edmond. *The Fall of the Dynasties.* Garden City, N.Y.: Doubleday & Co., 1963.

Terraine, John. *The Western Front 1914–1918.* Philadelphia and New York: Lippincott, 1965.

———. *To Win a War.* Garden City, N.Y.: Doubleday & Co., 1981.

Thoumin, General Richard. *The First World War.* New York: G. P. Putnam's Sons, 1964.

Tolstoy, Leo. *The Cossacks.* Boston: Houghton Mifflin, 1932.

Tschuppik, Karl. *Ludendorff: The Tragedy of a Military Mind.* Boston: Houghton Mifflin, 1932.

Tuchman, Barbara W. *The Guns of August.* New York: Macmillan, 1962.

———. *The Proud Tower.* New York: Macmillan, 1966.

———. *The Zimmermann Telegram.* New York: Macmillan, 1966.

Tucker, Spencer C. *The European Powers in the First World War, An Encyclopedia.* New York: Garland, 1996.

———. *The Great War 1914–18.* Bloomington: Indiana University Press, 1998.

Vincent, C. Paul. *The Politics of Hunger: The Allied Blockade of Germany 1915–1919.* Athens: Ohio University Press, 1985.

Ward, Candace, ed. *World War One British Poets.* Mineola, N.Y.: Dover Publications, 1997.

Weintraub, Stanley. *Silent Night.* New York: Free Press, 2000.

Welch, David. *Germany: Propaganda and Total War, 1914–1918.* New Brunswick, N.J.: Rutgers University Press, 2000.

Williamson, Samuel R., Jr. "The Origins of the War." In *World War I: A History,* edited by Hew Strachan. New York: Oxford University Press, 1998.

Winter, Denis. *Haig's Command.* New York: Viking, 1991.

Winter, Jay. *Sites of Memory, Sites of Mourning.* Cambridge: Cambridge University Press, 1995.

Winter, Jay, and Jean-Louis Robert. *Capital Cities at War: Paris, London, Berlin 1914–1919.* Cambridge: Cambridge University Press, 1997.

Winter, Jay, Geoffrey Park, and Mary R. Habeck, eds. *The Great War and the Twentieth Century.* New Haven, Conn.: Yale University Press, 2000.

Wolff, Leon. *In Flanders Fields: The 1917 Campaign.* New York: Viking, 1958.

Woodward, Sir Llewellyn. *Great Britain and the War of 1914–1918.* London: Methuen, 1967.

Zeman, Z.A.B. *The Gentlemen Negotiators: A Diplomatic History of the First World War.* New York: Macmillan, 1971.

Zuckerman, Larry. *The Rape of Belgium.* New York: New York University Press, 2004.

Index

About the Author

G. J. Meyer is a former Woodrow Wilson and Harvard University Fellow with an M.A. in English literature. His other books include *The Tudors* and *The Fate of Nations: The Story of the First World War, vol. 2* (forthcoming from Amberley). He lives in Goring-on-Thames, England.